OOTACAMUND
Mettucherri R.S.
Fernhill R.S.
Keti R.S.
Lovedale R.S.
Aravanghat R.S.
WELLINGTON R.S.
COONOOR R.S.
Karteri Road R.S.
Hillgrove R.S.
Runneymede R.S.
METTUPALAIYAM
G000151908
Mount Munro
8412
Government house
Kuntha chappe
Jennings Estate 7922
Kodapamund
Varnarappeltai
Dodahalla R F
Secretariat offices
Old Ootacamund
Kotagiri Trace No 1 R F
Kotagiri Trace No 2 R F
Dodabetta R F
Kotagiri Trace R F
OTACAMUND
Doddabetta
8650
(Dodabetta)
Observatory
Tallyattimund
Elk Hill
8092
Dodabetta reservoirs
Burnfoot Lake
Mainalai R F
8250
7945
Metre gauge
Branch
Nilgiri
23 Keti RS
Acchipakal
Thire
Keti
Yelfanhalli
PTO
Alada

JOURNEY OF A LIFETIME

JOURNEY OF A LIFETIME

Lionel Gregory

Northcote House

British Library Cataloguing-in-Publication Data

A catalogue record for this book is
available from the British Library

ISBN 0 7463 0865 5

First published in 1997 by Northcote House Publishers Ltd,
Plymbridge House, Estover, Plymouth PL6 7PY, United Kingdom.
Tel: (01752) 202368; Fax (01752) 202330

Printed by
Macdonald Lindsay Pindar plc,
Edgefield Road,
Loanhead,
Midlothian EH20 9SY

Jenny Walton.

For Annie

Dear Jenny

I hope some parts of this book may be of interest to you.

Yours. Reg.

Edinburgh

2001.

By the same author

CRYING DRUMS
WITH A SONG AND NOT A SWORD
TOGETHER UNAFRAID

CONTENTS

ILLUSTRATIONS

AUTHOR'S NOTE

I have to thank my brother, Lieutenant Colonel H. C. S. Gregory, OBE, KSG, of the late 10th Princess Mary's Own Gurkha Rifles, who was with me from the outset of this journey, Devon County Council for commissioning the model for the Commonwealth Green Pennant Awards by Garrard, and Hamilton and Inches of Edinburgh for redesigning it in copper – incorporating the African continent with the existing symbolism of the oldest and largest democracies in the world. I have also to thank David Burchfield of Devon County Council, Judith Parkinson of Comex 5, 6 and 7 and BAFTA, Norman Leigh of Comex 2, 3 and 11 and the British Council, Sydney Williams of Comex 5, 11, 12, 13 and Ten Tors, Kamaljit Singh Garewal of Comex 10 and the Punjab Superior Judicial Service, Promod Shanker of Comex 10 and 13 and a sarod player of distinction, Neṇa Vrbos Leibel of Comex 3 and Zagreb, now Jerusalem, Alan Waters of Comex 9 and 13 and Librarian in Essex, Hamish Paterson, MBE, of Glenbreck, Couter, and Ian McNee of Macdonald Lindsay Pindar of Edinburgh for casting a cautious eye over my enthusiasm at various stages of the journey before signalling me on.

L. G.

INTRODUCTION

Within history's memory there have always been flags –
Glittering gold banners, or worn tattered rags –
To proclaim the great victory, to acknowledge defeat,
At the crossroads where triumph and tragedy meet.
The rich and the poor, how tell them apart,
Where does one end and the other one start?
All are equal at the portals of sorrow,
United today, divided tomorrow.

– from *Flags*

During one of my many visits to India I stayed with an old friend, Shri Prithi Singh, and his family. The elder son of the princely state of Bharatpur, he had been studying in Britain when war was declared and, ordered to do so by his father, enlisted in the Duke of Wellington's Regiment. He now worked in the Ministry of External Affairs and lived in a house on Moti Bagh, the name given to a new colony on the outskirts of Delhi where the city fades into the great plain.

It was my habit, each morning, to walk from the house along Moti Bagh to Shanti Path (Avenue of Peace), a modern dual carriageway leading directly to the President's Palace and on to the Government Secretariat. Most of the foreign embassies and high commissions are located along Shanti Path, screened by an avenue of neem trees.

On the morning of 23 November 1963, I had set out on my usual walk. It was early, but that alone could not account for the singular lack of activity everywhere. There was an ominous silence in the air and the flags of all foreign missions drooped sadly at half mast behind the foliage of the trees. I had neither heard the news nor read the newspapers, so the obvious thing was to call on the British High Commission, opposite the American Embassy, and ask what had happened.

'President Kennedy has been assassinated,' I was told by the receptionist, who looked as though she had just suffered a personal bereavement. And that is exactly how it felt. As I continued my journey along Shanti Path, nursing a confusion of thoughts, I could see the President's personal standard at masthead high above the dome of his palace. It was like a sign of reassurance in a world gone mad. John Kennedy had been a good and generous friend to India, as Prime Minister Jawaharlal Nehru acknowledged in eloquent and moving terms to a silent Lok Sabha. Deep feelings were revealed on every face. Strange it was that death, brutal and wasteful, should have such a unifying effect.

In a spontaneous reaction I expressed my thoughts in verse for the *Hindustan Times* – which pleased my hosts – and although no part of this story it is not inappropriate to mention it here because it was in Prithi Singh's house that I first discussed the possibility of a Commonwealth Expedition, which later became known as Comex. The idea seemed to capture the public's imagination.

Twenty years later we were celebrating the success of the tenth expedition in the presence of the Duke of Edinburgh at the Commonwealth Institute in London hosted by Times Newspapers, and the late Sir Denis Hamilton, then Chairman, was there to welcome His Royal Highness.

'Times Newspapers have played a very insignificant part in the events that have led up to a morning we are looking forward to immensely. In publishing newspapers there are so many horror stories, so many terrible things we have to report, but there is the other side of it: to refer, to project and assist where we can the work of youth, and we are proud to have played a small part to help Colonel Gregory in this tremendous, inspirational story of the last fifteen years of Comex. But my duty is to welcome you sir, and it enables me to say something from my own heart. I have been a journalist and editor for thirty years and I have seen you at work; the way you have dedicated yourself to everything that is good and especially to events in the Commonwealth. Your involvement in Comex is just one more example of the extraordinary range of your activities, and if Times Newspapers, or the other newspapers in which I am involved, can do more to help in the future of Comex, let us do it sir.'

Thanking Sir Denis, His Royal Highness spoke of a world being torn apart by men of narrow ideological and nationalist horizons, men who seemed to believe that they could reform the world by violence and terrorism. And he went on: 'In this sad and depressing situation the Commonwealth ideal of the brotherhood of man, of peace and co-operation, stands out like the beam from a lighthouse on a stormy night.'

At the time, the Commonwealth consisted of forty-nine sovereign states, now fifty-three (with the return of Pakistan and South Africa, plus two new members) embracing nearly a third of the world's population of which the Queen remains the symbolic head – a position as unique as it is a tribute to her people. Any other country similarly endowed would make much of it, even claiming to be a super power; but that is not the British way. A lofty indifference dogs the passage of our history, with occasional bursts of spectacular energy and courage when disaster threatens.

Of course the Commonwealth is not about power, it is about people, and the brotherhood of man, and it takes someone of more than average courage to use such expressions today, which is precisely the message from the majority of the human family – the young.

When Prince Philip concluded his speech by saying, 'I hope that the spirit of Comex, represented by these LITTLE GREEN FLAGS [the green pennant of Comex with Prince Philip's personal cypher and the Asoka wheel embroidered in gold], will help to keep that light shining brightly', he not only illuminated this story but signalled the birth of the Green Pennant Awards: identifying, for the first time, the spirit of adventure with crossing the barriers that divide people.

That message was communicated to Edinburgh Castle to be recorded by Pipe Major Angus MacDonald in the form of a pibroch – a simple enough tune invented for the sole purpose of steering the unsuspecting Prince into the Commonwealth Institute – and relayed to India.

In Delhi, sarod player Promod Shanker and his tabla accompanist Kamal Kant Sharma set to work and turned it into a 'raga' for the Commonwealth. It was then passed to John Mwesa and the Heritage Singers in Zambia, where it was delivered to Kenneth Kaunda in song – the language of Africa.

The President responded enthusiastically: not only did he insist on singing with them but he invited the rest of the Commonwealth Heads of Government to join him 'in setting in motion a tide of goodwill from the Zambezi to reach people all over the world'. His initiative, endorsed by President Frederick Chiluba when he took over, drew an enthusiastic response from six African and five other Commonwealth governments, and encouraged Hamilton and Inches of Edinburgh to redesign the master model of the Green Pennant Awards in copper, incorporating the Zambian eagle (and thus the African continent) in the existing symbolism of the oldest and largest democracies in the world.

Modelled on the original in silver (commissioned by Devon County Council and designed by A. C. Styles of Garrard), the work was done by the young craftsman, John Hunt, and displayed on its own turntable in the window of Hamilton's during the Edinburgh Festival of 1992. To the casual passer-by it may have been no more than an object of curiosity; but for the thousands who had watched the little green flag passing along the Old Silk Route (now the Asian Highway) it represented the success of a series of expeditions from 1965 to 1992 aimed at India, Pakistan, Sri Lanka, Malaysia, Singapore, Canada and Zambia.

On 11 September 1992, the master model left Edinburgh in the hands of a smiling African, Love Mtesa (then High Commissioner), for its permanent home in Zambia to be copied thereafter by coppersmiths in Kitwe, while the pennants themselves would be embroidered in India.

The *Journey of a Lifetime* is essentially the story of THE LITTLE GREEN FLAGS but it is more: it is a pibroch; it is a 'raga'; it is a song; it is an award; and it is an adventure in all these respects. And the starting point has to be a small town called Ooty, in the Blue Mountains of South India, where my brother and I grew up, which I invite the reader to look at in some detail because it was here that the seeds of an idea were sown.

It was also in Ooty – discovered as a health resort for the British in South India by John Sullivan, the Collector of Coimbatore in 1819 – that Macaulay began his work on the Indian Penal Code, extant today, and Field Marshal Lord Wavell found the health and strength he was to enjoy in adult life. And there were many more of equal distinction. But our boyhood heroes were a market inspector by the name of Hugh Carson, who had a fine singing voice and collected butterflies; a head constable called Mariappa, who practised yoga and wrestling; and Anthony Nayagam: friend, philosopher, artist, musician, footballer and cook. Time and change have not blurred that perspective.

The market was a happy meeting place with ebullient good humour at every twist and turn. And, although we couldn't put a word to it at the time, comradeship. It was an adventure playground without fear or threat, and never to be forgotten.

Those early experiences, followed by war, a military career, and the endless forays into the wilderness of human relations, preserved the inspiration of childhood and endowed it with the comradeship that lasts a lifetime. It also kept alive for me the enduring excellence of the Empire, in its day, and its natural successor, the Commonwealth – hence the Green Pennant Awards.

When I went to war it was the unflappable brigade major, George Bolton, and the irresistibly cheerful Dogra, Havaldar (Sergeant) Achha Singh, who stiffened my morale and encouraged me not to let the side down. And there were those marvellous commanding officers who raised our sights above the squalor of war and inspired all who followed them. They were seldom in the news, and indeed never bothered about such things, but without them we would have lost many more battles than we won. To have had a place among the endless ranks of comradeship that came marching off the battlefields of the world remains for me what the Commonwealth is all about. And to have been present when hundreds of thousands of smiling faces welcomed India's 'tryst with destiny' by raising the words equality, freedom and friendship to the pinnacle of man's achievement, is to understand why an Englishman (Lord Mountbatten), was invited to be the first head of state of independent India, and Her Majesty's role as head of the Commonwealth.

Serving with Gurkhas during the emergency, in what is now Malaysia, extended those experiences and sharpened them with the resin of time. When the pipes and drums played me off the premises, the last sight I had was of my orderly, Purnaram Gurung, saluting the departing train. I was able to acknowledge that comradeship by sending a royal pipe banner – received in the company of my brother from Her Royal Highness, the Princess Mary – to Katmandu, there to be carried by Pipe Major Bhom Bahadur Limbu at the coronation of His Majesty King Mahendra Bir Bikram Sah Deva. It was the first such banner presented to Gurkhas.

The transition from Gurkhas to Junior Leaders stationed at Denbury in South Devon was a quantum leap into the unknown. The experience was different; and my time with them will probably be remembered for Ten Tors on Dartmoor – the success of which inspired the first Commonwealth Expedition – and singing given its proper place on the adventurous training agenda.

Ten Tors, pioneered by six hundred junior leaders, brought together thousands of young men and women from youth organisations all over the south of England in a joint venture in which all could succeed, or equally fail. It was described by the *Western Morning News* as 'one of the most challenging tests of endurance for young people in Britain.' The *Mid Devon Advertiser* went even further in a leading article with the banner headline: 'THEY WON THE FREEDOM OF THE MOORS'. I salute them all in the Ballad of Denbury Common.

When I left Denbury and set off on the long dusty road to the East, it was with the avowed intention of restoring old friendships eroded by time and neglect. Most soldiers leave the army with some such ambition and very soon discover that it is not as simple as it may once have seemed. But the universities of Britain responded to the challenge and together we mounted Comex 1 – trained by the Royal Air Force and armed with a combination of song, dance and drama as the means of meeting thousands of people. The efficacy of that treatment was tested at the Dartington Hall School of Music, in Totnes, under the supervision of the late Roy Truby.

Thirteen expeditions followed, the largest five hundred strong, trained by the Services and Industry and identified everywhere by the green pennant. The early successes and failures were reported in a book entitled *Crying Drums*, to which Prince Philip contributed the foreword.

The third expedition gave its final entertainment – after three months and twenty-five thousand miles – at the Royal Albert Hall, the fourth crossed the Bay of Bengal in the Landing Ships *Sir Lancelot* and *Sir Galahad* (later lost in the Falklands), the fifth camped and trained at Denbury, the eighth set out from the Royal Marines Depot in Deal (Kent) and celebrated the Queen's Silver Jubilee in Ooty. Devon County Council provided the base for operations to Canada and Zambia.

But it was not just the undergraduates; men and women from the Army, the Royal Air Force, police, medical and teaching professions, local government, industry, the fire services and Ten Tors veterans stepped forward to have a go.

And there were others on the road, ordinary folk who were genuinely interested in what we were doing, and helped in whatever way they could; among them a lawyer in Croatia, Ned Ivancevic, who defied the Communist authorities in helping to ensure a safe passage for Comex through his country, then part of the old Yugoslavia, and a Croatian postman, Nikola Vrbos, who entertained the whole of the Cambridge contingent – and many others feeling homesick after the first thousand miles away from home – and then sent his daughter Nena to represent Croatia on the largest expedition of all.

There were those simple men on the Turkish mountains, on the desert between Damascus and Baghdad, in Iran, in Afghanistan, on the Khyber Pass, in the tribal territories of Pakistan and in Baluchistan, whose cheerfulness and hospitality helped us on our way without thought of reward for themselves, who will never be forgotten.

The remarkable Franciscan, Father Joshua Sterk, provided hundreds of hot baths for weary travellers arriving at St Francis School in Quetta from the Great Sand Desert of Iran, and seemed blind to distinctions between Christians, Hindus, Muslims or Sikhs. He called everyone 'brother'.

A few hundred miles from Quetta, in Lahore, where Kipling once wrote for the *Civil and Military Gazette* and Kim's gun stands proud on the Mall Road, we found Mohammad Saleem, son of ex-soldier Mohammad Hussain, a genius with engines who was selected to represent Pakistan on the Queen's Jubilee Comex 8 as chief mechanic. Those twelve silver vehicles were his pride and joy. Saleem's presence was also a reminder of those humbler countrymen of his, the 'charwallahs' of the Empire, who in an earlier day served with British regiments stationed in the sub-continent, and were perhaps the most loyal friends those soldiers had.

From the old viceregal seat in Simla, to Ooty in the Nilgiri Hills, the reception in India touched new heights: the Garewals of Chandigarh, who never failed to appear at the frontier to welcome Comex, and entertained as many as their house could accommodate; the Agricultural University in Ludhiana, whose doors were always open to as many as descended on that hospitable campus; the Sikh surgeon, Pramjit Singh Grewal of Amritsar, who restored my injured leg to active service.

And then there was the tabla wallah, Kamal Kant Sharma, who drummed his way into the hearts of everyone he met, not only in India but in Britain and Africa too; the sarod player, Promod Shanker, who can claim to have heard a 'raga' for the Commonwealth in a tune written for bagpipes; and Chinnu, the cook, whose only sin was to enjoy a few glasses of toddy after sunset, but whose virtues were legion. And there were many more.

I pay tribute to the men whose spirit of adventure pervades the Grand Trunk Road in the narrative poem 'The Captains of the Road', to the bullockcart drivers moving on their unremitting way in the song 'My Friend', and to the hospitable face of India in 'Village Lights' (Gaon Ki Jyoti) – translated into Hindi and set to music by Kamal Kant Sharma and his friends.

When 'The Captains of the Road' appeared in the local press, there were calls for the author to appear on stage at the Tagore Theatre in Chandigarh and deliver the 'masterpiece' in person before an audience almost exclusively of Sikhs. Not being at all confident of the reception it would receive, I was immensely relieved when a resounding 'Sat Sri Akal' (Truth is Timeless) filled the theatre, reassuring me that I was among friends, and a minister came forward to present me with a kirpan and saropa (Sikh sword and sash).

In Kolhapur, my old friend Colonel Vasant Deshpande insisted that I was 'an honorary Maratha too' – for climbing the statue of Shivaji and garlanding the great Maratha chief on his birthday – and duly tied a 'kesar patka' (saffron turban) on my head to cries of 'Har Har Mahadev!' from his fellow countrymen.

Africa was altogether a new experience. I had always hoped to see the continent through African eyes, but hardly expected to be singing with the President of Zambia. Nor had I anticipated travelling from Kitwe to Livingstone serenaded all the way by the delightful voices of John Mwesa and the Heritage Singers. And it was in Africa, surrounded by the smiling faces of children and the sound of their singing enlivening every activity, that the idea of recording the story of Comex in song took root.

Twenty-five songs had been written about the Comex experience – I have already mentioned some of them – inspired by such disparate subjects as a journey through the desert lands of the Middle East; the Queen's Jubilee silver train; sailing to Malaysia and Singapore and back in the *Sir Lancelot* and *Sir Galahad*; from ocean to ocean in Canada; and the river of destiny in Zambia.

How and why these songs came to be written appears elsewhere in this story, but the origin of one of them, 'There Must be a Reason', belongs here: the idea of a Franciscan priest in Pakistan, arranged by a Brahman tabla player in India, and performed in Hindi by the University of Delhi Girls' Choir during the Green Pennant Awards in the capital.

By happy coincidence Prithi Singh was present – the last time I was to see him before he died – not only to represent the President of his country, but to receive a Green Pennant.

In all, sixty awards were made in London, Delhi and Lusaka, including: the Governor of Karnataka, Times Newspapers, a tabla player in Delhi, a mechanic in Lahore, the Prime Minister of Singapore, a weighing machine engineer in Australia, the Heritage Singers of Zambia, the Asian Service of the BBC, the Governor-General of Canada, the first Secretary-General of the Commonwealth, a British Council officer, a lawyer in Punjab, a teacher in Newton Abbot, the YWCA in Ooty, a doctor in Somerset, the LSL *Sir Galahad*, a Franciscan priest in Karachi and several Comex veterans.

I mention only a few to demonstrate the mix. Yet there were thousands more who helped 'to keep that light shining brightly' whose contribution has not been recognised. For all of them, wherever they are, I hope that the Commonwealth Heads of Government endorsing the Green Pennant Awards as 'THE COMMONWEALTH GREEN PENNANT AWARDS' at their summit in Auckland, New Zealand in November 1995 (the 30th anniversary of Comex 1) will be seen as a fitting and well deserved tribute.

Time passes swiftly, the memory short,
Our hearts wear the scars their anguish has bought;
But the memory remembered can lessen the pain
When our flags ascend proud to their mastheads again.

CHAPTER ONE

THE MARKET INSPECTOR

The town of Ooty

My brother and I had just walked into the Italian Produce and Wine Merchants, Valvona and Crolla, in Edinburgh; it was Christmas, and the voice of Luciano Pavarotti singing the beautiful old carol 'O Holy Night' over the speakers evoked memories that swept us back half a century. My brother looked at me and I knew at once that I had a task on my hands. But I did nothing about it until my wife and I happened to visit Iona, off the west coast of Scotland.

Now Iona is a gem in God's almighty universe that would gain little from any words of mine. But it was there, while walking from St Columba's Abbey towards the Atlantic to view the vast expanse of royal blue which surrounds the little island, that we came across a small, very small, secondhand bookshop, and in we went.

Under a table in an annexe the size of a cupboard we found a battered cardboard box – the sort more often than not the repository of unexpected treasure – and my hand was drawn to it like a child's to a lucky-dip. And out came a map, a map of Ooty: the very place and of the very period that had provoked my brother's look in the wine merchants'. It was a miracle, and all the divine intervention I needed to get started. So I photographed the relevant section of the map to give myself the satisfaction of completing the first page with the minimum effort, and then began making plans to visit Ooty and photograph the little town from the top of its highest mountain. That completed page two, and as my confidence soared the memory took over to complete the story.

Our parents knew Ooty well, my brother and I had the good fortune of spending some of our formative years there; and it was in those beautiful blue mountains (Nilgiris), which reminded Macaulay of Braemar, and my mother of Devon where she spent many anxious days watching over my father evacuated to hospital in Exeter from the bloody battlefields of Flanders, that my brother and I became aware of the Empire and Commonwealth, and of comradeship too. Even today, for anyone setting out to discover Ooty there awaits the bonus of discovering the Commonwealth (another word for comradeship?), and for me there is no better way of doing that than in the company of Hugh Carson, the Market Inspector.

Little enough was known about him, apart from the commonly held belief that his father had been in the British army and having completed his service had joined the South Indian Railway to become a grade-one driver in whose capable hands the Madras Mail ran from Madras Central to Mettupalaiyam. Moreover, Carson senior enjoyed the singular distinction of driving the Special that transported the Governor of Madras Presidency and his entourage once a year to the Nilgiris for the season, and the good of His Excellency's health (and Her Excellency's too no doubt!), in the rarefied, eucalyptus-scented atmosphere of Ootacamund – Ooty for short. It is possible too that Hugh Carson often accompanied his father on those journeys, which may explain why the roots of his childhood came to be buried in the little town, and his own determination to serve it with the labour of a lifetime. And this is not surprising, because everything that the Empire and Commonwealth stood for was to be seen at its best.

Everyone who visited Ooty fell in love with the place, and Hugh Carson knew most of them: the important and the not-so-important; the big and the small; the genuine and the hangers-on. All of them visited the market, if only to be seen or to gossip with friends, and not infrequently to consult him on a whole range of topics: the flower and dog shows, tips for the next race meeting, the prospect for game in the outlying forests, and an expert's advice on fly-fishing.

And if he knew a great deal about the regular visitors to the Nilgiris, it was nothing compared to his knowledge of the local people themselves, for he was as much part of Ooty as the Todas who lived in small hamlets, or *munds*, dotted among the hills with their herds of buffaloes; or the more common Badagas, a jolly tribe much addicted to the drinking of toddy, whose principal occupation was market gardening. All of them knew, feared and respected the Market Inspector.

He was so personally identified with the market that few people could tell you where he lived. It was his natural habitat, and he was to be seen there on most days dressed in an immaculate khaki drill or serge uniform, depending on the weather, with knitted tie to match, riding breeches, highly polished brown leggings, boots and Sam Browne belt. He wore a Wolseley helmet with patent-leather chinstrap, and a silver badge of office immediately above the centre point of the traditional puggaree. The buttons of his tunic, each embossed with the imperial crown, were also of silver. Attached to one of these, a silver chain draped across the chest supported a whistle tucked away in the left-hand breast-pocket.

He was in his early thirties, clean-shaven, of stern manner and given to few words – unless he happened to be talking about Ooty. He carried a riding crop for company, and as a symbol of authority, which he demonstrated from time to time with a smart stroke across the right leg producing a sound like a pistol shot. It was all the warning necessary for anyone foolish enough to be contemplating a little disorderly conduct within the precincts of the market.

His mode of transport was a bicycle, a beautifully maintained Rudge – as good as a Raleigh, he was quick to point out – with a three-speed facility and a newly acquired headlamp powered by a dynamo. The latter was mounted on the rear shaft, just clear of the back tyre, whence it could be triggered into action by a flick of the heel. The only disadvantage of this concession to modern technology was that the degree of light dropped alarmingly when travelling uphill in the dark. The old oil lamp was at least constant, if dimmer and less exciting. But the Rudge was a handsome vehicle. Parked outside the front gate and touched only by the hand of the leader of a gang of coolie boys answering to the name of Augustine, who cleaned it with the utmost diligence, the presence of the Rudge called for the same reverence as a Rolls Royce parked outside Government House or one of the Maharajas' palaces. It signalled the presence of its master.

The Rudge was to be seen in other places too: it was the link between the market and the rest of the town, and the activities that framed Hugh Carson's own. An evening ride through the botanical gardens was common enough, and as a member of the flower show committee he took a keen interest in the work of the malis (gardeners), most of whom he knew by name.

Sometimes, he would ride on to visit the Todas (a fast diminishing tribe of aborigines) in one of the principal Toda dwelling places called Kodapamund. The patriarch was an old friend: a large, powerful man with gentle eyes and long curly hair flecked with grey. Robed in crude homespun cotton tied about the middle like a kilt and falling to the knee, with the other end draped over the left shoulder, he could have stepped straight out of the Bible. The women wore a similar garment but in the manner of a sarong tied above the breast.

'He looks just like the pictures one sees of St Peter,' was how Hugh Carson described him. 'And I call him Prince Kodapa, after the name of his mund nestling under the protection of Snowdon at eight thousand three hundred feet, and Mount Munro a hundred feet higher where the Toda gods have their abode.'

The Toda home was a low-lying thatched hut, arched along its length, with a hole in the roof for smoke and a minute entrance. Living accommodation was below ground. Their possessions amounted to a few buffaloes, cooking pots and utensils; and for all the criticism levelled against their living habits, they were at least content. 'We are happy to see you,' was how Kodapa would greet his old friend, and the reply was always an assurance that Hugh Carson was happy to see them too. They would then sit together and look out across the valley, absorbing a scene that held for both of them the very essence of existence. For Kodapa it represented an eternity – he knew or cared about little else. For Hugh Carson it was the farthest point from his own origins and having reached it he would never return. The empathy between the two men made it unnecessary to engage in small-talk.

After the Todas came the Badagas, at the bottom of the valley. Here the culture was quite different: Badagas like to gossip, their shrill, sing-song voices crisscrossing each other with questions about anything that came to mind without waiting for an answer, which in any event would be drowned in laughter. It was not information they were after but companionship. As market gardeners, their main concern was to raise their crops, sell them to the earliest bidder and enjoy the proceeds. The womenfolk kept a watchful eye on these matters and, while being just as eager to gossip, were more interested in questioning Hugh Carson about the behaviour of their menfolk on market days. This also was cause for much merriment.

Both communities were enthusiastic about the flower show, the Badagas more so. Nor were they averse to the prospect of winning some sort of trophy if the Market Inspector could so arrange things. How he managed this was not their concern. And it was delicate work trying to explain that there would be lots of competition from all over India, and that the outcome, even in the matter of a pot of Toda honey or a single cauliflower, was in the hands of an expert panel of important people; judges impervious to local sentiment or influence. But as far as his friends were concerned, no one could be more important than the Market Inspector. Alas, with all the goodwill in the world, their handiwork seldom qualified for a prize. However, the flower show was an opportunity not to be missed of seeing visitors from foreign places, and there was always the prospect of a little retailing on the side.

The Rudge was no stranger to the racecourse either, where Hugh Carson sometimes gambled away a few rupees, following up a tip from the governor's or one of the maharajas' stables. Even so, he was not a habitual gambler; more to his liking was a day out on the Ooty Downs with butterfly net and fishing rod. Occasionally, a vintage shotgun would go along too, and that was bad news for the snipe and blue teal that made their seasonal retreat among the reeds and marshes along the water's edge.

But it was mainly the fishing that saw the Rudge heading for those parts. When he was really serious about snipe, blue teal or even butterflies, he would be off on a more ambitious adventure to the foot of the Nilgiris where stocks were plentiful and his conscience suffered less from reducing them. This could be either south, in the direction of Mettupalaiyam, or north, beyond the downs towards Mysore via Pykara, the Liddellsdale and Greenway tea estates, and down the steep descent to Gudalur – now one of the principal game reserves of India.

Of course, Mysore is usually identified with the military exploits of Tipu Sultan and Wellington. But those great events were only of passing interest; whereas the story of the river Cauvery (the demarcation line between the opposing armies of Wellington and Tipu Sultan in 1799) rising from the tears of a heartbroken princess appealed to Hugh Carson's romantic nature. And to the source of that great river he once made pilgrimage on the day and hour appointed to see for himself the tears that gushed forth once a year to commemorate her grief. It was early in the morning and a large crowd had already assembled to witness the miracle. So he didn't actually see her tears when they first appeared out of the minute little hollow at the head of the stream; but as the sun rose a great roar went up: 'Ayah! Ayah!' and the crowd dropped to its knees. The miracle lasted for a few minutes and then it was all over.

'Did you not see friend,' asked one of the lucky ones, 'how beautifully her tears are flowing? In this way God has given new life to a princess.' And Hugh Carson had to be content with that. But when he did check out the water her tears were certainly flowing.

After a visit to the racecourse, he usually made his way to the railway station to celebrate, or commiserate, over a bottle of Tennent's beer in the excellent refreshment rooms upstairs run by Spencer and Company, then the South Indian Railway's catering contractors; and very good they were too – on and off the trains.

The waiters wore white cotton 'chokas' – a long wrap-over tunic buttoned up to the collar – blue and green cummerbunds fastened with a large silver buckle, white turbans trimmed in the company's colours and a badge displaying the letter S ringed with the words 'Spencer and Company Limited'. The damask tablecloths and napkins were always spotless; the Sheffield plate and Crown glass polished to a sparkling finish.

Tuesday was market day, when the whole town met and mingled freely. The gates were opened for business the moment the Inspector arrived at six o'clock, and he remained on duty until the last market stall was closed and the gates locked at about nine o'clock. On other days the procedure was more flexible: he would appear about mid-morning and make his way home at tea time.

To comprehend fully the unique role of the market in the life of Ooty, or Ooty's in the Empire for that matter, one must try to imagine a time and place far removed from the noise, dirt and squalor of a modern city, and picture a small town about three to four miles across set among hills seven thousand feet above sea level. At one end, a little railway station – bordering a lake surrounded by arum lilies – marks the principal entrance and exit, and at the other, Government House. From Dodabetta, rising to eight thousand six hundred feet above sea level, one got a panoramic view of the whole town.

The journey from Mettupalaiyam to Ooty (a distance of about twenty-eight miles) took little under four hours by mountain railway, assisted part of the way by a ratchet between the rails to stop the little train slipping back. The most important train of the day was the *Blue Mountain Express*. But even this celebrated train had to give way to the *Governor's Special*; although it must be said that Their Excellencies themselves preferred to drive up the hills in a Rolls Royce displaying those symbols of imperial authority: a crown and the Union Jack. People were expected to turn out in large numbers to welcome them. It was an event that even merited a school holiday; thus ensuring a massive presence of children clutching their own little flags to add a quality of innocent enthusiasm to this annual ritual.

The season brought other visitors too. The princely states of Jodhpur, way up near Delhi, Jaipur, Baroda, Hyderabad, Mysore, Travancore, and others less well known, followed the governor in quick succession, conforming to long-established protocol, and usually in seniority, bringing their own Rolls Royces and racehorses. Jockeys accompanied the horses, and visitors from all over India filled the hotels and boarding houses vying with each other to be identified with the top set. It was like a game; but whether you were in the top or bottom set, or no set at all, Ooty had many attractions to offer and ample opportunities to compete for inclusion in one of them.

The Ooty races for example, though not in the same league as Ascot, attracted a dazzling display of royal saris, and on Governor's Cup day gloriously flamboyant turbans rose sky-high above the regulation toppers dusted and brought out in honour of an emperor far away. Dresses and hats too were not entirely unfashionable – the British memsahibs were not to be eclipsed by their Indian sisters – but it fell to such spectacular events as the Mysore Gold Cup and the Travancore Stakes to set the local pulse racing. And as to the racecourse, it could claim to stand higher above sea level than any comparable stretch of racing turf in the world, with extensive downs nearby for point-to-point meetings in a setting as beautiful as anything the mother country had on offer.

When 'Their Exs' were in residence, the governor's band was on hand to entertain their guests at garden parties and similar functions modelled on the London tradition. But to attend one of these an early and legible signature in the visitors' book was essential; and even then there was no guarantee that an invitation would be forthcoming – if some over-zealous official had managed to eliminate a worthy aspirant or two along with those unlikely to dignify such occasions.

However, there were compensations. When not employed on more important duties, the band was free to entertain the rest of the town at a series of promenade concerts in the Assembly Rooms – otherwise the venue of English-speaking films – and to help out at dances. And of course the botanical gardens, home to as fine a display of rhododendrons as might be seen anywhere, were open to all. Rising gracefully into the surrounding hills, a lush green carpet with exquisite floral designs was nature's reward to generations of malis who had spent their lives in the service of Kupani Thotam – literally the (East India) Company's Garden – since its inception in 1847, masterminded by Kew? And it was not just their labour that commanded attention and reduced conversation to a respectful silence. It was the sheer artistry and skill involved. These men understood their business and would be at home in a garden anywhere.

Just above a small lake covered with water lilies, and guarded by two cannons long retired from the business of destroying the King Emperor's enemies, or firing blanks less ferociously in honour of his representatives, was Government House (commissioned by the Duke of Buckingham in 1877), the governor's residence, standing alone and aloof from the rest of the town. By night, two little red lights at either end of the spreaders on a ship's mast signalled the continuing presence within of Their Excellencies after the imperial standard had been lowered. At the main entrance to the gardens, stone-built gate-houses sold flowers, seeds, postcards and other memorabilia associated with the Nilgiris. And in front of these, two more artillery pieces of the same type and vintage as their cousins above completed a picture of peace and tranquillity with a sharp reminder of war.

This was the setting for the annual flower show, followed shortly after by the dog show. Meticulously planned and organised by groups of enthusiastic volunteers, both events attracted nationwide interest, the governor and his lady usually attended, and there was no shortage of royalty.

At the opposite end of town, the downs invited visiting anglers to risk their reputations in a succession of well stocked trout streams; while in the calmer waters of the Ooty lake an abundance of the more docile carp lay in waiting to ensure that everyone, at the end of a long day, would have something to take home and boast about. Those bent on capturing a few rare butterflies found this the ideal environment for pursuing their more modest ambitions; and there was room enough for picnicking parties too, particularly during point-to-point meetings. But above all it was the Ooty hunt that trumpeted its importance into society magazines all over the Empire as it thundered across the downs, hounds in full cry in pursuit of the humble jackal. It must have left the latter wondering what on earth all the fuss was about.

Well out of the path of hounds and horses, the most exclusive site was reserved for the finest golf course anywhere in the East. Every green had the quality and finish of a billiard table, owing as much to the richness of soil as to an ancestry of special seeds imported from the mother country. Its history is preserved on the club-house walls and in several albums of photographs. A young professional largely responsible for developing the place had established a record for the course including an amazing hole in one about which there were varying accounts, embellished in the telling no doubt. But it was a record nonetheless, and would stand the test of time because his popularity was such that the feat was etched into the memories of those who followed, and upgraded whenever necessary. Such is the loyalty of simple folk.

Apart from his initials on the back of an old photograph (H.E.G.), only the stories about his prowess remained. In a remote corner in Flanders, while serving king and country with the 1st Battalion of the Royal Scots, he was wounded – and died of those wounds. His widow and two sons later returned to Ooty, where life had been rich with promise and where there had been so much love and happiness. There was a daughter too, but she had been left hostage to circumstances in the care of her grandmother.

As a designer there was a ready welcome for the soldier's widow at Bailey Brothers, the leading fashion house in the Nilgiris and perhaps the whole of southern India. In the market, where she often came with her young husband in their carefree days, she was known simply as the 'Golf Club Madam'. They were well liked and had many friends; friendships that stayed close to her in her widowhood and continued to associate her with the golf club although she was no longer part of it. To those who came to indulge their vanity at Bailey Brothers she was just Maud. Her family, ship merchants of the Honourable East India Company, had built St Mary's Cathedral and St Andrew's Church in Madras around 1850, and helped in establishing those two notable institutions of learning, St Joseph's College and St Joseph's Convent, standing on opposite hills between Wellington and Coonoor, about twelve miles south of Ooty.

But to return to the golf club for a moment, there remains one feature that added greatly to its popularity: the food. It surpassed anything served up in any other comparable establishment. And, humble though he was, the head cook was not entirely unaware of the miracles that emerged from his kitchen. With a disarming smile he put it like this: 'If master give order for jungle fowl, this one [meaning jungle fowl in general] is coming like volunteer sir!'

A bicycle tour

To tour Ooty in the company of Hugh Carson was a unique experience. For one thing, a hired bicycle was no match for the imperial Rudge; for another, at each stage it was like looking through a window and reliving a small part of the story that has given Ooty such a special place in the life of the Empire and Commonwealth.

And a good place to start is the little station by the lake where Macaulay got his first glimpse of Ooty on 25 June 1834, having travelled all the way from Madras on men's shoulders – a distance of four hundred miles – in nine days, ensconced in a palanquin, to find 'a climate equable as Madeira and invigorating as Braemar'. So he was not exactly speeding when he arrived, and his *Life and Letters* (Longman's, 1893) describes his passing through 'a wilderness where for eighteen miles [the downs presumably] there was nothing more human than a monkey, until a turn of the road disclosed the pleasant surprise of an amphitheatre of green hills encircling a small lake whose banks were dotted with red tiled cottages surrounding a pretty Gothic church'. At first glance that Gothic church might have been the much loved St Thomas's tucked into the hill immediately south of the lake, but it was not built much before the turn of the century so the reference is probably to St Stephen's, nearer the town centre, built in 1829. And, as Hugh Carson explains, the railway was not in existence then – hence the long journey from Madras on the shoulders of men. It arrived in Coonoor in 1898 and was extended to Ooty in 1908. But a Ghat road (descent to a river) is to be seen on old maps from 1825, becoming fully operational in 1847. The lake was created in 1823. Half a century after Macaulay, a boy destined to be a great soldier and later Viceroy of India (Field Marshal Lord Wavell) came to embrace the health and vigour he was to enjoy in adult life, and there have been countless others.

With these facts established, the Rudge moves off smoothly with its hired companion following at a respectful distance. Rider and vehicle are much admired, friendly greetings are exchanged and the commentary picks out essential features as they present themselves.

Moving west to east along Commercial Road, the high street of Ooty connecting the two ends of town, is a comparatively easy ride. About half-way along and to the south, directly opposite the market, are the racecourse and the two Elk Hills known as 'little' and 'big'.

From the Nilgiri Hairdressing Salon a voice calls out: 'Good morning Mr Carson sir,' laying claim to his patronage for a neat trim, shampoo and brush-up at four annas a time, or the equivalent of about five pence, and is rewarded with a friendly wave.

Along a covered walkway to the left a string of identical little shops in uniform white on brick offer pots and pans, spares and repairs, and bric-à-brac to please all comers. A bakery-cum-tea shop at the far end is there to provide the needs of the shopkeepers and hospitality for their customers. 'Of course,' speaks the voice of authority, 'the shopkeepers receive discounted rates, which is common practice, and the customers pick up the difference. And you see ahead there, on the right, the Modern Emporium and the Novelty Stores? Well, modern suggests we are moving with the times, and no Indian bazaar is complete without a novelty stores.'

A large department store, Kishinchand Chellaram, Ladies' and Gentlemen's Tailors and Dress Makers, is singled out as 'the pre-eminent store on Commercial Road. It is privately owned and the family have been here ever since I can remember. They are very rich people.'

The tour leads directly to Charing Cross: the sight that first catches the eye on entering Ooty by road and the last when departing. Hugh Carson slows down. 'This is a site of historic importance,' he declares, bringing the Rudge to a halt with his left foot dragging along the pavement, 'which is probably the reason for that enormous fountain and the spectacle of lions spewing water in all directions. As far as I know it is the only Charing Cross in the whole of India, and never ceases to remind me of that little poem by Francis Thompson (1859-1907) in which he says:

"But (when so sad thou canst not sadder)
Cry; – and upon thy so sad loss
Shall shine the traffic of Jacob's ladder
Pitched between Heaven and Charing Cross."

We call it "Cheering Cross" in deference to those dancing cherubs poised above the lions to express a welcome, or farewell, to visitors in and out of season. However, the colours are jolly and don't you think it was clever of Wren Bennett and Company Limited to locate itself in full view of the fountain and without the threat of competition? It is as typically British as Chellerams back up the road is so delightfully Indian, and both in a class by themselves.'

Wren Bennett's certainly presented an imposing façade standing well above ground level, its wooden verandah decorated with hanging plants and tubs of exotic shrubs. But everything inside was imported and therefore much more expensive than anything comparable manufactured locally.

Hugh Carson was now in full flow: 'Buses and bullockcarts bound for Mettupalaiyam turn right here and go past Stonehouse on the hill to the left [he points] – the first house built in Ooty by John Sullivan in 1823 – and the main garage and workshop on the opposite side of the road owned by George Oakes. He was largely responsible for bringing the motor car to Ooty, and with it the seasonal immigration that fills the available space outside the Assembly Rooms (during the proms), at the races, and outside the market on market days when there might be as many as a hundred parked cars. The Assembly Rooms is straight ahead, past the Crown Bakery on the right there; the botanical gardens and Government House are about half a mile further on, just beyond the Sacred Heart Church [now a cathedral]; and Kodapamund lies in the opposite direction – in old Ooty – on the road to Dodabetta. But we shall be turning left here up the hill to St Stephen's Church,' saying which he changes deftly into climbing gear and moves forward slowly, erect and dignified, leaving the hired transport heaving and weaving behind.

Three-quarters of the way up there is a brief stop to admire Spencer and Company, where produce of the highest quality was sold to satisfy the tastes of the rich. On the verandah outside, Badagas of known good character were licensed to squat selling strawberries (which they called 'starberries') in beautifully constructed wicker baskets lined with fern. There is instant rapport.

'The trouble with my friends here,' he says, shaking his head sadly, 'is that they will persist in overdoing the fern to give a false impression of the number of strawberries in the basket, and that leads to all sorts of problems.'

Hugh Carson exchanges a few words with the Badagas and the climb continues to St Stephen's Church. 'This church,' he observes pensively, 'is a memorial to the men and women who came to Ooty not only to live here but to be buried here. Nor is the cemetery the end of their story: that hill behind the church (once Club Hill now Church Hill) is the guardian of their secrets.'

Leaving the church on the right, a comfortable ride along Club Road (where the Savoy Hotel and the Ooty Club claim pride of place) passes the Tea Rooms of D. R. Davis perched precariously on a steep bank on the opposite side of the road between church and club. Here morning coffee, afternoon teas, ice cream on frosted glass plates were once dispensed along with well-informed gossip about the goings-on in town.

The Ooty Club, built in 1830 by Sir William Rumbold, stands comparison with its peers the Madras Club and the Bengal Club in Calcutta, and remains a landmark in the story of Ooty. Apparently, it was here that Macaulay began work on the Indian Penal Code; it was here that snooker was invented by Colonel Neville Chamberlain in 1875; and it was here that the Ooty Hunt Ball earned its reputation as an outlet for the spirit of adventure.

Hugh Carson had a lot to say about the club, and his views are well summed up in an old scrap book found in the library:

For soldier or horseman or planter or sportsman,
The club is a place within call:
For dating and mating and bar room debating,
Or shaking a leg at the ball.
And a global dimension comes with the invention
Of snooker, for sahibs one and all,
But the memsahibs are furious, if none the less curious:
'What are they doing with those balls!'

Within a stone's throw of the club, the Savoy was home for members in transit and celebrities of one sort or another, offering the same excellence of comfort and service as its namesake in London.

At the far end of Club Road, the Nazareth Convent still preserves the nimbus of convents all over India, and, just above the convent, St Mary's Church looks after the spiritual wellbeing of the local Roman Catholic community. And it was from this church on a hill that the bearded Father Crayssac, a dedicated parish priest of the French Foreign Mission, distributed goodness and kindness in abundance, oblivious to distinctions of colour, class or wealth, and bore stoically the burden of a heavy limp in memory of a leg contributed to the First World War. Legend has it that this holy man had gone to the downs in search of a piece of land for a new cemetery, and in a deserted spot beyond Kandal village had come upon an enormous boulder. It was a sudden and startling reminder of Christ's holy sepulchre, and compelling enough for a life-size cross to be erected on the spot which came to be known worldwide as the Kandal Cross, attracting pilgrims from far and wide. Ironically, a chapel had been built near the same site between 1826 and 1828 for the pioneers who came to work on government buildings. And to local people this was all the explanation necessary for the presence of the cross, and the legend about the departure of a serpent when the cross arrived.

Be that as it may, there is a more recent account of a visitor who, on entering the little chapel next to the cross, made a mental resolution to give a substantial sum of rupees to the first beggar he encountered on leaving the place. There was no one around when he entered, and the cross is in a remote, isolated corner; but as he walked out a little old lady in a worn grey sari appeared near the cross. She said nothing, nor was she begging. Who was she and where had she come from? He handed over the money, which she accepted without a word and faded into the background before he was aware that she had gone. Seriously disturbed, he looked everywhere but there was no sign of her.

Hugh Carson explains that the word Kandal responds to translation as 'burning light', and if that is so it suits the message of the cross admirably, but he was unable to say whether this had anything to to with the choice of the site.

On the way back, he had something to say about the schools in the Nilgiris: 'Children from all over India (and now from abroad too) come to the schools. Some, like the Nazareth Convent, are expensive, others less so, but all share an enviable reputation if only for the reason that the children enjoy good health. The Municipal High School, behind the municipal offices overlooking the market, absorbs the largest day scholarship. Breeks School, half-way up the hill above Charing Cross, serves the Anglican and Methodist communions as a fee-paying grammar school.' And so he went on. About two miles from Ooty, the Lawrence Memorial Royal Military School in Lovedale was a boarding establishment for Service families and a place well known to Hugh Carson, which probably accounted for his military bearing and sense of discipline.

There were others less well known, and one of these was an orphanage in the Keti valley (midway between Ooty and Coonoor), the valley of fourteen villages and arguably the largest and most beautiful unspoiled valley anywhere in South India, where Hugh Carson hoped eventually to find a place for Augustine – the coolie boy charged with cleaning the Rudge. But this was not the only contact Hugh Carson had with Keti. Armed with his shotgun – on the off chance of meeting a few 'volunteers' – he would look in on the Keti Brewery (flourishing at the time and supplying the whole of the Nilgiris with its own local brew more cheaply than the imported Tennent's and Beck's) for a little refreshment.

Pedalling back towards the market via St Stephen's Church, Hugh Carson heads for the Collector's Office, a formidable building opposite the church, where the sound of typewriters oiling the wheels of bureaucracy testified to the importance of the man inside, second only to the governor himself. 'The collector is no ordinary person,' the Market Inspector acknowledges with some respect. 'He is the chief administrator and collector of revenue with magisterial powers dating back to the East India Company in 1772.'

Behind the Collector's Office, the post and telegraph offices and the law courts carried the collector's business into other fields. The law courts in particular attracted much public attention: land disputes, the ownership of livestock, excessive drinking, wife-beating, and the occasional case of theft was about the sum of the litigation on offer and much enjoyed both outside and inside the court. A preliminary discussion of these matters by a coterie of lawyers huddled together – like penguins in their black jackets and white collar bands – usually took place outside, and the public were welcome to join in. More often than not the litigants were Badagas, and their favourite lawyer a character by the name of Smidth.

He was a scholarly man, eccentric in his habits, and wore heavy tweeds. With a gold hunter and chain draped across his waistcoat, jingling a selection of gold coins, he looked very distinguished indeed. His head rejoiced in an abundance of dishevelled, greying hair protected from the elements by a trilby hat a size or so too small. But it suited him. Unfortunately, he was habitually drunk and had to be escorted to and from the law courts by his clients, one on each side, to steady his progress. But once inside, and whether a case was conducted in English, Tamil or Telegu, his performance was brilliant and the Badagas loved him as much as his adversaries feared him.

A few steps down from the courthouse, the Imperial Bank of India with its imposing gates and long drive with flower beds along either side occupied pride of place, as might any offspring of the Bank of England. The rupee was a sterling currency trading at 13.25 to the pound. Beside the bank, a red-brick Victorian building displayed the words Nilgiri Library on a large arched sign over iron gates. This was the place to learn all about the origins of Ooty and the pioneering spirit that brought the rest of civilisation to the land of the Todas. There were some watercolours too of Todas and the early days by Captain Richard Barron (1837). Hugh Carson always spoke of the Todas with special affection: 'They have been here since the sun first shone over these hills, and while all the enterprises you have seen were inspired by eminent people caught up in the excitement of discovering Ooty, and carried through, not unlike Macaulay himself, on the uncomplaining backs of coolies, very little has been said about the Todas.'

Opposite the library, and catering exclusively for the Government House set and the princely states, was Bailey Brothers, the home of Nilga: patented waterproofing guaranteed to withstand the severest monsoon on the backs of policemen and postmen, and other government employees expected to carry on despite the weather. Next door, P. Orr and Sons claimed its place of honour as jewellers and silversmiths by appointment to H. E. the Governor, and, further along, Higginbothams the booksellers.

The Rudge moves cautiously down a little road scuttling away behind Bailey Brothers, and its master calls out with an accompanying laugh: 'This may be a minor road but it is important because it enables me to freewheel all the way to the station – but that is not the only reason for its importance!' At the head of the road, on the left, the municipal offices occupied a commanding position with an uninterrupted view of the market; while, directly opposite, the *South of India Observer* – a weekly tabloid of eight pages controlled by a remarkable Englishman, Harold Davis, who had decided to live and end his days in Ooty – represented the voice and conscience of Ooty. Fluent in the regional languages, he could evaluate local news as comfortably as he chronicled events around the Empire, or published his letter from London.

Beyond the *South of India Observer* and skirting half a mile of embankment to the right was St Bartholomew's Hospital. Small but well appointed, it once enjoyed the services of a distinguished surgeon by the name of Colonel Paton, the very mention of whose name had a rejuvenating effect on his patients – helped maybe by a climate 'as invigorating as Braemar'! Leaving the hospital, the road dropped steeply to the station where a widely respected celebrity by the name of Bob Hill was regularly called in to play host to visiting dignitaries. He was a sort of part-time station master; but that he was distinguished there is little doubt, judging by a portrait of him – still to be admired in the Station Master's office – dressed in plus-fours with a peaked hat worn at an angle and displaying a magnificent moustache.

Passing a member of the local constabulary and exchanging the obligatory salute prompted a few words on the Ooty season, when traffic was heavy enough to require the presence of policemen at the five cardinal points in town: outside St Stephen's Church, at the cross roads between the bank and Bailey Brothers, at Charing Cross, the botanical gardens and the market on Tuesdays.

The governor of course had his own mounted bodyguard. They wore gold and green turbans and carried lances. But the policemen too presented a handsome sight in their navy blue uniforms with three silver buttons securing the tunic from breast to collar. A silver chain, with a whistle on the end, disappeared into the single breast-pocket, and a brown leather belt kept the tunic in place around the waist. On the head, a dark red toque helmet – reminiscent of a well shaped strawberry – with a broad strip of black tasselling on the right-hand side added a distinctive quality to the rest of the outfit.

Approaching cars would attract the policeman's attention by squeezing firmly on the rubber bulb attached to the horn outside the driver's door and signalling the desired direction. In the more modern cars the squeezing could be done from inside, while personalised horn-blowing was common practice, depending on the rank of the passenger or the disposition of the driver. For his part, the policeman would turn smartly in the direction of the oncoming car to wave it on with a spectacular signal followed by a smart salute – if the occupant happened to be someone of importance. This would be acknowledged by raising a forefinger half-way to the right eyebrow; or ignored by those not well up in the local etiquette.

The bicycle tour ends as it began, over a bottle of Tennent's in the station refreshment rooms, with Hugh Carson declaiming passionately: 'Ooty is nothing if not the queen of hill stations, and the market is the jewel in her crown.'

The market

The market owed its origins to the involvement of the whole town, the collector digging deep into his official pocket and the chairman of the municipality being obliged to follow with an equally substantial sum if only to secure his own position in office. Architects and artisans had given their services at a fraction of the going rate and coolies in large numbers turned out to labour for little more than the day's food on site. But most of the money came from the surrounding states for whom Ooty was an escape from a south Indian summer.

For geographical reasons, and convenience too, the market had to be in the centre with ample accommodation for all who wished to hire a stall. These included the Todas who brought buffalo milk and honey, Badagas trading exclusively in vegetables, and others from further afield with fruit, fish and toddy to sell. Catering for more royal families than would normally be seen in one place at any one time, and the multinational retinues that accompanied them, standards had to be very high indeed. And although shops along Commercial Road catered for the more general needs, when it came to freshness and variety the market had no equal.

It was oval in shape, not unlike the town itself, about half a mile long and a quarter wide, surrounded by green railings. Two small entrances at either end allowed for the regular users to filter in and out, while the main entrance, with its double swing-gates – where the bicycle was parked – welcomed seasonal shoppers with more to spend and a public image to maintain. Outside the main entrance there was a large well-surfaced free car park. At a discreet distance, on less hallowed ground, bullockcarts were allowed to line up in an orderly fashion, shafts raised protectively over their own team of bulls relaxing in preparation for the long night's journey to come.

Opposite the market, the Blue Mountain Theatre – a huge corrugated iron barn of a place painted green – offered such delights as Eddie Polo in *Daring Ways*, and Al Jolson in *The Jazz Singer*. And, to reinforce the message displayed on large posters near the entrance to the market, Al Jolson's voice serenaded the public through external speakers. For customers beyond the range of even that resonant voice, a ponycart, known locally as a jutka, with billboards on either side and a trumpeter on board, his feet dangling out behind and blasting a medley of well-known tunes, galloped through the town.

The market itself was on two levels, the up market and the down market, making a distinction between the permanent dwellers and those who operated on Tuesdays only – a detail important enough to be included on most old maps. Inside, and to the left of the main entrance, a number of small stalls selling row upon row of brightly coloured glass bangles, postcards, eucalyptus oil, confectionery and Nilgiri tea was the first ambush into which the coolie boys steered the patrons cheerfully and with well-practised skill. In the centre, facing the entrance, a large covered area with a concrete base was marked off in equal sections for fruit and coconuts: bananas, mangoes, mangosteen, papayas, oranges, jackfruit and pineapples were usually available in abundance, and all of excellent quality. Clockwise around the upper level was first the Royal Dairy where butter was churned on site, patted into the desired portions and embossed with a crown by means of a wooden die. An inner circle of grain shops followed: large stalls with corrugated iron roofs pitched steeply to ward off the rains and supported by stout pillars.

But this was no place to be satisfied with an indulgent glance. Here was a fortress in the heart of the Ooty market; a quadrangle sealed off by high walls with large doors set in place like a drawbridge against the tide of humanity seeking a share of the treasures within. This was the home of the true professionals who eschewed corruption as much as they disliked charity. They wore their turbans with a careless disregard for fashion and were not much interested in bright colours either. A loose cotton shirt and a dhoti, or lion cloth, wrapped round the body with the end passed through the legs and tucked in at the waist, sufficed to complete a singularly unenterprising appearance.

All the stalls were identical and each had its own clearly defined territory. They sold rice and pulses, spices, sea salt, kerosine, cooking oils and jaggery – little blocks of coarse brown or black sugar made from wild date palm. To prevent a sudden gust of wind disturbing the spices, these were housed in old kerosine tins with hinged lids, and Hugh Carson was quick to point out that, while the combined force of powdered red chilli, black or white pepper and coriander, may be a cure for many ills, set free to wander at will they can have a devastating effect on eyes, nose and throat. The innocent-looking turmeric alone can leave its mark for life.

The rest of the stock, being relatively harmless, was stored in gunny bags made from the fibre of jute and fully exposed to public view. These bags have travelled far and wide and no one has yet come up with a better, or less expensive method of transporting the merchandise for which they were invented centuries ago. They were stacked neatly on a raised wooden platform about a foot off the ground for protection from the damp, and to allow easy access for a squad of cats employed to pre-empt unwelcome incursions from a colony of rodents resident below. The tins of oil were arranged along the front of the sacks for convenience, and a series of shelves on the back wall made space for ancillary items dictated by custom and experience. Prominent among these were Sunlight soap, matches, cigarettes and the traditional beedie – a tobacco leaf rolled into a cigarette and tied with a coloured string after which it was named: red string or green string beedie.

The owner of the stall usually positioned himself a little off centre on a dais raised to the level of the surrounding sacks and covered with a folded cotton dhurrie which served as a depository for petty cash between its folds. A thick hanging strap with a large knot at the end enabled him to launch himself in any desired direction to the farthest outposts of his little empire.

Who and what were these men who held such sway over the business community in Ooty as elsewhere?

'They belong to the Chetty (or Chetti) caste of Hindus,' says Hugh Carson. 'Chetty means merchant; but tack an 'ar' on the end and you have Chettyar, meaning merchantman. Not unlike the word Swami, or Swamy, meaning Lord. Add an 'ar' there and you have man of God. Of course British soldiers were responsible for reducing Swamy to Sammy, but I don't suppose God minded very much; and it could be that the word chitti, as an IOU, is a derivation of Chetty attributable to the same source. You should consult *Hobson Jobson* by Colonel Henry Yule and A. C. Burnell,' he advised. 'You'll find a copy in the Ooty Library.'

And that remarkable glossary of Anglo-Indian words and phrases published in 1886 certainly has a lot to say. A member of any trading post in south India is known as a Chetty. In Tamil the word is Chetti, in Telegu Shetti, in Singalese Seddi, and there are more variations, all denoting a plain shopkeeper. But it was also used for merchantmen in the nautical sense. According to one account there is no other authority for the use of the word analogous with 'merchantmen'.

One could also read about the 'vessels of the Chettyars, known as Chettils, sailing along the coast of Malabar', and that 'the Chettis are men with such a genius for merchandise and so acute in every mode of trade that when any man is to be praised for his business acumen, he is called a Chettyar. But although very rich, the Chettis rank with the left hand caste' – meaning perhaps that they were not quite the equals of Brahmans.

There follows a brief comment on status: 'The strength of the Brahman is knowledge; the strength of the king, courage; the strength of the cultivator, revenue; the strength of the Chetty, money.'

'So, as you can see,' says Hugh Carson, 'these are no ordinary people. They are a special sect, feared by the rest of the market but respected by all. And being the money men, as well as money lenders, they exercise considerable influence.'

Hugh Carson goes on to illustrate his discourse with another anecdote: 'In the north of India the Chetty equivalent is the Baniya, from which word we get the banian tree. It is an enormous tree with large oval leaves and reddish fruit. And it has aerial roots that grow downwards into the soil to provide a defensive framework around the main trunk, not unlike the high walls here,' he laughs, pointing with a sideways gesture of the thumb. 'That is why people say that once you are trapped inside a banian tree (in debt with a money lender) there is no escape.'

Around the corner from the Chettyars, a line of shops uniformly fronted by sliding wooden panels sold glass, crockery, kitchenware and pharmaceuticals, with a 'Toys and Fancy Goods Emporium' at the far end. Heading the line was the Empire Stores, in a class by itself and living up to its name with stocks of everything from home and abroad that one might expect to see in a grocery of international standing. There was also a tea shop and a coffee shop.

And there is a distinction here, for whereas the tea shop catered for all comers regardless of creed or wealth, the coffee shop was run exclusively for and by the Brahman fraternity, but with a special dispensation for the upper classes who invariably gravitated towards them. There was some difference in the service too.

Both shops were strategically placed so that a well-targeted shout would fall on attentive ears. Message received, the tea shop would launch a highly motivated assistant at the double balancing a wooden tray laden with cups – some without saucers, others chipped or minus handles, but all serviceable. A large aluminium pot of boiling tea with milk and sugar already added unless otherwise ordered would be held in the spare hand ready for action on site.

The coffee shop observed a more conservative tradition. For one thing, a shout did not please the Brahman ear and, while no order was entirely ignored, there would be a noticeable absence of enthusiasm. And any semblance of doubling was considered undignified. On the other hand, an order delivered in a polite and proper manner, with due deference to the status of the management, would be rewarded with a welcoming smile and the coffee transported at a brisk pace in a tin-lined brass vessel, sometimes called a 'lota', with accompanying brass mug to complete the necessary ceremony in the presence of the customer. This amounted to pouring the coffee from one into the other as often as necessary, with arms fully extended and without losing a single drop, until the coffee was thoroughly mixed and the temperature suited to the customer's taste. The demonstration would normally be observed by one or two passers-by who might feel disposed to pause and bestow a word of praise on the dispenser of the coffee and congratulate the consumer thereof. When customers of appropriate rank and status visited the larger shops, the ceremony might be activated with many skilful variations as a mark of high esteem. And under these circumstances, the more stringent codes of etiquette, including the doubling, could be set aside to the more compelling demands of good public relations.

Of equal standing, though larger, was a sweetmeat stall without which no market community could hope to prosper, because the giving and receiving of sweets has a special significance as Hugh Carson explains: 'Not having heard from his son away at boarding school, a father dispatched a brief telegram, "no news worried" and received the reassuring reply, "worry not, colours got, sweets distributed". "Colours got" meant that a place in the hockey eleven had been secured, and "sweets distributed" merely confirmed that heaven's role in the matter had been dutifully acknowledged.'

Another pointer to this was the variety of religious pictures on display: Brahma, the creator; Vishnu, the preserver, present everywhere and in every living thing; Siva, the propitious, with three eyes and four arms, mounted on a bull; and the popular Parvati, daughter of the mountain, in all her sublime beauty.

Then came Skanda, a warrior with six heads, astride a magnificent peacock; Ganesa, the god with the head of an elephant; and Rama and Sita, hero and heroine of the romantic *Ramayana*. Special places were set aside for the terrible Rawana, king of the monsters; Hanuman, the huge ape who could leap prodigious distances and is worshipped for his great devotion to Rama; and not least Kali, the mother of all who gave birth to the world.

But the place of honour was reserved for Lord Krishna, the human incarnation of so much mythology, playing a flute with right foot crossed over left, who was singled out for special treatment with a garland of marigolds.

Devotional aspects apart, these deities were present as guarantors for the excellence of the goods on offer, and perhaps to remind the faithful that the passport to nirvana was available right there.

Seated within easy reach of his masterpieces, and adorned in little more than the sacred thread worn by all Brahmans and a lungi, with caste marks on his forehead, the maestro presented to his customers a smooth, well-developed stomach as evidence of his own prosperity.

The sweets were beautifully displayed on brass trays arranged about him in tiers, with joss sticks at work along the top in order to hold the attention of the gods in whose honour they were destined to be bought and 'distributed'.

In the centre, a flat, white sweet known as *dudh bera*, about an inch in diameter and stuffed with pistachio nuts, was stacked high in the shape of a pyramid. One of these, Hugh Carson's favourite, would be waiting for him on his first round of the day, but always paid for in order to preserve a proper relationship.

If accompanied, he would insist that his companion join him in this act of communion, drawing attention to the fact that no fewer than a thousand sweets went into creating the splendid edifice on view. Each tray boasted its own artistic arrangement based on variations of the central theme: a fortress of large yellow blocks, not unlike fudge but of rougher texture, identified with the state of its origins and known as Mysore pak.

Several varieties of the curly *jelabi* – an early emigrant to the four corners of the world – were very much in evidence on home ground, and both cheap and popular. Halvahs abounded: Madras, Bombay and Karachi varieties, mostly of a rubbery texture (not unlike Turkish delight) and incorporating nuts of one sort or another, most commonly pistachios or almonds. There were many kinds of *burfi*, very similar to what one might expect to see in fudge shops anywhere but displayed with oriental extravagance and panache. The oval shaped *gulab jamun*, dark brown on the outside with a soft spongy centre, made of semolina and dipped in syrup, and as yet untainted by foreign influence, was much sought after but difficult to handle on site unless presented on a piece of banana leaf.

Yet, however popular, sweets cannot survive without those accompanying savouries that have crossed international frontiers to make their debut in today's supermarkets and wine shops under the pseudonym 'Bombay mix'. In Ooty they were to be found in the original: nuts fried and sprinkled with ground red chillies, spiced banana chips, gram and split peas, layer upon layer of what looked like vermicelli – light yellow in colour and crisp – and another item, in appearance not unlike chopped spaghetti, that tasted much the same. And finally the *samosa* and the *pakora*, as common today as fish and chips.

At the far end of a walk around the upper level, fishmongers occupied an exclusive area in full view of the entrance. And to this point Hugh Carson conducted visitors of influence to demonstrate that there were no flies around, and that the technique of laying-out fish on marble slabs covered with sawdust and blocks of ice under dried banana leaves, was a guarantee not only of freshness but of good hygiene too.

An amateur fisherman himself, admitting to some responsibility for the dwindling stocks of carp in the Ooty lake, he had more than a passing interest in what went on at this end of the market, and reserved a special affection for the men who made the long journey from the Western Ghats every week, first by train and then by bullockcart, to sell their fish. He would talk to them about their families, and their adventures in the Arabian Sea fishing from catamarans (from the Tamil 'kattu', meaning bind, and 'maram', tree) for the pomfret, mahseer, begti, lobsters, crabs and prawns they brought to Ooty. And in an aside for the record, he makes the point that the begti, an excellent fish found in the mouth of most tidal rivers in India, was known also as 'cockup' – in all probability a corruption of the Malay word for the same fish, *kakup*.

The Market Inspector's private army, the coolie boys, were under strict instructions to lead their patrons in the direction of the fishmongers early on, and he encouraged Government House, the Ooty Club, the Savoy Hotel and the various boarding houses to place their orders early as a guarantee of likely sales.

Occasionally, before they set out for home having first satisfied a fisherman's thirst for toddy, he would coax them into singing the song of the fishermen at sea, 'The man who gives us life', and he frequently joined in. Once started, the singing continued all the way down the lonely ghat road.

A walk about the lower level of the market was a different experience altogether. A short distance from the main entrance, and down a few steps, led to the chickens. Here a great cacophony of protest rose from hundreds of hens and their consorts against incarceration in overcrowded, three-storey cages, without any attempt having been made to segregate the sexes. The protest was vigorously sustained, interspersed with screams of outrage as one or other of the protesters was dragged out for inspection, and the prospect of a worse fate. And the odds were usually shortened by their owners claiming personal knowledge of the ancestry of each bird.

At the bottom of the steps, tucked into the foundations of the upper bazaar, a basic lean-to provided cover for large baskets of eggs that testified to the level of production, and cried out for justice against the death sentence on such conscientious workers. The eggs themselves could be tested by holding them up to the sun, cupped tightly between forefinger and thumb with one eye closed, not unlike taking aim; or by floating them in a pail of water: the good to sink and the bad to swim.

The remainder of the lower bazaar was perhaps the most crowded, with row upon row of small stalls selling vegetables, greens and betel nut. This was a hornet's nest to be approached with some caution, as Hugh Carson was quick to advise, particularly when accompanied by unwary visitors. The ladies who manned these stalls were no respecters of persons.

They advertised their produce with a frightening display of vermillion teeth achieved by continuous mastication of the betel nut, and they could spit great distances with uncanny accuracy, targeting the back of a pretty sari, skirt or pair of trousers without the wearer being aware of what was going on. Only a very brave man would dare to give offence here. Their conversations were conducted in high-pitched, rasping tones, earthy and loud enough to reach all ears in the lower bazaar, with embarrassing overshoots higher up accompanied by bursts of raucous laughter. The effect could be unnerving. No blushing maidens these. A young man passing might qualify for a remark such as: 'Hey woman, what about this one for your daughter?' And back would come the answer: 'Never mind my daughter, I could put him to good use myself.'

For the Market Inspector they reserved a more genteel approach: 'He is much too good for one woman, just you wait and see; I am biding my time with the best betel nut he has ever tasted.' Understanding the language, he would sometimes risk a reply: 'I must remember that,' to be rewarded with wild cheering, much spitting and the clapping of hands.

Beyond these ladies, the butchers were locked away in an enclosure of their own, waiting for the Market Inspector's stamp of approval before meat could be sold. And behind them, along the length of the outer railings, small mobile booths set up at ground level sold secondhand books and junk from the godowns of the big houses.

Between the shops, the stalls, and the customers, the coolies played an indispensable role. And the qualifications for employment were nimble feet and a large basket with a dent in the bottom big enough to accommodate a human head. In these, cushioned with a piece of old towelling and beautifully balanced, the day's purchases would be carried from market to car or home as required. Both men and women were thus employed, but the coolie boys were special: the corps d'élite. As regulars, they were always on parade outside the market when required, and for them Hugh Carson devised a special code of conduct. In addition to a basket, for which he usually advanced the necessary capital, each boy was required to maintain a slate and pencil to be carried, when not in use, in a cloth satchel over the right shoulder, leaving the left arm free to steady the basket.

When not attending a customer, they were required to remain together and write English words picked up in the course of duty, or dictated by the Market Inspector, on one side of the slate and the Tamil equivalents on the other. The same procedure was followed for sums: problems on one side, answers on the other. As they made progress, leaders were appointed. A few even qualified for enrolment in St Mary's Sunday School. There was also the prospect, however remote, of serving mass for Father Crayssac and the joy of exchanging the working clothes of a coolie for the red and white surplice of an acolyte. The senior of these was Augustine, a name given to him on behalf of his parents when he was christened in St Mary's Church, where he now attended Sunday School and occasionally served at mass.

Similar opportunities were sought for the non-Christians, but the trouble was that they had no religion at all and it was better to send them up the hill to St Mary's than nowhere. Moreover, it was very rare indeed to find an orthodox Hindu or Muhammadan boy employed as a coolie.

Hugh Carson explained that it was not his intention to convert these boys to Christianity but to make decent citizens of them. However, from this unorthodox schooling outside the market, many of them moved on to more permanent employment or a better education, and one did become a priest.

Leaving aside the special instructions in regard to the fishmongers, the boys had their own favourite shops and stalls, and a well-cultivated understanding of market forces. Some of them were skilful enough to record the purchases made by clients on their slates; a practice shopkeepers were aware of, and the likely consequences if those slates were inspected. But the shops needed the customers, the provision of which brought rewards in cash or kind for the coolie boys, and, of course, customers were always willing to pay for exceptional service. So everyone turned out a winner.

Market day

On Monday evenings the operation got under way with the fishermen bringing the day's catch into Mettupalaiyam from the coast on what was known as 'the fish train'. Meanwhile, amidst scenes of much confusion and shouting, the bullockcarts were loaded and marshalled in readiness for the night drive to Ooty aimed at arriving sometime before first light.

Thus the whole community was involved: the fishermen who lived close to the sea, their less adventurous brothers who grew fruit and vegetables further inland among the coconut groves, and the bullockcarts with their drivers. Apart from convoy duties and routine maintenance, the latter enjoyed a free and easy existence: the bulls provided the driving power and, in those fertile conditions, largely looked after themselves. A convoy might consist of anything up to twenty carts, sometimes more, and each had a complement of two or three, depending on the load.

The early morning shuttle from Mettupalaiyam brought kerosine and cooking oils, sacks of grain, spices, lentils and a good supply of toddy taken down by toddy-tappers at four o'clock the same morning and transported in the original pots. These were destined for the toddy shops tucked away discreetly behind a Hindu temple outside the west gate of the market. At the same time, in Ooty itself, the Todas and the Badagas would be making their own way to market with milk, vegetables, honey and clarified butter. By nine o'clock everything would be in place, ready and waiting for the customers to appear.

Asked why the fish were not transported by train all the way, Hugh Carson explains that the day's catch might be brought ashore at any time up to sunset and then accompanied to Mettupalaiyam where it would have to wait for the morning shuttle. Despite the ice, this was not a good prospect; whereas the bullockcarts could set off immediately and reach the cool of the hills within a couple of hours. They were also cheaper.

As he walked about the market inspecting stalls at random, and occasionally picking up a mango, a chicken or a side of beef, Hugh Carson's approach disturbed the nervous system: anxious eyes followed his movements and the grapevine passed them on. To be caught operating outside the accepted norms was very bad for business. On-the-spot sanctions began with confiscation, edging up in stages to the much-dreaded bonus of a visit to the local police station, just two minutes up the hill from the main entrance, where anything could happen.

Listening to a customer being offered a hundred mangoes for ten rupees – less then fifty pence at today's prices – Hugh Carson would turn on the vendor: 'Did I hear something?'

Brilliant actors, whatever the circumstances, a look of credulity would spread across the protesting face. 'No, no, sar; you are hearing nothing, if I tell madam hundred mangoes five rupees, madam will give two and a half rupees, so I am saying ten rupees. Please see sar, how good it is' – a piece would be cut out skilfully with a single-bladed penknife and offered for tasting – 'how can I sell for cheaper price?'

Hugh Carson would ignore the evidence, advise the lady not to pay more than four rupees and move on, leaving the stall owner feigning distress by moving his head from side to side.

The poultrymen were rougher, tougher and more elusive; they did business on their feet. It was judged fair game for a newcomer to the market to be persuaded to buy a chicken at an exorbitant price by raising and lowering the bird by its legs until it squawked loud enough to intimidate the customer into buying. If Hugh Carson happened to come upon such fancy work and intervene, he would be confronted with an indignant defence and challenged to feel the thighs and breasts of the bird: 'It is fatter than His Highness sar,' to which Hugh Carson might respond with: 'If I tell His Highness what you said, he will cut off your head.'

In an instant a look of great alarm would be assumed, with hands outstretched in a plea for mercy. 'No, no, sar; I have wonly one head sar, and what chickens will do if I am be killed? Please take it sar (placing the bird in the coolie's basket), nevermind, you pay me you like' – a masterly tactic to which customers invariably succumbed with a magnanimous gesture.

On those rare occasions when the governor or one of the maharajas, with attendant ladies and gentlemen, decided to make an appearance in the market, three long blasts on the Market Inspector's whistle were all that was necessary to activate emergency stations. Shopkeepers and stall holders would leap into action; coolies not already committed would begin cleaning up; hidden merchandise would appear as if by magic; displays of fruit and vegetables would be rearranged in a trice and all minds switched on to the possibility of some unforeseen opportunity in the offing.

Thus did the market prepare itself to welcome Their Excellencies or Their Highnesses, as the case might be, though the wives seldom accompanied their husbands on such expeditions. When they did, however, all but their presence was forgotten. It was, in Hugh Carson's words 'the ultimate reminder of the gulf between VIPs and VOPs' – very important and very ordinary people.

The party would be accompanied by two policemen, one a head constable – easily identified by the silver piping running in two parallel lines from front to rear over the top of his red helmet – not for any reason of security but to add a little colour to the procession and to emphasise the importance of the visitors. The head constable singled out for this duty was a magnificent figure of a man by the name of Mariappa: tall, powerfully built and greatly admired. He was about the same age as Hugh Carson and they were good friends. Children of the Nilgiris, they had grown up together; one the son of Tamil parents and a Hindu, the other of British parents and a Christian.

Indeed, Hugh Carson often sat beside his friend in the Hindu temple on major feast days and joined in the celebrations afterwards, and Mariappa invariably accompanied him to midnight mass on Christmas Eve because he liked the atmosphere.

These were great men, and greater perhaps than many of the people they served. The bond between them was a shared love of Ooty. As Hugh Carson explains: 'I like fishing, collecting butterflies and shooting. Mariappa is keen on weight-lifting, yoga and wrestling. But we both like to play or watch cricket, and when I have a good tip for the races I always pass it on to him.'

During these VIP walkabouts Hugh Carson usually fell in beside Mariappa – behind the collector, the district superintendent of police and the chairman of the municipality – but with his ears tuned to pre-empt casual criticisms gathering momentum and wandering about recklessly! As the party progressed, with a question here, a nod of the head there, sometimes a smile, everyone stood up with hands folded respectfully and bowed low. It was the sort of obeisance that may have pleased the governor, but not the Indian princes, who were surrounded by an excessive amount of this sort of thing every day of their lives.

For any VOP caught in the eye of a VIP, pausing even for a moment in front of a stall, or a shop, opportunity knocked, and nothing less than the hand of heaven was seen to be pointing at the owner for exceptional treatment. The knocking became even louder if the all-embracing gaze could be held by making elaborate obeisance and offering a special fruit or some other morsel for inspection. And it was not unknown for Her Ex to disrupt the formal procession by exclaiming ecstatically at the sight of a particularly fine display; even an unsuspecting bunch of bananas might find itself raised up in the delicate hand to be suspended before the uncertain smile of a dutiful spouse.

This, of course, was rare, and all the more reason for savouring the moment and reliving it at every opportunity. Intoxicated by the experience, the owner of the bananas would join his hands and bow his head low before the lords of heaven and earth for such unexpected good fortune, yet daring not to offer the fruit as a token of abject gratitude. For him the hour of destiny had struck; henceforth the bananas would enjoy a place of honour, not only for themselves but for their offspring, to be admired by one and all for as long as myth or legend would allow. The accompanying mark-up was no more than a gesture of respect for the hand that had so recently touched them, and the upgrading of the rest of the stock a concession to market forces. 'Tell me sar, why big Excellency is looking this side?' – the inference being that Their Exs knew a good thing when they saw one – was how Hugh Carson's attempts to put a brake on such inflationary practices would be challenged. For the rest of the market, hoping for similar blessings to look its way, the matter had a certain logic and was accepted philosophically.

In this quarter of the market there was little prospect of such an event being recorded; but when it came to the larger stores round the corner, beyond the Empire Stores, a much more sophisticated strategy would be set in train and a photographer commissioned to stand by with his tripod at the ready. His task was to capture the precise moment when the VIP party walked into the lens trained on the front of each shop, while the owners thereof adopted the most flattering pose to show off their personalities to the best advantage. The result had to be good because it was destined to grace the shop for years to come, and to be garlanded at festival time along with the appropriate deity, regardless whether of Hindu, Muslim or Christian origin, in order to reflect the status of the shopkeeper vis-à-vis his maker, and his governor.

One of their number would be chosen to go forward and welcome Their Excellencies with a garland of marigolds for the governor and one of jasmine for his lady. The man so chosen became – until the next time round – the governor's official spokesman.

During these goings-on the shopping public stood well back, waving politely; the governor might raise his white pith topi and his lady smile with an accompanying nod.

Maud

The 'Golf Club Madam', Maud, came early, accompanied by her sons. Most of the ladies in the governor's party wore her dresses and hats, and she learnt a great deal from watching the way they were modelled.

Her sons had eyes only for Hugh Carson and Mariappa. These men were the boys' heroes, and infallible ones at that. Hugh Carson's opinion on birds, fishing and butterflies was the last word on those subjects, and he often parted with a rare butterfly or two to help their collections along. To own a Rudge such as his was their most treasured ambition.

Mariappa, on the other hand, would invite them to visit the police station as a special treat which included collecting them and taking them home. Here there would be sweets, fresh from the market, and coffee served in the 'Brahman way', followed by the awe-inspiring visit to two small cells with heavy bars in which they could imagine the presence of dangerous criminals. But Mariappa was always careful to erase such thoughts by explaining that the cells had only ever been used for jolly Badagas unable to make their way home after drinking too much toddy. It was their hotel, he told them, and the name stuck. For all practical purposes thereafter, the police station was the Badagas' hotel.

He sometimes allowed them to watch him wrestling, or doing yoga, both of which they enjoyed immensely and afterwards practised at home. If the wrestling got out of hand, as it occasionally did, a reminder that Mariappa would have to be informed brought about an immediate truce. Loss of approbation from that source was too great a price to pay for continuing hostilities. And anyway the boys were the closest of friends.

Maud's house stood alone at the head of the valley sweeping up past the Blue Mountain Theatre to within a few hundred yards of Bailey Brothers, so the walk to work took no more than five minutes. The rendezvous for mother and sons at the end of each day was the lawn outside the library. The house itself was a charming red-tiled bungalow, brick built, with an enclosed glass verandah and matching winged extensions. The woodwork was painted green. It was built on a raised foundation about three feet above ground level, with a series of low steps extending well into the surrounding garden, and provided the ideal accommodation for dozens of potted geraniums.

The house faced south, looking towards the market, the racecourse and the Elk Hills beyond. It was dominated in front by a giant eucalyptus tree leaning against a granite revetment, and overshadowed by conifers on the grassly slopes behind. The eucalyptus tree was something of a landmark in that, on 24 December, an enormous star, made of bamboo and coloured paper with an oil lamp inside, would be raised to the summit as a reminder that the miracle of Christmas was not confined to Bethlehem.

The architect of this piece of artistry was Anthony Nayagum, a member of the household staff which rotated around five brothers, Ambrose, Andrew, Agusty, Anthony, Christy (there was a sister too, Ruth, who married a lamplighter from Mettupalaiyam station) and their parents. They were a talented family of drivers, mechanics and electricians with experience of working on tea plantations, and all were excellent cooks like their father, the legendary chef of the golf club.

Anthony and his wife Asu were more or less permanent fixtures, and to his occupational skills he brought the additional attributes of musician, artist (though a Christian he painted mainly Hindu deities) and footballer, captaining the local team known as the Centurions. The origin of that name was to be found on the sailor caps worn by the boys.

When it came to fishing, catching butterflies or flying kites, the widow's sons were in his sole charge; he even manufactured the fishing rods and butterfly nets, and made the kites. When he played football they were among his most vociferous supporters.

On the way home from an expedition to the downs there would be a special treat in the form of tea in a local teashop near 'finger post', at the crossroads between Ooty and the downs, so named because the fingers pointed the way to St Stephen's Church, the club, the railway station, St Mary's Church and the downs. The tea was brewed from a bag dipped repeatedly into boiling water and served, very sweet, with lots of milk. As host, Anthony would remain standing and decline to take tea himself. This was intended to teach his young charges the nature of true hospitality which often dictated surrendering personal convenience to the needs of others – at least that seemed to be his view of the matter.

Fishing and catching butterflies on the downs led naturally to exploring the depths of the water, and the boys insisting on learning to swim. Anthony did his best to deflect their enthusiasm away from the swimming to the more important business in hand. But two small boys determined on a course of action are not easily dissuaded, so the long-suffering Anthony is forced to take to the water and allow each in turn to ride on his back, and later to be reminded that they had learnt to swim on the back of India.

The football occasions were less hazardous. The boys were positioned near the home team's (Anthony's) goal and the goalkeeper instructed to keep an eye on them. But while their own eyes were glued loyally to their hero's every movement, what they really looked forward to was the retelling of events – including all those extravagant details they had not actually witnessed – when the game was over.

One of the more popular rewards for good behaviour was a bullockcart ride, when they were allowed to steer the bulls to the end of the drive and back. Although Maud never actually accompanied her sons on these expeditions, she invariably watched their performance.

On Tuesdays the boys would accompany Anthony to St Mary's Church to deliver loaves of bread for the poor. This was known as St Anthony's Bread, and in response to their questions the boys were told that it would one day make them very strong. That explanation may well have been beyond their comprehension, but coming from their mentor it had to be true.

Work on the Christmas star would begin in early December, and the dedicated Anthony was assured of the unwavering attention of two boys wrapped in admiration. Whenever he played the harmonium he could count on an audience of two.

The valley between Maud's house and the market, about a mile long and half a mile wide, was made up of small-holdings of potatoes, cabbages and cauliflowers, supplemented with stocks of free-ranging poultry destined for the market. A few of these fell prey regularly to packs of hungry jackals on a cold night out from their normal habitat in the hills.

Their high pitched howling not only disturbed the peace, but sometimes signalled a more sinister menace – a hyena or a tiger – confirmed when the dogs in the area observed a strict silence. Sometimes a shot would ring out, which meant that the Market Inspector had had enough, and that the adventurous spirit of at least one marauder had been brought to a close. The silence following signalled that the jackals had got the message.

The ghat road

At the end of a long day, the petromax and hurricane lamps, and the more common oil lamps with exposed wicks, transformed the scene in the market, giving it an intimacy that drew everyone closer together in that magical atmosphere characteristic of any Indian bazaar after sunset.

And there was a noticeable reluctance for people to go home as they gathered in groups about the shops and stalls to gossip about their experiences during the day. For Hugh Carson, however, there was still much to do before he could mount his Rudge and pedal home to the Tennent's waiting to restore his energy, and the voice of Gigli to soothe his nerves via the latest His Master's Voice gramophone.

The bullockcarts resting contentedly outside the market had to be marshalled for the long journey down the ghat road to Mettupalaiyam, and cleaning operations set in motion to ensure that the accumulation of litter from a busy day was not around to greet the first customers next morning. Stalls and shops had to be checked for the last time, and the names of those intending to sleep where they worked, which included most of the coolie boys, had to be noted, and each provided with a 'chit' authorising him to do so. And last, but not least, the several groups of Badagas tuning up to sing their way home had to be warned to go quietly until out of earshot of the police station. It was a warning unfailingly greeted with cheerful good humour and promises of prayers for the everlasting health and prosperity of the Market Inspector.

Only once did Hugh Carson allow himself to express sympathy for the long and tedious journey that lay ahead of the convoy of bullockcarts, to which the lead driver responded instantly: 'What sar, no difficulty; you please don't vurry. To this Coonoor (the town twelve miles south of Ooty and about two thousand feet lower) traffic is coming. Then ghat road, cars and lorries will not coming there; it is too much narrow sar, and how many steps? You come see sar, it is very nice.'

He had travelled back and forth on the mountain railway often enough, and had cycled to Mettupalaiyam; so why not complete the experience and do it by bullockcart? On impulse he decided to go, and elected to travel at the head of the convoy sitting beside the driver. One of the fishermen, Muthu by name, was the other passenger.

It was a clear moonlit night. Each cart had a hurricane lamp suspended from the yoke, between the bulls or from the axle, the position being interchangeable, though the lead cart normally opted to have the lamp in front. Despite the grinding of wheels, conversation flowed easily between the lead driver, Chinnapulai, and Arikyaswamy, bring up the rear, in a high pitched sing-song voice that translates from the Tamil something like this:

'Arik-ya-swa-myeee!' – the 'eee' sustained and rising – calls Chinnapulai.

'Haaaaah! Tell what!' comes back from Arikyaswamy.

'Water are you hitting?' (Are you drinking toddy?) asks Chinnapulai.

'Not now, you will see there on the ghat road,' warns Arikyaswamy, meaning that toddy would be available on the ghat road.

The lead driver then turns his attention to his own crew: 'Now this Muthu will singing one song sar.' Hugh Carson readily approves.

'Dai Muthu!' (You Muthu!) Chinnapulai checks that Muthu is still present.

'Tell, what!' says Muthu.

'Put on a song fellow.' Chinnapulai uses the word 'da' for fellow.

Hugh Carson explains that the word 'fellow', used as to an inferior, or lightheartedly to a friend is 'da, dai or dee' and is very common in colloquial Tamil: In a typical example, 'why fellow how are you?', the word for fellow would be 'da'. Calling a male at long range, in similar circumstances, 'dai' (dai-eee) – sometimes followed by the name – would have the desired effect.

By contrast, a small boy caught spending a penny behind someone's car would jump six feet and button up with alacrity at the sound of a short sharp 'dai'!

For one woman addressing another thus: 'What dear, is there any gossip?' the appropriate word for dear would be 'dee'.

Having been told to 'put on a song', Muthu obliged with the standard favourite, 'The man who gives us life', and whether fisherman or not they all joined in.

That the Market Inspector should be singing with them was of far greater significance to Chinnapulai than his own role as captain of the 'flag bullockcart', and the expression of contentment that spread across his face said as much.

There were five toddy shops between Coonoor and Mettupalaiyam, but none between Coonoor and Ooty, and the reason for this was that the latter section of the road was open to all traffic and drinking and driving – even for bullockcarts – in those far-off days was inadvisable. Furthermore, most bullockcart drivers were accustomed to sleep, particularly after taking toddy and when travelling in convoy, leaving it to the bulls to follow the leader who, under normal circumstances, would be expected to remain awake and alert. But quite often the leader too would place his reins in God's hands and trust the bulls to find the way home.

Three to four miles an hour is by no means excessive, and it took a little over three hours to reach the ghat road. But the singing continued, most of it directed towards heaven and the Headdriver living there; and there were some solo performances of high quality up and down the line which filled the air with the sound of simple men enjoying life. At one point Muthu came up with an extemporaneous offering about market inspectors: the supreme Market Inspector, whose market was the universe, had sent his personal representative from Ooty to accompany them on the ghat road, which was a measure of his generosity and a good omen for them all. The rapport between Hugh Carson and his companions of the sea and soil was something that governors, collectors and others in high places rarely, if ever, experienced. In a way it was a closer, a more intimate comradeship than might exist even in the army because it grew out of a deep and abiding affection in which discipline played only a voluntary role.

At the first toddy shop, the convoy pulled in, a simple enough manoeuvre because it moved nose to tail, and Hugh Carson was confronted with the hospitality of fifteen drivers, fishermen and others. He was also well aware that the sweet innocuous toddy of the morning would be the bitter fermented toddy of the night.

The toddy shop was a mud hut with a thatched roof made of dried banana leaves, and a crude wood-panelled front. Two of the panels allowed for an entrance, but to enter one had to stoop. The inside was illuminated by a single hurricane lamp hanging from the ceiling, and the action took place around a large wooden table surrounded by seats made from old tea chests. As a precaution against unwelcome insects, the walls and floor had been treated with a coating of cow-dung; on a built-up ledge, several pots of toddy held the promise of the house.

The toddy was served in a variety of glasses, tough enough to stand the test of boiling tea when required, and the most impressive of these, the largest, was passed from hand to hand for inspection before being filled and presented, with both hands

– it being considered impolite to offer anything with one hand – to Hugh Carson. 'This one, best one toddy sar,' Chinnapulai assured him with the confidence of a true connoisseur. 'You taste and see sar, don't vurry.' Hugh Carson accepted the glass and stared long and hard at the white opaque liquid inside. Several ants floated on the surface as guarantors that the pots had not been tampered with since they were taken down in the early hours of the morning. Having risked all in search of the sweet liquid, the ants had left some of their comrades behind, hostages to fortune: to be swallowed or spat out according to taste.

The hospitality on offer was heart-warming, if excessive, and it would have been churlish not to respond in the same spirit. But it was also self-evident that if he accepted a glass from each one of his hosts he would be a dead man (or very nearly so) and the convoy would be unlikely to make Mettupalaiyam on that or perhaps any other night.

He had to take the initiative at once and the best option was a brief speech in colloquial Tamil. Translated literally, this is what he said.

'We have a common interest in the Ooty Market. Is this right?'

'Ama! Ama!' (Yes! Yes!) they acknowledged in unison.

'For this reason,' he continued, 'I must look after the market with happiness for everybody.' There was no dispute about the propriety of that sentiment either.

'It would be good, and I would happily drink a glass of toddy with each one of you.'

'Ama! Ama! good it will be,' they cried in unison before he could finish the sentence.

'But please see, would I ask you to let me drive a bullockcart on the ghat road at night? Like that you must not ask me to hit too much toddy my friends – because I am inexperienced.'

In the half-light he took in the expressions on those serious faces, so full of trust and understanding. They were clearly pleased to hear him speaking and avoided any further interruption. So he continued: 'Looked at like this, I will take one glass of toddy from Chinnapulai. And why? because I am sitting in his bullockcart.' There were smiles all round.

'After that from all of you I will take one glass. Then you all one, one glass from me will take.'

'Ama! Ama!' they conceded; the proposition went down well.

'Doing like this,' said Chinnapulai, 'we will all very happy be.' And with that the serious business began; three glasses each, no less, no more!

Hugh Carson then raised the question of boredom travelling by bullockcart.

Chinnapulai cleared his throat, while his companions waited for him to speak. His Tamil had room for the occasional English word.

'We are simple people wonly sar. When we going from here you will looking up sar and see the stars – you may also count. No cars is dashing sar,' he laughed. 'In car you cannot do like that. In day time sar, everything God is make you can see. That car is too fast going sar, he is too much hurry and 'fraid for accident. We can also sleep sar, bulls is knowing how can go home. When he want there is plenty grass for bulls, no need petrol sar,' this produced a laugh all round, 'and no accident sar. What else we can ask from the God?'

Hugh Carson absorbed this bit of ghat road philosophy, moving ever closer to a perfect understanding of the people in whose country he had learnt the meaning of true humility. The notion of the brotherhood of man held no fears for him.

It was not long after they had moved on from the toddy 'stop' that Hugh Carson heard heavy rustling in the undergrowth to his left and then, suddenly and without further warning, an enormous object leapt down the bank and into the road – blocking it completely. In an instant the thought crossed his mind that Tiger Hill comes all the way down to the river below the ghat road, and here was one of its permanent residents heading in that general direction with no more sinister intention perhaps than its own nightly refreshment.

The tiger stood perfectly still with a frown on its face, the healthy shine on its coat reflecting the colours and pride of a prince of the jungle. It continued to look in the direction of the bullockcarts, blinking slowly as if puzzled by this intrusion into its nocturnal habits, and, turning slowly, presented a better view of its magnificent proportions and the stripes that picked them out to such perfection. It was a majestic sight. For a moment Hugh Carson regretted not bringing his gun, but as quickly dismissed the thought; to shoot such an animal would have been little short of a sacrilege, the very worst kind of destruction. For his part, Chinnapulai's reaction was to go for the bulls' tails – a sharp twisting of the same being the time-honoured means of accelerating in an emergency – with the clear intention of charging the tiger at full gallop. Acting instinctively, Hugh Carson dropped his hands on Chinnapulai's and stopped him. Sensing danger the bulls came to a halt; the convoy closed in and remained still. Like a general reviewing a parade brought to attention, the tiger continued to glare, its large eyes flashing red in the moonlight, and then moved slowly off the road and down towards the river.

'Strangely enough,' says Hugh Carson, 'the silence was not broken, every man was alone with his own thoughts, and not only about the glory of God's stars in the sky, but of His tiger on the ghat road. It was an experience I shall never forget.'

As if their emotions had been held in check on a time clock, a great cheer was released: 'Arik-ya-swa-myee,' cried Chinnapulai, 'did you see?'

'Hah!' came the response, 'very well I saw, we all saw.'

Turning to Hugh Carson, Chinnapulai gave his opinion on the scene they had just witnessed together: 'This very much good luck sar. This big one tiger is strong like God. So what means sar is we all peoples will be look after by the God.'

There was a long pause and then, 'I think so sar because you come with us.' The sincerity of that remark, its stunning simplicity, left the Market Inspector speechless.

Chinnapulai now insisted that the entire convoy of fifteen bullockcarts should escort Hugh Carson to Mettupalaiyam station to catch his train. Nothing less would do justice to the comradeship they had shared. The curiosity of the station master, other officials and the passengers on the platform was ignored. This little band of brothers had come through the night together and Chinnapulai spoke for them all when he addressed Hugh Carson.

'Numbo Dorai,' he said, meaning literally, 'Our Gentleman' – not unlike the use of the word 'Sahib' in the north of India, and a rare accolade of its time – 'happily please go.'

He boarded the train a wiser man, tired and overwhelmed by emotions that were difficult to control. He felt bound to his companions of the night with something like the bonds that might bind kinsmen, and there were many more like them waiting for him in Ooty.

As the train puffed its way up into the hills, each little station seemed to hold out its own personal greeting: Kallar, Adderley, Hillgrove, Runneymede, Karteri,

Coonoor, Wellington, Aravanghat (or Aravankadu), Keti, Lovedale, Fernhill and then his beloved Ootacamund. What wonderful names they were! They too were his friends.

A few lines took shape in his mind which many years later were incorporated into a song dedicated to the bullockcart drivers of India:

My Friend, I have passed you by a thousand times,
And your image comes vividly to my mind:
With unaltering pace, grace, patience personified
You rumble on content, while I am left behind.

The creaking of your cart, the bumps, the grinding wheels,
The rhythmic footfalls of your bulls portend
The tenor of an endless way
Beneath your gentle hand, my lonely friend.

How is it with you at night, when heart and limbs are tired
And all your hopes lie stilled within your breast?
Do you lay down you reins and trust in God
Asking of Him the blessing of some rest?

The hurricane lamp swings gently, beckons still,
Symbol of comfort, courage, hope and light,
To scatter all your doubts and fears forever –
Forever shining brightly through the night.

Move on your unremitting way, farewell!
We shall meet again; but parting I confess:
Of all the things you see and others miss,
I treasure most your memory – timelessness.

The fire

It was on such a night that one of the coolie boys spotted some sparks rising above the inner courtyard where the grain stores with stocks of cooking oil and kerosine were located.

The leader, Augustine, went to investigate and found the large doors, rising to the height of the surrounding wall, locked and bolted. The Chettyars had gone home. Mindful of the instructions dinned into their heads time and again by the Market Inspector on what to do in the event of fire, one of the boys moved as fast as his legs could carry him to the first station on Commercial Road, half-way between the market and Chellarams, while a second raced away to warn Hugh Carson.

The others raised the alarm within the market and began collecting fire buckets (empty kerosine tins) and stacking them near the three standing taps available: one by the fish stall, one at the bottom of the steps leading to the poultry cages, and a third in the butchers' yard. There was no fire hydrant in this part of town.

There were no lights in the market either. Electricity had only just begun to appear in Ooty and street lighting was provided by oil lamps, which brought out the lamp lighters at sunset every evening. But, romantic as this undoubtedly was, the spread of light was limited. Apart from the general area outside the main entrance, everything was in darkness. However, aroused from their slumbers and shocked into action, those shopkeepers who had made a night of it in the market got to work on their petromax lamps and soon the whole area in front of the grain stores was ablaze with light.

Properly dressed for duty, Hugh Carson arrived on his bicycle, the light from his new headlamp bouncing in front and a coolie boy riding on the cross-bar.

To the sound of a wild clanging of bells, despite the total absence of traffic, the residents of Ooty were informed that their fire engine, with four helmeted men on board draped from head to toe in Nilga waterproofing, had arrived and was ready for action.

The Market Inspector was now in control. He directed the fire engine carefully past the fruit stalls and into position in front of the wall by the grain stores. At the request of the fire engine commander a few men were co-opted to help work the hand pump while the professionals connected up the hose and moved towards the wall, nozzle at the ready. It took a little time for the water to appear, and when it did the result was disappointing, posing little threat to the fire; but with some vocal encouragement the tempo of the pumping improved, the jet of water began to creep up the wall with growing confidence and the crowd cheered. But cheering was not enough.

Meanwhile, Hugh Carson was being urged to break open the doors and salvage as much of the stock as possible; but he was quick to point out that if the fire got out of control the wall offered everyone the best possible protection. The right thing to do was to act quickly, pump hard, and keep the water supply coming in buckets to top up the trailer.

People started to arrive in numbers; among them Maud, who had heard the fire engine and could see the smoke rising above the dimly lit market where she had been shopping that morning. Leaving her sons in Anthony's care and summoning the rest of the household, she headed for the market as fast as she could. Like all the others, she was intent on helping her own favourite shopkeepers; but this was no time for picking and choosing – her squad simply did as they were told, helping to clear the shops under greatest threat and stacking the goods well out of harm's way in easily distinguishable lots.

The spirit of the day returned to the night, as men and women sweated over their labours. All spare hands were put to running a chain of buckets from the fish stall to the fire, while others continued to bring single buckets at the double. The water was having some effect, but the smoke and the sparks, and an occasional tongue of flame, rose ominously above the wall to cries of consternation from the workers below as they urged the men on the pump, now working in relays of four, to redouble their efforts. As the fire gnawed into the timbers the crackling and snapping grew louder; explosions followed as kerosine tins succumbed to the heat and were torn apart; black smoke billowed over the quadrangle, swirling and weaving and diving through the market in a sudden downward sweep pursued by the naked fury of fire unleashed on a mission of destruction; apprehension took hold of workers and watchers alike.

It was at this point that Hugh Carson had an idea. Conceding only the removal of his helmet to the exigencies of the situation – the helmet was new and it was easier to scrub a head covered in soot and grime – he got hold of a ladder and climbed to the top of the wall. Outflanking the smoke, he secured a position of vantage from which he was better placed to direct operations. The water was raining down into the smoke, but his concern was, by moving along the wall, to try to locate the source of the fire as it spread laterally.

It was a bold move. He called for buckets of water to be brought up the ladder and discharged right and left simultaneously, working inwards from the outer fringes of the smoke, while the more professional effort continued to attack the centre of the target. Alas, at this point, his little army faltered.

Fortunately, at that precise moment Mariappa arrived and, removing his red helmet, was up the ladder in a flash to join his friend. Aroused by his example, others found their way up, each bringing a bucket of water. Gradually the pattern evolved into a chain, the head of which moved back and forth along the top of the wall – 'like the hood of a cobra' was how Hugh Carson described it – attacking the fire at source with undiminished vigour, and not a little courage.

Through the night the battle continued. Slowly, but quite surely, the fire was brought under control, and miraculously without any casualties. Although the tins were alarmingly hot, most of the oil survived. That was a miracle in itself. But all the sacks of rice and lentils stacked nearest the wall had been destroyed, the burnt contents scattered far and wide like a last desperate offering to appease the wrath of the gods.

Roof timbers were savagely scorched, shutters burnt to ash; but, amazingly, no lives had been lost. And, as Hugh Carson stepped down from the ladder, he noticed the tall figure of Kodapa standing well back from the crowd – his presence exuding an aura of royalty – clutching a shepherd's staff. He walked over to him quickly. Kodapa's expression betrayed nothing of the concern he might have felt – it was calm and emotionless. In his world, everything was part of a universal scheme beyond the hand of man. Perhaps the Toda gods looking down from Mount Munro had sent him, simply to be on hand, bringing a few of his tribe with him to fetch and carry. Perhaps! And now that that duty had been accomplished it was time to go, and they had grouped around their leader.

'I see that you are well,' said Kodapa.

'Yes,' replied Hugh Carson, 'I am well.'

There was along silence, broken by Kodapa: 'That is good.'

That brief exchange was enough; nothing more needed to be said. Kodapa turned and began to walk away without a single backward glance, while Hugh Carson just stood there watching him depart – leading the long walk back to the hills.

Devoting its front page to the fire the *South of India Observer* proclaimed Hugh Carson a hero which indeed he was. But his own treasured memory was of everybody helping, the coolie boys carrying out their instructions to the letter, and no one having been hurt or worse, killed.

The market was soon back to normal, even improved, with generous donations from Their Excellencies, Their Highnesses, and the permanent residents. It now boasted a brand new fire hydrant sited on the most conspicuous spot as a kind of memorial to the fire.

Festival time

Whatever happened inside or outside the market, the seasons continued on their way, but always with the assurance that they would be coming back. Autumn had already arrived, turning the attention of the whole community towards the festival of Diwali.

Apart from Christmas and Easter, the feast days of Christian saints arouse little interest, given only a mention in church notices, unless they happen to wear a national label. In India it is different; not only is the Hindu calendar filled with a rich variety of feasts and festivals, all widely proclaimed and celebrated, but those of all other religions are generously included. The result is that India enjoys more holidays, and has more experience in celebrating them, than any other country in the world. Of these, three – in the order they appear on the calendar – call for a special mention because they were the favourites of Hugh Carson and Mariappa: Diwali, Muharram and Christmas.

'Diwali,' as Hugh Carson explains, 'is a Hindu festival that arrives when the leaves begin to fall and the old gives way to the new. It is the festival of lights when millions of tiny oil lamps light up the hospitable face of India. And that face is to be seen everywhere: among the rich and the poor, on every street, in every home, and in every stall and shop in the Ooty market. It is a time when the debris of the past year is swept out of the hearts and minds of the people. Goodwill abounds; sweets are distributed; there are no strangers on that day.'

Asked about his own activities during Diwali, Hugh Carson passes the question to Mariappa.

'Together we visit my friends and my family. But first we tour the market to greet everybody and then go to the stone temple; the one with the red and white stripes near the station. After that the celebrations continue all day and through the night. Everybody is happy.'

Although Mariappa is a Hindu, and Hugh Carson a Christian, they always shared the ten-day ritual of Muharram (the sacred month) with the Shiite community co-ordinated by the owner of the Empire Stores known as the 'Sait' (adapted perhaps from the Arabic Sayid, for Lord).

Mariappa explains that the Shiite (or Shiah, meaning follower) are the minority sect of Islam and followers of Ali, the cousin and son-in-law of the Prophet Muhammad.

'Ali's younger son Husayn, the grandson of Muhammad, became the third Imam (Abu Abdullah Husayn ibn Ali, to give him his full name) who was martyred for his faith at Karbala in October 680 and was thereafter known as Sayyid ash-Suhada (Prince of Martyrs). So, while Muharram is the commemoration of that tragic event, to the casual observer the ceremonial can be altogether confusing.'

In Ooty the first signs come from the sound of drums, floating into the town centre from every direction. The basic rhythm is quickly assimilated: 'De dum-dum, de-dum; de dum-dum, de-dum,' and remains constant despite periodic variations in a more vigorous and aggressive style. The sound grows in volume as the parties close in.

The drumming heralds the coming of human tigers in what seems to be a display of disguise, defiance and courage. They are dressed and painted with exceptional skill and artistry to fill the part: tightly fitting yellow loin cloths and headdresses, silver whiskers, heavy eyebrows, claws attached to wrists and ankles, and the exposed parts of their bodies painted yellow with appropriate markings. From the more affluent sectors of town the quality of costumes and the painting, and the rest of the paraphernalia, display more expensive tastes and larger pockets. Apart from that, the tigers are no better than their poorer relations.

The lesser ones might make their debut with no more than a single drummer and half a dozen acolytes. Those from the direction of Government House and surrounds would be escorted by ten times that number and a proportionate corps of drums.

The tigers themselves, hoisted proud on poles held at different levels above the heads of the crowd lining the approach route, display a fearsome image. As they close in on the market square the effect is spectacular, even frightening. The tigers confront each other, bodies crouched, heads and shoulders poised for battle.

The drums step up the volume and tempo; the tigers slip into a variety of threatening postures and look ever more menacing; the sweat begins to roll. The crowd is driven into a state of high expectation, and although the fight never actually takes place, they have seen it all and for days afterwards recall with relish the fights and the fighters.

The culmination of Muharram is a procession around a replica of the tomb of Husayn. In India it is referred to as 'Ta'ziya' (or Tazia) and is a highly stylised theatrical presentation of the Karbala tragedy not unlike the Christian passion play.

But winter has come, the visitors gone, and Ooty settles down to enjoy the advent of Christmas. Each morning brings a spectacle of frost, filling the valley and contrasting vividly with the surrounding hills. Peace and goodwill abound. For the children of those who could afford it, Wren Bennett's features all the attractions of an Oxford Street store complete with pretty lights, Christmas tree and Father Christmas. For the majority, the market provides an equally jolly scene with a variety of less expensive toys and seasonal presents.

Carol singing fills the night air, dedicated hands raise the great star to the top of the eucalyptus tree outside Maud's house, and Christmas arrives a few hours earlier than in Britain. Wrapped up against the cold, families and friends set out, not unlike those three kings of centuries ago, each to pay homage at the crib in their own parish church.

The walk to St Mary's on the hill is yet another expedition filled with excitement. To secure a place in the pew next to the crib when the doors open half an hour before midnight, Maud and her sons arrive early to take up their positions under the porch outside the west transept. The rest of the church is carpeted, without pews, because the majority of the congregation squat on the floor. Men, women and children, however lowly their means, wear new clothes in honour of the joyful mystery of the Nativity.

By midnight the church is packed; the choir arrives, full of confidence after an extended rehearsal during the afternoon, and occupies the gallery overlooking the aisle.

Standing unobtrusively at the back, and on duty by choice to help with the crowd and to share his friend's Christmas, is Mariappa. His presence means that Hugh Carson too is in his place with the choir.

But for a cough or two, there is silence; all eyes are focused on the crib.

St Mary's was one of the early beneficiaries of electricity, and expresses its gratitude in the clusters of coloured lights around the figures of Mary, Joseph, the three wise men, and the farm animals, with the brightest single light, like a star, in place over the spot reserved for the Son of God. All is beautifully arranged on a pallet of straw.

'Is it not remarkable,' commented the Market Inspector later, 'that the king of kings should have been born in a stable, and that this scene is tonight the centre of adoration in hundreds of thousands of churches all over the world, and will remain on view until the singing of Auld Lang Syne ushers in a new year.' Amen to that.

But it was the flickering of a thousand candles: on the main altar, in front of the side altars, the many statues and the crib that filled the church with the light of hope.

As Father Crayssac, robed in cream satin vestments and cradling the infant Jesus, followed a small procession of acolytes in their red and white surplices, led by

Augustine carrying a thurible, the organ began to play the first haunting notes of a carol long to be remembered.

The congregation stirred, there was a palpable air of expectancy as the procession moved slowly towards the crib and Father Crayssac, bending low, laid the infant in its place. On cue, the clear tenor voice of Hugh Carson rang out through the church: 'O Holy Night, the stars are shining brightly, this is the night the dear Saviour was born,' and Christmas had arrived.

Apart from the fire in the market and the encounter with the tiger, two other events had marked the year: Mariappa had been promoted to sub-inspector which meant that he no longer wore the blue uniform or the red helmet; instead he and Hugh Carson dressed exactly alike in all but two minor respects. On his epaulettes Mariappa wore the insignia IPS meaning Indian Police Service, and on his head a magnificent khaki and gold turban moulded in the same fashion as his old red helmet.

The other event was Mahatma Gandhi's one and only visit to Ooty. Apparently, a dais had been erected for him in a large field opposite the racecourse, high enough to be seen from the market. A very large crowd, including Sub-Inspector Mariappa and Market Inspector Hugh Carson, had gathered to hear him speak.

'He was dressed in the usual loin cloth of homespun cotton (khadi) with a warm shawl about his shoulders, and he spoke in a clear resonant voice,' was how Hugh Carson recalled the event. 'He talked about the time having come to end foreign rule in India, and he spoke in English, which didn't seem so strange to Mariappa or me. After all, Gandhi could not be expected to speak every language in India, and English was the accepted lingua franca throughout the country.' He paused for a while before finishing what he had to say: 'You see, to men like Mariappa and me it didn't really matter who did the ruling, a British viceroy or an Indian president. It was India that mattered, and the people. So long as their lives were not disrupted, or ours in Ooty, it made little difference.'

What happened to the principal characters in this story is shrouded in the mists of time; but for the widow's sons (and of course I was one of them), the army, the war and the transition from Empire to Commonwealth still lay ahead, as I am about to recount. For the moment, however, the final word is best left to Father Augustine.

'I was an orphan with no known relatives. My parents had been labourers, and the first thing of any use I learned to do was to carry bricks on my head – an important qualification for the next stage in my working career as a market coolie. That move made a dramatic improvement in my standard of living: at least I had enough to eat. But much more important, it brought me under the influence of Mr Hugh Carson.

The ad hoc school he organised for the coolie boys outside the market gates in Ooty I shall remember always with pride and affection. It released in me the desire to learn, and taught me how to set about getting started; and in that sense compared favourably with the college in Madras where I completed my education. It taught me also that when it comes to choosing His priests, God is not concerned with colour, class, or wealth.

The children for whose parents I so often carried a basket of shopping on my head, grew up to call me "Father". That was my personal reward and I pray for them every day.

I am sure there were other men like Mr Carson, all over India, whose contribution to this country can never be measured fully, or adequately rewarded; but it will be remembered in Heaven, and certainly if my prayers have any influence there.'

CHAPTER TWO

THE LAST NOTE LINGERS

The battle of Hyparabyn

Pursuing butterflies on the Ooty Downs, fishing its trout streams, or climbing Dodabetta in the reassuring company of my brother armed with nothing more lethal than a picnic, may not have been the best preparation for going to war, but the memory of it often came to the rescue when morale was low.

And while there are all sorts of reasons for going to war, the only lasting benefit to come out of it – certainly from a soldier's point of view – is the kind of comradeship to be seen when the Gurkha Brigade Association makes its annual pilgrimage to Sandhurst. They come in their hundreds, erect and steady as when they left the place a quarter, or even half a century, before. The singing in the college chapel resounds with the quality of confidence, bugles sound the last post and reveille, a lone Gurkha piper plays a lament and the collection plate is filled. Duty done, the doors of the Indian Army Room are thrown open – its own history lit up by the sun shining through stained-glass windows – and the serious work of compressing a whole year's hospitality into a single hour begins.

It was in these circumstances, after a lapse of many years, that I met George Bolton, a friend of long standing. The face was the same, kind and amiable; the inquisitive blue eyes still twinkled with humour. We talked about Hyparabyn where both of us had learnt at first hand what war was all about, and had come away alive but unconvinced.

He told me of his own saddest experience, after the battle of Monte Casino – the monastery founded by St Benedict in 529 and used as a fortress by the Nazis in World War Two – when he climbed to the top of the hill and found his young Gurkha orderly dead. He was not a British subject; his country was not even a member of the Commonwealth. He was nevertheless one of the King's soldiers – as many of his fellow countrymen are today the Queen's soldiers – and had come all the way from his home in Nepal to prove it.

The glow of comradeship sent my own thoughts winging back to a memorable day long ago when, not much older than George's orderly, I had walked alone, suitcase in hand, to swear allegiance to the same King for the same purpose.

The sound of a demoniac voice greeted my arrival: 'Mar-kars Stead-oi!' And steady they were looking more like statues than living soldiers, and as the words exploded over their heads ordering the rest of the battalion to march on to those same markers – 'in close column of companies' – the barracks square splintered into a thousand moving objects and the parade got under way. The regimental sergeant major's voice had been trained in the Irish Guards and, when that voice spoke, men listened: turns to the right and left, marching forwards and backwards, rifles raised and lowered, sloped, trailed, shouldered and presented like one man. Only perfection was good enough.

No doubt the memory of that voice would one day drive out fear when it gripped the stomach and raised the pulse, and perhaps even make the difference between victory and defeat; but the experience then was frightening enough. I just watched and wondered. How many years of my life would be spent in such surroundings? I was a soldier's son, my mother was a soldier's widow: what if I should find the going too hard and too long? I would not be the first to fail. But, like all the others, I came to admire and fear the RSM.

The lessons learned on the square would one day be tested in the field. When the bullets flew and the shells burst, that voice would come through from the past, 'Mar-kars Stead-oi!' And steady it would be, all the way.

However, an interest in heliographs and all the other paraphernalia of signalling attracted me, and, come the day, I found myself preparing for war on the bleak mountains that separate Afghanistan from the Indian sub-continent with a signalling troop attached to the Dehra Dun Brigade. The troop consisted of eighty-five men, mostly Dogras from the Kangra valley – where the exiled Dalai Lama currently holds court in Dharamsala – eight horses and thirty-two mules.

We had wireless sets too: the No 1 for short range work and the No 6 for more ambitious operations. These were designed for voice and morse code, and came complete with carrying equipment so that they could be operated off the back of a mule. Fitness and efficiency were the words drummed into us every day, and the closer we got to the enemy the more relevant they became. Instant dialling around the world and satellite communications were beyond the dreams of signallers fifty years ago; but to operate a heliograph from mountain top to mountain top is still the closest man may ever get to operating exclusively with the sun.

Mounted orderlies galloping with their dispatches, rifle buckets strapped tight and turban tails flying, are a very different sight from motor cycles performing the same function and making a hell of a noise about it while at the same time belching carbon monoxide into the atmosphere. To be up and away with all your possessions – guns, equipment, blankets and rations on the backs of mules, who had a stake in carrying those loads because they included the day's fodder for the animals – in the knowledge that to make or break camp was only a matter of an hour, is altogether a more exciting experience than being part of a convoy of trucks rattling along an uneven track.

But loading up was not entirely trouble free. The loads would be laid out in parallel lines and the mules moved into position between them in strings of three. To this well-practised drill the mules invariably offered some resistance, either by breaking ranks to foil the loaders, or by performing a high kick or two powerful enough to send one of them into hospital, or simply planting a savage bite on the most convenient target. It was all considered good fun. The mule handlers, however, had their own procedures for dealing with such behaviour: a half-nelson around the nearest ear, a tweak of the testicles or, if available, bringing in a white lead mule which for some reason had a calming influence.

The brigade moved to Jingagacha, a sad derelict little village on the waterways of the Ganges Delta. Here, notwithstanding the formidable obstacles nature had placed between ourselves and the enemy, we built an anti-tank ditch around the village – if only to prove that war is no ordinary business and that there is a certain drill to be gone through.

And new wireless sets were on the way. The No 22 would do the trick whatever the conditions: 'Just throw a piece of wire over a tree old boy, and Bob's your uncle,' the signals would come through loud and clear. I was much too inexperienced to question any such statement, so it came as something of a surprise when Bob turned out to be a most unreliable uncle; he had forgotten about humidity in the jungle, and that there was no carrying equipment available for these new miracles of invention. When the problems came, the 'salesman' was absent.

We were learning quickly that improvisation is as important to winning a war as negotiations are to preserving the peace – dreaded words both but central to our existence – and the brigadier (his name was Hungerford, which I mention here by way of saluting a brave and popular man) ensured that we would have time and resources to design our own carrying equipment and practise men and mules in their use.

As added insurance against unforeseen eventualities we were reinforced with a loft of carrier pigeons. These were prize birds, conscious of their status, temperamental by nature and not easily taken for granted. Like any other soldier, each had its own regimental number and commanded an equal share of paperwork. Their administration had to be spot on, and their training conducted with infinite care so that, in the last resort, they could fly back to Calcutta with a message of farewell.

All in all we were as ready as anyone ever is to take on the enemy, and it was at this point that George Bolton joined us as brigade major – a key step on the ladder to high command. And a great blessing he proved to be. With his Gurkha felt hat worn jauntily off-centre, chinstrap behind the head, a fine blonde moustache and a brisk pace, he was just the sort of action man we needed. His ready smile and unflappable disposition impressed itself upon us in a matter of days. If I had to go to war, I was glad to be going with him.

Now, if war is a bloody business, the frustration and confusion that go hand in hand with it make matters even bloodier. 'Mar-kars Stead-oi!' evoked in all sorts of different ways may drive out fear perhaps, even replace it with a greater one, but those insidious parasites creep into the very soul driving a wedge between the givers of orders and the recipients thereof.

We were full of confidence, ready for anything, anywhere, anytime; but that was before the news burst upon us that the brigade was to be mechanised.

The first vehicle to arrive was a jeep – we had not seen one before – for the personal use of the commander. This was clearly a sweetener from those in authority who must have known that they had served a death warrant on the finest pack brigade in the Indian Army.

For me, the end of the world had arrived. In a very real sense, we had grown up with our animals. We knew them and loved them, and, in their way, they knew us, and maybe they loved us too. We had reached the highest pitch of readiness and were fit and efficient; very fit, and very efficient. To retrain mule handlers as drivers, mounted orderlies as motor cyclists, and re-equip ourselves psychologically for what lay ahead seemed shortsighted, stupid and dangerous. Whatever confidence one felt in higher command evaporated. It seemed to me that the general staff were too far removed from everyday events, nursing their own ambitions, to be concerned with the simple fact that it had taken years of training to perfect the animal pack expertise in which we prided ourselves. We knew little else and were to be mechanised in a matter of weeks.

And it says a lot for the brigadier and George that they contained this crisis and steered us through it without serious mishap. The animals and the pigeons went, and some of the men went with them; their replacements were of a different caste.

The havaldar (sergeant) in charge of the animals, a marvellously cheerful Dogra by the name of Achha Singh (achha means good), whose trade was 'Signals Assistant Animal Transport', or SAAT, elected to stay if I could employ him as a general duties sergeant with the trade of lineman. This was easy enough to arrange, and general duties covered a multitude of sins. My own orderly, Prasinder Ram, also a SAAT and a fine horseman, volunteered to stay with me and learn to become a lineman too.

Achha Singh's knowledge and experience with horses and mules were legendary, – he had done little else for eighteen years, and was sometimes referred to as 'Kachha Singh' (kachha meaning mule), which made him a 'lion' among mules. He was also an excellent soldier.

Among the higher trades, mainly wireless operators and technicians, the best remained, including broad shouldered Naik (Corporal) Gian Singh, with a fine moustache that curled up at the ends, who came from the same district as my orderly, Hoshiarpur. He was due for promotion and would in due course take over as the troop Indian Officer.

When the vehicles arrived we were in for another shock. Most of them were cast-offs from a retreating army, camouflaged for desert warfare and quite unsuitable for the jungle. Like everything else, they were simply statistics on a staff officer's pad, bearing little resemblance to what was actually wanted on the ground.

We were still trying to cope with this situation when orders came to proceed to the Arakan, and help to stop the rot before it degenerated into a wholesale rout. Our army there was retreating fast. En route, we were hardly encouraged by the sight of an endless line of bedraggled men, some without weapons, drifting aimlessly on the tide we were sent to stem. And yet our own condition was no less hopeless, except that we had so far only tasted the bitterness of defeat from our own side.

There had been some rain. The narrow dirt road was a quagmire. It was neither the time nor place for wheeled transport, and by the time we had organised a makeshift assembly area near Buthidaung, on the west bank of the Kalapanzin river, we had abandoned the lot. So what now?

The brigadier had received fresh orders. We were to revert to animal pack and move down the Kalapanzin valley to halt the Japanese advance south of Hyparabyn. This was like Balaclava all over again; I couldn't believe it.

Only a fortnight ago, a couple of hundred miles from this God-forsaken corner of an old map, we were the 'fittest and most efficient' animal pack brigade that the army was ever likely to see. Now we were reduced to a state of moral desolation, almost as bad as our retreating comrades, and ordered to do what we had been trained to do but deprived of the means of doing it. It was like asking sailors to sail without ships!

That, in the end, is the reality of war. It could be argued, and was at the time, that we had to respond to circumstances, to improvise and outwit the enemy. But a bugger's muddle by any other name is still a muddle – even if it is sometimes mistaken for ingenious staffwork.

Such equipment as we had was strewn about the place, dragged in by one means or another. It was raining, there were no proper arrangements for feeding the men, rations had not caught up with us and perhaps never would. The brigadier kept his own counsel, concentrating hard on what he had been instructed to do, and summoned us for orders. George took most of the flak from the rest of us.

'How and when are we expected to move?' I demanded to know.

'I think at about 0500 hours,' he replied, 'and we can expect a troop of the Jaipur Pony Company around midnight.'

'Jaipur Pony Company!' I spluttered in disbelief. What was the point of talking; little good would come out of it and there was so much to be done.

Rations did arrive, and we fed ourselves on a quick brew of corned beef stew and Shakapura biscuits. These war-winning biscuits may have been named after Shaka, an outstanding Zulu war leader, and deliberately coupled with 'pura' – which in Indian Army parlance means complete – as a confidence builder, but the ingredients, apart from an infusion of dried weevils, remain a military secret. Had I waited a little, Achha Singh would have been a willing and generous host over dhal and chappaties.

Cheerful whatever the circumstances, he was delighted to hear about the ponies and was full of enthusiasm, which made me feel not a little ashamed, and my own confidence began to pick up. 'Kuch parva nahin sahib' (it does not matter), he called out. In all probability, he assured me, the ponies would come complete with 'universal carriers' (not unlike Venetian blinds made of bamboo slats and held together by strong leather straps with metal rings at one end for hooking on to a pack saddle) and into these everything could go – wireless sets, batteries, Bren guns and all. But there would be no possibility of operating on the move.

Then he came up with a bright idea. The largest pony could carry the big No 9 Set mounted on top of the pack saddle and held in place by two supporting ropes on either side. Four men, all operators, could take turns hanging on to these or operating as they went along. A second pony, roped to the first, would carry two sets of batteries (each a larger version of today's car battery), with one connected up for operating so that we might at least be able to tell the world what was happening to us.

The Jaipur ponies duly turned up. Those wretched animals and the men accompanying them deserved a better reception than they got. They had marched a long way from Maungdaw – a distance of about fifteen miles in filthy conditions – and they too had a sorry tale to tell, having been switched at short notice from the daily routine of carrying rations to a blind date with us.

The whole business seemed such a gigantic farce, and it was just as well that Achha Singh was around to cheer us up. The scene was reminiscent of a Hollywood movie, with Achha Singh cast in the role of trail boss.

At dawn we began to march, for no other reason than that somewhere, far away from the action, a big white chief had given the necessary orders – having been assured no doubt that the Dehra Dun Brigade was in position, fighting fit and raring to go – and was probably even now waiting for news of the victorious outcome to be communicated to Whitehall. The skill lay in the giving of orders; whether they made sense, or whether they could be carried out was a gamble often taken in the dark, plucked out of the air, leaving the outcome to brave and desperate men.

These same orders a fortnight ago would have been welcomed; there would have been a sense of elation, of adventure, of absolute confidence in making short work of the opposition. In the event, we were stripped of what Field Marshal Bill Slim once called 'the greatest single factor in winning wars' – morale. Be all this as it may, we had a date with Hyparabyn, which was – though according to John Bartholomew no longer is – a tiny hamlet on the Kalapanzin river in Burma. We were headed there via Buthidaung, a landing stage of sorts for sampans and other local craft.

Hyparabyn could boast little history and posed less threat to the rest of the world: the men caught fish and the women mostly worked in the rice fields. A few buffaloes supplied the milk, free-ranging hens laid eggs, and that was about it. Once a week a sampan would set off upstream to Buthidaung to barter away some of these things for other essentials.

It is a strange irony that, in the pursuit of some greater objective, Britain and Japan should choose this fragment of God's earth to slaughter each other and in the process obliterate Hyparabyn from the map for ever. Like so many thousands of such fragments, Hyparabyn too had its hopes, its dreams, and, like them, is no more.

Achha Singh had one of the ponies saddled for riding just in case it should be needed; he probably saw himself as a mounted orderly delivering that final dispatch when all else had failed. At one point I did suggest to the brigadier, exhausted from lack of sleep, proper food and the strain of the past fortnight, that he might like to ride for a while, but his pride would not let him. I instructed Achha Singh to stay close at hand in case he should change his mind, and for Gian Singh I reserved the simplest and most important order: 'Jemadar Sahib', I cautioned, placing a trusting hand on his shoulder, 'stay with the No 9 Set no matter what happens. Don't let it out of your sight for a second.' He understood and replied simply, 'Ji Sahib.' I had no doubt that our mobile 'radio station' would remain in communication come what may – if only to receive fresh orders!

Prasinder Ram, no longer required to accompany me as when we rode from battalion to battalion to ensure that our customers were satisfied with the service they were getting, dashed off to join the cable laying team moving behind the leading battalion. It was this enthusiasm, a readiness to volunteer and have a go at anything, that cost him his life, when a cable detachment ran into an ambush. There had been just four of them, lightly armed and carrying a mile or two of cable each; and although they were, like all linemen in the Arakan or anywhere else, the most resourceful of men, it was a lonely and hazardous mission.

Prasinder Ram himself was always as cheerful as a cricket, and moved as quickly; a little man with a big heart and dancing, mischievous eyes, he was a great companion and friend. I have to recall the days when, having saddled our horses of a morning, he would dispatch mine (a chestnut mare by the name of Mona) with stirrups crossed, a flower to brighten up the head harness and a slap on the haunches to send her trotting in my direction.

I shall remember always an occasion when we set off together across the northern tip of the Mayu Range in Burma to find a battalion of the 9th Gurkhas holed out in a place called Goppe Bazar. It was a lonely ride with not a single living creature in sight, when suddenly out of the blue a Japanese Zero fighter appeared on the horizon. The pilot had clearly spotted us, judging by the upswing of the plane as it went into a sharp turn. Prasinder Ram reacted instantly, delivering the familiar blow to the back end of Mona and an equally effective signal to his own horse, and we were into the bushes, dismounted and under cover before the pilot could do us any harm.

The plane swept up and down the valley a couple of times and, frustrated no doubt, released a few random bursts of fire which sounded like crackers thrown in the air, bringing forth from Prasinder Ram the comment that it reminded him of

Diwali. When he was killed, he left behind a fifteen-year-old wife – another tilt in the fortunes of war – and who knows how many more Dogras from Hoshiapur died in the service of the King Emperor.

However, the march to Hyparabyn had to go on. To the right, along a line of hills separating us from the sea, a Gurkha battalion watched our flank. Ahead, the Punjabis provided the advance guard and the Sikhs followed behind as rear guard – covering the ever-growing space between us and any well-wishers. And by now it was perfectly clear that our movements were being closely monitored.

I hesitate to mention the names of the commanding officers, but in order to satisfy the reader that they are real, and as a small salute from me, perhaps there is no harm in mentioning that Robbie Fawcett commanded the Gurkhas: a strong, stubby man with a crusty sense of humour, who once gave me a brief lesson on how to take cover with dignity by going to ground in the upright position with head held high. On one occasion, when he was returning from temporary command of a brigade whose brigadier had become a casualty, I asked him how things had gone and he told me: 'Like a sour sweet I have been sucked and spat out.'

Sir John Austin commanded the Punjabis. He was a quiet man of great charm and gentleness, for whom this war was a distraction from a more congenial and civilised way of life at the regimental centre. Johnnie Childs, commanding the Sikhs, was a cheerful character. His favourite story was about how he came to be wounded in the buttocks calling to those around him to get down under shell fire. He alone received a bit of shrapnel. The courage and personal qualities of these three officers, who spoke the language of their soldiers fluently, had a direct influence on the conduct and steadiness of the rest of us, novices, inexperienced and anxious not to let the side down.

To each of these battalions I sent a wireless detachment. Unable to operate on the move, they could however be set up quite quickly and meanwhile tap in to the main cable on the general line of advance – in the laying of which we had already suffered our first casualties. For the Gurkhas, this meant sending a signalman at the double to find that lifeline, reeling out a drum of cable from a spindle as he went. Though the distance was seldom greater than half a mile, the difficulty lay in retrieving the cable after use, which was sometimes left to those coming up behind, or our opponents, depending on who got there first.

If the signalman happened to be in a hurry, the wires might be left bare, invariably causing a short circuit to be sorted out later and often with greater ease than calming frayed tempers. It fell to Achha Singh to ride the range as mounted patrol and check these shortcomings, a job he enjoyed and carried out with great panache and courage, whatever the circumstances. He was often to be seen riding patrol when the line was in perfect order, and with him around bad tempers could not be sustained for long. Throughout that memorable day, the Dogras kept us in touch with each other.

By sunset we were in Hyparabyn. There was no sign of the enemy – not yet anyway – and there were no booby traps either. One of my Dogras came forward with a mug of tea brewed in his mess tin; I waved him on towards the brigadier. Night was upon us, there was little time to get organised, man the perimeter and establish where everyone was.

It was a dark night, and there could be no question of using lights of any description. A few drums of cable were reeled out to sector commanders on the

1. Todas in Ooty. From a watercolour by Captain Richard Baron, 1837. (*Nilgiri Library*)

2. A Todamund. From a watercolour by Captain Richard Baron, 1837. (*Nilgiri Library*)

3. Ooty in mist from Dodabetta. (*Lionel Gregory*)

4. Ooty on a clear day from Dodabetta. (*Lionel Gregory*)

5. The Denbury — Later Ten Tors — Cross. (*Sydney Williams*)

6. Hay Tor from Denbury and close up. (*Sydney Williams*)

7. Ten Tors. (*Ministry of Defence*)

perimeter and field telephones connected. The Japanese, who had clearly been observing these activities, chose their moment well and welcomed us with a few bursts of small arms fire – just enough to heighten the tension. The encore followed with more firing, this time from several directions, and a display of tracer bullets streaking through the trees supplemented by a few hand grenades tossed about for good measure. It was enough to provoke an angry response from our own side searching for confidence in a wild outburst of firing which achieved little – apart from disclosing our own positions without inflicting any inconvenience on the enemy. The Japanese were presented with a target tightly locked into a well-defined area and took full advantage of it; they had probably targeted all the likely fields of fire before our arrival. We were shooting in the dark.

The firing continued, interspersed with human and animal noises as contact was made, injecting into the confusion a psychological element for which the Japanese were renowned. And although our own troops had been briefed on what to expect, the actual baptism of fire is very different from the theory: a man shot at wants to shoot back.

It was an unnerving experience, and we just opened up with everything we had. This was the moment for all living creatures to beat a hasty retreat if they had somewhere to go; but we were stuck without visibility, without room for manoeuvre, and without alternative accommodation.

Nippon was having a field-day at our expense, enjoying a fireworks display unlikely ever to be repeated on the banks of the Kalapanzin. Sitting not ten yards from George Bolton and me, one of my own men decided to relieve his feelings with a quick burst from his Sten gun. We ducked instinctively, while I reached out quickly to grab the hand on the trigger and enquire of its owner what exactly he had in mind. And he told me. He was quite clear about what he had in mind: 'Sab log fire karthe hain, to him bhi fore kartha hun' (everyone is firing so I'm firing too), which seemed fair enough, but he was persuaded not to subject us to a repeat performance.

By morning, stocks of ammunition were dangerously low. Having seen us through the best part of that terrible night, the brigadier, now a very sick man, had to be evacuated by sampan, followed a few hours later by some of the more serious casualties of the night in similar transport. This was a feat in itself, made possible no doubt by the blessings of heaven falling upon the doctors and medical orderlies, but for the rest of us there was little reason for self-congratulation.

A month later I got a note from the brigadier recovering in hospital in Bombay: 'I will always remember your cheerful Dogras, and that life saving cup of tea,' he wrote.

In the morning a new commander arrived on foot, escorted by a section of Gurkhas. We were ordered to assemble at once and then told to go away and get shaved. Well, leadership manifests itself in many different ways, so we got ourselves shaved and returned. There had not been much eating, sleeping or washing in this part of the world for some time, but no doubt our new leader would put all these things right and defeat the enemy to boot.

He ordered the Punjabis to advance between the range of hills on our right and the river, while the Gurkhas stood fast to hold the flank. The Sikhs would remain at Hyparabyn on standby to follow through the success of the Punjabis.

My task was to get the communications 'buttoned up' with wireless and cable, 'and there is to be no breakdown. I want you up front to make sure things work.' I was not sure whether this was an expression of confidence or a threat – one never knew – nor was it necessary to acknowledge such orders; they simply had to be carried out. But now that we had had a shave anything was possible, including our unprotesting readiness to march into glory at first light.

The perimeter was better prepared for the second night, patrols were out and a degree of order restored. Strict orders were issued to conserve ammunition and, although there was a lot of firing, most of it was on the enemy's side. We had learnt our first major lesson: not to fire unless the target could be seen, and then only at the last possible moment. Every bullet had to count.

The Punjabis moved out on time and into thick mist, with my Dogras behind reeling our cable as they went. With Achha Singh in charge they would go all the way to hell and back if necessary. The brigadier followed with George and his tactical headquarters. I avoided accompanying them and concentrated instead on the wireless detachments deployed with the battalions, at tactical headquarters, main headquarters, and the Sikhs at Hyparabyn. Thoughtfully, dear old Achha Singh had left the saddled pony with me in case I should be forced to charge the enemy single handed or gallop away to freedom.

Blinded by the mist, the Punjabis infiltrated the enemy's forward defences. It was not intentional, and the Japanese, disturbed in their early morning ablutions, were far from pleased. Instead of inviting their unexpected guests to breakfast, they opted to express their displeasure in the most inhospitable manner. And the guns began to roar; fighting was close in. Having lost contact with everyone, a not surprising development in the circumstances, and furious at having a few well-aimed mortar bombs falling about him, the brigadier accused one and all not only of incompetence but cowardice as well, whereas, in the confusion of battle, we were all searching for something courageous to do.

Although my own search lay in the direction of the Punjabis, it was just possible that the Japanese would interfere with my freedom of movement and deny me the pleasure of their company. In the event, however, I caught up with Achha Singh laying out drum upon drum of cable regardless of the growing tempo of this extraordinary battle, I think he found the situation highly amusing, and greeted me with a broad smile, but there was no time for small talk, the work had to go on. Communications were working well enough, but as far as I could see there was open space on all sides and no one around to make use of them.

Despite the brigadier's remarks, these were brave men, very brave men, and while they could always march to the sound of the guns, what if that sound was coming from all directions! But all sorts of things happen and are said in the heat of battle.

A fold in the ground offered suitable cover for the ponies and here they remained with the wireless detachment. The rest of the cable laying continued without them, my own role being that of Number 2 to Achha Singh. When I mentioned this to him he laughed happily and said it was a great honour.

The next large hole in the ground revealed the headquarters of the battalion, and there I was happy to hand over the end of the cable with a field telephone attached to it, but there were no takers. I watched with pride as Achha Singh turned the handle of the telephone and reported that tactical headquarters and Hyparabyn were answering 'loud and clear sahib'. The brigadier was on to it at once, demanding to know what the hell was going on. Hell had to come into it somewhere although he knew perfectly well what was going on, and he could hear the firing, but having no one else to fire orders at he aimed them at me. 'Find John Austin and tell him I want to speak to him.' I could hardly reply that Sir John was otherwise engaged and would call back later.

All the portents signalled a major calamity unless we were very careful. It was important to cool it. George came on the line and I described the scene to him as best I could, promising to keep looking until I made contact with the appropriate authorities on one side or the other. His patience was remarkable, his quiet voice eased the tension; he even offered me a few words of encouragement in Urdu, calling me 'respected brother' and urging me not to let the confusion get me down or, worse, add to it.

The mist had lifted, firing grew in intensity, mortar bombs fell about us and a mountain battery, attached to the brigade, went into action. I had last seen the like in Waziristan, on the North West Frontier – Kipling's Screw-Guns – and by God they were good.

The appearance of the guns, arranged by some unseen staff officer who had undoubtedly earned his promotion (they had in fact followed us from Buthidaung on the backs of mules), was an instant boost to morale and they wasted little time getting down to business. The sound of the howitzers blotted out the rat-a-tat of the machine guns, but they were still there, like rattlesnakes in the grass, and deadly. Sir John had established himself in a bomb crater with his adjutant. A brave and good man, a gentleman in every sense of the word and a popular commanding officer, he was trying desperately to get to grips with the situation and to regroup his battalion. C Company (I think it was), somewhere in the bowels of the Japanese positions, was engaged in a deadly duel from which there was no escape until one side or the other gave way – and it was not going to be the Punjabis.

Casualties were heavy. I offered Sir John a friendly chat with the brigadier which he declined politely. But a chat there had to be and a decidedly one sided affair it was.

'Yes, yes, yes brigadier; I know; I see; OK sir, yes, yes, yes, right-o!' was about the gist of it.

As seen from tactical headquarters the situation was indeed a bugger's muddle, and Sir John's orders, not unlike mine, were to 'get things buttoned up', the meaning of which was becoming all too clear, embracing the entire code of tactical doctrine from praying to charging the enemy single-handed.

We had by now established reliable radio contact back and forth, with someone in authority permanently at the sending and receiving ends, and a clear line. But this only encouraged the giving of fresh orders, distracting attention from the murderous struggle going on all round. Having said that, however, it is at such times that a wireless set mounted on a pony, or anywhere, becomes the most potent single weapon in the winning or losing of a battle; it is not only the principal means of redirecting effort and resources to the point where they are most needed, but enables leadership to play the crucial role. One day guided missiles may prove the point conclusively.

We were just settling down nicely when George sent a message to say that the brigadier was demanding my presence. I made some unfortunate remark, adding that I was quite happy with the Punjabis and preferred to remain with them. 'No,' said George, 'that simply won't do; I too should like to be up there but can't, and your place is here. Besides, the brigadier wants to see you at once.' One could be shot for disobeying such orders – so back I went. Just over the brow of a hill, and sitting under a ground sheet stretched across some bushes, sat the brigadier with a glass of rum and water in his hand – a little camp comfort which accompanied him wherever he went. He poured some into a second glass and offered it to me. I was a non-drinker at the time, but thought it might be undiplomatic to mention the fact.

'Are your Dogras OK?' he asked. I replied that they were.

In his hand he had a piece of paper which he passed to me. 'Have you seen this message?' I hadn't.

It had come in on the good old No 9 Set and was marked Most Immediate – a priority that drove most praying men to their knees – and I recognised Gian Singh's writing. 'Well done. The situation elsewhere demands you break contact with the enemy immediately and return via Buthidaung to Maungdaw. Further orders to follow.' That was it then! I looked at the brigadier and realised there was nothing more to be said. His was a thankless job. We had done little apart from inflicting some casualties on the enemy and sustaining a few ourselves, and in the process demoralised a lot of good men. On the credit side we had learnt a few lessons, not least about improvisation.

'You had better get back to John Austin and stay with him,' he said, and he didn't have to add anything like this being a bugger's muddle.

This time I made use of the pony and enjoyed the ride. It was the quickest way of covering a couple of miles and the enemy was unlikely to be interested in my movements. In the back of my mind was the thought that while making contact with the enemy was difficult enough, breaking contact and turning your back on him was a very different proposition altogether. And this is precisely what we were now called upon to do.

However, what had to be done, had to be done, or, as Achha Singh put it: 'Jo kuchh hoga, hoga' (what will be, will be) and we enjoyed the march back together, wrapping miles of cable around each man in turn – much simpler than trying to reel the stuff onto a drum – and connecting up every time we were forced to stop and express displeasure at being followed, and to report progress. Unwanted baggage was dumped on the pony's saddle.

In the early hours of the morning we got back to Hyparabyn. As we approached, I could hear the brigadier asking George whether anything had been heard of me, and when told that I had returned he came across to greet me with a mug of tea laced with rum.

'You'd better drink this,' he said. There was no such welcome for Achha Singh, but he understood, and I made amends later.

The brigade withdrew as instructed, turning south along the coast towards Akyab island with orders to stop the enemy advance and to hold the line for Christmas. If both the letter and the spirit of these orders were to be obeyed, some tangible form of compensation there had to be, and to a resolution of that problem we bent our minds.

As it happened, the latest Japanese adventure had been to overrun one of our own Field Ambulance units situated a short distance from our new positions, and, as everyone knows, Field Ambulances are usually well equipped with all sorts of good things. The thought that the dreaded Japanese, who had caused us so much inconvenience, might even now be enjoying their illgotten gains was too much. Something had to be done, and here the brigadier rose to the hour; all his military training had prepared him for just such a situation.

He summoned the Gurkhas for war talk and drew up a plan that would take them around the unsuspecting Japanese, whence a blow would be struck to send them scuttling back to Akyab, or face-saving suicide in the waters of the Bay of Bengal – it was up to them. For the brigadier there were weightier matters to consider.

Our own intelligence had established that the booty (loot is too crude a word) the enemy would be obliged to abandon included large stocks of brandy and rum – which was incentive enough to ensure success. The operation was launched accordingly, the brigadier never putting a foot wrong – even in the matter of placing the padre and the doctor in charge of distribution.

We were comfortably established about a mile from the beach in a long winding gully full of scrub – a combination of stunted trees, bushes and an assortment of wild plants common in the arid hinterland of Burma – supplemented by heavy-duty tarpaulins tastefully deployed. It was a congenial setting, providing cover from the elements and public view, accommodation for the brigadier's headquarters, a medical centre, Officers' Mess, a cookhouse for my Dogras and an unlimited choice of personal sleeping quarters – provided they were tactically sited and the occupant undertook to dig a hole beside his bed big enough to accommodate his person in an emergency, and to do some firing.

Downwind from the gully a few trenches with bamboo poles down the middle for squatting, and screened from view of enemy and own troops alike by hessian screens fluttering gently in the wind, were the public latrines. One was reserved for the brigadier, who attended the place solo, but all were sparsely protected in order to ensure that visits there were not unduly prolonged.

At the far end of the gully, where all our worldly goods were stored, distribution of the spoils of war was taking place: items and quantities announced by the padre – according to the drinking habits of the recipients – and handed over by the irrepressibly cheerful Achha Singh (who as usual had found a place for himself in the middle of the action) with accompanying words of encouragement, and gratefully received by small working parties from the battalions.

George Bolton and I were sitting on the bank overlooking the brigadier's headquarters watching this scene; there was no firing, and I opined how marvellous it was to see Christians, Hindus, Muslims and Sikhs (the King's men all) preparing to celebrate Christmas together in the hallowed name of comradeship.

George agreed with this, but his own thoughts were much more down to earth: 'All over Burma, throughout the Middle East and Europe, countless thousands of these incomparable men from all over the Commonwealth are similarly employed' – and he was not talking about loot! It was our last conversation before he moved on to command his battalion, and I became an adjutant – long held to be the traditional perch for high fliers!

The Arakan

I suppose it is reasonable to assume that our lives are shaped by events, good and bad, that influence our judgements and opinions in later years. If that is true in general, it is even more so in the particular, at least in so far as a soldier's life is concerned, where prevailing orders take preference over everything else and there is no room for negotiation.

As an adjutant, for instance, I learnt that to keep my desk tidy, the files in good order, and the riotous behaviour of my fellow officers out of sight and earshot of my commanding officer, would be reflected advantageously in my confidential report.

I learnt, too, that while I was conducting a regimental parade at my master's behest on the art of saluting – longest way up shortest way down, upperarm parallel to the ground, fingers close together and all that – 'to smarten things up', as he had decreed, there was always the possibility that he would suddenly turn up and position himself in full view of the troops. There was no great harm in his being present of course; but when his reponse to the entire regiment being immobilised and riveted to the ground while I performed the customary salaam of welcome turned into a cheery greeting, 'morning dear boy', with an accompanying salute delivered skywards off the right eye, fingers distended, and at an angle of forty-five degrees, it altered the whole atmosphere.

It may also have been his way of raising morale by demonstrating that, while the adjutant was a slave to the handbook of military drill, he, the Colonel Sahib, strode on a much higher plane, and would not have been responsible for anything so disagreeable as a saluting parade when there was a war on. One never knew!

I was to learn many lessons in this way. For example, if a particular officer's personality and general demeanour was such as to offend the commanding officer at every turn by his very presence, his every word and deed, despite being perfectly competent in all other respects, the solution lay in putting his name forward for posting on promotion.

If the CO (the abbreviated form comes simpler) happened to like riding through the countryside of an evening, indulging in an occasional blast on his hunting horn to remind him of home, it was incumbent on the adjutant to accompany him with matching enthusiasm.

These experiences are set in an all too short period of retraining in Chittagong before returning to the familiar battleground of the Arakan in Burma.

The colonel was a jovial man, well over six feet tall, with bushy eyebrows brooding over bright blue eyes that were difficult to read because they twinkled with amusement even when he was angry. He wore a magnificent moustache that swept across his face, connecting up with equally heavy sideburns. Together they contrived to conceal a mildly cynical smile. The first signs of that smile could be detected from the lines outside his eyes and, as these increased, the smile itself would emerge from under cover of the moustache to beam and glow. But only the very foolish would dare take liberties with him.

At morning stand-to – the daily ritual prescribed for just before first light – the rest of us were expected to cower in our trenches in readiness for a dawn attack while he strode above the ramparts like a latter-day Duke of Wellington surveying his troops and offering good counsel. The poncho cape he wore was the largest available, but too small for him. His steel helmet sat on his head like a Chinese coolie-hat. For the enemy he had contempt.

I thought he must have been pleased with my progress, unless of course he wanted to get rid of me, for, summoning me to his presence, he confided that the 7th Division had got itself boxed in at a place called Sinzweya, in the Mayu Hills about fourteen miles south of our own positions, and he wanted me to get a line out to them as quickly as possible. This would not normally have been part of an adjutant's duties, so it was either a compliment or something much too sinister to contemplate.

'Dear boy, take a gang of coolies with you (locals who had lost their homes and belongings and tagged along with the army for survival); they can carry the cable, and some linemen. Follow the Kalapanzin [river] to Taung Bazaar and then turn west. The place should be obvious enough because there is a lot of activity going on there. Report in at intervals and let me know how you're getting on.'

'Yes sir!' That was the only response he expected, and the only one he got. But there was a lot of ground between his orders and the box, and it was highly unlikely that I should be the only visitor in those parts. What's more, some serious battles had been fought in the area over the past month the evidence of which was plain enough to see.

There were dead bodies propped up in grotesque attitudes decomposing in the sun, some with arms raised and fingers pointing the way home; tattered mosquito nets hanging from bushes whence their owners had escaped in a hurry; bits of burnt paper floating in the air above piles of the stuff hastily destroyed – a couple of cypher officers had died in that desperate exercise – and an assortment of bottles, tins, ragged clothing, and even a pair of pyjamas, bearing witness to an undignified débâcle. This was no place for men with a preference for the quiet life.

My little army consisted of sixteen coolies, trotting rhythmically under the weight of two drums of cable each bouncing on the ends of a bamboo yoke balanced across their shoulders, and eight linemen. The latter were busy reeling out the cable as fast as they could off similarly improvised bamboo spindles, tucking the stuff into the long grass along the river bank to avoid detection and the attentions of a careless boot.

By nightfall we had covered about ten miles. I called my master to report progress, and to warn him that we would be going to ground for the night and would prefer not to have any calls for the duration. But I left the field telephone connected to the cable just in case some emergency arose at either end. The site I had chosen was well protected by trees and shrub. Anyone approaching could not avoid betraying his presence long before reaching us. The coolies huddled in the centre and the linemen, armed with Sten guns, manned the perimeter. Of the eight two remained on guard at a time.

After a bowl of whatever was on the menu at headquarters, and a final glass with the general, the colonel's thoughts turned instinctively to his adjutant crouched at the end of a field telephone somewhere in no man's land.

That telephone had an unusually large bell capable of making a big noise; if not loud enough to arouse the dead, then at least to invite any Japanese patrols in the vicinity to move in and recruit a few reinforcements for them. The colonel duly rang the bell.

In a panic I grabbed the telephone and whispered into it.

'Hello dear boy, how are ya?'

I told him as politely as I could.

'Speak up,' he went on, 'this line doesn't sound too good to me.'

I explained that local conditions were not conducive to conducting a normal conversation and that I was anxious to avoid announcing our presence to unfriendly ears.

'Oh, I see,' he sounded disappointed. 'Well, keep up the good work and call me in the morning. Good night dear boy, sleep well.' The possible presence of any enemy in the area was to him an irrelevance.

We had little difficulty finding the way and made contact at journey's end with the Lincolnshire Regiment preparing to assault Hill 315 (I think it was called) and to open a way into the box. That task was given to Charles Hoey and his company.

It was a simple enough mission on paper, but very different on the ground. The preliminaries by the divisional artillery had already begun and were soon followed by heavier guns farther back. The outcome is best described in the Supplement to the *London Gazette* of Tuesday, 16 May 1944.

> The King has been graciously pleased to approve the posthumous award of the Victoria Cross to Captain (Temporary Major) Charles Ferguson Hoey, M.C. (71106), The Lincolnshire Regiment (Vancouver).
>
> In Burma, on the 16th of February, 1944, Major Hoey's Company formed part of a force which was ordered to capture a position at all costs. After a night march through enemy held territory the force was met at the foot of the position by heavy machine-gun fire. Major Hoey personally led his company – still under heavy machine-gun and rifle fire – right up to the objective.
>
> Although wounded at least twice in the leg and head he seized a Bren gun from one of his men and firing from the hip, led his Company onto the objective. In spite of his wounds the Company had difficulty keeping up with him, and Major Hoey reached the enemy strong post first where he killed all the occupants before being mortally wounded.
>
> Major Hoey's outstanding gallantry and leadership, his total disregard of personal safety, and his grim determination to reach the objective resulted in the capture of this vital position.

However briefly, I was proud to have known such a man. He died opening a door into Sinzweya through which lesser mortals could carry the means of survival.

The rum run

Away from the reality of war at its sharpest end, another mission awaited me. We had returned to Chittagong for a wash and brush up when I was summoned to the presence. 'Take a section of Gurkhas with you dear boy and make your way to a place called Mandya, near Mysore. There is a large distillery there. Contact Indian Railways and arrange for three wagons to be shunted into the place and load up with fifteen hundred gallons of rum and an equal quantity of gin.'

Not for me to reason why. This was obviously the secret weapon for winning our war; the stuff to make men follow the path to glory against all odds. In the face of such a strategy I was not going to bat an eyelid. He went on: 'Make sure the wagons are properly sealed and that they remain that way.' There was a cunning little twinkle in the eyes as he brushed his moustache upwards, adding that the seals were not to be tampered with by anyone, anywhere or at any time, however compelling the need for a casual inspection. 'And you better get back here as soon as possible.'

He was not interested in the paperwork involved or the bureaucratic obstacles likely to be encountered between Mandya and Chittagong. He just wanted the job done, and had given me my orders, and that was that.

The man behind this spirited initiative was none other than a certain lieutenant colonel answering to the name of Cariappa. He was the AA and QMG (Assistant

Adjutant and Quarter Master General) – a title that might lead a man into all sorts of indiscretions – and had a friend who ran the enterprise in Mandya. That he was destined to become a field marshal and commander-in-chief of the Indian Army surprised no one; but whether the rum and the gin played any part in that meteoric rise to fame is anybody's guess, though they must surely have been subtle pointers in the desired direction.

Escorting that quantity of hard drink across India at war was a hazardous journey and one of legendary proportions. All along the line good men with sensitive noses and well-developed instincts were anxious to assure themselves that everything was in order inside those wagons.

'No, no, sir, we must simply see that everything is "woh k!" What is there in breaking seal? It can be replaced with another one.'

I stood my ground, and the Gurkhas, armed with rifles and kukris, stood theirs. But none of these confrontations called for violence; they were friendly and good humoured.

In Calcutta, however, it was very nearly a different story. The stationmaster had heard about the wagons and was no doubt aware of their contents. He insisted on their being detached from the train and shunted into a siding for inspection.

'You must open these wagons for inspection,' he said. 'Otherwise they will be impounded and you will have to proceed without them.'

He seemed to me to be a pompous little ass, determined to display his authority in the presence of his subordinates, and to undermine mine in the presence of the Gurkhas. But I was wrong. All he really wanted to do was to be seen to be playing his part in the war effort by helping to clear an important consignment destined for the 'war front'.

Realising this in the nick of time I responded accordingly. 'Stationmaster,' I said, loading the word with respect, 'you place me in a difficult position.'

'Why so? You tell me, I am here to help you.'

'Well, you see, when I left the war front, Colonel Cariappa gave explicit instructions that these seals were not to be broken until the wagons were officially handed over to him in Chittagong. Now you want to open the wagons, I can explain my problem to you, and I am sure you will understand. But what happens when I get to Chalna, where the railway ends?' I asked, looking at him appealingly. 'I will have to trans-ship onto the steamer bound for Chandpur and pick up the train from there for Comilla, and then change again for Chittagong?' This was a railway problem and one he could handle with relish.

'No, no, you do like this. I will order wagons to be hitched up with twenty-one up mail, extra two-three hundred miles, to connect up with Kaliganj-Tripura Express. From there it is wonly one day to Chittagong, also via Comilla.'

'That sounds wonderful,' I said.

'Riverboat route through Chalna is three days, my suggestion is wonly two days, and, my dear sir, you will be saving one day, and the seals.' He laughed happily.

'Who is this Cariappa?' he asked, and when I explained that he was the most senior Indian officer on the war front he seemed impressed. 'Come on, don't vurry, we will have a cup of tea.' Thus spoke the hospitable heart of India.

Crossing the Ganges Delta was then, and still is, a complicated business, but we did save a day, as the stationmaster had predicted, and I was confident that something more substantial than 'well done dear boy, is it all there?' lay in store for me at journey's end.

And it did. My next confidential report made a brief reference to the matter, concluding with: 'Can be relied upon to deliver the goods', or something of the sort. It was the kind of laconic remark common among senior officers, intended to camouflage their real feelings about the ambitious young officers under their command.

Combined operations

No two COs are alike; that much one learnt early on. Each has his own treasured set of values, his own idiosyncrasies, and his own foibles that have long awaited their hour, biding their time for opportunity to knock.

'Dear boy' had moved on to higher things and I was waiting for a new CO. There would be changes, and some reshuffling no doubt; but one hardly expected his arrival to be delayed because the aeroplane transporting him into our lives ran out of fuel.

He had set off happily enough from a Royal Air Force base equipped with parachute – by pure chance – that a squadron commander friend had given him as a souvenir, and was looking forward to a pleasant flight over the Burmese jungle, when the little two seater Auster began to cough and splutter. Having established that they had run out of fuel – whether through carelessness, over-consumption or a leak in the system was never established – the pilot asked my future CO if he would mind stepping out onto the wing and jumping off. It was an invitation not easily refused.

Even so, it came as something of a shock, but there was no alternative and little time for discussion. The parachute was adjusted and away he went into a free fall finishing up on the branch of a tree from which he was later brought down safely by a rescue party; his final thoughts before jumping were for an unpaid mess bill. However, thus to be cast afloat in thin air and to survive was no ordinary feat, for which he was made a member of the 'Caterpillar Club', a privilege of which he was immensely proud.

He was an excellent soldier too, dedicated to the welfare of the troops and the efficiency of his regiment – as it happened his first. He was also extremely conscientious on matters related to sport, rugby in particular, and he enjoyed a well-organised party.

The two lessons I learnt from him were never to set a limit on your horizons, and if confronted with an emergency to react at once, but as casually as possible, and start thinking hard. I select two examples to illustrate the point.

Having promoted me to second-in-command, he invited me to join him one morning on a tour of the camp, during the course of which he introduced me to a broken down old barn doggedly hanging on to the evidence of its most recent occupants.

'Wouldn't it be marvellous', he said, 'if we could turn this into a general purpose theatre for the troops?'

He was just thinking aloud, but in my new-found importance I was anxious to appear to be tuned in to his thoughts, and agreed at once, fuelling his enthusiasm by adding that it was an inspired idea. I had grasped the nettle before it was thrust towards me, and, in addition to thinking hard, spent the next month learning a great deal about the restoration of an old barn.

'Ye Olde Barn' was officially opened by the general officer commanding, and I received many plaudits on passing my first major assignment as a new second-in-command.

Somewhere within the same calendar of events, I found myself sitting beside the colonel and the general at the divisional sports under an unblemished sky – in every sense – until the 220 x 4 relay race began lining up in front of us. There appeared to be some confusion caused by one of the teams (it turned out to be ours) missing a fourth runner.

'Do be a good chap and strip old boy' was not the sort of solution I had in mind, but other ears were listening. Moreover, I had only recently taken to wearing a crown on my shoulder and felt quite comfortable with it there. My thoughts naturally flashed to my undergarments which, fortunately, were in good nick and reasonably clean. So, casting caution aside, I stripped and ran the first leg barefoot.

The general's obvious pleasure in this display of leadership was later reflected in my confidential report in a single telling phrase: 'Can rise to an occasion.'

There were to be other occasions too, and one of these came under the heading of 'Combined Operations'. That was big medicine; big enough to make the chest swell and eyes light up with a vision of distant horizons beyond the reach of ordinary men. All it meant, in fact, was that the navy, the army and the air force, the traditional enemies, would for once be planning and doing the same thing, only together. We were preparing an assault on the island of Ramree off the west coast of Burma.

There had been much advanced planning, most of it behind barbed wire – to protect those in the know from those not – and it had all taken place in a tented camp on the Arakan coast between Cox's Bazaar (heaven knows who Cox was) and Maungdaw. Now the time had come for action.

We landed on a clear day and in very good order. Apart from the naval guns covering the landing there was not much sound of anger. The Japanese, seeing little point in hanging around, had withdrawn more willingly than expected and our own troops had advanced through the first line of defences in hot pursuit.

However, according to the plans drawn up behind barbed wire, the next instalment of the bombardment was due to be delivered by bombers based in Colombo, and the area mapped out for this display of allied resolve was no longer occupied by the Japanese. We had moved in.

My orders came thick and fast: 'Get hold of a set, chuck a piece of wire up somewhere and make contact with the Fourteenth Army Guard Wave.' Here again, the thing to do was to start moving fast and switch to 'think hard'. I got a set, found a hole in the ground and settled into it. A young signaller, who would have done the job with less fuss given the opportunity, was directed to climb the nearest tree and fix the aerial wire in the desired direction.

Under Bill Slim's much-loved command we were entitled to use his guard wave – an arrangement whereby a powerful transmitter would signal the first three letters of the day for five minutes before the hour, and then stand by for any distress signals for a further five minutes. But we were no longer a part of Fourteenth Army – combined operations having placed us in more select company – which meant returning cap in hand like the prodigal son and, as gratefully, to be welcomed back.

Identification had to be established by using the call sign allocated to every headquarters. We still had the frequency, and it was Wednesday. Spectators of all ranks gathered above, which made me feel very important, but not a little insecure too: supposing the good Lord failed to hear my prayers, what then?

That was a singularly disturbing thought which encouraged me to listen with the maximum possible concentration. And suddenly, there it was, by heavens, the unmistakable signal: dit-dar-dar, dit, dar-dit-dit, repeated over and over again. The moment it stopped, I got in fast with the same three letters and my own call sign. Wonder of wonders! Miracle of miracles! From a thousand miles away came the reassuring signal to go ahead.

The message was ready and waiting: 'Forward troops moving ahead of first line of opposition. Cancel bombing programme. . . .' It was acknowledged first time and I came out of my hole in the ground like a man truly risen; even more, like a man who had just won the war single-handed. The colonel snapped his fingers in the air, a habit he had whenever something especially impressed or pleased him, and showered praises on me while I, with great difficulty, adopted a suitably humble demeanour. Capturing Ramree so brilliantly put us among the top contenders for the assault on Rangoon to be followed by operation Zipper, the invasion of Malaya.

I had once seen a beautiful drawing by John Moore of the landing at Rangoon by the combined forces from Bengal and Madras under the orders of Sir Archibald Campbell on 11 May 1821; and here we were at it again. What's more, the job was accomplished with equal success and few casualties; but, before we could turn our attention to operation Zipper, the atom bombs had already been dropped on Hiroshima and Nagasaki. The war with Japan was at an end.

The pectoral cross

Our convoy was quickly diverted to Padang in Sumatra – still occupied by the Japanese – with instructions to play everything by ear. Such a strategy is not unusual when one is not quite sure what to do, and may explain why my orders were to make contact with the headquarters of the Japanese guards division in Sibolga, on the west coast, and thence to proceed to the capital, Medan, with a letter for the Indonesian governor.

'Your first contact will be at Bukittinggi, about forty miles up the road; avoid shaking hands, and don't be tempted to acquire any trophies, such as a sword for instance.' (The swords were to remain fastened to their owners' belts until relieved of them by more worthy claimants.)

These instructions were clear enough, and my own colonel added that the rear elements of our division would be arriving in Medan shortly after I got there. 'Look after yourself,' he said, 'and do whatever you can for any Dutch prisoners of war you may come across.' I wanted to ask whether the lads along the road had been informed that the war was over, but thought better of it, and climbing into my jeep set off with a brave wave of the hand. It was not so much the escort – a whole platoon of British infantry looking thoroughly professional – that gave me confidence and a bit of status, as the large Union Jack fluttering over the bonnet of the jeep. It lifted my spirits and made me feel invincible.

The journey to Medan was about three hundred miles. Welcoming crowds waved us through Bukittinggi and I responded with a viceregal gesture or two as we pressed on to the first enemy outpost manned by a company of infantry. The company commander, who spoke a little English, was polite, very correct and a good host. He was a good officer too; I could see that by the way everything had been arranged. We were of the same rank and understood each other's position. Between us there was no longer a war, and given time we could have become friends.

Sibolga was less comfortable; not for any lack of hospitality, if anything there was too much of it, but from the point of view of protocol. Here I was, a young, temporary major, confronting a general, and a distinguished soldier at that, bowing to the inevitable. His staff stood beside him in order of seniority on a beautifully manicured lawn outside their headquarters.

Enemies we may have been, but we were soldiers too, and the barriers between us were not of our making. Most members of his staff were senior to me and I would normally have been on the receiving end of their orders. I like to think that the general understood my dilemma for like good military men everywhere he set out to make my task as easy as possible. Stepping out of the well-formed line, he stood rigidly to attention and bowed in that crisp, deliberate fashion of the Japanese in all walks of life. His staff did likewise. No hand was offered and in any case I anticipated any such gesture by saluting, which was within the rules. The general returned my salute.

Briefing my escort to stay put, and emphasising that they should do so in good order, I accompanied the general into the building. We sat in a circle in what was obviously the briefing room, and, speaking on behalf of the general, an interpreter explained that the Indonesians were inclined to resent our presence. There had been a disturbance earlier in the day culminating in a raid on the armoury. 'The raid was foiled,' he went on, 'but they are armed and the general wishes to know your intentions and your orders.'

I replied that we would be proceeding to Medan in the morning, that my escort and I would benefit from a good night's sleep, and that I would have to rely on the general for our comfort and safety. I was anxious to avoid saying anything like 'I will hold the general personally responsible for our safety' because it would have sounded both trite and pompous. That this was appreciated became self evident as orders were issued for a cordon to be thrown around the building for the duration of our stay, my escort led away to a meal and accommodation elsewhere in the building, and a sentry posted outside the door of my sleeping quarters. On the table in my room was a bottle of vermouth and a glass; on the floor by the bed a pair of slippers.

In the morning we were escorted to the outskirts of the town and bade farewell with the same correctness and courtesy we had experienced the evening before. There had been no crowds to welcome us to Sibolga and none to wave us goodbye which may have been ominous but failed to register at the time.

In Medan the governor didn't seem over-pleased to see me either, perhaps because the presence of allied troops meant that his own plans to take over where the Japanese had left off would be frustrated. There were neither smiles nor any other form of hospitality.

I simply handed over the letter, dignified his office with a smart salute and made my way to the Medan Hotel. It had until recently been occupied by the Japanese and was now cleared for our use. A few members of staff remained and were hanging around; there was lots of accommodation but little else. Naturally, I saw it as my duty to display a little leadership and gave instructions for the army rations we had on board to be opened up. A cup of tea and whatever else came out of those mysterious tins seemed the best way of breaking the ice and making friends.

It also dawned on me that until the remainder of the division arrived at Belawan, the port serving Medan, I was no less a person than the allied commander Medan, the highest position I would ever attain in life. When I put this to the troops they responded with instant enthusiasm – the hallmark of all good soldiers: 'Congratulations sir,' and followed that up with a spontaneous rendering of 'He's a jolly good fellow'. Our Indonesian friends smiled politely.

The first call on my services came from a Franciscan priest, Father Wap, a stocky little man with a ginger beard wearing a dark brown soutane and a girdle made of white cotton rope with a series of knots at the end. 'Major,' he said, 'the Indonesians have declared war on the Dutch. Our nuns are in a small convent near Toba Meer [a lake in the hills some distance from Medan] and in great danger, you must please rescue them.'

For the allied commander Medan this was no big deal. I might even have said: 'Father, my moment has come.' It most assuredly had, for under my command was a large garrison of Japanese troops, armed and with implicit instructions to do my bidding. So I sent for a liaison officer. He arrived, bowed and waited for his orders.

'I want you to send an armed escort with sufficient transport to the Franciscan convent at Toba Meer and bring the nuns and all their baggage back to Medan today. Father Wap here will give you the details.' He bowed sharply and uttered the one word 'hai!' – short and sharp like a controlled hiss. The operation was carried out successfully and acknowledged the following morning by a delegation of nuns, led by Father Wap, marching into my office on the verandah bearing an enormous cake. They had baked it immediately on returning to Medan.

Power is a heady thing, which is probably what prompted me to ask if there was anything else I could do. 'O yes, many things,' said the mother superior, 'but our greatest concern at the moment is that our dear bishop no longer has a pectoral cross. It was melted down in prison to buy food.'

Now this was altogether a different proposition, but I had taken the plunge and had to swim. What's more, looking into the smiling face of that good and holy woman, I saw at once that she knew she had got me hooked. 'Leave it with me mother,' I said, 'I'll see what I can do.'

'O thank you,' she beamed on her champion.

I passed the word around that any spare guilders in search of a good home would be warmly welcomed. But it was an operation likely to take some time, and meanwhile the incoming 'allied commander' would see to it that my authority was diminished as soon as possible in order to establish his own – especially in regard to those Franciscans. But I was wrong; as my importance declined so did their loyalty rise, and I remained their man.

When the rear echelon arrived, it brought fresh light in the person of one Mohammad Khan, a havaldar major (sergeant major) of real stature. He stood over six feet tall, with a moustache that commanded universal admiration. He wore a magnificent khaki turban tied around a gold cap with one end standing erect, raising him yet another six inches above his fellow men.

He spoke in Urdu, a language I had been at pains to learn under threat of demotion. 'Major sahib,' he said, 'they are saying that the big padre sahib was a prisoner and had to sell his gold cross to buy food for the prisoners. We are very sad to hear that bad thing and very happy that you are trying to buy a new cross. The Muslim, Hindu and Indian Christians in headquarters would also like to contribute towards buying this cross.' Now this was the sort of man one would readily accompany into a mosque, and a man who would similarly honour a Christian church. When the colonel arrived I told him about Mohammad Khan and operation Pectoral Cross. He snapped his fingers and, typically, offered to make good any shortfall.

Although we were not aware of it at the time, this was a bit of ecumenism prompted by circumstances that brought people together and made them help each other – even across the barriers of religion.

The cross was ordered from India and in due course arrived: bright and shining in a beautiful presentation box with a large ruby in the centre. It was handed over to Father Wap without ceremony. Caught off guard perhaps, his face began to glow with the light of faith in a battered world, and he was visibly moved. 'What shall we do now?' he asked.

To diffuse the situation, I came up with what seemed to me an outrageous suggestion: 'Why not erect a large wooden cross on the football field, Father, so that the bishop can say mass in the open and bless everybody?' But as far as the Franciscan was concerned this was far from outrageous.

'That is an excellent idea,' he said, and off he went to recruit the nuns and the priests and anyone else who might be persuaded to lend a hand. And so the work was done, and the day and the hour set for the bishop to return to his fold, properly dressed.

A great crowd gathered to witness the event. And as that good man turned to face the sea of faces watching and wishing him well, his left hand moved across to the pectoral cross while his right hand rose high above his head. Slowly and deliberately he began to bless all who had made the day possible – Christian, Hindu and Muslim alike. I had little doubt that the experience would remain with him as one of the more hopeful aspects of war, not just for the day, but for ever.

Seconds-in-command are not usually found at the centre of big events. Their role is to serve others; looking after the welfare of the troops for instance and, occasionally, the colonel's. I remember standing in the ante-room of the Officers' Mess on one occasion, listening to the adjutant recount an incident involving the use of a pistol. We all carried pistols, whether going on duty or not, and were expecting a jeep to arrive at any moment for the duty officer.

As the adjutant drew his pistol to demonstrate the point he was making, the jeep driver appeared at the door and the pistol went off simultaneously hitting the driver in the middle of the stomach. Acting instinctively, I grabbed him under the knees and around the shoulder, concertinaing his body to seal any wound, and jumping into the jeep with the driver on my knees instructed the adjutant to drive to the hospital as fast as he could.

Once there we got the driver onto a bed, but when the doctor examined him he found nothing more than a bruise just above the navel. The bullet had hit the brass buckle on his web belt slap in the middle, so precisely in fact that it had not been deflected into any other part of his body. It was a miracle certainly, and one up for the pectoral cross. Of course the colonel had to be told, but with the sequence of events reversed in order to lessen the impact and limit the damage to a quiet word with the adjutant, and a new standing order on the wearing and use of firearms.

Shortly after this incident, we were having a drink in the mess when the telephone rang. I answered it. The orderly sergeant was on the other end reporting from the Sergeants' Mess that a young soldier, seemingly drunk, was outside demanding to see the regimental sergeant major in a most unfriendly manner.

'Send the bastard out and I'll kill him,' was how he put it.

Once the orderly sergeant had reported the matter, he was off the hook and I was on it.

'Call out to the man,' I instructed, 'speak clearly and firmly, and say that the second-in-command wishes to see him right away in the Officers' Mess' – the mess being about two hundred yards up the road. The message was passed on and the orderly sergeant duly reported back that the man was on his way accompanied, he might have added, by a massive sigh of relief. The other officers were unaware of what was going on and I thought better than to enlighten them because it would only have caused confusion. After all, this was not the sort of subject likely to benefit from general discussion.

As I emerged from the main entrance, so did the would-be assassin appear outside the mess gates at the far end of a gravel path. I beckoned him forward. 'Come along,' I called out in a friendly manner and as calmly as possible, 'don't be afraid. I want to talk to you.'

I must have conveyed more confidence than I felt for, holding the rifle in front of him, he advanced to within a yard of me, and when I put my hand out to take the rifle from him he handed it over meekly. It was a tricky moment, and I could see that he was not drunk.

'Would you like a cup of tea?' I asked, greatly relieved.

'Yes sir.'

'Then come along in and let's talk about this business.'

I led him into the mess office, organised the tea and then examined the rifle. It was loaded right enough with one round up the breach and four in the magazine.

'Why do you want to shoot the sergeant major?' I asked.

'He's a bully sir.'

'But you can't go around shooting people simply because you think they are bullies!' I spoke quietly because the lad was obviously distraught.

'No sir, sorry sir.'

Well, there was nothing for it but to place him in detention and get the doctor to visit him. Maybe the cumulative effect of the landings in Ramree and Rangoon, the dropping of the atom bombs and the sudden ending of the war – tinged with a little home sickness perhaps – had thrown him off balance. How could one tell?

But sick he certainly was, and evacuated soon afterwards to the military hospital in Singapore to be sent home on medical grounds. The regimental sergeant major didn't remain long either, but that is a separate matter.

Delhi

When anyone came to the mess with a problem, it seemed the second-in-command was always there to oblige. The other officers were usually deployed on more important duties, and the best place for me, particularly in the evenings, was the mess, opposite which there was a workshop built of atap and bamboo.

Here, one evening, Sergeant Joseph, an Indian Christian and a highly competent technician, was at work when he noticed a cobra reclining at full stretch on a beam just below the eaves of the atap roof. Its intentions were unclear, so he nipped over to the mess thinking that I would be interested.

Now I had a special relationship with Sergeant Joseph – sealed during the recent divisional sports when boxing was included as part of the evening's entertainment. I was matched against Joseph and for both of us it was something of a dilemma: he had no wish to batter the face of the second-in-command – despite vociferous encouragement from the audience – and for my part, the last thing I wanted to do was to inflict bodily harm on a good Sergeant, particularly one from the state of Tamil Nadu.

I accompanied him back to the workshop, and there right enough was a cobra in full bloom, seemingly unperturbed by our presence. It was probably the permanent occupant of the hut, and regarded us as squatters. But now that its presence was exposed, the status quo was no longer an option. One or other had to decamp.

We were not entirely sure what to do, but Joseph thought I ought to shoot it, adding, with the hint of a smile, that if I missed it would pursue me for ever, and if I killed it there would be a major change in my life. It was not the kind of mythology I felt comfortable with, and I suggested that he might like to have a go.

'No sir,' he said, with the smile of a man about to win the argument, 'you are the senior officer and a better shot,' after which he handed me his rifle and turned the hanging lamp onto the target. The cobra raised itself to full alert, beady red eyes fixed angrily on its adversaries, and ready to spit venom into our faces. It was an easy target and I suppose I had to shoot it.

'Good shot sir,' said Joseph, but sir felt distinctly unheroic.

Within a few days of this incident, orders arrived for the division to move to India, and for me there came notice of a posting to Delhi.

My new commanding officer was a tall, elegant man, highly intelligent, who kept aloof from the rest of the herd, which had the effect of stifling the slightest breach of regimental protocol the moment he appeared. If he had a sense of humour, it was not immediately obvious. But he did teach me a lesson which I am happy to pass on to others.

Returning from a long and difficult night watching over transmissions to London, I was summoned to his office and asked, among other things, whether I had a servant. Thinking he was expressing concern for my welfare, I answered, maybe a little nonchalantly, that I did share the services of a batman.

'Then get him to clean your buttons,' he said, and he was not joking.

It must have been a little trick he had learnt somewhere, but at the time it failed to amuse me. The grin vanished from my face and I delivered the best salaam in my repertoire. Of course, he was only reminding me that, even when tinkering with global matters, the basics of soldiering were not to be neglected. And he was right.

The upheavals in the Indian sub-continent were bursting over our heads; communal rioting on a scale the world had not seen before swept through the great city leaving a trail of death and destruction. The Muslim community was moved into the old fort (Purana Qila), about one hundred and twenty thousand at the earliest count, and chapatties were airdropped to feed them.

How could such a thing happen? This 'unofficial' war accounted for more casualties than the official one we had just left behind, and it was done in hand-to-hand combat between brothers; men who had been born and bred in the same city.

Yet it was a remarkable achievement that the situation was contained and brought under control – excepting of course that for the hundreds of thousands made homeless in their own country the matter was not so simple.

The partition of India which followed erected, in effect, a barrier between old friends. And not just old friends: my brother, who had also survived the war, was stationed at Alhilal – the summer residence of the raja of Baluwalpur in Pakistan – commanding his regimental centre and assuaging communal tempers with the promise that the Gurkhas under his command were there to protect them all.

It was not easy going to see him: a couple of hundred miles by train, bus and jeep through endless columns of refugees – all wretched but none hostile; nor did they attempt to obstruct my freedom of movement. But what a joy to be among the first to cross the Indo-Pakistan frontier – so often repeated in later years – and the only threat to my person came when I arrived at my brother's quarters late in the evening to be confronted by an angry Alsatian by the name of Nuts. Like my brother, he had not been prewarned of my visit and came at me through an open window; but when reassured that we were indeed brothers, he called off the attack – however reluctantly.

These events were eclipsed by India coming 'to her tryst with destiny', Lord Mountbatten's arrival as viceroy and that great soldier, Field Marshal Sir Claude Auchinleck, going on air to tell us what to do, in a broadcast to the Indian Army delivered in Urdu.

'Indian Officers, do not cut your own foot with your own mattock. Do not take or connive at any action which may impair the discipline, efficiency or loyalty of the army to the government of the day.

British officers, serve the new India as loyally as in the past your Indian comrades have served the present India. It is your duty to your country, and to the army to which you belong, to pass on to your Indian comrades, who are to follow you, all the experience and knowledge that you have gained in the past, so that they, in their turn, may serve the Indian Army as faithfully and truly as you have done. Thus may the Indian Army lead the way.'

When the hands of future generations turn the pages of history, I hope they will find that not a single soldier broke ranks to join the riots, and that the Indian Army remained steady and firm, as its commander-in-chief had instructed, guarding the dawn of the largest democracy in the world.

We had played a small part in the independence of our soldiers' country, and left them to continue the good work with their own officers, while those of us departing followed on the heels of the Somerset Light Infantry (PA) as that fine county regiment slow-marched through India Gate, in Bombay, to the waiting ships.

The memory returns easily to that scene; nor will the last British regiment to leave India ever forget it. The bands, the pipes and drums, the colours, the centuries-old traditions, and the thousands of Indian voices singing 'Auld Lang Syne' will remain a testament to comradeship long after politicians have had their say.

Edinburgh

That comradeship had come marching off the battlefields of the world, triumphant in its finest hour; an hour shared by the hundreds of thousands who did the actual fighting, and the millions who had endured the horror of it all with anxious hearts. It was now called upon to break ranks and go its separate ways.

Mine led me to a nissen-hutted camp in Fairmilehead (now a Marie Curie Home) on the outskirts of Edinburgh and within a twenty minutes' tramride of Princes Street. There was a camp next door for German prisoners of war hanging on to what remained of their own dreams of home.

They shared with us a view of the Pentland Hills and provided a ready-to-hand labour force – little else. Nor was it theirs to reason why; they did as they were told, while the leaders who had brought them to this sorry pass were facing a more serious fate elsewhere. It was here then that I took up my new appointment, once again a heartbeat away from the seat of power, serving a man who enjoyed shooting and fishing.

This was a much more agreeable existence, and as he enjoyed nothing better than carving a well-hung pheasant and entertaining his friends, there was little cause to worry. He was a small, well-proportioned man with dark hair and sharp features. His goodness of heart warmed to the idea of bringing the prisoners of war over to our side of the camp to share part of our Christmas festivities, and the Germans responded by producing an excellent choir to entertain us.

I doubt whether I shall ever again be so moved by the singing of 'Stille Nacht, Heilige Nacht'. Nor do I need to elaborate on the scene that followed: we were all soldiers and had experienced the same things. The only difference was that they had lost.

But the army could not rest on its laurels for ever. It had to be seen to be preparing for something – goodness only knows what – and the best way of doing this was to embark on an ambitious programme of sporting activities. And there is always the man to match the hour. An otherwise idle staff officer at Scottish Command must have got carried away by working in the castle and proposed, off his head so to speak, that it was time to stage the army boxing championships, and as reputations have been known to rise or fall on the outcome of such contests, feverish activity was generated, and not least at Fairmilehead.

My own records revealed that I had been driven into the boxing ring in my earlier career, and, being the right weight, in went my name not only to captain the regimental side but to make a personal appearance in the light heavy-weight class. This was no laughing matter, it had to be taken seriously. So I took myself off to the Army School of Physical Training at Scarborough and got into good shape to win honour and glory for my master and a good confidential report for myself.

When I returned to Fairmilehead it was to a hero's welcome. I was presented with a seventy-five-pounder shell either to kill myself or to beef up the training – whichever came first. If I could manage a hundred situps, with the shell across my shoulders, I was told, a devastating punch would be the result. So I pursued that target, exercising morning and evening, and it never occurred to me to ask why some of the other officers had not been persuaded to volunteer. Possibly it was that although I was young enough, they were even younger and less experienced. One never really knew about such things.

As luck would have it, and perhaps fortunately for my reputation, there were no other officer contenders in my class – the troops maintained that they had been frightened off, a view I was happy not to discourage – so while I could not claim victory, I was at least the unchallenged champion and, in that capacity, attended the boxing to demonstrate a keen interest in those less fortunate from a ringside seat.

For all the experience I had gained while being groomed for command – if grooming is the right word for the hard labour that leads to command, if lucky, or early retirement if not – the process was by no means complete. The final assignment was yet to come, and this time with a cultural twist.

We had moved from Fairmilehead to the stone-built splendour of Redford Barracks with its luxurious accommodation, gymnasium, playing fields and enormous parade square. It was a move that warranted some kind of celebration but, sadly, as a hastily thrown together unit we had few possessions to show off. The moment had therefore arrived for the 2 I/C to display a little initiative.

The new Officers' Mess had a magnificent entrance hall, empty but for a passable chandelier. It was so grand in fact that we had turned our backs on an old friend, a cable drum – the sort one sees outside British Telecom storeyards measuring about five feet across the top and four feet high – that had served us well in a nissen hut, but for which there could be no place at Redford Barracks, apart from the ante-room fire. Unless? And here one of those rare flashes of genius came to the rescue: if the Chief Ordnance Officer could be won over, perhaps the old drum might be given a facelift? A veneer of mahogany on top, bottom and middle, with the large steel bolts silver plated, would transform its appearance and give us a whole new perspective on what to do with it.

But what sort of story could we concoct to bring this about? A full-blooded lie could backfire and do more damage than the project was worth; a half truth on the other hand, if propounded with skill and confidence, might do the trick, and on that premise we secured an appointment with the COO. He listened patiently as we explained our attachment to the drum which, as far as we knew, was the first across the Rhine during the Second World War, sinking its armoured cable into those heavily mined waters to provide communications for the allied forces. How else could it have finished up at Fairmilehead with the remnants of several Royal Signals units?

'You're joking,' he said.

'No, sir! That's how the story goes; and if old guns, and swords, and commanders' caravans can finish up as museum pieces, why not an old cable drum?'

I don't think he was convinced. But the novelty of our approach must have impressed him for he became part of the conspiracy and suggested we cart the drum off to the Royal Ordnance Depot in Glasgow to see what could be done.

And very much was done. Six weeks later the drum returned, recognisable only from its shape. It was in a class by itself, a dazzling piece of furniture that added an aura of distinction to the entrance hall. A small silver plaque recorded its brief, if not too accurate, history, and a silver statuette of the Winged Mercury (the only trophy of any value we possessed) found a home on top.

Now this figure has one leg cocked up behind and one hand raised above the head, forefinger pointing skywards, ready for take-off, and that wholly innocent gesture gave birth to an idea: 'The ceremony of the drum'.

It was a bit of harmless nonsense for the benefit of newcomers who would be required to walk onto the drum (barefoot of course) over a bridge of officers, the most senior touching the edge of the drum with his forehead and the most junior hanging on to the tail. On reaching the drum, the less than enthusiastic victim would take the place of the statuette, adopting exactly the same posture for a period of one minute, while all others present would consume as much drink as they could at his expense.

It was quite clear that my new boss approved of the piece of furniture, but saw little merit in the ceremony as a means of promoting the leadership qualities of his officers. Indeed, I took particular note of the fact that he failed to express himself delighted with it.

But he did like music, and played the piano tolerably well, while his Senior Woman's Royal Army Corps officer (she was in charge of a squadron of girls attached to the regiment and wore the rank of major) was less musical and had a preference for conducting drill parades for the girls. This became a regular feature on the barracks square and did not please the colonel one bit. The challenge confronting me was how to coax those two well embedded cultural instincts towards a more productive occupation for the WRAC without the combined wrath of the protagonists descending on my own head.

That I managed to do both at a stroke suggests that opportunity does indeed knock – if one is in tune with events and ready to grasp the opportunity when it comes along. Thus was I delivered from the bondage of the oppressed classes into the free-ranging world of command.

It came about like this: Her Royal Highness, the late Princess Mary (the Princess Royal), who was Colonel-in-Chief of my father's regiment, and closely associated with my brother's regiment and mine, was coming to Edinburgh to visit us – then the sole occupants of Redford Barracks.

Two things had to be done: the first of these, despite rationing, was to provide luncheon of a quality to match the occasion, without recourse to any underhand practice; and the second, a more lasting impression of the visit involving as many people as possible.

The matter of lunch was easily solved. The officers tightened their belts and loyally agreed to their bacon rations being frozen – a little mortification to be rewarded, if not in this world then certainly in the next. And it was rewarded – in Edinburgh at that – in the form of a whole ham, the very sight of which restored morale in anticipation of better times ahead.

As to the longer-term objective, the regiment could present a Scottish Reel, specially choreographed in honour of the royal visit, with a little help from the Royal Scottish Country Dance Society of which I quickly became a life member. This would involve the colonel taking a personal interest in the music, and the WRAC learning to dance – in the gymnasium.

So far so good, but convincing Whitehall that dancing was an essential element in military training north of the border was more difficult. The only course open to us, therefore, was to remind the bureaucrats scrutinising the programme that too much interference from London would play straight into the hands of the Scottish National Party!

The great day dawned. Her Royal Highness, always thoughtful and kind to anyone who had the good fortune to meet her, was pleased with the programme. There were no disasters during lunch, although she did ask about the ham and was delighted with the explanation of how it came to be on the menu in such stringent times.

The dancing followed, and to my eternal relief, without a hitch. That great Pipe Major, Willie Ross, then master of piping at the castle, had arranged a suitable tune and the pipers of the 51st Highland Division did justice to it.

All that remained was for a friendly reporter to be coerced into writing a flattering account in the *Evening News* under the headline: 'Princess Sees New Dance'. A month later my posting orders arrived.

The Brigade of Gurkhas

For me the gateway to Malaya (now Malaysia) was a night ride from Singapore through bandit country in the company of my old friend Hamish Paterson. He was then a subaltern fresh out of Sandhurst, a citadel of leadership to which he had contributed the rugby skills acquired on the battlefield of the Borders Sevens while deep in his heart harbouring the more ambitious dream of being capped for Scotland. And it was by no means an impossible dream . . . but duty called.

I had had enough experience to leave dreams alone, enjoying or rejecting them as they happened. We were both the same height and carried the same weight. We had just disembarked from the *SS Devonshire* and were bound for the Brigade of Gurkhas.

On the voyage out, much of our time had been taken up learning Gurkhali, with the result that we developed the habit of tossing newly acquired words and phrases into the air to see how they sounded afloat and, perhaps unconsciously, to impress our fellow passengers headed for less prestigious assignments. But when we first displayed this newly acquired skill for real by wishing a Queen's Gurkha Officer 'ramro bihan' (literally, good morning), a greeting unheard of in his language, it elicited a broad smile but the tactful and correct rejoinder 'ramro chha' which, while agreeing that the day was indeed good, really meant that he was well.

The overnight train from Singapore was, and I am sure still is, an exhilarating experience. The sleeping accommodation was air conditioned and spotlessly clean, with all the requisite facilities to hand. In the restaurant car, approached without difficulty along a corridor, the service was superb and on call all night. So much so that few of us opted for a good night's sleep in air-conditioned comfort. Excitement had something to do with it too.

And it was not just the stengas, the horses' necks, the Carlsberg Lager, the Tiger Beer or the excellent cuisine, dispensed by a single Chinaman dressed in the regulation red ochre uniform, that we found so irresistible. Outside, in the dark, stalking the train from the cover of rubber plantations bordering the line were bandits, real bandits with real guns bent on derailing the train and killing its passengers. It was the prospect of this sort of activity that concentrated our minds and drew us close together around the bar.

A few warning shots as the train passed through Johore Bahru had already signalled the possibility of something bigger to come. A decoy engine moved in front of the train, heavily weighted to trigger any explosives on the line – a well tested device that would certainly derail the engine, but save the train, and allow for the troops to dismount and give chase, or take whatever other action was necessary. Though well protected in an armour-plated cabin the driver of the decoy engine was a brave man, and always the first to meet the enemy.

We had been briefed before leaving Singapore by a competent looking officer who probably had some experience of jungle warfare, because he warned those of us not armed to get on the floor and to stay there, preferably out of the way of running feet, in the event of an ambush. The troops deployed ad hoc along the length of the train would dismount immediately, he assured us, and take up firing positions along the railway embankment, while the official escort consisting of one officer and fifteen men would move further afield to investigate and engage the enemy. It all sounded highly plausible.

We were well into the night when the firing began, quite a lot of it and at fairly close quarters along the side of the train. The officers around the bar put down their glasses and rose to a man. The OC troops demanded to know what was happening but no one could tell him.

The train stopped. There was an immediate exodus, all heading in the same direction, and an excellent demonstration of running feet for the green horns among us to avoid from the prone position. It was pitch dark outside and no one could possibly see what was happening; voices were raised giving orders and counter orders. But there had been no explosion on the line, which meant that the decoy engine was still on the rails; and an angry burst of firing ahead warned any bandits lurking in the bushes that our side was ready for them.

Meanwhile, the Chinese barman put his own emergency plans into operation by going to ground behind the bar – he was too experienced in jungle warfare to remain standing and present his head as a target – but he was first and foremost a businessman and was not going to stop serving drinks or food so long as there was someone around in need of those services and prepared to pay for them.

His hand appeared over the top in response to each order, and he popped up occasionally to check on customers beating a hasty retreat from the bar without paying. He kept them all in his sights and scribbled the evidence on a piece of paper in a display of operational accounting worthy of the most diligent staff officer. Excitement stimulated demand, but he remained unperturbed, doing what he had to do from a crouched position, until the train began to move again.

The troops re-embarked. The officer in command returned with a heroic look in his eyes and announced that all was well. Someone said 'well done old boy' and the rest of us nodded. The train started and normal service resumed. The same procedure was repeated later, and apart from a Gurkha sergeant with a bleeding ear there were no casualties. Hamish and I had become part of the Emergency, and with that sombre realisation disembarked in Kuala Lumpur.

The scene awaiting us was more comforting. The magnificent railway station, a fine example of Islamic architecture, with a built-in luxury hotel and excellent restaurant seldom short of customers, was a sight to gladden the heart and welcome the weariest of travellers to the Malayan capital. But any inclination to explore the available delights was scuppered by the appearance of a tall immaculately clad military figure in jungle green wearing a Gurkha hat. This was no ordinary hat: a sort of double terai, not unlike the Australian bush version, but two in one without the traditional turn-up. Cocked to one side and anchored to the chin by means of a strap it lent an air of distinction to the wearer and made us feel uncomfortably 'operational'.

'I'm Ian Parkinson,' he said, his expression betraying a mixture of compassion and humour, 'welcome to Gurkha Signals.'

We greeted him in turn and shook hands enthusiastically but with the deference due to the old from the new.

'How far is it to the camp?' I asked for want of something better to say.

'Not far,' he replied, 'about a couple of miles,' and with that led us to his car – a Ford Consul I seem to remember – for the final leg into the exclusive world of Her Majesty's Brigade of Gurkhas.

A short distance from the railway station the Selangor Club occupied a position of some importance, dominating the largest padang (sports field) in the city. It was long and flat, like a very large colonial bungalow, with wide open verandahs overlooking the padang, and protected from the elements by blue, cotton-lined bamboo blinds.

The prospect of a rugby pitch occupying the best part of the padang forced a question from Hamish and the reassurance from Ian that the Selangor Club was very keen on rugby (news that had an immediate effect on Hamish's confidence) and hockey too – a game more to Ian's liking and, as we later discovered, he could wield a hockey stick as no other man we were ever likely to meet.

The whole site was once a swamp, where Police Superintendent Sayers is reported to have done much of his shooting way back in 1883, while his wife 'presented a formidable sight out shopping with two Dalmatian hounds trotting behind her carriage'. From this, it appears, the idea was coined of calling the club the 'Spotted Dog'. The spots were soon dropped; the 'Dog' however remained and is so called to this day.

It was a curious irony that the Selangor Club should dominate the top end of Batu Road and the Gurkha camp – hutted, not unlike the origins of the club – the bottom end, on the banks of the Gambok river, while ladies in tricycle rickshaws, or trishaws, their inscrutable expressions looking for all the world like painted dolls, patrolled the mile between, disporting the principle that there can be no adventure without risk.

Situated well below the level of the road, the camp attracted the overflow from the river and all that came with it; the all pervasive smell of refuse from countless dwelling places and restaurants lay heavy on the air. Previous residents, including an assortment of refugees, prisoners of war and others had complained to little avail. In this fertile soil the seeds of the Queen's Gurkha Signals were sown.

We were ushered into the presence of George Cox. He was a bulldog of a man: strong, determined and accomplished. Even more important perhaps was his popularity on the Kuala Lumpur social circuit, which was a good thing because it brought much solace to the smellier end of Batu Road, with invitations to drink, and to dine, and to dance.

Our suitability for such benefits must have been uppermost in his mind for having delivered a brief lecture on this and that, and most particularly on how lucky we were to be there at all, he pointed us in the direction of the Selangor Club for initial indoctrination and training. As Hamish and I soon discovered, membership of the club, where the 'tuan haru', or gentlemen (tuan is Malay, to which we attached the Gurkhali appendage haru in a display of linguistic know-how), whether Malay, British, Chinese or Indian, foregathered in the forenoon and evening to review the day's events over their stengas, was a passport to social contacts at all levels.

'Hullo, old boy, have a stenga!' was the standard welcome and as near being a club signaure tune as anything. I became member 3403 and Hamish 3404; and when next we visited the club to test the validity of our signatures, 'Head Boy' Dhew Heck Mitt, who had worked in the place since 1908, remembered them.

He was the true measure of the quality and the importance of the place, and when he retired at the age of eighty after sixty-two years' service his thoughts were expressed quite simply: 'My life would be nothing if the Selangor Club didn't come into it. Even when I'm no longer wanted, I will come here every day for as long as I can walk the mile between my house and my club.'

In a Moorish style brick pile opposite the club, with its hundred-and-thirty-foot clock tower, the government offices faced the Dog's canine antecedents. And, as we learnt from the prevailing gossip, these two bastions of power were locked in competition, dating from their origins in the 1890s when the government had lent the club one hundred dollars to effect certain improvements.

The club had done just that, appointing at the same time a Count Bernstorff as its first salaried secretary; but the count departed abruptly, leaving eleven hundred dollars unaccounted for. The government offices, on the other hand, had financed themselves more generously in undertaking improvements costing a mere fifty-two thousand dollars, none of which had been syphoned off – not officially anyway. On that basis the competition was a little one-sided, but the club still had the edge, because what went on in one place was discussed in the other, and vice versa, and at the end of the working day all government officers were still members of the club, and the majority on the Dog's side.

We were learning fast. And as we became acclimatised the camp did not seem too bad, the wonderful opportunity presented to the officers – both British and Gurkha, brought in to mastermind developments there – overshadowing the less promising aspects. But in keeping with age-old tradition, it was good to have something to complain about at the outset which would later enhance the achievement.

The first challenge confronting Hamish and myself was the wearing of the Gurkha hat. It was hard, heavy and uncomfortable; but once the head was beaten into shape to accommodate it, the owner was considered fit for any adventure, however great the risk.

The Gurkhas came mostly from those already serving in the battalions who perhaps saw this as the ideal repository for men earmarked for disposal. But a small percentage of original material trickled in from the recruiting depots. Nevertheless, the very idea of Gurkhas being trained as anything other than infantry failed to please traditionalists. This despite the fact that Gurkhas had distinguished themselves as signallers in the First World War, and, anyway, every battalion had a platoon of them. The only difference now was that they would be trained to much higher standards.

The Royal Artillery had tried and given up because, or so rumour had it, the men were too small to handle the guns, although Gurkhas have been known to carry pianos, and even cars over the mountains into Katmandu in the past. The real reason was the need for more infantry to cope with the Emergency.

The Royal Engineers too were having a crack at training Gurkhas as builders of bridges, and layers of mines, and all the other tricks of their trade in Hong Kong. And being far removed from Malaya, they enjoyed a certain freedom from interference and made a good showing as a result; whereas soldiering in the rich milieu of a century and a half of well-cultivated tradition was altogether a different matter.

And yet the day would dawn when the badge of the Queen's Gurkha Signals would rise from the unsalubrious end of Batu Road like a sphinx – the figure of Mercury balancing precariously on a world cradled in a lotus flower – protected by the sharp ends of crossed kukris named Certa and Cito (Swift and Sure). Thus did the messenger of the gods wing its way into the heart of the Brigade of Gurkhas.

But why were Hamish and I sent here? Surely it was not intended that he should start teaching Gurkhas to play rugby! No, he was simply a very good officer. As to myself, a possible explanation was that my brother belonged to the 10th Princess Mary's Own Gurkha Rifles, affiliated to the Royal Scots – sharing the same colonel-in-chief as Royal Signals, Her Royal Highness the Princess Royal – in which our father had served.

At least that is how I liked to think about it, but without giving too much weight to the lunch and the dancing that presaged the move from Edinburgh! The truth was probably much less romantic: there was simply nowhere else for me to go. Or perhaps we too had been earmarked for disposal!

Whatever the thinking in higher places, there was work to be done. Good signallers are not just plucked out of the air, they have to be trained long and hard, and for this purpose two officers of outstanding ability had already been appointed from a long list of hopeful candidates in Malaya Command. I have already mentioned their names: George Cox and Ian Parkinson.

When these two men had finished with the motley collection of would be signallers assembled in the most unsavoury environment the army could find – no doubt with the avowed intention of spicing the challenge with an element of squalor – the potential of each individual was drawn to the surface, and there remained little that text book, parade ground or class room could teach them.

Having thus completed their mission, George rose rapidly to higher things, wearing a brigadier's hat to prove it, while Ian departed to the Depot of the Brigade of Gurkhas, then in Sungei Patani, whence to continue training recruits and to wield his hockey stick into the leadership of the all Malaya eleven.

The assignment left to Hamish and me was to muster the finished product – the Independent Gurkha Signal Squadron to give it its full name – and deploy it within the 15,000 square miles of Pahang State, at the time an operational hotspot of some repute. And the time for action had arrived.

But first there had to be an inspection – an 'in-is-spection' as the Gurkhas cheerfully called it – and we accordingly invited Major General Osborne Headley DSO x 3, the first Major General of the Brigade of Gurkhas, to do the honours. He had last seen me in action at the divisional sports in Sumatra.

Kuala Lipis

We had organised the squadron in such a way as to reflect the home country of the men. For instance, the detachments (each consisting of a wireless vehicle with commander, driver and crew of three) were named after towns and districts in Nepal: Baglung, Tansing, Dhankuta, Okaldunga and so on. The command vehicle, in which I hoped to sit, was named Katmandu.

Everything was in order. George and Ian made a final appearance to witness the first public performance of the show they had put together. The vehicles were moved into position with their crews standing in front of them; but the wretched Katmandu refused to budge. Repeated attempts on the self-starter succeeded only in making matters worse; several hands took it in turn to crank the starting handle with equal success. The only thing to do was to push her into position and hope for the best.

The general arrived, the inspection went well, and then my heart sank: he asked the driver of Katmandu to take his seat and demonstrate a manoeuvre or two. 'Dominus meus, et Deus meus' was all I had time to say. But it was enough: Katmandu started first time. Expressionless from the outset, the driver did as he was instructed and returned to base triumphant. Let no man ever tell me that God is not interested in humble squadron commanders!

The general spoke words of praise and encouragement. He had served with Gurkhas for twenty-eight years he said, and had never known them to fail. 'You will not fail!' That last bit was an expression of confidence and an order. For me he had a more personal message: 'If you don't pass the Gurkhali examination within the year you are no good to me. But if you do, then you may visit your brother at the recruiting depot in Lehra [just south of the Nepalese border] and accompany him to Katmandu.' There was no need to say more; next stop Kuala Lipis, the state capital of Pahang.

The convoy was formed up and inspected, final farewells exchanged and the vehicles began to roll out of the Batu Road Camp for the last time. The road ahead was one of the blackest in Malaya and had claimed many victims, among them Sir Henry Gurney, the governor, who was ambushed and killed on the mountain pass separating Selangor from Pahang.

Every convoy ran the risk of a hostile reception from angry and hungry men lurking in the jungle – I doubt very much whether the majority understood what they were angry about – but we had practised our skills and drills and carried them out at regular intervals, if not to impress the bandits then at least to instil a little confidence in ourselves.

Apart from a single shot, which could have been one of the vehicles backfiring, we arrived without incident. It was wild country, shared by four battalions of 48 Gurkha Infantry Brigade, an equal number of bandits, and a large population, mainly Malays, who never knew where or when to expect the next ambush. But in our armoury we had many weapons.

To link up these operations we began by deploying Baglung in support of the 10th Gurkhas at Bentong, Okaldunga with the 7th in Raub, and Tansing with the 2nd Malay in Triang. It had a winning ring about it, and I must say that the men were a credit to themselves and to those who had trained them. Each deserves a chapter of this story, and they will all understand why I have chosen just two.

Birendrasing Gurung, struggling to emerge from the shadows of an illustrious father, was our Queen's Gurkha Officer. Chunke Gurung, the father in question, was a Gurkha major of legendary stature who had served a lifetime with the 4th Gurkha Rifles and retired before the Second World War; but he was recalled when the balloon went up, and soldiered on to the end.

Chunke's influence over his son can only be appreciated by glancing at the man himself through the stories told about him. On retirement, Chunke built himself a house just outside the gates of the regimental centre in Bakloh, in Himachal Pradesh, and from that point of vantage observed on the comings and goings of his regiment whether invited to or not.

He had a large family of seven or eight children – Birendra was the oldest – and the discipline practised in the household was modelled on the training given to recruits. Chunke himself had joined the regiment as a boy, played the clarinet in the regimental band and remained much attached to the instrument.

Around sunset, he would change into regimental mufti (undress) and proceed to the Gurkha Officers' Mess, where he would make short work of half a bottle of rum while regaling an attentive audience of serving officers on how things used to be in the 4th. He would then return to the house and entertain the family to a short programme of martial music concluding with the regimental march, when all members of the family, including Birendra's mother, were expected to stand. He would then return to the mess and finish the remainder of the bottle.

While I cannot vouch for this story, I do know that when Chunke died, Birendra felt compelled to go home and have a photograph taken of himself wearing his father's uniform. In this way, he maintained, his father would always remain close to him.

Birendra's most endearing quality was his enthusiasm. At its peak it was irrepressible; but his mood often swung the other way plunging him into deep depression. Rum, he insisted, was not good for one, and yet he found comfort in a tot or two most nights and would always finish up by repeating the same injunction. He was a remarkable man, certainly, and today occupies his father's house in Bakloh.

The other character I have in mind is Man Bahadur Gurung, a corporal. His job was to drive an armoured personnel carrier armed with a remote-controlled Bren gun, centrally mounted above and behind the driver's seat, as a deterrent against any bandits attempting to interfere with his freedom of movement.

A radio transmitter-cum-receiver was fitted in the back with two large aerials in the shape of a 'V' – not unlike fishing rods – swinging out freely behind. Volunteers to man this equipment, however, had to be pressed into service because failure to make contact, for whatever reason, fell outside Man Bahadur's comprehension and he would express himself accordingly, calling the operator a *janta* (pubic hair) or something equally uncomplimentary.

He was more than a driver; he was the captain of that APC, and unfailingly managed to enlist the services of a No 2, as co-driver. Stories about Man Bahadur are legion. It was claimed, for instance, that he could lift the APC single handed.

Before setting off on a lonely patrol – he was totally unafraid and would go anywhere any time – his No 2 would start the engine; only then would Man Bahadur take his place behind the wheel and wave goodbye to well-wishers gathered to see him off. Once the APC was on the move, the radio operator would report contact loud and clear, and repeated that assurance every few minutes even when it was weak and unclear. Driving through bandit country he would sometimes take it upon himself to steer with one hand and trigger a few random bursts into the jungle with the other to warn any bandits in the vicinity that it was Man Bahadur who was passing.

After such a display the No 2 would automatically jump to his feet and replace the magazine in readiness for the next bit of action. At the end of a journey, Man Bahadur would dismount first, leaving the engine running; the No 2 would switch it off.

When I first saw a buffalo's head removed at a stroke during the Dushera festival celebrations, his hands held the ceremonial kukri. I can also affirm that he drove my brother and me from Johore Bahru to Kuala Lipis through some of the worst bandit country in Malaya and we never felt safer.

I have not known any other man who could fry an egg in a mess tin and then scoop it out with his bare hands. As the beneficiary of such an egg on more than one occasion, and despite a little engine oil deposited on the white from his fingers, I never had the courage to decline his hospitality.

All the others, falling between these two, deserve at least a mention, so I salute them with pride from this distance in time. And does it not say something about the quality of those men that every detachment commander was to become a Queen's Gurkha Officer!

However, it is not only about those actually serving on the day that I wish to write, for they have honours enough, and history will accord them a better place than is to be found in any story of mine, but those unsung heroes, in the shadow of events, who gave their loyalty and their support, each in his own way. One of these was Chem See Lu.

He was a Chinaman and owner of a general store in Kuala Lipis, then capital of the state of Pahang. It was here we learnt that any convoy with one or more vehicles tagging along behind with supplies for Chem See Lu was unlikely to be ambushed – which may even account for our safe passage to the state. True or false, such an operator one had to meet. He was a fat man with a large tummy, a round face and very little hair on top. His smile reminded one of the laughing Buddha in a cautious mood. His shop stood at the entrance to the main street in Kuala Lipis, built of timber with a corrugated iron roof. The front door opened directly onto the main street.

A few planks nailed together served as a footbridge across the gutter running past the shop, which in turn facilitated the flow of filthy water picking up refuse as it made its way to the end of the street and down a steep embankment into the Pahang river. The back of the shop, mounted on several stout beams, overlooked the river and the fringe of the jungle beyond. In front, seated shoulder to shoulder along the length of an untidy mess of electric and telephone wires, thousands of house martins took up their daily abode, risking life and limb for a ringside seat from which to observe the activities below. And they were not entirely safe from Chem See Lu's kitchen either.

The shop was stocked from floor to ceiling with everything from pressed Peking Duck to Scotch Whisky. Anything could be negotiated here; a seat to fly from Singapore to London; a new car registered and taxed for the road; suits, shirts and dresses made to order and delivered on time, and a whole host of other things.

Nothing was impossible. Every festival – Christian, Muslim, Hindu or Chinese – was marked up on the calendar and anticipated with perfect timing, the more distinguished citizens receiving gifts appropriate to their rank and status.

Chem See Lu's favourite expression was 'vely nice', and it served for 'good morning', 'goodbye', 'thank you', and, above all, 'I have got what you want'. And as far as we knew this represented his entire vocabulary, but coming from him it unfailingly fitted the occasion. He probably understood English but saw little benefit in wasting business time communicating unnecessarily.

Hamish often visited Chem See Lu's to indulge a youthful addiction to nougat dating back to school in Edinburgh, and the conversation would go something like this: 'Good morning Mr Chem See Lu, a box of nougat please.' Chem See Lu's hand would move at once to the precise spot and a box would be handed over accompanied by 'vely nice, vely nice'. Hamish would say thank you and probably add a casual goodbye to which he would receive the standard reply, 'vely nice', with a smile and a not too excessive bow.

After sunset, his clients from the other side of the river would call for their own emergency supplies, their approach less polite and more demanding, underlying a tacit understanding that generous discounts would be included for services rendered on and off the road. He probably said 'vely nice' to them too.

Chem See Lu accepted the reality of the situation philosophically, recouping those discounts from the rest of us, a little here and a little there, confident that we too would understand. He was a shopkeeper, no more, no less, and if his activities did run close to the wind, he never betrayed one side to the other. And what would we have done without him?

It was on a Saturday morning, while I was reading the *Malay Mail* in the Officers' Mess, that a telephone call from the town hospital enquired whether anyone with a blood group zero positive might be available to help out. Acknowledging ownership of such a blood group, I volunteered and found myself giving blood to a bandit's wife who had lost a lot of blood after a difficult delivery. The baby seemed well enough but the father was not around.

Apparently he had approached Chem See Lu, who had advised him to bring the mother in and that he would have her taken to the hospital. Once there, he claimed a fake relationship with the woman and, on being told that she would probably need some blood, persuaded the dresser, also a Chinese, to contact the Officers' Mess as the most likely source of supply. He was astute enough to know that help, if available, would not be refused.

A few days later, I happened to be going to Chem See Lu's to collect a couple of shirts when Hamish asked if I would get him some nougat. I collected the shirts and asked for a box of nougat, but Chem See Lu handed me two. 'Only one, thank you,' I said, returning the second box, but he pressed it on me with an unusually broad smile. 'Vely nice, vely nice,' he insisted. So I left it at that. It was only when the whole story found its way around town, after mother and child had returned to the jungle, that the reason for the second box was revealed. One mother and child had been spared the consequences of the emergency; the nougat was the pay-off!

But it would take a lot more than a smiling Chinaman and a box of nougat to help me through the Gurkhali examination for which I was listed as a candidate in order to avoid being returned to my native land as the general had promised. I simply had to have a go, but that did not prevent me feeling decidedly nervous at the prospect, and it was too late to back off.

The Gurkhas, however, saw things differently. To them I was already a hero, because many officers, while speaking the language fluently, did not bother to take the exam – or they knew how to avoid doing so – and as far as the Gurkhas were concerned the outcome was a foregone conclusion. If I should fail, therefore, which was more than likely, there would be no hiding from the disappointment, perhaps even scorn, in their eyes.

As I had noticed earlier in my career, miracles do sometimes happen: confident of failure, I gained a pass, and what's more with credit, which could only have happened through divine intervention, and that was reason enough for a celebration far in excess of anything warranted by what was after all an obligatory qualification.

It was at about this time that John Ridge came to join us: a fine specimen of an Anglo-Saxon with light hair and blue eyes, endowed with boundless energy which he demonstrated admirably when playing rugby and hockey, and projected off field by cultivating a serious visage with the merest suggestion of a frown.

This tended to conceal a boyish enthusiasm that would reveal itself every time a burst of laughter lit up his features and filled his eyes with merriment. He was a loyal officer and an everlasting friend, and was quick to grasp that it was not the

British officers, flitting in and out of the regiment, who would shape its personality, its traditions and its customs, but the Gurkha soldiers themselves for whom the regiment would become the whole of their lives, not only while serving but afterwards as pensioners.

He came to understand this better than most officers and, as it happened, the regiment was to become a way of life for him too. Not unlike all good officers, he enjoyed an empathy with the men, responding to the trust, the loyalty, the comradeship and the legendary good humour that are the hallmarks of Gurkhas, and he identified fully with them.

Naïvely perhaps, he expected to find those same qualities blooming in the upper echelons of the army, only to discover that they often withered on the climb to the top; and he was inclined to express his disappointment in a manner least likely to advance his career. But the men took to him; they liked him and respected him, and I was glad that he was chosen to join the squadron when I left to form the regiment.

John and Birendra got on like a house on fire – if the fusion of two men of boundless enthusiasm can be so described. Both were argumentative and utterly committed, and they were fast becoming firm friends. One liked rum and declaimed against it; the other preferred Carlsberg and praised it. Both aimed at the highest standards and guarded the independence of the squadron jealously.

I have known John Ridge to shed a tear when a Gurkha child died, and to raid his personal resources in order to provide something extra for his men and their families during the festival of Dushera – the triumph of good over evil – when the past and the present come together in a union of renewal.

(Over a quarter of a century later he was still making an annual pilgrimage to Nepal to visit the men I have been writing about and to spend a few days reappraising the old arguments with Birendra in Bakloh. It is, in its way, a special story and one requiring much more space than is available here.)

Lamjung

Hamish and I returned to Kuala Lumpur. The old camp on Batu Road had been allowed to return to grass and the smells seemed to have disappeared. We set up headquarters on the hill adjacent overlooking the Gambok river running between ourselves and the old camp.

It was also hidden from view by a barrier of pampas grass running along the banks of the river. This was the habitat of a large population of waterfowl, regularly culled to supply the QGO's Mess from stocks surplus to requirement, while at the same time providing the owners of shotguns with a little practice before proceeding on long leave to Nepal.

The new camp called for an imaginative name, and what better choice could there have been than Lamjung, the home district of Gurkha Major Parsuram Gurung who had just been posted to us from the 2nd King Edward VII's Own Goorkha Rifles. His coming was a sure sign that we were edging towards becoming a regiment. I mention Parsuram because without him we would have got into difficulties dealing with the sudden influx of men from east and west Nepal – the traditional dividing line between the existing regiments: the Seventh and Tenth recruiting Rais and Limbus from the east, and the Second and Sixth Magars and Gurungs from the west – brought together in the Queen's Gurkha Signals so that we could identify (at least in the tribal sense) with all the regiments of the Brigade of Gurkhas. So proud were we of the name Lamjung that when the Officers' Mess was built – albeit of atap and bamboo – it had to be modelled on Lamjung Darbar (the governor's house in Lamjung). The regiment had arrived.

Grasping the prevailing mood, as Gurkha majors usually do, Parsuram set about choosing a lesser site where first a tent and then a hut were erected for my personal use, with a connecting bridge to the mess reminiscent of a similar situation in Nepal. And here I took up residence.

It was during a routine visit to the headquarters of the Brigade of Gurkhas in Seremban that a telephone call came through for me from Malaya Command. Any call from there had a disquieting effect, being usually concerned with some complaint or other but, happily, this was from Guy Tucker, then the Chief Signal Officer. A call from him was always a pleasure because he was a very old and trusted friend, and always cheerful; a man with what would today be called a 'caring disposition'.

'I called to tell you that you are now a lieutenant colonel,' he said.

Thus to be anointed over the telephone came as something of a shock. How does a man react to being elected Prime Minister of Great Britain or President of the United States? This was much bigger medicine, as every commanding officer knows, and had to be absorbed in easy doses.

Guy was still speaking: 'That is the news and I am delighted to pass it on with many congratulations.'

Driving back to Kuala Lumpur, I found myself sitting up straight, seeking altitude from which to appraise the new responsibilities vested in me. I had the distinct feeling that the Queen herself had singled me out for this honour.

The first person to be told was the Gurkha major. He weighed the matter thoughtfully and came to the conclusion that there would have to be a party (at my expense) if I felt equal to it. But he assured me that no more than a hundred bottles of rum would be required – to be mixed with two parts water in fire buckets and dispensed on demand – supplemented by rice and lentils, known more commonly as 'dhal bhat'.

Suddenly all work stopped. The casual offer of a drink in the Officers' Mess was spread over the rest of the day and into the night. The QGOs were called in. Rehearsals got under way on the little parade square at the top of the hill as preparations began for an evening of celebration.

As the regimental dancers (male dancers dressed as women, 'marunis', accompanied by their male partners in traditional costume) weaved and bobbed, moving back and forth in step with a line of madals (drums), singing as they went, I could not help marvelling how simple it was to organise a party for several hundred people when those people happened to be Gurkhas.

Elevation to lieutenant colonel meant that I was now welcomed into the inner circle where generals and brigadiers and senior staff officers met regularly to discuss strategy for war and peace. These gatherings were sometimes referred to as 'morning prayers' and someone of my rank was not expected to disrupt proceedings with unsolicited comments. More in keeping with my function was to implement the decisions taken.

Let me illustrate that point. A growing number of Gurkhas coming to a place like Malaya from the rarified atmosphere of the Himalayas had fallen victim to tuberculosis, and common sense dictated that they should be isolated together in a special ward in the military hospital.

It came as no surprise to me that I was 'ideally placed to co-ordinate their administration and welfare'. Of course! And when the first Gurkha to qualify for thoracic surgery expressed doubts about the efficacy of such treatment, it automatically fell to me to reassure him, wheel him into the theatre, and remain in attendance for the duration. Similarly, when it was discovered that there were a few cases of leprosy among the Gurkhas, my experience with TB patients qualified me to look after them too.

But these duties were not without reward: when the first Gurkha was returned to full active service sans TB, and the first case of leprosy sent home to Nepal cured, the credit belonged to the doctors and nurses responsible for their treatment, but a great deal of satisfaction came my way too.

When the ADMS, assistant director of Medical Services, Alex Drummond – a powerful man then and later, as well as an ear, nose and throat specialist – tried to browbeat me into involving the Gurkha families in a research project dictated by the incidence of tuberculosis among Gurkha families (which called for an analysis of mothers' milk) I declined on the grounds that it was too sensitive a subject to discuss with the Gurkha major.

On reflection however, I remembered that the 'Dhai-ama's' daughter – that is the daughter of the Gurkha midwife recruited in Nepal to look after our families – who was well educated and spoke excellent English, had expressed a wish to be trained as a nurse. So, at the very next gathering I put it to Alex Drummond that if he would arrange for the girl in question (Rada Rawat) to be trained in the UK as a QARANC sister, it would prove very popular and attract enthusiastic co-operation for his project. It was not exactly blackmail (greymail perhaps!), but the bargain was struck and the career of the first Gurkha nurse set on course.

But the first ambassador dispatched to London from Lamjung to represent the regiment at the Queen's coronation was Parsuram. In fact he very cleverly volunteered before anyone else could stake a claim, arguing that as I had already been to Nepal and had met King Tribhuban, it was incumbent on him to undertake a similar mission to the United Kingdom to meet Queen Elizabeth. What he did not know at the time was that Hamish had relinquished his own claim in favour of the Gurkha major's.

I can still recall Parsuram's address to the officers on his return. What he had to say found its way into a little book of verse which I gave to his son Suk Bahadur Gurung when he came with Hamish to see me in Edinburgh many years later. It is simple and, for that reason perhaps, captures exactly the essence of his feelings:

> Flames leap about the memory's pyre,
> Ashes of music moan the passing lyre,
> The last note lingers, fades, and all is still;
> Sweet winds blow fresh on recollection's hill.
>
> The seer must see, the dreamer dream again,
> The curtains rise before an endless plain.
> To the watchers let some passing spirit say
> 'That star beyond the star was once today.'

Drums, trumpets, pipes and marching feet,
Those noble tunes their ceaseless rhythm beat,
As onwards, upwards, distant echoes cry:
'We crossed beyond the grave but did not die.'

Behold the stage, the great parade of stars;
Footlights on earth, and backcloth draped in Mars.
Of such array would critic dare to write:
'The drama of God's day thus turned to night.'

From here a single tale I will relate
That faith so kept with faith, but not so late
As when the old, in fading from the view,
Would leave but tattered glory for the new.

My mother, I recall, once said to me
As child I sat upon her peasant's knee:
The world we know, but Heaven or Hell must be
Man's goal beyond life's dreams and imagery.

I have lived these years, illusions I have few,
Man must live and by his living rue.
As Heaven abides beyond the sky and sea,
So Hell lies sunk below man's dignity.

I stood (as others stood) guard upon that day.
The mist had spread its gloom, the skies were grey.
The rain had washed the streets, now fresh and clean,
Had London thus prepared to greet her Queen!

The sun it seemed had never shone before,
Nor thunder sound as did her people roar:
Sword, sabre, hands and kerchiefs waving, cheer,
Love in a smile, a courtesy, a tear.

On came that golden coach with horses proud,
As hoof and harness warned the straining crowd;
Expectant, adoring, behold the scene:
A million hearts were strewn before the Queen.

A rose thus set within a golden frame,
Her people hushed and scarcely breathed the name.
The hand that waved, the smile that spoke to me
Left me to wonder – here might Heaven be.

Progress can be measured in many different ways. The first step was the arrival of a Gurkha major. I was now to have an adjutant of my own, a resolute young officer by the name of Able Dacre. No longer was I free to rely solely on the informal advice and criticism of my old friend Hamish; but, although operationally employed elsewhere, he was never completely out of range.

Able – the name suited him well – was one day to hold the much sought after appointment of brigadier, Brigade of Ghurkas, and for him the journey to that distant peak began in Lamjung Camp.

Over the brow of our hill, the Gurkha families were quartered in tents and in urgent need of some basic facilities. There were few taps about, and the latrines had long since served their usefulness. They had in fact become a health hazard. For the men there was accommodation enough.

The garrison engineer had in his possession authority to build some additional huts in Lamjung, and favoured extending the living quarters for the men. This would have been 'vely nice', of course, but there was a more pressing need for the families, and it was upon this matter that I instructed Able to have a word with the garrison engineer.

This was the first major call on him as adjutant, and when the garrison engineer refused to be persuaded, he naturally turned to me for a decision. I sent him back with more detailed instructions and suggested that he should invite the garrison engineer to accompany him on a tour of the camp in order to explain our needs on the ground.

But the garrison engineer had his budget and his plan. He declined Able's invitation and informed him that the work as scheduled on his piece of paper would go ahead. This was clearly stuff of which wars are made, and Able returned to me protesting that his position as adjutant was being undermined. The garrison engineer had probably judged that here was a new boy, as was the colonel, and that he could brush aside our objections. But he was sadly mistaken. The lessons I had learnt from those remarkable men who had helped me along the perilous journey to Lamjung were alive and well enough to be alerted in an instant. They had been designed for just this sort of emergency!

I told Able to inform the garrison engineer that unless he decamped immediately, taking with him labour, tools and materials, he would be locked up in the guard room. Without a moment's hesitation Able delivered that ultimatum. For his part, the garrison engineer was inclined to assert his own authority by ignoring Able until the alarm bells began to ring, when the guard commander was ordered to open up for business.

The story spread, not entirely to our disadvantage, and the expected riposte came in an unheralded visit from the chief royal engineer (a brigadier) and his general (not Headley, I hasten to add) and many words were spoken that are better forgotten. But the upshot was that within a week work was started on building washrooms and lavatories for the families, and Able Dacre had notched up his first success on the road to high office. There was more to come.

The thought of a few pipers marching through Lamjung had crossed our minds more than once. Hamish and I had even ruminated on that distant day when the regimental pipe band would be 'Beating Retreat' at sunset to entertain our friends.

But thoughts are not enough; they have a way of hanging around and disturbing one's sleep until released to express themselves in some practical form. So, a few chanters were scattered about the barrack huts to test the soil. Nor was this a casual off-the-cuff ploy; it had a sound strategic base. Most Gurkhas spend part of their young lives tending herds of goats and buffaloes, or, less commonly, cattle and sheep, whiling away the long hours with the aid of a bamboo flute. They would surely recognise an old friend in the chanter!

When Able was brought in to flesh out the scheme from the accumulation of staff duties he had absorbed since the garrison engineer episode, he was instantly alarmed and warned of the possible consequences of disturbing another hornet's nest. He also wanted to know how the pipe band was to be financed, and precisely what signalling trade could be ascribed to a piper.

That was much too down to earth for our thinking; but, like it or not, down to earth is where all great ideas have to take root, and the earth needs to be fertile. What about a regimental farm – pigs, chickens and turkeys, that sort of thing – to finance the band, and as to a trade, since bandsmen have traditionally doubled as stretcher bearers, why not pipers as linemen?

'And a tartan?' asked Able, a note of incredulity creeping into his voice.

'Yes,' I beamed on his anxious young face, 'we have an informal affiliation with the 51st Highland Division so why not start by drafting a letter to the Countess of Seafield?'

It was fortunate too that my brother, now back with his battalion, had an excellent ex-piper in his company, one Bhom Bahadur Limbu who, having had a disagreement with the pipe major was back in his rifle company sharpening up his skills on bandit hunting. He was a dour character and I cannot remember ever seeing him smile; but when he got working on our pipers they had to blow, and blow hard and long, regardless of personal comfort, or of disturbing the peace. Moreover, performing on a chanter while marching uphill at a good military pace is not something that trainee pipers are normally expected to do. But our situation was not entirely normal; over a hundred years of tradition, and who knows how many pipe tunes, separated us from the other regiments. To bridge that gap called for extraordinary measures.

With a little help from our friends, the farm was established, the pipe band formed, and the marching began – up and down our hill more often than they or the rest of us would care to remember. And it must be admitted that the noises they made, in the early days at least, were not entirely harmonious – each piper intent on pacing himself regardless of what was going on around him.

In the fullness of time the pipers were dressed in the tartan of the Clan Grant by courtesy of the Countess of Seafield, and the Queen graciously approved an affiliation with the 51st Highland Division. These distinctions brought with them the crowning accolade of a regimental march: 'Scotland the Brave'.

To mark the event, the 51st sent us a quaich, and many are the times I watched Bhom Bahadur raise it to his lips with these words: 'Suk santi ra dirgaiyu hos' (meant to convey the spirit of peace, happiness, and long life – with a drop of poetic licence) which I am still not convinced he really meant. Similarly, the officers dutifully responded with 'Tatahastu' (so be it) and watched the whisky go down in a single gulp. The quaich was then turned on its head to receive a kiss of appreciation while the remainder of the bottle accompanied Bhom Bahadur back to his quarters to complete the libation.

A proud day

Another of our unsung heroes was Rahim Bux. He had come to Malaya as an enlisted follower with a regiment of Rajputs and was wounded during the Malayan campaign. As a tailor, he was no great loss and found himself abandoned to make his own way home to Lahore, then a part of India. But he hung on to his Singer sewing machine and that, in a manner of speaking, saved his life.

When he came to Lamjung, seeking employment as a tailor, he could neither read nor write, but he could turn out half a dozen pairs of shorts and shirts in forty-eight hours flat – a level of production that suited us perfectly – so we employed him and set up a tailor's shop in a tent behind the quartermaster's stores. There he laboured day and night.

Like the regiment, Rahim Bux started from the bottom; with the patience and perseverance for which his countrymen are renowned, he got to the top. Soon he was upgraded to regimental contractor – an event marked by the opening of a canteen, a grocery shop and a laundry service. Such a major expansion, however, was beyond the means of a poor tailor, as Rahim Bux was quick to point out, but if an interest-free loan from regimental funds were to come his way anything was possible. And so it was, once the bank was satisfied that he could sign his name. In his old regiment, the thumb impression sufficed for all purposes, including his weekly wages, and he naturally thought that this would be good enough for the bank too. However, that problem was quietly solved by Parsuram, under whose tutelage Rahim Bux learnt to pen a credible R Bux, and with an assurance that even the Hong Kong and Shanghai Bank found convincing.

In accordance with Indian Army custom he was now entitled to display his proper status outside the tailor's shop. It read: Rahim Bux Kichi (an additional name brought in to mark his elevation and share the honour with the family back home), Master Tailor. And he was as proud of it as we were of Lamjung when that name first appeared outside the front gates by the guardroom.

(Fifteen years later, Rahim Bux handed over the contract to members of his family and boarded a plane for Pakistan a very rich man, to open an electrical goods shop in Karachi.)

There are two others unlikely to find a mention in any book, or even on a gravestone, unless I remember them here. The first of these was Pakri – at least that was the name he went by – a Tamil whose grandparents had come to Penang in domestic service. He went to a small mission school on the island, where his studies seemed less important than his prowess as a boxer.

His mentors accordingly encouraged him to take up the sport professionally, first in Ipoh and then in Kuala Lumpur where he appeared in the ring in an amusement park off Pudu Road billed as 'Battling Pakri'. Unfortunately, as so often happens, success opened the way to new and hitherto untried luxuries and he developed a taste for Tiger Beer which he indulged to such an extent that his performance in the ring began to suffer. He was too slow, and his punching lacked the crispness of earlier days.

His final contest was with an up and coming pugilist from Ipoh, answering to the name of Ping On, whose speed and dexterity had earned for him the pseudonym Ping Pong. A courageous performance, witnessed by members of the regiment out for an evening's entertainment, cost Pakri a broken nose and considerable bruising to other parts of his face and body. But he remained upright – on his feet to the last – and lost.

It may have been the sympathetic attitude of the soldiers, or perhaps a conversation with them, that led Pakri to Lamjung in search of employment as cook or waiter; I do not know. But he told his story well and was taken on as the Officers' Mess cook with the understanding that he would double as waiter whenever necessary. It was an arrangement that suited him perfectly, and he also volunteered, without encouragement or promise of extra reward, to make himself available as a sparring partner for the regimental boxers. Though his culinary skills were limited – apart from curry lunch on Sunday, when he came into his own – he was a trier and made rapid progress. There were occasions, however, when old habits caught up with him and he fell from grace, finding himself unable to get home without the aid of a couple of Gurkhas.

One morning, while I was working in my office tent situated in isolation under a large mangosteen tree just above the mess, a little figure burst in, breathless it seemed, and stood by the entrance with an appealing look on his face.

'Who are you?' I demanded to know, my sanctuary having thus been violated.

'Sammy sir,' he replied, raising both hands to the point of his chin in a gesture of supplication common among Tamil people.

'What do you want?' I asked, not unkindly.

'Please sir, give some good job.'

I was experienced enough to know that this was an act of supreme courage. Sammy had thrown caution to the wind in a single bold attempt to improve his lot, or perish in the attempt, and was relying on me to treat him as I had treated his fellow Tamil, Pakri.

He was in his early twenties, dressed in a torn vest and tattered khaki trousers, and had been working in the camp in charge of a gang of Chinese grass-cutters, otherwise known throughout Malaya as 'swing sisters' for the manner in which their scythes went up and around their heads in a graceful swinging movement to the accompaniment of a tuneful melody. Acting on impulse, he had seized his moment when no one was watching, and now it was up to me.

How could I forget that, as boys, my brother and I had known boundless kindness, courtesy and affection from our Tamil servants in the Nilgiri Hills of South India? They had taught us so much, and not least good manners.

Sammy's family had immigrated from Ceylon as rubber-tappers. Poor pay and the constant threat from bandits demanding protection money had driven him to grass-cutting, a profession in which he had risen to the position of foreman. Now it was time to move on, and he had decided to put his fate in my hands. He had chosen wisely; I decided to employ him as my personal servant.

When news got around about the presentation of the new badge, Pakri and Sammy formed up to ask whether they could wear one too. This would have been irregular, but what about new uniforms with a large badge embroidered on the pocket! How would that do? Sammy answered for both: 'It will be very good for us sir, thank you sir,' he said, while Pakri raised his hand to remove what looked suspiciously like a tear. But before leaving them, I must record my indebtedness to Sammy in particular for his help before the badge parade.

For us, it was an event of immense importance. The badges had been manufactured by Garrards of London and were flown out in a sack, as accompanied baggage, to save space and prevent damage. And the intention was that these would be paid for, and presented to the men, by their officers, marking the beginning of a tradition now buried deep in the hearts of everyone present on the day.

My brother was coming to inspect the rehearsal before the real thing later in the day. The Gurkhas naturally approved of this because 'jeto' (the elder brother) wields very special authority within a Gurkha family.

My role was to repeat the speech by the Major General Brigade of Gurkhas, a long one which began with 'This is a proud day and one long to be remembered . . .' in Gurkhali, without the use of notes. Sammy's mission school English was good enough to follow the Roman script and rehearse me before, during and after breakfast, steering me through each line until I had mastered the text to his satisfaction.

Parade concluded, I returned to my hut to find Sammy in his immaculate white uniform, proudly displaying the new badge, waiting to greet me – his face alight with pride.

'You speaking so nicely sir,' he said. And after a brief pause added: 'I am so glad for that sir.'

'So am I Sammy,' was the best I could manage, adding a more eloquent slap on his shoulder.

Sammy would continue to work all day, and late into the night, serving food and drink, and cleaning up as he went along. What's more, he would be enjoying every moment of it without expecting any reward. What is it, I wondered, that makes humble men, such as Sammy, rejoice in the happiness of others! Is it just goodness, or a way of expressing gratitude for the little they have? Perhaps both.

What would happen to the badge in the future no one could tell, but the day would certainly be long remembered, and not only for the badge but for the party that followed. It was 23 September (now the regimental birthday), and there was much to celebrate.

To start with, Lance Perowne, then the Major General Brigade of Gurkhas, a brave and dear friend, had played the key role in approving the proposal to have the badge made by Garrards of London, on the grounds that it would be difficult to sack both the general and the colonel for the same offence!

Moreover, he silenced the more dubious critics with the passage in his speech that read: 'You are young in history, but old in tradition and rich in inheritance. In the new badge, the Winged Mercury of the old-established Signal Service of Her Majesty's Army is joined together with the crossed Kukris, symbolic of the martial traditions of Nepal; and above all is set the Crown which is the symbol of our united loyalty to the Queen. So henceforth you will bear upon your heads three times the honour and carry in your hearts a threefold pride. . . .'

(Forty years later, in a souvenir book of photographs compiled by Sean Dexter, Her Royal Highness, the Princess Anne was able to say: 'Your Regiment's reputation stands high, and your badge can be worn with even greater pride.)

The pipe band, resplendent in full ceremonial dress, played in tune to welcome the hundreds of guests headed by Sir Donald MacGilvery, then the High Commissioner in Malaya, and at a given signal the trumpets sounded sunset from the bridge connecting my quarters to the mess.

Sir Donald played his part by fixing the regimental pipe banner to the pipes of Bhom Bahadur Limbu – who accepted the honour with tolerable good grace – and then proceeded to christen a jolly reel specially choreographed for the occasion, and danced by the Gurkhas, as 'Gregory's Frolic'.

The prototype ceremonial outfit for officers had arrived only a few days before the event, and Able Dacre was kitted out, with the aid of Rahim Bux, to model it and give our guests a foretaste of how the officers would appear on such occasions in the future. If anybody had to be credited or discredited with the result it had to be the adjutant.

Parsuram was not going to be left out of this. He had plans of his own: when the QGO's wives made their appearance, they were all dressed in royal blue and gold saris. And not only that; according to reliable sources, the Gurkha major had rehearsed them in the art of imbibing cocktails the evening before.

More was to come. A troop of 'marunis' and their partners performed the Andikola Salijo which is nothing short of an epic in song and dance about the triumph and tragedy of Andikola, or Andhikhola (in western Nepal) when the snows melt and the rivers flood. The haunting rhythm of the madals, and the voices pitched high in unison as the dancers bobbed and turned to the changing mood of the drums, uplifting one moment, downcast the next, had a hypnotic effect on the audience. They clearly could not understand what was going on, but were aware that this was something special, and for the best part of an hour gave it their full attention.

To my astonishment I noticed that Parsuram's wife's eyes had filled with tears, and quickly took my place beside her. It seems the great man had chosen the Andikola Salijo and trained the dancers to such perfection because she came from there.

The night was already ushering in a new day as my brother and I made our way to my hut to find Sammy and Pakri waiting to see if there was anything else they could do for us. On impulse, I told Pakri to make a pot of tea, which the four of us shared before retiring for the last hour before dawn.

Having seen us safely through the badge parade, the time had come for Parsuram to return to his native Lamjung on retirement. For him, the only cloud on an otherwise unblemished horizon had been the possibility that Hamish, then on a course back home, might miss out on the badge parade.

Anxious that he should complete his service on a high note, I had suggested a telephone call to Hamish, well knowing that such calls were then both unusual and expensive. But it was worth it to see Parsuram's face light up with pleasure when I informed him that he was probably the first Gurkha to speak to the United Kingdom from Malaya. However, I had not bargained on the rest of the Queen's Gurkha Officers falling in behind him to deliver their own personal messages, ending in each case with: 'Tethi ho hazur, janu paryo' (that's all sir, I must go).

That duty accomplished, it was left to the Gurkha major to announce, in time-honoured fashion: 'Hazur, raksi khanu paryo,' meaning that the time had come to drink rum. And the rum must have done the trick, for Hamish did return in time to receive his badge on the little hill where we had first laid our plans.

The last note

Parsuram's successor was another Gurung by the name of Dhan Bahadur. He was a jolly little man whose laughter, always lurking just below the surface, was powerful enough to carry its message to every corner of the camp.

I have a mental picture of him stalking waterfowl in the pampas grass along the banks of the Gambok. It was fun to call out to him and see the movement stop abruptly and his little head appear above the grass with a broad smile. 'Hazur,' he would cry out, restoring his single-barrel shotgun to its place on his shoulder ready to present himself at the double unless signalled otherwise. His sole purpose was to carry on where Parsuram had left off; he had no ambitions beyond that unique role of Gurkha major.

I can only hope that these brief stories will capture something of the spirit of the regiment, and the comradeship we came to take so much for granted. It made better men of us all – the few I have mentioned and the many I have not – and with that thought uppermost in mind I must leave the reader with this final anecdote.

Serving with us from the very beginning was an exceptionally fine soldier, our first regimental sergeant major, Bir Bahadur Rawat.

He was on leave in Nepal when he was recommended for promotion to lieutenant (Queen's Gurkha Officer), and, as his promotion had come through earlier than expected, he was instructed to return as soon as possible. He replied to the effect that he was on his way and bringing his young wife with him.

Within a year, while he was on operations in the jungle, his wife was admitted to hospital to have her first baby. There were complications and the doctors decided to operate. Rawat was contacted by radio and asked for his consent, which he gave.

He returned to Kuala Lumpur by the first available train, and I met him at the station with the desperately sad news that mother and child had died. We drove to the hospital in silence, and later that day they were buried. In accordance with custom, Rawat went into fast for twelve days. Six months later, during a mass X-ray programme, it was revealed that he had tuberculosis and was admitted to hospital. I spent a lot of time urging him to display the greatest patience and discipline in complying with the doctors' instructions so that he would be the first Gurkha to be returned to duty after having had TB. It would be a tribute to himself and his regiment, and give hope to all other Gurkhas similarly afflicted.

He was a model patient, and I was invited to attend his operation at the British Military Hospital in Singapore. It was a brutal affair: his back was opened up and parts of several ribs removed so that the rib cage could be compressed to allow the affected part of the lung to heal. Recovering from the anaesthetic, his first request was for a cold beer. When I put that to the surgeon he replied: 'If he wants a cold beer, for goodness sake give him one.'

He made a remarkable recovery and the following year married his late wife's sister. The marriage took place in Lamjung – the bride having come to Malaya with families returning from long leave – but fate had not finished with Rawat. A few months on and his wife was found to have TB, and that all but finished him.

He came to see me in my little hut on the hill and we went over all that had happened in two short years. His morale was at rock-bottom and I had to dig deep to find the right words. 'Nothing else can happen to you,' I assured him. 'If you can somehow find the strength and the courage to fight once more, just once more for your wife's sake, and see her through this ordeal, I am sure that God will have some special blessing in store for you.'

I had to convince him and to leave him in no doubt that the regiment would do everything possible to help. We were friends; he had to trust me. And, like the good soldier he was, he remained steady and firm and saw his wife restored to full health at the Lady Templar Hospital in Kuala Lumpur. In time he was himself to become the Gurkha major.

But there was a bigger reward waiting: just before I said goodbye to the regiment, his wife gave birth to a son, Bijay, and that boy was destined to be the first Gurkha cadet ever to win the Sword of Honour at Sandhurst.

The time had now come for me to go, and to say goodbye is always to die a little. I sat beside my driver-orderly, Purnaram Gurung, who had been with me all the years I spent with Gurkhas, as we drove to Kuala Lumpur station. In keeping with the great traditions of Gurkhas, his impeccable appearance and loyalty had never faltered. And the only request he made of me was that I might find time to send him an occasional letter.

Immediately ahead of us, standing up in an open Landrover and showering rose petals on the car in a traditional gesture of farewell, was Gurhka Major Dhan Bahadur Gurung.

A bar had been set up on the station platform. Pakri and Sammy were there to dispense hospitality to all comers: friends, well-wishers and strangers alike. Rahim Bux appeared with a dozen garlands destined to be strung around my neck by those who felt this final gesture would stiffen my morale.

There were many new faces on the platform, corralled from outposts in Sungei Patani, Ipoh, Kuala Lipis, Seremban, Muar, Johore Bahru, Singapore, and even Hong Kong, to witness my departure and to enjoy a celebration on the very site where Hamish and I had first set foot on Malaysian soil. For all of them there would be a bigger and better platform when the history of the regiment is written.

(And because names mean so much more than mere words, I feel compelled to list them here: Sidney Allaway, Mike Barrett, Ted Baxter, Bob Benbow, Zackaray Clark, Alan Dexter, Reggie Glanville, Todge Griffiths, Frank Lettin, Tom Livingstone, George Lynam, 'Mac' McCormick, Peter Mussebrook, Aubrey Rawson, Val Swindale, David Willett, Ted Winn, Sam Young – and the Queen's Gurkha Officers: Aslal Rai, Birkhababahadur Gurung, Krishnabahadur Gurung, Maniraj Rai, Motilal Thapa, Maniratne Thapa, Namgyal Tendup Sherpa and Narianprasad Limbu. They were the torchbearers upon whose heads would fall the wrath of irate staff officers and their masters.

In the event, comradeship won the day, spreading its effervescence through the Ministry of Defence and into the cities, towns and villages of the United Kingdom and Nepal – and this from only one regiment still in its infancy. But carry the hypothesis further to the rest of the Brigade of Gurkhas with a proven vintage, and further still to the old regiments of the Empire and Commonwealth, and there at a glance is the true measure of Commonwealth friendship.)

The pipes and drums marched up and down the platform playing for the first, and perhaps last time a march specially composed by Pipe Major Willie Ross – no doubt recalling our earlier association – called 'Gregory's Pride'. After I left, it was quietly shelved; even so, how could I fail to remember such a touching farewell?

The train began to move, noticeably trying to keep pace with the music. The last sight I had was of Purnaram standing rigidly to attention saluting the departing train.

Caught in the emotion of the moment, my final thought was for a promise I had made to Hamish that I would somehow get a royal banner into his hands in time for the coronation of His Majesty, King Mahendra Bir Bikram Sah Deva in Nepal, at which Hamish was to represent the regiment. It was a matter of no little pride that the youngest regiment of the Brigade of Gurkhas should have been the first to possess a pipe banner bearing the royal arms, and the first to display them in Katmandu on such an occasion; nor could there have been a better man to fulfil that historic mission. Hamish told me years later of the pride he felt, as a Scotsman, in seeing the banner he had personally attached to the bagpipes of Pipe Major Bom Bahadur Limbu, picked out in scarlet and gold in the floodlit stadium ahead of the massed rifle green of the Brigade of Gurkhas.

For me, there remained the personal satisfaction of receiving the banner, in the company of my brother, from Her Royal Highness, the Princess Royal, in the throne room at St James's Palace, while our mother watched the ceremony on television over a cup of tea.

Her Royal Highness's brief address, ending with these words, lingers like the last note in an unforgettable experience:

'May this banner serve to remind all who have the honour of belonging to the regiment of the intimate association which brings together, in this regiment, the great traditions of my Corps, and of Her Majesty's Brigade of Gurkhas.'

That was enough for me: it was the fulfilment of a dream and I was ready to pack my bags and go. But the Ministry of Defence had other ideas, and decided that the privilege of a boyhood in the Nilgiris, or Blue Mountains, of south India, and the comradeship I had enjoyed as a member of the armed forces of the Commonwealth and Empire qualified me for a more down to earth assignment on Dartmoor, via a preparatory stint on the staff, to freshen up my thinking in the company of junior leaders. The mood and the experience were quite different, but it was a fortuitous move.

(I next met Hamish Paterson and John Ridge when I returned to Edinburgh many years later. The trams had long since gone; the festival still beckoned to the rest of the world to come and enjoy itself; and the cold winds from the North Sea blew fresh, enlivening the spirit of the people. There was much to learn here too: Hamish was back in his old habitat, Coulter, in Lanarkshire. John Ridge takes the train north from time to time to regale us with an account of his latest travels in Nepal, and the names spill out in an endless litany of friendship.

The latest of these included a visit to a remote village in the west of Nepal called Masina to persuade my orderly, Purnaram Gurung – who I had last seen on the station platform in Kuala Lumpur – to present himself at a reunion in Pokhara (two days' march from Masina) to do with the regimental badge where John arranged for him to speak to me. His news was brief and to the point.

He had ten children – his second son, Haribahadur Gurung, with the Royal Gurkha Rifles in the UK. His house lacked piped water, electricity and sanitation, but the family was self-sufficient in food, milk, rice wine and honey – a pot of which he would be sending me by hand of John. His wife and children were well and he hoped that my family was well too. His son would give me a full report (which he did while staying with us for a few days in Edinburgh, and before leaving presented my wife and me each with a miniature regimental badge in gold).

When I asked Purnaram whether he needed or wanted anything, he replied: 'Hoina hazur, Baghwan ko kirpale sab kura chha' (By God's grace I have everything).

It was against this background that we were also talking about 'Options for

Change' and the sinister message that lay in store for Her Majesty's Brigade of Gurkhas: the old regiments had been abandoned (their badges scrapped) and replaced by three (soon to be two) battalions of the Royal Gurkha Rifles. For nearly two hundred years the hill men of Nepal – Her Majesty's soldiers but not her subjects – have forged a link between the people of these islands and the people of the Himalayas which today commands the admiration of the entire civilised world. Is it so easily expendable?

They had served with distinction in the front ranks of the armies of the Empire and Commonwealth and added lustre to their achievements – particularly in the British and Indian contingents – and yet Nepal is not (but in my view should be) a member of the Commonwealth.

And could there not be a place for our Gurkha friends – recruited, trained and administered as they have been since 1814 – as a permanent force for the United Nations? With bagpipes and military band would they not prove to be a reassuring investment, and even bring a little cheer to the poor old world organisation?

From my lowly perch there was little I could do to influence events, but when asked for a contribution to Forty Years On, *a pictorial record of the Queen's Gurkha Signals compiled by Sean Dexter, I was able to say this: 'You have travelled far, your achievements are many. You have been judged as men and measured as soldiers. And you can claim to be the heart of the Brigade of Gurkhas. But if the heart stops the body dies; and should this happen, a much loved part of Britain and Nepal will die too.')*

CHAPTER THREE

THE DENBURY STORY

Balaclava General

From the window of my hut, I watched the day draw to a close over the great stone mass of Haytor silhouetted against the evening sky like some giant Buddha at the far end of the valley. Slowly the night engulfed Dartmoor. But the presence of Haytor lingered, fuelling the imagination as it had done on every single day since that winter's evening, three years ago, when I reported for duty with the Junior Leaders' Regiment at Denbury.

Occasionally, the notoriously unpredictable weather on Dartmoor would drop a curtain of mist between us, isolating the camp and investing it with uncanny loneliness, and then as quickly draw it aside. And Haytor would still be there, watching over the welfare of the young – all six hundred of them. This is their story.

They were junior leaders, destined to provide a corps of non-commissioned officers for the army. And for them Denbury was home, far removed from the bustle and confusion of the outside world. There was time and space here to reflect on the elusive quality of leadership – claimed by many but found in few – which usually manifests itself in the art of bringing out the best in others.

That principle was put to the test across three hundred square miles of Dartmoor: over rocks and cliffs, through bogs and streams, and not infrequently in the mists that add mystery to its majesty. And there were many examples to prove the point; one of these, reported in the *London Gazette* by the Queen's Order, in November 1960, might serve for all.

'On the evening of 28 May 1960, Junior Sergeant Major Ronald John Butcher was one of a party of junior leaders in a truck which left the road, fell over a fifteen foot bank and ended up partially immersed in a stream. Half of the twenty-two junior leaders were injured.

Due to the suddenness of the accident, and the darkness, there was a risk of dangerous confusion, but Butcher took control, maintained order and then helped to organise relief. This he did in spite of the fact that he himself had received injuries to his face which subsequently required one hundred and twenty stitches. At an age less than eighteen years he displayed courage and fortitude.'

Denbury too had its own story, beginning with the Anglo-Saxons who built the original camp. And it had a castle, still to be seen on old maps that give the little village bearing its name an aura of antiquity.

At the end of the main street, past the church with its single-handed clock and the high walls of Denbury House, stands the Union Inn, a repository of tales about the affairs of the village and the drinking habits of its citizenry since 1812. Looking every bit like a picture-postcard cottage with white gables and thatched roof (since tiled) it is well placed to welcome all into its hospitable sanctuary. Harry Lark, one of a long and distinguished line of landlords, filled me in on much of the detail.

Apparently, the walls about Denbury House had been built high enough to erase the rectory and the person who lived therein from the field of view of the then squire. Current relations were less hostile, but the walls remained a salutory reminder of the past. And if a stone wall can qualify for a mention in legend, surely there is space for an old army camp too – if only in an abridged version of the accounts I heard from Harry Lark and his customers. After all, most of them had at some time found employment there.

The fifty acres of lovely grassland, soft and flat below the village, first came into prominence as a springboard for the pioneering aviators of the twenties and thirties. It was the clearest signal that the adventurous spirit had arrived, and was to remain, in one form or another, at the heart of the Denbury story and all who played some part in it.

The flying men brought merriment and tales of exploits over the Devon skies to liven up the evenings in the Union, and they were popular. But that happy state of affairs was rudely interrupted in May 1939 when hundreds of workmen were brought in, at a weekly wage of about three pounds, to build a new camp within a stone's throw of its Anglo-Saxon forebear.

Within three months it was ready for occupation. The cookhouse was regarded as one of the best of its kind, and there were no old army kit boxes for the soldiers either. No indeed! Their personal possessions were to be housed in steel lockers – not unlike filing cabinets.

But soldiers have a reputation for accelerating the pace of life, whereas Devonians are by nature more inclined to the pervasive influences of the moors and the farmers who struggle to make a living on them. So, depending on the rumours fed into the Union, wise voices expressed doubts or approval until time and experience settled these differences.

On 15 August 1939, the Argyll and Sutherland Highlanders moved in – reason enough for a full turnout at the Union to discuss contingency plans – but there was no cause for alarm; before the local side was called upon to face the drinking men of Scotland across the Union bar, war intervened and all minds switched to higher things.

In 1942 the first Americans arrived; on Dartmoor the allied troops began to prepare for D-Day, and three weeks before the momentous 6 June 1944 some very important people came to inspect them: Prime Minister Winston Churchill, and Generals Eisenhower and Montgomery. Although they did not actually stop off at the Union to test the local resolve, they had come and that was enough. In the hearts of the locals, Denbury was now the launching pad for the liberation of Europe. From here the King's men hurled themselves against the Normandy beaches; casualties were high and Denbury became a hospital for the wounded.

1945 brought victory, celebrated in the Union with the attendant honours, and the hospital wards were converted into classrooms for several hundred members of the Women's Royal Auxiliary Corps. 'It was like a bleeding convent,' commented Harry Lark, but they stayed only a short while before handing over to a contingent of Polish soldiers – part of the famous Warsaw Guards Unit – who had elected not to return to Poland under Russian occupation, and instead devoted their time to clearing Dartmoor of live ammunition. When they left, civil servants nosed in with the threat of demolition.

It was now 1947. In far away India, the British Empire had reached the beginning of its end, the new Commonwealth was born and the words equality, freedom and friendship raised to the pinnacle of man's achievement.

Despite the rows of huts rotting in the wind and rain, and the long grass creeping over the once neat pathways, the old camp stood its ground, stubbornly refusing to surrender – to time, to neglect, or to the weather.

Homeless after the war, scattered units of the Royal Army Service Corps found a refuge in Denbury. Five years on and the Depot Regiment of the Royal Signals ousted the RASC, setting up a transit camp for wild men, which prompted Harry Lark to remark that this was worse than the bloody war!

It was at this point that Denbury became the home of junior leaders. 'Junior Leaders!' It had a good sound, a departure from the norm but new and untested: too new for the Union to pass judgement. The regulars would have to wait and watch, and perhaps deploy a few spies.

To prevent them wandering off limits, the junior leaders were quickly organised into a hundred patrols made up of one from each of six terms, plus a leader. Each patrol member was allocated a specific task to be performed and perfected over one term, before moving up one. The leader's job was to keep a close watch on his patrol and generally to coordinate its behaviour.

Out on the moors, the second-in-command was responsible for navigation and understudying his patrol leader, while the others, in descending order of importance, were answerable for first aid, communications, stores, cooking and litter. Individual successes and failures in all these activities, calculated on a points system – which included work on the parade square and in the classroom – was the criterion by which the champion patrol was selected.

The Union approved these arrangements regretting only that the newcomers were barred from using the facilities of the place which was a major disadvantage, reducing the takings at the till. However, such strictures did not apply to the officers and the permanent staff, of whom there were many, and they were cordially welcomed.

One interesting innovation which seemed to please the locals was that everyone, regardless of rank, was required to wear a coloured Balaclava helmet for identification at long range: black for the most junior and moving up through the colours to white for the finished product about to graduate.

The practice was not wildly popular with the Ministry of Defence, and some quite unfriendly words were spoken over the telephone. But the Junior Leaders' Council (JLC) – the ten most senior junior leaders – moved quickly to pre-empt any practical expression of displeasure by presenting the Adjutant-General (Sir Hugh Stockwell) with a white Balaclava for his own use, and a black one for his wife. And when that great man later visited his budding young comrades he was wearing it, earning for himself an accolade of dubious distinction, 'The Balaclava General', which of course had little to do with the actual number of junior leaders, or the Balaclava's association with the Crimean War, but was intended as a compliment.

Litterbugging

Needless to say the younger officers had been dazzled as much by this display of leadership as by the bright red tabs of a real live general, and their ambitions were aroused. So much so that the colonel decided to exhibit a little leadership of his own by channelling their energies towards setting up a nightclub.

Initially the idea was dismissed as fatuous, but on closer examination didn't seem at all bad. Besides, there were all sorts of moth-eaten precedents for this kind of thing dating back to the Second World War, and in particular the one about officers with impeccable reputations learning the art of all round defence from the belly dancer at Groppe's, in Alexandria.

And nearer home, the prevailing practice of incorporating a night out at the Hammersmith Palais in London for senior officers attending leadership courses at Eltham Palace – in order that they might observe their young countrymen and women in action – was another pointer to the adventurous thinking in high places. Against that background, a nightclub seemed not only appropriate, but highly desirable.

That then was how Denbury Castle, alias the flea pit, came into being. But a castle without a prince would not do, hence the legend that having lost his way on Dartmoor, the Prince of Denbury returned as a flea to make his presence felt. This led to the abolition of scratching for any purpose whatever (or, more specifically, gossiping about each other) on the grounds that it might endanger the life of the prince. When this latest bit of news reached the Union, there was some consternation among its members. Perhaps an epidemic of 'moordom' was creeping into Denbury, in which case they had themselves better take the precaution of wearing Balaclava helmets just as the general and his lady had done.

Unlikely as it may seem, the project did take off: two small storerooms and two disused lavatories were commandeered for the purpose, and the intervening walls placed at the disposal of the younger officers for demolition. And when a hole large enough to dance through had been created, the clerk of works was invited to view progress. Not surprisingly, he was taken aback. But when told that no less a person than Her Majesty's General in the Southwest had approved a generous sum to finance the project – from the adventurous training budget – he relaxed and commented favourably on the work already done. He went even further in pronouncing that it would save time and money.

The project was thus raised to the level of a combined operation and work resumed: one of the lavatories earmarked for upgrading to wine cellar, and the other, with a minute door constructed in deference to the patron of the establishment, restored to its original function. The decor was a much admired silhouette of officers in the guise of fleas on salmon-pink walls. There was also a serving hatch and piped music.

Opening night was distinguished by the presence of the Balaclava General dancing with the 'Chair' of the Dartmoor Preservation Association – no doubt hoping thereby to persuade her to adopt a more conciliatory attitude towards the army playing war games on Dartmoor. Alas, it was the coming together of two opposing forces and dancing was not enough. She too was a leader and saw through this bit of chicanery. Nevertheless, they clearly enjoyed themselves and there was thereafter a noticeable improvement in relations between the Ministry of Defence and the Dartmoor Preservation Association.

The big guns, however, would not be silenced and remained targeted on the military planners in London. And although this helped to divert the attention of ambitious staff officers from Denbury, some of the fallout landed on the junior leaders, identifying them with litter, spent cartridges and unexploded mortar bombs. The riposte had to be swift, and decisive. Bravely led by the officers – including such non-combatants as the chaplain, the doctor and the dentist – an expedition known as 'Operation Litterbug' was mounted with orders to retrieve, in a single litterbugging sweep, no less than six hundred sacks of prime garbage as a practical contribution towards defusing any lingering animosity between the MOD and the DPA before it erupted into open warfare.

When the word 'litterbugging' reached the Union it was assumed there that the junior leaders had invented a new dance; and although that misunderstanding was soon cleared up, the idea of the dance was kept alive as a suitable project for joint examination at some future date. But the operation itself was a complete success, and the accumulated spoils transported to a nuclear free zone for public viewing before being handed over to the leader of the Newton Abbot District Council. It was a spectacular event – talked about to the present day – with all the trappings of a victory parade, and enhanced by the presence of the regimental pipes and drums. That final touch raised the matter from the gutter where it began to a place among the stars.

And one might have thought that this was precedent enough to make the collecting of litter within Denbury itself an adventurous occupation. But not so; while junior leaders were perfectly willing to collect litter for the council during a national emergency, there was a statutory obligation on the part of the council to do as much for junior leaders on a regular basis.

The problem was resolved without recourse to a public demonstration when two advertisements appeared simultaneously in the same weekly magazine: one offering a second-hand ponycart for sale and the other seeking a good home for a donkey. Negotiations followed and at an agreed price cart and donkey were brought together. The latter was named Prince and had a junior leader's badge fitted to his harness; the former was restored to showroom condition, painted green and provided with a registration number plate – DEN 1.

The first public engagement for DEN 1 was a courtesy call on the Union where the villagers turned out to express their approval in the usual way, marking a new phase in relations between the new Denbury camp and the old Denbury village. Harry Lark took it upon himself to applaud this unique event, eulogizing that it had taken a donkey to bring it about. But there were others present to remind him that this was simply an extension of a proud tradition of service among the brotherhood of donkeys dating back nearly two thousand years.

Some initiatives fall into place naturally, and leading Prince around Denbury was one of these. His popularity was such as to earn for him a place of honour on all graduation parades – recognising that he too deserved some credit for the product on display. There were six hundred junior leaders, but only one donkey, or was it the other way round?

Adventurous training

Something still remained to be done about filling the idle moments during weekends and public holidays, and that was how pigeon racing came to be written into the curriculum under the heading 'extra mural activity'. And very soon there were almost as many birds around as there were handlers for them.

Nevertheless, the sport was taken seriously and dominated the summer term culminating in a race from Whitehall to Denbury. It was feared at first that the opposition concentrated around Trafalgar Square might ambush its country cousins en route, but that was before reconnaissance revealed that the flight path to Denbury lay in the opposite direction.

When news of the London-Denbury race got about it attracted a wide following and the offer of a suitable trophy: a pigeon in repose, sculptured in white maple in Oberammergau.

Of course, the more conventional forms of adventurous training there had to be, and not least because this was the new catch phrase in Whitehall the very utterance of which sent shock waves down the spines of staff officers and their political masters scuttling for cover. And all because no one knew exactly what it meant.

It may also explain why three hundred pairs of special boots were supplied for six hundred pairs of feet. But, the show had to go on – if only in shifts – allowing scope for imaginative initiatives elsewhere.

And where else but at the Royal Albert Hall.

In such matters the support of heaven can usually be relied upon, unlike the bureaucrats on earth whose training is of a different ilk aimed at blocking any initiatives likely to cause extra work. To convince them that there was as much adventure in singing a song – if one had never sung in public before – as in say climbing a mountain, would require more than just prayers.

However, if they could be so persuaded might they not shower blessings upon Denbury for adventuring beyond the call of duty, while at the same time saving the taxpayer the cost of three hundred pairs of boots? Maybe; but how does one secure admission to the Royal Albert Hall from this tiny backwater of the universe? There was no need to worry; a man shrewd in such matters rose to speak:

'Form a choir,' he advocated, 'and have it auditioned for the Festival of Remembrance.'

For better or for worse, Ralph Nye had served a long time in the Royal Army Education Corps and made a habit of climbing on the Cornish cliffs in search of inspiration. He had already earned universal respect for voting in favour of a period of 'inwardbound' training – a well intentioned device aimed at depriving the individual of his freedom – for those falling behind in their studies, and it had worked so well that very few qualified for it. And now this!

What could be simpler? he insisted. It would take about a year to train a choir, allowing time to muster the necessary support to outflank the Ministry of Defence and convince those who favoured a quiet life that a choir of junior leaders appearing before the Queen was an adventurous activity within the meaning of the act. Surely it was worth a try.

Yes it was; and selecting suitable voices was surprisingly simple. All six hundred were assembled in the gymnasium and the regimental sergeant major, Fred Pavey, posted at the only exit. There was no way of getting past him without attempting the tonic sol-fa in transit. Fifty per cent true was the standard prescribed and, according to Fred Pavey, a hundred and ten passed muster – the precise number required.

In the months that followed, the growing pains of a choir in embryo were heard beyond the narrow confines of Denbury and suffered with equanimity and sympathy; while at the Union Inn the law was gently bent to encourage the nobler aspirations of leadership bound for the Royal Albert Hall. But to get to that point many ancient skills known only to RSMs had to be employed including weekends off, disagreeable fatigues set aside, free tea and cakes on call, and other inducements guaranteed to raise morale and stimulate the vocal cords. It was a well balanced prescription for success.

Now came the hard part: an application to the festival committee begging for an audition. That task was allocated to the adjutant, a resourceful man by the name of Peter Davis, who was instructed to drop everything and begin drafting – and to include an invitation to lunch.

His place in history is assured for securing an immediate response: not only would the festival committee be coming to hear the choir for themselves, they were actually looking forward to lunch. Ah! So something more than just the singing would be judged in clinching the deal, and that something was hospitality.

It was conference time. After much heart searching, one of the colonel's hottest favourites was chosen to dominate the menu, supplemented by pink gin and pearl onions – an infallible Indian Army tipple – and a continuous supply of ice-cold lager during the limbering-up process.

And did that treatment work? It transformed a motley collection of junior leaders, each with a fancy for outshouting the other on the higher notes, into a choir of angels – but not without a little help from the padre.

Ronnie Wood well understood the higher purpose of his calling, and junior leaders singing was certainly part of that purpose: the pews in the wooden hut that served as St George's Church were so arranged as to place the choir in a central position grouped around the smallest boy. The boy in question had been borrowed for the occasion, but the visitors were not to know that. He had a particularly good voice well rehearsed in the verses of 'Land of Hope and Glory', and as the auditioning party staggered into the church, the singing began.

The tremulous young voice rising above the choir humming softly was instantly effective; but when they burst into the chorus en masse, any audience would have been forgiven for thinking that Denbury was indeed the land of hope and glory. It was like watching a miracle unfold. The low ceiling helped to amplify the sound while Ronnie Wood stood with arms folded and eyes turned heavenwards in a final appeal to his boss. That too worked.

The producer stepped forward, visibly moved by what he had seen and heard, and drunk: 'You're on boys,' he said, 'you're on,' embracing those nearest to him with outstretched arms, and was rewarded with a cheer he is unlikely to forget. So far so good, but one snag remained: train fares and logistical support for so large a number would be expensive and there was as yet no provision for this sort of activity in the adventurous training budget.

But the scent of success was already in the air, and with victory within his grasp, Peter Davis was already preparing to confess all and plead with his brother officers in high places for a little help. Judging from past experience however, it was more than likely that they would choose to cock a snook at him by delaying, ignoring or even refusing the application. What then eh?

Having come thus far the journey simply had to be completed: the fateful moment had arrived for the leader to make a decision, or at least take the chair. All eyes focused on the colonel.

'If the Royal Albert Hall can accept the Junior Leaders Choir to sing at the Festival of Remembrance,' he declared with steadily mounting eloquence, 'the least we can do is to get them there. My personal army number is available for use as a temporary authority.

If the choir is a success,' he went on, 'approval will be forthcoming. If not, well, we'll just have to leave it to God.'

It was impressive stuff, his subordinates had been waiting for something like this – 'the Holy Ghost coming down upon the Apostles' as one of them put it – and were now convinced that they had at last found the real meaning of leadership. It was a masterstroke, and thankfully one that would not land anyone of them in trouble.

'Young soldiers sing for the Queen,' was how the media reported the story. Her Majesty was obviously pleased, she even waved to them, and watching on television parents saw the poppies come cascading down on the heads of their sons.

It was a moment that caught the imagination and opened the way for the choir to appear at the Victoria Palace in London with Gracie Fields in aid of the Army Benevolent Fund. After that, starring in the forces Christmas broadcast was a mere formality and singing took its place on the adventurous training programme.

(Eight years later the success of those junior leaders re-echoed through the Royal Albert Hall when Comex 3 made its debut there.)

Nijmegen

In less exalted circles, a story was going the rounds that a number of British soldiers in Germany had been taken out of circulation for a brief spell of detention, but had been offered the option of taking part in the international marches in Nijmegen as an alternative punishment – a hundred miles to be completed in four days with a suitable load on their backs. It was an inspired offer and from all accounts they had found the prospect more congenial than contemplating the future from the cells of a cold, concrete guardroom, and to prove the point had completed the march in record time.

One of these reformed sinners had reported for general duties at Denbury (some clear thinking there!) bringing with him a first hand account of his experiences for the edification of the regiment – revealed during the course of an adventure training discussion.

The idea of marching a hundred miles in Holland fell on fertile ground, and there were boots enough. But how to transport the wearers thereof to the appointed place called for an enterprise out of the ordinary.

Extensive enquiries revealed that a popular air vice-marshal had recently moved into a large white house in Salisbury, and if he could be persuaded to find a corner in one of his transport aircraft to lift half the marchers, hired coaches could look after the rest. But that sort of persuasion would require something more convincing than a friendly letter.

So, despite some reservations, a plan was drawn up and the house surrounded. As luck would have it, the night chosen was one on which the unsuspecting AVM was playing host to a minister from the Ministry of Defence, and that vital piece of information was received too late to call off the operation.

Right on time, therefore, the plan was put into effect and the ADC informed that unless his boss acceded to their demands the junior leaders would be obliged to enter the house and take him hostage. Had the ADC reacted by inviting them to go and eat fish and chips they would probably have done so. But he was so taken aback by the suddenness of the event that he rushed into the adjoining room to warn his master.

'The house is surrounded sir,' he reported, the urgency of the matter all too apparent in his speech, 'and a party of junior leaders on some kind of crazy mission want to take you hostage.'

'Good God,' responded the AVM, but conscious of the presence of an important guest in his house stepped out to face his would-be captors – now looking a trifle cowed.

'And what had you in mind to do with me?' he demanded.

'Nothing sir,' replied the leader, and was immediately aware that it lacked the smack of leadership.

'What!' he snapped, quick to seize the initiative, 'come all this way and do nothing!'

'We had hoped that you would agree to have us flown to Nijmegen.' This was an improvement but not much 'smack' there either.

'Oh you did! I see.' The AVM was now in control. 'And how would you get back from Nijmegen? Walk?' There was a long and embarrassed silence; things were not going at all well. When junior leader confronts senior leader there are strict lines of engagement, particularly on how far the former dare go, and it was up to the latter to throw out a lifeline.

'Perhaps you had hopes of being airlifted home as well?'

'Yes sir!' came the grateful response.

'Very well then. I'll do what I can. But next time think the operation through, and choose somebody else.' Having thus demolished any threat to his person, he instructed the ADC to dispense some hospitality and returned to regale his guests on the importance of adventurous training. So he too got something out of it, and for the junior leaders there was at least a crumb of victory.

In addition to the pipes and drums, the choir and the dancers, there were several volunteers for each of the two hundred places for the Nijmegen Marches, and those who failed to qualify were guaranteed places the following year. Nor did the RAF renege on the promise made by their commander. All that remained to be done was for the marchers to complete their hundred miles in four days. While most people spent the evenings dealing with blisters and preparing for the next day's twenty-five miles, the choir sang for all who would listen, some played football, and the pipes and drums, with the dancers in tow, had a full list of engagements. They were the youngest of over ten thousand marchers and not one failed to complete the course.

Watching these events from not far away was the 'Balaclava General'. He was now Deputy Commander NATO at Fontainebleau and was reminded, if indeed he needed reminding, that in an unguarded moment he had invited the junior leaders to call on him should they ever be passing his way – little thinking that they would take him up on the offer. But here they were, over two hundred of them, and true to form he honoured that invitation with lavish hospitality and a briefing in the Operations Room. As they marched out of his headquarters singing 'Land of my Fathers' for a great Welsh Fusilier, and the 'Marseillaise' for a wider audience, the locals joined in – unaware that these were potential hostage takers!

With Nijmegen out of the way attention switched to the junior leaders themselves playing host to other youth organisations clamouring to test themselves against the rigours of Dartmoor.

Once again, Ralph Nye was called in, along with John Joyner, for consultation. The latter was known as the Yeti for his obsession with Dartmoor, dating –

according to the junior leaders – from the time his parents had spent their honeymoon at Cranmere Pool, which is not so much a pool as a large dent in the peat where a pool might once have been.

Ten Tors

On a cool autumn night a disparate group of junior leaders made their way through the moors in search of the right formula. The stars shone brightly, conversation was barely audible.

But Dartmoor is notorious for whispering messages to the uninitiated, which may explain why the words 'Ten Tors' entered their consciousness. And in the absence of any record of how many tors were climbed ten seemed to fit and it stuck.

By mid-winter an expeditionary force of three hundred junior leaders was mustered to put the matter to the test: not only because one of the unwritten rules of military operations is that there should be a trial run wherever possible, but to ensure that they would be equal to doing themselves what they planned to inflict on others. Apart from the more practical considerations, the rule book stipulated that junior leaders should put their faith in each other first, and then call upon God to straighten things out if necessary. And that is exactly what they did, only to be rewarded with the heaviest snowfall Dartmoor had seen in years.

The snow began to freeze, visibility fell to zero, and suspicion began to grow that someone in heaven was deliberately misreading divine orders in order to make monkeys out of the junior leaders on earth. Unless, of course, the intention was to enhance the success of the operation by the conditions under which it was achieved. Anyway, that was the encouraging hypothesis communicated to all concerned, but it was as well to be armed with a little practical advice too: 'Stick together chaps; don't lose sight of your patrol leader; and if lost go to ground, batten down in your bivouac tent, get into your sleeping bag, tuck into your emergency rations, pray and wait.' At the head count next day eight were reported missing.

'Eight Junior Leaders Lost On Dartmoor. Colonel To Retire.' Thus headlined, the news spread. The BBC broadcast regular bulletins, the General Officer Commanding Southwest District sent his ADC to enquire whether the Royal Marines should be called in, and a string of hungry reporters sat in the Officers' Mess tent enjoying regimental hospitality and sharpening their pencils. With the prospect of courts of enquiry and other unpleasant procedures in mind, the officers responsible were already on their way back into Dartmoor, moving on pre-determined bearings and in radio contact with each other. Operating on the same frequency, a naval helicopter was launched to help in the search and, if necessary, to evacuate any casualties.

The first sign of life came in response to a boot making contact with a mound of snow: 'Hey!' The owner of the voice announced his presence loud and clear, but the much relieved owner of the boot still thought to ask if anyone was at home. 'Yes sir!' came the reply, and three junior leaders emerged. Safe and well they were given the option of accompanying the search party on foot or evacuation by helicopter. They chose the latter – perhaps because they had never flown before! Others were similarly rescued and no one was any the worse for the experience.

Thus Ten Tors was launched on its historic flight into the future. The challenge lay against self and the environment, not one another, a principle dramatised on the floor of the Union Inn in thirty-eight cantos entitled 'The Ballad of Denbury Common'.

The Ballad of Denbury Common

A long time ago, on Denbury Common,
As the sound of massed trumpets splintered the air,
A thousand young faces, weary and yawning,
Crept out of their dreams while day was still dawning.

Overnight the base camp had mushroomed to life,
Hubbub, and confusion, and tents everywhere:
'Like pigeons in a loft,' the RSM said
As he counted them in and tottered to bed.

Not far from the centre, by Denbury Cross,
The momentous briefing on Ten Tors began
To wild cheers and applause, and maybe because
Ten Tors was considered a cheerworthy cause.

The reception over, we turn to review
How Rothwell of Ogwell and his merry crew,
Having weathered the storm from morning till night
Turned up to continue the watch at first light.

As the chattering streams poured into the yard
A voice could be heard, like the ghost of a bard,
Speak words of caution then go silent until
They heard him again up on Haytor's fair hill.

Back at Denbury, pilots checked out the start
And the military men consulted the stars.
From Salisbury a staff-car moved south through the night
Praying for good weather and a trouble-free flight.

The flags flutter gaily, trumpeters in red –
The same scarlet warriors that roused them from bed –
With a priest in his cassock to bless the day
That God sent to help launch Ten Tors on its way.

And so the appointment with many events:
The move, the assembly, the striking of tents.
Everyone to his task and all in its place;
But try as one might they'll still call it a race.

The men raise their faces, the women just smile,
The sun plays its part in celestial style.
Then out of the heavens and haloed in light,
A whirring bird glitters and hovers in sight.

The cabin door opens, the steps are in place,
An officer stands by well briefed just in case,
As stepping out briskly and looking his best:
Behold the Queen's General commanding the West.

'Just a thousand this year but two thousand next;
Well done and good hunting,' the gist of his text.

The trumpets then sound, a brief moment for prayer,
And again that voice speaks: 'They conquer who dare!'

Now watch the action-men, patrol leaders stand
Astride maps on the ground compasses in hand;
They talk and they argue, some grumble, some dance:
Why march on a bearing – let's leave it to chance!

Away to the moors, every hill, every glen,
Beckoning young leaders, brave girls gallant men.
Well trained to resist any thought of retreat
From the weather or time, the tors or the peat.

Swift as the rushing winds and clear crystal streams,
By pastures and meadows in sunshine and beams:
A trek across Dartmoor's bewildering scene
To Hexworthy bound, thence to Colin's own green.

And there stands the leader at the entrance gate,
For once he is early, thank God he's not late:
Balaclava set right, bright toorie on top,
Saluting the general – and one word of shop:

'We're through sir on FM to every tor;
Conditions are perfect – could not ask for more.'
A moment's reflection, then just one more word:
'Eh, by the way general, your breakfast is served.'

That was the sitrep around eight hundred hours;
Some marching to the moors and some to the bars:
For VIPs, of course, how could they refuse
The Council's kind offer of 'dutyfree' booze?

As maps, tapes and checkboards are moved to and fro
Plant's giant display-chart takes Ten Tors in tow;
While Chandler works upwards, then down and around:
A flag for the lost and a pin for the found.

There's Willmott and Osborne and Simmonds in turn,
Wirelesses humming as the midnight oils burn.
Such dedicated men are happier this way
Which means working long hours without extra pay.

The sum of their figures progressively grew
As each one of Ten Tors was conquered anew.
Relentless, the timewatch goes on to the end
And wonder of wonders they're not 'round the bend!

Across yonder field called the devil's delight
The pricker of blisters now limps into sight.
You may think what you wish, but shout while you can
'A most hearty welcome old medicine man.'

Behind the red crosses the pots start to boil

Watched over by cooks as they babble and toil.
Ask Stacey, he knows that apart from their feet
Sooner or later even leaders must eat.

Bear with me a moment: 'Up toories and cheer!'
The men and the women who year after year
Come to help where they can, and always on hand:
For them hoist the bunting and turn out the band.

Ah! here a strange message the radio speaks
A patrol has collapsed on one of those peaks:
'Symptoms exhaustion; feet blistered and tender;
Negotiate terms for abject surrender.'

How many patrols from Haytor first started,
How many since from their leaders departed?
With the urge to compete still setting the pace
Three hundred are forced to abandon the 'race'.

To digress once again, and ponder a while
Those stout-hearted women, the girls with a smile,
Who merrily, cheerily, right from the start,
Held no fears for Dartmoor and captured its heart.

Now that story's moral must have its own tale;
Did the women pitch camp near Princetown's old jail?
Ask Joyner, he's mum; there are rumours for sure
But what were they up to those guardians of law?

Throughout these proceedings, perhaps just as well,
The press played its part as Mike Hartnett will tell:
Reporting each up, but more fully each down
Then judging it time to retreat from the town!

The founder's own ruling must now state the case
That the men up in front did not win the 'race'.
And those coming home at the pre-stated time
Most merit approval in reason and rhyme.

The endless procession, all tired, some lame,
Patrol after patrol homewards they came:
Juniors from Teignmouth and the Royal Marines,
Bravo! and again for Ashburton's 'Toreens'.

As the hard night wore on and threatening frost
Officials worked on to account for the lost.
And Rothwell's reception once more came alive
Till the last half dozen clocked-in at O five.

There are members of staff too many to name,
Indispensable in this annual game
Of pickets and rescue, in base camp and out,
And leadership on call: that's what its about.

To those men and women warm thanks are here due
For the bulk of the work well done by the few.
Yet asked if they'd rather be elsewhere, maybe?
Speak up in unison: 'O no sir, not me!'

Such comradeship merits a grass-green silk tie
With something quite striking to capture the eye:
The old tinner's symbol, three rabbits, three ears,
Yet each displaying two to allay their worst fears.

Here comes the Admiral, spot on at six bells,
To present the awards and say the farewells.
'Remarkable,' he says, 'a jolly good show:
Its tough in the heat but much worse in the snow!'

Such wisdom and foresight brought forth a loud cheer
As he steered a brave course 'round courage and fear.
And having thus planted a thought for the day
Hopped into his staff car and went on his way.

Designed by Hugh Ridge of St Ives Artists' Guild,
With Haytor and Ten Tors emblazoned and milled,
A medallion in bronze is honour enough
For all who are born with the best British stuff.

Perhaps VIPs, who preside on the day,
Could bear this thought in mind and mark what I say:
'Weighed down you may be with high honours galore,
But a Ten Tors medal could weigh even more.'

(With acknowledgements to the officers, staff and junior leaders who were present on the day, and all who have since supported Ten Tors. Actual names are given throughout. The success of Ten Tors was marked by the patronage of His Royal Highness The Duke of Edinburgh, KG, KT. And there were other patrons too: The Lord Lieutenant of Devon, Lord Roborough; Brigadier Sir Ralph Rayner, MBE; Lady (Sylvia) Sayer; Admiral Sir Nigel Henderson, KCB, OBE; Air Marshal Sir Donald Evans, KBE, CB, DFC; Major-General F. J. Swainson, OBE; Major-General J. R. Holden, CBE, DSO; Brigadier J. B. Ashworth, CBE, DSO, ADC; Rear Admiral D. J. Hoare, CB, who together formed a ring of encouragement around the junior leaders from which they could emerge with confidence to take the risk and adventure.)

Meanwhile an encouraging message arrived from Sir John (now Lord) Hunt of the 1953 Everest Expedition: 'Ten Tors has achieved the distinction of being a remarkable success story in a very short time.' He went on to talk about discovering nature, concluding with 'I note that this aspect is reflected in the Ten Tors prayer which I especially commend.'

It reads:

'O God, who has made the Earth of wondrous beauty, and planted in Man the Spirit of Adventure, we thank Thee, for the beauty of the earth, for the joy of life, for the courage and vigour of youth, for friendship and friends, and the opportunity to enjoy all these gifts. Go, we pray Thee, with all who today set forth on this Great Adventure among the tors of this ancient moorland. And grant that, overcoming every frailty, we may meet each challenge and difficulty with unselfish courage, and in the companionship of honest endeavour find that spirit of true brotherhood which alone can serve our God, our Queen, and our Generation.'

Setting the seal of approval on Ten Tors with his patronage, His Royal Highness, the Duke of Edinburgh went straight to the point: 'Living as we do in an overcrowded and highly regulated island, it requires considerable ingenuity to find an outlet for the spirit of adventure. Ten Tors provides just the right mixture. . . .'

The Junior Mercury

The growing list of activities added to the regular celebrations in the Union – now an established conference centre for the permanent staff – and many good ideas blossomed there including the Ten Tors tie depicting three rabbits in a triangle. That each was missing an ear but together displayed six (the old tinners' symbol) was cause for much speculation: was there a hidden message here? But the motif was popular and the green background suited the environment. The tie sold well.

One of the less radical suggestions was that a newsletter might serve a useful purpose in keeping friends and well-wishers informed. So, the *Junior Mercury* was launched with the hugely ambitious slogan: 'Leadership in the cause of peace.' Sadly, even in the cause of peace an early edition misfired and was reduced to carrying this moving leader:

The printer's impatient, the editor's tough,
Our hacks lack experience and clout:
The JM is late and we're all in a state,
Pull your finger out chum! Pull it out!

Those ivory towers, invested with powers
To order, to abuse and to shout;
Blinking or winking we know what they're thinking:
'Pull your fingers out chums! Pull them out!'

The Queen's junior leaders were shocked and appalled
When the colonel said 'be a good scout'.
For fashion led crazes the popular phrase is:
Pull your finger out chum! Pull it out!

And so it went on, attracting a swift riposte: 'The recalcitrant behaviour of junior leaders does little harm when confined to Denbury or Dartmoor, but given wing in a newspaper it could start a revolution in the Southwest.'

The editorial staff, headed by the big hearted WO 11 Wheatley of the RAEC, assembled in the Union to weigh up the likely consequences. Did the *JM* pose a threat to the *Mid Devon Advertiser*, long established in Newton Abbot? Or that other great county newspaper the *Western Morning News*, based in Plymouth? Did the editorial policy tend towards inciting a mutiny?

'Indeed not,' came the reassurance, with generous praise for the editor as a man of peace! Yet the view from above was much less sanguine and complaints were received at regular intervals. For instance, a headline 'Junior Leaders See Off Teds' set the telephone bells ringing. Another offering 'Genuine Litter Twenty-five Pence A Bag' to local councils was condemned as a waste of time and not strictly legal. But when the junior cartoonist extended himself with a well-shaped female figure wearing a G-string with JAN 1 precisely sited and captioned 'New Year's Eve', he very nearly did for himself and for his commanding officer.

Of course the reporters doubled as paper boys, which brought them into contact with their readers; and this was good for both in that it created opportunities for unsolicited interviews, a little farmhouse gossip, and generous kitchen hospitality. And perhaps it was this practice that inspired the next headline to hit the streets, 'By These Standards Forward', suggesting that it might be advantageous for the bagpipes to carry banners displaying the heraldic bearings of the local councils. Once started, the talk did not stop until the mayors of Totnes, Paignton, Torquay and Newton Abbot were invited to dinner in the Officers' Mess. For them it was an adventure into alien territory across barriers that would normally prevent the leader of one authority visiting another (while wearing his chain of office) without special dispensation. But once the word got around anything was possible: the dinner was a success, and by the time the party was over all had signed up to present a banner.

Referring to these leaders in a subsequent issue as 'The Chain Gang' very nearly scuppered the project, had it not been overtaken by 'Girls For Denbury' – which might have caused even bigger problems but for the reassuring message in the subtitle, 'The Largest Youth Club in South Devon', explaining that untried and untested first termers would be ineligible to join, and that sixth termers would be stationed at every known venue likely to encourage a breach of good order and military discipline. As to the girls, it was made clear that they would be expected to produce the written approval of their parents and the local vicar, and would thus be assured of escorts from and to the bus stop outside Denbury. What happened after that was their affair.

The time had now come for the growing popularity of junior leaders to be marked by something more than the dreary high buttoned khaki uniforms of pre-war vintage that did little for their image. Regimental undress there simply had to be, distinctive and in keeping with prevailing fashion. Gieves and Hawkes of Plymouth, makers of smart uniforms since Wellington's day, were consulted and they came up with single breasted blazers over cavalry twill trousers (sixteen inch bottoms!) to be worn with chukka boots and a scarlet tie. It was cool, if a bit of extravagance that cut deep into the modest pay of junior leaders. But pride has its price; and regimental undress (informal uniform) was a part of that price.

What went on below the head soon influenced what went on above it: hair on the junior leader's head! It filled a productive evening at the Union, and Fred Pavey came away with an idea. The days of short back and sides had long passed into history; hair was growing longer even to the length of concealing the back of the neck from the regimental sergeant major's gaze. Something had to be done about this absurd situation so he despatched three volunteers to Glenshaws of London whence they returned to model the Devon, the Denbury and the Dartmoor in the gymnasium.

The reception there was jolly enough; but the story had to finish where it began – before a packed audience expressing its approval in the usual way – in an abridged version of what later became known as 'Next Please' when performed by the Denbury Amateur Dramatic Society.

Scene 1. The RSM addressing his volunteers:

'You're off to Glenshaws in the morning,
And once you get inside that door
Your heads on your block for the asking:
Or you'll not outward bound any more.

If a queue is already waiting,
Like athletes poised for the gun,
Well nursed in the sporting tradition
Of protesting when others have won:

Keep your nerve! Your leadership training
Will help, if you call it to mind,
To beat that 'next please' by a whisker
And leave the less nimble behind.

Should the barber make any comments
Sit still, and don't utter a word:
I've told him to do what he must do
And your views are not to be heard.'

Scene 2. Junior Leaders resigned to their fate:

'Where now democracy and freedom,
The flag of the red, white and blue,
When RSMs and barbers conspire,
There is nothing mere JLs can do.'

Scene 3. Junior Leaders at Glenshaws:

'Inside all is charm and sweet smelling,
The receptionist dainty and chic,
But gentlemen! We junior leaders
Don't meddle with any old chick?

Some want an old fashioned haircut,
Others a more modern hairstyle,
But whether haircutting or styling
They'll just have to wait for a while.

Now here's a marvellous example
Of courage, and confidence too:
A man snaps his fingers demanding
A massage, blow-wave and shampoo.'

Scene 4. Junior Leaders in the barber's chair:

'We'll clean up this mess in a minute;
A trim and a singe here and there,
Or a short back and sides with clippers,
Is that sir how you'd like your hair?

Now here's a new style for a leader,
The Denbury, what a haircut:
Just look at those spikes rising sharply
On your junior leader's hard nut.

Ah, this one is more a creation,
Each strand set with patience and care:
The Devon, O yes sir the Devon's
The answer to your maiden's prayer.

But wait, here is something more special,
With lines sleek and trim and as free
As the heather that grows on the moorland:
It's the Dartmoor, or Ad-venture-T.'

Scene 5. The RSM has the last word:

'When you see yourself in the mirror,
Starry eyed and with stiff upper lip:
Resist the impulse to get even
And by unhappy chance under-tip.'

This bit of light entertainment was soon forgotten when news spread that Her Royal Highness, the late Princess Mary, would be visiting Denbury, and that Alexandra Pavey, the RSM's daughter, had been chosen to present a bouquet. It was the first time that royalty had set foot on Denbury soil and the details were reviewed in the Union before and after the event. Apart from the importance of the visit, this was a very special royal lady.

The Princess was well briefed, certainly on the thoughts and aspirations of her junior leaders, which probably explains why she specifically asked to meet the Junior Leaders Council – raising the self esteem of its members to dangerously high levels. But it also had the effect of a controlled explosion, driving the whole camp into a fever of activity. The junior leaders took her coming in their stride; it was in the higher echelons that the flapping was most evident.

Not least was the problem of moving a full size billiard table from a small annex adjacent to the ante-room in the Officers' Mess to provide a suitable rest room for the royal guest who would be spending the best part of a day at Denbury. Then there was the delicate question of adding on a toilet suitable for her exclusive use. The decor had to be right, and although it could not be expected to compete with St James's Palace there would be no forgiveness for bad taste. Promotion was often retarded by a lack of attention to such details.

The ceremonial parade went like clockwork: the pipes and drums, the choir and the Scottish dancers earned excellent marks for appearance, enthusiasm, and a little more. But the star performance came from Alexandra Pavey. When told over tea and cakes in the colonel's office that she was to present a bouquet to the Princess, she displayed all the qualities of a junior leader – although only seven at the time – and went through the briefing with assured self-confidence. All that remained was for her mother to provide a beautiful dress.

The presentation was due to take place before tea in a huge marquee at the top end of the camp. The place was packed with families and friends, a sizeable delegation from the Union, and an anxious looking RSM. As the Princess sat down Fred Pavey could be seen urging his daughter forward but, firmly shaking her head, she was having none of it. However, once HRH was comfortably seated, and all eyes were turned on her, Alexandra marched forward, dainty, composed and confident, and prostrating herself before the Princess handed over the flowers. Many of those present may have seen presentations of this kind before and since, but never one to capture the heart of the matter so completely, or to win a happier expression of royal pleasure.

The upshot of that visit was an invitation to the Junior Leaders Council to parade at St James's Palace and receive a royal banner for the pipes and drums from Her Royal Highness: 'I am very happy to see you at St James's Palace and I hope you will tell all my Junior Leaders that I am very proud of them. With your Ten Tors Expedition and many other activities, you have set a fine example to youth all over the country. You have a great responsibility and a duty, which, I am sure, you will discharge with good humour, discipline and efficiency. And now, I am very pleased to hand to you, Junior Corporal Etherton, this banner, bearing my Arms, to be carried by you as Pipe Major.'

May your rice bowl never be empty

It was a singular coincidence that a pipe banner should have marked the end of my service with Gurkhas and with junior leaders: both received from the hands of Princess Mary. Perhaps it was a good omen for the Green Pennant Awards yet to come – who knows!

I was due to leave Denbury in a few days and test the many lessons I had learnt in a wider, Commonwealth context. And as my thoughts lingered for a moment on the little hill above the camp, and the Union Inn, the sound of marching feet reminded me of the present. It was time to get dressed for dinner. The lights went on around the square picking out the scarlet tunics of the pipers and drummers as they moved in a block towards the Officers' Mess, followed by the trumpeters and the choir. Suddenly the voice of Drum Major Yates reverberated though the camp. 'Arlt!' Perfectly timed, the pipes and drums came to rest within saluting range of the adjutant standing outside the mess. Peter Davis had long since gone, handing over to Michael Hartnett, an enthusiastic sailor and hockey player.

'Band present saar!' yelled the drum major. A simple sir would have sounded too familiar; moreover, as a member of staff he felt obliged to impress his authority upon the junior leaders who always responded well to the power of a commanding voice. Both men knew how to act and to react as circumstances demanded. If the drum major had to arrive an hour early to begin a long stint of extra regimental duty, he would see to it that his voice was heard by all concerned.

Here, however, there was a minor mishap. Yates, otherwise immaculately turned out, was wearing shoes. He had been excused boots on account of an accident sustained years ago, at least that was his story. Others maintained that this was a smoke screen for varicose veins. Whichever it was, his socks had slipped their moorings and were draped loosely about his ankles. This should have been no problem because his trousers would normally have concealed them; but on raising his right foot to the regulation height before smashing it down beside the left, his trouser leg got tangled up with the crumpled sock and remained there, spoiling his appearance and sending a boyish flush into his cheeks. Yates twitched his muscles, slightly relaxed and then stiffened his knee, and even tried wriggling his toes. All to no avail. He was at the mercy of the adjutant, his pride laid bare, and the blushing persisted as he waited. The junior leaders giggled.

'Bastards,' he thought, 'I'll have their guts for garters' – a threat they had often heard but never seen carried out.

Bending slowly Mike Hartnett adjusted the trouser leg with excessive care planting a gentle tickle on the exposed Achilles tendon. It lasted for only a moment, but that was long enough; a revolution took place inside Yates. He could neither laugh nor say thank you, but prayed instead that on some dark night on Dartmoor his moment would come.

Across the square, meanwhile, the persistent knock of what sounded like a diesel engine announced the arrival of the second-in-command, Malcolm Scott, in his immaculately maintained old Humber. Out he stepped with Ralph Nye, both dressed for dinner and in earnest conversation. They had arrived early to go over a few points arising out of the recent 'Firelight Fantasy' over which Malcolm was particularly sensitive. 'That bloody bonfire extravaganza in November,' he was saying, 'it was the way the buck was passed to me that still rankles, and now we are inundated with requests from all manner of organisations that end up on my table marked 2 I/C to deal.'

It had happened like this. The officers had been called to a conference – a regular friendly affair, with coffee and walnut cake supplied by Madge Mellors of Newton Abbot helping matters along – to preview the following week's programme, when out of the blue someone drew attention to Guy Fawkes night and suggested that some improvements might be made on the previous year's effort. Alarm spread across Malcolm's face. Great files grew out of such things and usually landed on his table. He had to act quickly: 'What was wrong with last year's bonfire? Each squadron makes its own arrangements, the colonel visits all, and a prize is awarded for the best Guy.'

But Harry Rothwell, one of the squadron commanders, had seen a way of offloading some of the chores and had formed an alliance with Colin Bound, a fellow squadron commander, to push the buck upwards. Harry was on top form having received a boost to his confidence that very morning in a letter from Field Marshal Slim agreeing to his name being associated with Harry's squadron – now Slim Squadron. Colin had matched his chum's initiative with a letter to Field Marshal Alexander and was now commanding the Alexander Squadron. These two men made a formidable alliance.

Harry kicked off with: 'We should make a really big occasion of it this time and invite the whole of Newton Abbot. After all, we won't be here for Christmas and the locals have been good to us.'

'I quite agree,' chipped in Colin.

'And I disagree!' Malcolm was determined to strangle this one at birth. 'Why do we always have to get things out of proportion? There's a graduation to be thought about, and parents day – which means a hell of a lot of work – and the orderly room staff are pretty pushed already.' Warming to his case he pressed on: 'And I should like to warn everyone (nothing like a threat to dampen ardour) that if we persist in

8. Presentation of a Royal Pipe Banner to Queen's Gurkha Signals at St James's Palace.

9. Alexandra Pavey presents a bouquet to HRH the Princess Mary. (*Fred Pavey*)

10. The Union Inn in Denbury, South Devon. (*Sydney Williams*)

11. Lionel Gregory and Gurkha Major Karnasher Tamang at Garelochhead. (*Gautam Gurung*)

12. Chief Mwanachingwala, Lionel Gregory and John Mwesa. (*Alan Waters*)

overdoing things we might end up with a few locals getting burnt, and that will take some explaining.'

The colonel observed a discreet silence. Malcolm had one shot left: 'It's a positive hazard having six hundred junior leaders around a bonfire, without providing other attractions to stretch control and supervision. What do you think John?'

John Smith-Owen was the doctor. His preference for wearing fancy civilian socks with uniform necessitated occupying a chair at the back of the class to avoid the colonel's eye falling on them, and his inclination was to say as little as possible on these occasions. He had learnt his lesson from lodging a protest against the farm hobby in which Harry Rothwell had a personal interest.

The geese were Harry's particular private army and they were accustomed to marching past the medical centre before opening time every morning leaving considerable evidence of their passing for all to see – not least the doctor. One fateful morning he had telephoned the adjutant to inform him that at that very moment a 'whole battalion of Rothwell's bloody geese' were passing his front door pausing, deliberately so it seemed to him, to desecrate the entrance to what was after all the centre of health and hygiene. 'Doesn't the colonel care about such things any more?' Once started he just had to go all the way. 'As medical officer I've had enough!'

Mike Hartnett dutifully passed on the message suggesting that in future a detour behind the cookhouse might avoid unnecessary aggro to which Harry Rothwell agreed. But when John Smith-Owen arrived next morning he was to find, seated in his chair and as still as a stuffed dummy, a goose with a stethoscope dangling around its neck, glasses balanced on beak, a small white apron around its middle and a card strapped to its chest with the words 'Dr J S'O, MD. Phurr'! The goose didn't seem to mind and the junior leaders working in the medical centre saw to it that the story spread.

John Smith-Owen hadn't forgotten. 'Well,' he said, not quite sure where to go from there, 'yes, of course any event of that kind would need to be carefully planned and supervised.' It was a modest enough offering, but Harry picked it up at once.

'Exactly,' he beamed at John. 'That is why it must be done at regimental level.'

Colin Bound nodded. 'A sort of firelight fantasy,' he suggested, obviously pleased with the sound of that.

To demonstrate that he had a staff officer's grasp of what was afoot, Mike Hartnett came up with: 'That would read well on a publicity poster.'

Malcolm was furious, they were all ganging up against him. 'The trouble with adjutants and squadron commanders is that they haven't the first clue about what is involved at a higher level. You force the regiment into situations without thinking – if you can think that is! – about the consequences.'

Any further discussion had to be blocked before an irreversible decision was taken. So Malcolm made his final throw: 'Colonel, may I talk to you about this later?'

In the event, the Firelight Fantasy did take place, about 1,500 people from the town attended, and it was judged a success. The organisation and administration were superb; even the weather smiled on Malcolm's labours. But the problem for him was that having opposed the idea in the first place he could hardly take the credit for it – which went instead to his protagonists. And now, together with letters of congratulation, came requests for help in planning similar fantasies throughout the Southwest.

One of these, which could not be ignored, came from the well-heeled burghers of Bovey Tracey who were organising a county fair and thought the pipes and drums, with a team of dancers, might fill a useful spot in the programme.

The centre piece of the fair was a concrete Maltese cross and Malcolm thought this might make a useful presentation to Denbury after the event – much to the amusement of the organisers. For as it turned out, the cross was made of plasterboard washed over with cement. However, so touched were they by Malcolm's request that the committee decided to have a proper cross made and presented to the junior leaders in the name of the town and people of Bovey Tracey. A high powered delegation accompanied the cross to witness its erection in the centre of the main crossroads within the camp. And henceforth it was to become the accepted rendezvous for meetings and greetings better suited to the open air than a dreary office. Thus did providence bless the labours of a long suffering second-in-command.

The sound of trumpets brought my thoughts back to the present. The officers began to drift towards the mess. Uniforms were impressive; those entitled to wear medals wore miniatures displaying the range and nature of their military experience.

Pride and self-consciousness stalked their confidence as they wheeled bravely into the anteroom, paused briefly to pick up a sherry or a whisky and soda, and joined their comrades round the fire. Conversation grew in volume, hearts warmed, enmities were forgotten. Rank was reflected in greying hair, crowns and pips; conversation was initiated accordingly. On cue the mess sergeant reported to Malcolm as President of the Mess Committee. He in turn glanced towards the colonel and on a nod from that quarter passed the signal on.

The doors leading into the dining room were thrown open revealing two lines of trumpeters in scarlet and gold, trumpets at the ready. The first perilous notes swelled into a confident blend of harmonies; the drum major relaxed for a moment before raising his right hand to perform the best salute in the regiment. The adjutant obliged him with a wink as the officers passed through in seniority. In the darkness, above the supporting candelabra, a hundred flames swaying gently cast ghost-like images onto the flat ceiling. Reflected in the French windows the long table carried the illusion on into the distance, to other places and other comrades, and a world of memories that are forever the life of a soldier.

For me, it was not only a journey into the past, but into the future too. Six hundred pairs of young hands would tow my estate car out of Denbury, out of the army and out of Britain. Their pipes and drums would cheer me on my way down the long dusty road into the Commonwealth. As a reminder of the mission I had set myself, they had given me, carved out of Dartmoor Maple by the eight junior leaders who had been lost on the quest for Ten Tors, a set of wooden bowls with one of the following words on each: 'May Your Rice Bowl Never Be Empty.' On the eighth was a flea – the Prince of Denbury.

Dinner was over, the health of Her Majesty toasted. Relieved of his more formal duties Malcolm was reviewing the events of the past few years, much as I have been doing, concluding with these words: 'And when you return there will always be a warm welcome awaiting you at Denbury.'

I did return, after ten years, to find the old camp desolate, the junior leaders gone. Denbury had been sold to the highest bidder to become one of Her Majesty's prisons. The Denbury Cross was nowhere in evidence.

I called at the Union Inn. John Spence was now in charge, and he told me that it had been removed to Dartmoor where it remains today, standing on the hill above Okehampton at the start to Ten Tors, as a permanent reminder of the young leaders who opened up those ancient moorlands to the spirit of adventure 'in an overcrowded and highly regulated island'. Fortified with a ploughman's lunch and a bowlful of nostalgia I sat at John Spence's hospitable bar and wrote an article for the *Western Morning News*. It was published on the 28th of May, 1973 and headlined 'The Denbury Dream'.

And that was the original title of this chapter. But a dream come true is reality, so I settled instead for the Denbury Story, and in the years to come the Union will still be able to claim that 'it all began here'.

(That tens of thousands have since answered the call of Ten Tors must be the measure of that dream, and the pioneering spirit of those junior leaders – though they would not have been aware of it at the time – that made it come true. Numbers applying to take part grow year on year, but the total, in any one year, is limited to 2,400 for safety reasons and provision is made for young people with disabilities to be included. The founders still celebrate the spirit of adventure in a new establishment called the Ten Tors Inn in Kingsteignton.

According to Sydney Williams, one time teacher in Newton Abbot and master of Carvean (Cornish for a little manor on the hill) who took to Ten Tors like an eagle to the air – as he did Comex when he joined me on four expeditions – followed by his pupils and his family as they grew up (just as so many other families in the Southwest have done) the Ten Tors Inn began life in what was called the Five Ways Filling Station ('fuel and not beer') set in three and a half acres of moorland with beautiful views all round. It was built in 1953 with two semi-detached houses.

The houses were later turned into a transport café, but the filling station remained. In 1977, the whole complex was purchased by 'a devious managing director' on behalf of the South Devon Farmers; but he moved on to prison, for fraud, leaving the estate in the hands of receivers. It lay idle for three years – 'going to seed like Denbury in the early days' – providing a seasonal habitat for gypsies in transit to and from the west country. At this point, a young man by the name of Chris Stockman and his wife took the risk to fulfil a childhood dream – which is now the popular and successful Ten Tors Inn. In due course they sold out to Chris and Helen Edwards.)

CHAPTER FOUR

BETWEEN EAST AND WEST

The long dusty road

(Picked out by camels and donkeys centuries ago, the Asian Highway starts at the border town of Bazagan on the Iranian side of the Turkish-Iranian frontier, within sight of Mount Ararat. This ancient highway serves over a thousand million people and was once known as the silk route (more recently dubbed the long dusty road) operating between Venice and Hanchow.

Wise men, holy men, conquerors and rogues have pursued their ambitions from one end to the other, war has disrupted progress, frontiers have been moved. Engineers with bulldozers, and gangs of labourers with picks and shovels, have had to make way for the more pressing needs of tanks and soldiers with guns.)

Travelling alone on the Asian Highway can be a salutary experience, concentrating the mind and focusing the attention on ordinary, everyday values: words, gestures and actions that uplift the spirits and kindle afresh love and respect for one's fellow human beings.

I was destined to travel this road many times and to experience the kindness and hospitality of the people whose lives are inextricably bound up with it. The stories they have to tell would fill many volumes, and in some instances they already have. But my aim is simple: to draw attention to some of the men I was privileged to meet; men whose enthusiasm fired my own and made possible the Commonwealth Expeditions that were to follow. And although I have recounted some of these experiences elsewhere, it is not irrelevant to refresh the memory here.

In eastern Turkey, for example, the driver of a snow plough, Hassan by name, helped me over the snow-covered mountain of Kop despite considerable inconvenience to himself. Those who know that part of the world would know also that there is no way up or down Kop when the snow falls. 'If there is to be peace in the world,' Hassan said, as we talked for a while before he encouraged me to be on my way before conditions got worse, 'man must learn to call his friend brother; and to find our brothers we must return to the ancient landroutes that made us what we are before the aeroplane came.'

In token of appreciation I gave him a multi-coloured balaclava – one I used to wear when serving with the junior leaders at Denbury – which he immediately put to use, replacing the woollen scarf wrapped around his head. My last sight of him was through the driving mirror, waving me on with a broad smile of farewell.

Driving in the opposite direction a few months later, I had passed Ararat and was heading for the Tahir Pass with chains clanking heavily about my wheels when a peasant signalled me to stop and asked for a lift. He settled down comfortably and looked round the car but didn't touch anything. We had travelled for some time and were approaching a village when my friend indicated he would like to be set down. I stopped and got out with him to go through the formalities of leave taking.

One can thumb a lift in Turkey much the same as anywhere else, but there is a difference: in Turkey a driver will always stop, and it is customary to pay for a lift.

So when I declined his offer of payment he indicated that I should wait, ran down to the village and returned accompanied by an older man who may have been his father. A small boy followed carrying a brass tray with glasses and tea. Together they set to work on my snow chains and when these had been fixed to their satisfaction, we drank tea together. 'Tamam!' said the older man with the friendliest of smiles as he bowed towards me with his hand on his chest, while at the same time placing the rug he had been carrying on his shoulder on the passenger seat. He was repaying a small kindness, as honour demanded, with a present that had to be accepted.

When it snows in Turkey it is more than likely to be snowing in Iran. My inclination was to travel from Tabriz to Tehran by night; but at the time the road was little more than a dirt track, over four hundred miles of it, and would now be covered with snow all the way. So I pulled into the nearest hotel for a night's shelter and there met Touradj Kenani. He spoke excellent English, had recently completed a degree course at Tehran University and was now apprenticed to the Iranian National Tourist Organisation. I suggested light-heartedly that he was more than welcome to practise on me! Touradj had come to Tabriz in an INTO car so we arranged to travel back to Tehran in convoy, which was just as well because without his help, and willing hands to give us a push when all other means of progress failed, we would not have made it. The journey took three days and remains in my memory wedded to Iranian Reisling No 12, a local wine to which I was introduced as a suitable accompaniment to chello kabab.

In Tehran he insisted I stay with his family because his parents would not approve of a friend staying in an hotel – I had only known him five days – and besides, his wife was a good cook. In fact we did become firm friends and by a stroke of good fortune he was made responsible for the safe passage of all eight Commonwealth Expeditions hosted en route by the Government of Iran.

As a parting gift he gave me a beautifully bound volume of *The Philosophy Behind the Revolution* by the late Shah of Iran. It has been overtaken by events, but is still of interest as a prelude to the upheavals that followed.

Near the border with Afghanistan, at Fariman, I met Dr Fereydoun Chameli. I was driving through the town and had stopped to buy some grapes. He was on his way home from the hospital and, out of curiosity I suppose, stopped to ask if he could help me in any way. I was in no need of any help but thought it particularly gracious of him to take an interest in a stranger. He had visited Britain and was pleased to welcome me to Iran with an invitation to lunch with his family. I was sent on my way with a supply of grapes and melons way beyond my most extravagant needs.

(When the third Commonwealth Expedition arrived at the Afghan-Iran border it was faced with an outbreak of cholera and the prospect of quarantine. The five hundred members of the expedition were led away to Fariman by Dr Fereydoun Chameli and his staff, and how beautifully the Iranians behaved! This small town in the middle of a desert evacuated the hospital and made it available exclusively to us. The towns-people provided Persian carpets to cover the floors on which we slept, and the laboratory tests were speeded up to reduce to a minimum our period of incarceration.

Our initial reaction to quarantine was hostile, our last was regret that it was all over.)

At the time it was a relatively short, but rough, journey from Fariman to the border post with Afghanistan – Torbat-e Jam on the Iranian side and Herat on the Afghan. The actual crossing was at Eslam Qalah, a bleak wilderness at the lowest point between two deserts and a thousand miles from the Khyber Pass. Here I met a young police officer, Zahir al Haq, working in the passport section. He liked the look of my car and thought he might ride with me to Herat. I did not bargain on the trunk that followed him into the car. However, in this part of the world, so long as there is physical room there is space for passengers and baggage.

Initially he was going as far as Herat, but he enjoyed my company 'too much' and decided to accompany me all the way to Kabul – which was just as well. About thirty kilometres from Kandahar the car ran out of fuel; but I had, or thought I had, a spare tin of Super Shell bought in Austria. What I had failed to notice were the words 'motor oil' in small black letters. Too late, my policeman friend had tipped the lot into the tank, and when I explained what had happened he just roared with laughter. 'Now' he said, 'I will put on my hat and use my power to help you. The first lorry will do everything for us.'

It was a clear night, the silence of the desert was all around us and a million stars shone brightly in a black sky. It was the night before the new moon, the eve of Eid, and cold too. To pass the time my friend began to teach me an Afghan dance, but we had not progressed far before the first truck arrived and the sight of Zahir's hat brought it to a halt. The driver was informed that we would like the tank drained and refuelled with a gallon of petrol.

'Did you attempt to start the car?' he asked immediately. Reassured on that point, the driver crawled under the car and the draining began. To help matters along the driver's mate removed the petrol cap and blew into the tank – the full force of this initiative finding its target and bringing forth a great roar from the unfortunate man trapped underneath. I fully expected him to be very angry, even to assault his co-driver when he emerged covered in oil, but not a bit of it: he joined in the laughter as though it was a huge joke, and, depositing a hearty slap on his mate's back, proceeded to clear the oil out of his eyes and mouth. The tank was duly drained and flushed, a gallon of petrol added, and we were ready to go. When I raised the question of some kind of remuneration for services rendered, Zahir shook his head, 'No, they are happy to help you, and I have told them to take the oil in exchange for the petrol.'

We drove on to the old rest house in Kandahar, now called Hotel Kandahar. Zahir had been fasting since sunrise and nursed his appetite with promises of a large helping of pilau but, alas, it was too late, the cooking pots were cold and the kitchen empty. He sat on the bed next to mine with a disconsolate expression drained of its earlier enthusiasm.

I produced my camp stove, a jar of Ovaltine, heather honey, a tin of bully beef and a packet of biscuits. Zahir was fascinated. 'We are friends,' he cried, and setting to, morale completely restored, pronounced the coffee good. I didn't bother to explain. When I awoke, shortly before five o'clock, Zahir was already inspecting a breakfast of omelette and tea which he had organised. I enjoyed his company all the way to Kabul.

Returning just before Christmas, I ran into very heavy snow a few miles beyond

Herat. In fact the countryside was white as far as the eye could see leaving a line of telephone poles as the sole means of orientation. As if from nowhere a donkey appeared, staggering under the weight of a rider twice its size. 'Follow me,' he said. 'Don't be afraid, the donkey will keep to the centre of the road.' For more than an hour I followed that donkey through the snow; and it was as sure footed as though it had a built-in compass. The scene was almost biblical, nothing else moved. Gradually the road rose above the surrounding snow and I was able to make my way without further help.

At Eslam Qalah, Zahir was waiting, and when I told him about the donkey he was delighted. 'In Afghanistan, donkey is very special animal,' there was a significant pause followed by: 'Like good Afghan it also helps you.' And not only in Afghanistan, all over the Middle East there are donkeys galore, and while one associates camels with deserts, donkeys are to be found where the camel tracks end, their status rising all the way to Jerusalem.

I was heading in that general direction and stopped for the night in a hotel called Baron, in Aleppo, run by an Armenian by the name of Coco and his Scottish wife. Syria had just extricated itself from the United Arab Republic and an Egyptian diplomat absconding from his embassy had alarmed the authorities sufficiently to cut Aleppo off from Damascus. Only one man had the influence to secure an exit permit for anyone wishing to leave Aleppo, and that man was Coco. How he did it one would never know, but I got my permit and left with the good advice that if I wanted to cross the Syrian desert the best course would be to drive south to a place called Douma, just north of Damascus, then turn east and set my compass for Baghdad.

Baghdad was then General Kassim's capital. The bridge across the Tigris was shining new and the largest poster I had ever seen in my life informed me that this was the 'cradle of civilisation'. However, it was not until I met Hashim Abdullah Taha, head of many government organisations in Iraq including the equivalent of the AA in Britain, that I got a closer look at that cradle. He promised me that if a Commonwealth Expedition were to include Iraq in its itinerary, whether it approached from Turkey, Syria or Iran, and no matter what the state of relations with those countries, there would be a warm welcome in Baghdad.

(The sixth Commonwealth Expedition, of two hundred men and women from Britain and Canada, did in fact approach Iraq via Midyat and Zakhu (Kurdistan), and depart via Basra and the no man's land between Iraq and Iran attended all the way by Hashim's men.

The eighth expedition was even bigger, consisting of three hundred members mounted in ten silver vehicles in honour of Her Majesty's jubilee. That it was allowed to cross the Syrian desert by moonlight, escorted by outriders from the outskirts of Baghdad to a special camp on the banks of the Tigris and welcomed with a civic reception, was not only a gesture of friendship but a perfect example of hospitality in an ancient civilisation.

None of this would have been possible without the patient and painstaking efforts of my good friend Hashim Abdullah Taha.

'I very much admire your "silver train",' he said before we parted company. And the last message I got from him, broadcast over the intercom as the convoy moved across the desert towards Iran, was as typical: 'Relations between governments are

one thing, between people quite another. You are always welcome. Enjoy your stay in Iran and God go with you.')

Baluchistan

The southern route through the Great Sand Desert of Iran comes out at Quetta, in Baluchistan, the most western province of Pakistan. And anyone who knows Quetta knows St Francis School; not so much the school, perhaps, as the man who built it in the thirties out of the rubble of an earthquake, and masterminded its operation for forty years. His name is Joshua Sterk, a Franciscan priest who embodies all the qualities of his order in everything he says or does: goodness, kindness, unselfishness, consideration and humour. Once, when I credited him with some of these qualities, he laughed out loud and assured me that I was wrong on every count.

I first met him when I came out of the desert one evening and drove into his school, because it seemed the most obvious thing to do. I was a stranger and needed a little information on the road ahead and the difficulties I was likely to encounter.

(Over forty years, many others have needed a lot more information and got it from Joshua as he helped them on their way to the top of their professions. Today, the ex-pupils of St Francis School occupy most if not all the important posts in Quetta, while Joshua himself serves his Maker in a poor parish in Karachi.

There was always a hot bath and a place to sleep in his school, and not only for me but for the hundreds who later passed through Quetta as part of the eight Commonwealth Expeditions representing Britain, Canada, Pakistan, India, Sri Lanka, Malaysia and Singapore. Whenever he heard we were coming he would order the boilers stoked, doing much of the stoking himself, and offer everyone a hot bath on arrival. And to appreciate fully that kind of hospitality one must first travel twelve hundred miles in a desert. 'Welcome brother, the water is hot,' is not the initial greeting one might expect from a friend, but, in the circumstances, what a greeting it was! The brother part of it was an instinctive adaptation of the traditional use of 'bhai' (respected brother) common in India and Pakistan.

For all his help and kindness over the years, Joshua was awarded a Green Pennant. He was ill at the time and could not receive it in person when the awards were made by Kenneth Kaunda at State House in Lusaka, as his letter from St Anthony's Church, Karachi, explains.

'I have been in hospital with a massive infection in my leg and have to be very careful, and do a lot of resting. Things were rather low but, in this gloom, whence did a little ray of sunshine come? From the good old Commonwealth Expedition. How well I recall the first expedition nosing into the Grammar School.

We enjoyed having you stay in the school. Do I get the honour of a Green Pennant for having you as my guests? For an honour it is, and I am proud of it, and show it off to anyone stepping into my room.

It is a pity you are unknown in Karachi. I wish I could invite you here to show them. But you are not coming to Pakistan any more, and I am only a poor parish priest with not enough showers! But if Pakistan rejoins the Commonwealth, you must come. We will find a place and showers.

I thank you for the honour you do me with this Green Pennant. The boys in the

School always remembered, and now they have grown up they will still remember. When they come and see me I will show them the sign of your appreciation, which is for them too.

Thank you once more. I am not a very good thanker; but what can a man say more?')

Near Quetta, my radiator sprung a leak and I was in desperate need of a small quantity of water to keep the engine topped up for the rest of the journey. It was after sunset and dark. Out of the gloom a tall figure appeared dressed in those flowing garments that help to keep the body cool and healthy, and he wore a beard. I spoke Urdu tolerably well and explained my predicament. Without a word, he withdrew to his house, a mud hut standing alone in that vast expanse of desert, and returned with a bucket full of water. It was more than generous, considering the limited supply he received once a week from what must be the loneliest outpost in the world, Nokundi, about twenty miles away. I thanked him profusely and asked if there was any way in which I could help him. 'How can you help me,' he smiled, 'when God has already blessed me with the opportunity of helping you.'

Apart from the well-known film, *Northwest Frontier*, starring Kenneth More and the incomparable engine driver Gupta, not a great deal has been written about the exploits of the British-Indian Army in the tribal territory through which invading armies descended into the Indus valley. The points of entry – the Bolan Pass near Quetta and the Khyber Pass between Peshawar and Jalalabad – rightly have a special place in Vincent Smith's *History of India.*

(The third and largest Commonwealth Expedition chose the Khyber route and camped on the pass under the watchful eyes of hospitable tribesmen. The fifth and sixth followed the same route as those earlier invaders through the Bolan, camping first at Jacobabad, claimed to be the hottest place in the world, and then near Multan – one time punishment station for British regiments serving in India! – on the way to Lahore.)

As I approached the Bolan Pass, night had already fallen and the air was filled with a great noise. It had range and depth, a great chorus of noises, similar yet different. A bright moon touched the surface of the road winding its way into the valleys beyond, and it was alive – alive with sheep moving to summer quarters.

It was two o'clock in the morning when I finally bade farewell to the sheep and pulled in to a small clearing before a tea shop, or *dhaba*. It was built of bamboo with a thatched roof, and erected on a brick platform painted white to ward off ants. All was quiet within, but the faintest chink of light from a hurricane lamp encouraged me to knock on the door.

'Who's that?' came the sleepy voice.

I asked if hot tea and and some food might be available.

'Why not?' The wick was turned up, a few quick orders brought two others to their feet and the door was thrown open. It was made of wood, perhaps for better protection. Conversation followed the usual pattern about health and fortune and the purpose of my journey. When I mentioned the Commonwealth Expedition there was instant enthusiasm and extravagant promises poured forth. I was wise enough to know that these were expressions of genuine goodwill well beyond the means of my friends on the road. But what they could do to help they would, and judging by the first instalment of chicken, vegetables, chapaties, hot milk and the offer of a charpoy to sleep on, this little dhaba on the road to Lahore was unlikely to let Pakistan down!

At six o'clock sharp a wooden tray with a cracked china tea pot, a cup and saucer with pretty pink flowers, a brass mug with milk and a small clay pot of sugar, all neatly arranged was placed beside me. I asked him how much I owed for the night's board and lodging and he replied with a smile, using words I was to hear time and again: 'Kuchh parva nahin sahib,' meaning, 'It does not matter sir.'

I asked him if he would accept a box of lavender soap as a gift. 'If it will please you,' he replied.

Kipling's country

One of the tasks I had set myself was to explore the cross country route through the Sulaiman Range from Quetta to Multan via Loralai and Dera Ghazi Khan. It was a dirt road through tribal territory, but in Loralai (once the home of famous British regiments) I found an excellent rest house near a deserted barracks.

Naik (Corporal) Mohammad Umar, late of the Baluch Regiment, was in charge. His son and the assistant caretaker, together with the sweeper – whose main interest was football – and the night watchman, introduced as the captain and who turned out to be captain of the Loralai football team, had been watching a British Information film of an English cup final and wanted very much to talk about it. It was a pleasant way to spend an hour with men more interested in us than our interest in them merits. At dawn they were all present to see me off.

I had an appointment to keep in Rawalpindi, one time capital of Pakistan, and on arrival treated myself to a night in Flashman's Hotel on the Mall. As I approached my room in the annexe, a Kashmiri salesman cornered me. He was pushing a bicycle with a heavy load strapped on the carrier.

'Please buy something,' he pleaded. I had little time, didn't want anything, and told him so. 'Just look sir,' he went on, 'what good to make things if people don't see?' He had me there, so I invited him to come in and show me his things while I changed, repeating firmly that I did not want anything.

'OK, OK, sir.' In a trice the floor was covered with shawls. To my eye they were all beautiful. 'Which one you like best sir?' he asked, and I was trapped. It was a question that could not be ignored, so I pointed to a black shawl with pretty patterns in silver thread.

'Take it,' he cried. 'This is present from me.' He knew of course that I would not accept such a present without paying for it.

'How much?' I asked.

'Two hundred rupees sir, but no need to pay. It is present sir.' I gave him the money and he gazed at it for a while.

'You are good gentleman sir. Please sir, you come and take tea with my family tomorrow.' And I did, before departing for Lahore and India.

Lahore has not forgotten Kipling. The seat he used when editor of the *Civil and Military Gazette* is carefully preserved in its old offices on the Mall Road where Kim's gun occupies a place of honour. But my meeting was with Mohammad Saleem, owner and principal mechanic of a small garage off the Mall Road.

I had known his father, Mohammad Hussain, an ex Indian army soldier who had set up shop after the Second World War. Following his death, the elder brother Aslam moved on leaving Saleem in charge, and in his house there was always a bed for me. Only once did I dare to stay at the Intercontinental, and when Saleem heard of this he arrived hotfoot to tell me there would be a revolution in the house if I failed to change my abode.

(His personal responsibility for the Commonwealth Expeditions was to ensure that all the vehicles – on one occasion there were as many as twenty-one – were thoroughly inspected and serviced by the expedition's own mechanics, but under his supervision. From childhood he had learned all about engines: he loved them, understood them and cared for them.

With the approval of the Pakistan government, Saleem was allowed to represent his country on the seventh expedition as chief mechanic, and he was good, not only at looking after the vehicles but at badminton, a game he introduced among the drivers and mechanics to while away the off-duty hours with equipment imported from his home town. Unfortunately, relations between Pakistan and India had deteriorated into open hostility, and Saleem was not admitted across the frontier with the rest of us. But when we returned, two months later, he had already arrived at the border post on his motorcycle, his wife riding pillion, with a souvenir box of matches for every single member. These had been specially made in the expedition's colours of green and gold, and printed on top were the words, 'Welcome to Pakistan, the Seventh Commonwealth Expedition'.)

The river doesn't want a bridge

Jawaharlal Nehru once reminded me that it takes a lifetime to learn all there is to know about India. It has taken Britain more than two centuries, and the lesson is by no means over. My own learning process began with the people I met, whose opinions I learned to value, and on whose friendship I came to rely.

On one occasion I was obliged to embark on the river steamer *Chetla* for the journey from Muzaffarpur to Patna where the muddy waters of the Ganges flow through a flat, barren landscape. I sat on a bench on the upper deck and an elderly gentleman who had been the librarian of the government library at Patna sat beside me.

'Will you join me?' he asked, offering some grapes from a piece of newspaper.

Inevitably, we began talking about the Commonwealth: 'You must come and speak in Patna,' he said. 'We have a very big field there; at least a hundred and twenty thousand people can be accommodated.' When I assured him that I had no such ambitions, he replied: 'Why not? Other people must go and find out about the moon, but we should concentrate on making this planet a better place.' He reflected on that statement for a moment, as the steamer chugged along slowly down stream. I said nothing. Then, and maybe with those thousands in mind, he raised his voice a little: 'The head of the Commonwealth is a beautiful lady and she is in London; but the heart of the Commonwealth is here,' he embraced the whole of India in a sweeping gesture, 'no other place.'

There were many encounters to follow. I once asked a bullockcart driver if he would stop while I took a photograph. He was moving at about three miles an hour on the Grand Trunk Road about fifteen miles from Delhi and had been singing happily to himself until I spoke when, with a broad grin, he informed me that he would be late getting to Delhi. I asked him if five rupees would serve as adequate compensation. 'O yes,' he said cheerfully, and reined in his bulls. He then proceeded to retie his turban and adopt a more striking pose for the photograph. Any thoughts about delay in getting to Delhi were forgotten as he told me about his daily travels from one village to another, some ten miles apart. 'Sahib,' he said, 'if you are considering to send me copy of photograph, it is better to send two, one to each place, so that at least one will fall into right hands.'

The little shops in India could give the rest of the world a few useful lessons in enthusiasm, courtesy and salesmanship. But the technique that lies at the heart of a centuries-old culture is not easily transplanted, nor does it always thrive in foreign soil.

Noticing my interest in the bales of coloured cottons stacked high in his little shop on Janpath, the nearest thing to a high street in New Delhi, a shopkeeper invited me to 'take a cup of tea', making room on the wooden platform on which he squatted, resting against a bolster, so that I could join him. He was critical of the government: 'These people know only how to take money.' But when I responded by talking about the goodwill and the hospitality I had encountered he seemed pleased; and the more he criticised his country's shortcomings, the more I reminded him of its achievements – including the fact that the new Commonwealth was born in India. 'That is no doubt true,' he said, 'so we must do something.'

That 'something' was not meant to be anything in particular, so I refrained from asking what he thought ought to be done and instead pointed to the limitless beauty and good humour that attracted visitors to India, emphasising that it was for the Indians themselves to deal with the ugly and the bad. 'O yes,' he replied instantly, 'we must do like this,' and promptly switched tack: 'How is Her Majesty?' It was a question to which he neither expected nor wanted an answer, and after a while announced quite simply: 'She is very nice lady.' India is an ageless country; questions and answers, however illuminating, are much less important than attitudes. So I changed the subject quickly and asked him about his business and the economy in general. 'O, now you are asking; it is so bad sir, it is nearly bloody! But I am so happy you came to our India. You are like my own family member.'

Two days later, attempting to cross the Nabada river near Nagpur, I twice came to a dead end. There was a lot of water but no bridge. And the third time was not lucky either; there was a bridge right enough, concrete and complete but for a single span. The impulse in such circumstances is to toy with the possibility of having a go at flying over, but wiser counsels usually prevail. In my case, the wiser counsel appeared in the form of one Balram. He was a little man, very dark, dressed in loin cloth and turban which is not merely a colourful form of headdress, worn to stave off the adverse effects of the sun; it is frequently used as duster, towel, bed sheet, towing-rope and carrier bag, and is stored on the head for convenience. Balram had come to inform me that the bridge had been like this for two years. But why I asked.

'Because the river doesn't want a bridge here,' he replied.

'Have you told the authorities?'

'No,' he said. 'If I tell them they will catch me by the ear' (the inference being some kind of punishment), 'but they cannot catch the river by the ear, it hasn't got one,' he laughed.

For a few rupees per head, thirty volunteers were recruited to construct a raft and ferry me across. Ferrying meant that they got into the water and propelled the raft, and although Balram had suggested that I should sit in the car I decided to join him in the water. That gesture must have forged a bond between us because on reaching the far bank he asked if he might accompany me as far as Nagpur, to visit his brother who owned a tea shop there.

(A few years on, the seventh Commonwealth Expedition came to the same place. The bridge was still incomplete, but there was a ferry of sorts in operation. I asked after Balram and was told he was no longer around. But in his brother's tea shop I found him, and he recognised me at once. Clearly, I was a brother too.)

Chinnu

Arriving in Ooty, the turnaround point in my travels, was a profound experience. I had known the little town as a child of the Empire and had now returned as a man of the Commonwealth to honour the memory of those years.

Comparisons are invidious, but the place did seem a little tired, and perhaps overcrowded, although the hills I loved were still there and the people just as cheerful. The ghosts of the past rose up before me, I could feel the pulse of Ooty in my veins but resolved to rediscover the Eden of my youth through the eyes of my hosts.

A small figure seated among the arum lilies that border the Ooty lake caught my attention. He was in deep concentration with his fishing rod thrust out in front of him and protected from the midday sun by a khaki topi. I slowed down instinctively and he looked up, raising his hat as he did so, and I waved back with a cheery 'hello, having any luck?'

'Not bad,' he said, and I then asked him if he could direct me to Anandagiri.

'Straight on, beyond the racecourse, you can't miss it. But wait a minute, I'll come with you,' he said. I opened the door to let him in and we drove on together. It had crossed my mind at the time that the reflection of his rod on the water would frighten away the fish and when I put that observation to him he just smiled and said: 'There are enough carp in the lake prepared to commit suicide.'

His name was Denis Dique and his love of fishing came second only to his lifelong interest in railways; his favourite spot on the lake could have had something to do with its proximity to the railway line which made him feel completely at home. I grew to like this man and admired his quiet, unassuming manner, and the way in which he supported his wife, Rowena, who ran the YWCA at Anandagiri where I was to meet a character by the name of Chinnu. More about him in a moment.

Rowena had written to say that the Queen's Jubilee Commonwealth Expedition – involving some three hundred people from Britain, Canada, India and Singapore – would find a ready welcome at Anandagiri if we could make it to Ooty. And not only that; she thought it might be possible to organise a Silver Jubilee Ball in honour of the event, and had already been in touch with the Military Staff College in Wellington (a few miles down the road) catering for officers from all over the Commonwealth. It seemed an entirely desirable proposal, and one well worth a journey of a little over fifteen thousand miles.

(The ball did take place – preceded by an impromptu entertainment by members of the expedition – and was a huge success; so much so that, in the euphoria of the morning after, a telegram was despatched to Buckingham Palace.

'Anandagiri Ootacamund 9 April 1977. Please convey to His Royal Highness the Duke of Edinburgh that the Commonwealth Expedition Comex 8 arrived in Ooty on the appointed date to celebrate Her Majesty's Silver Jubilee at the opening of the Ooty season. We send loyal greetings to Her Majesty coupled with the warmest good wishes of our hosts in this beautiful town in the Nilgiri Hills.'

The Telegraph Traffic Supervisor, V. Pichai, insisted on appending his signature to the telegram and his own hand transmitted it. Hugh Carson and Mariappa and Anthony Nayagam would have approved of that.)

It was in the kitchen that I met the entire staff of Anandagiri, and chief among them Chinnu: short and stockily built, with a balding head and bright anxious eyes. He was dark skinned and belonged to that group of Tamil people (Dravidians) who seldom, if ever, leave the south of India. For him the rainbow settled in Madras, the capital of his dreams, and if there was a world beyond that horizon it was not for him. Generations of his family had worked for and with the East India Company – the John Company as it was called. He was a cook, like his father and grandfather before him, and was content with his lot.

But he had heard about London, where the 'King Emperor' lived, and his most prized possession was a manually operated mincing machine, made in London, with the hallmark of its origins stamped on the handle. The diameter across the top was exactly four and a half inches – a figure fixed in his mind from the teachings of the head cooks before him and his earliest experiences in the kitchen – which was important because four and a half inches meant perfection, and only London could produce such a machine. At least that was Chinnu's view of the matter and he would not exchange it for any other type, electric or otherwise. To him a vintage mincing machine and a vintage Rolls Royce belonged in the same class and commanded the same respect.

With the coming of Indian independence, many of the families Chinnu and his sisters (Danam and Anthonyamah) worked for returned to their native Britain. Circumstances changed, opportunities for people like Chinnu grew fewer. The combination of climate and a British way of life, had spawned Ooty's claim to first place among the hill stations of India. And the list of those who had played some part in the discovery, growth and distinction of Ooty as an oasis of enduring charm and tranquillity – starting with John Sullivan, in 1819 – would be endless.

But times were changing; the old sparkle, as vivid in my memory as the scent of eucalyptus, had already begun to fade. The eucalyptus trees themselves had been cut down to keep pace with twentieth-century progress. Wren Bennett's, Bailey Brothers and D. R. Davis had served their purpose and gone; there were many more schools, and hotels had proliferated. And yet, the good humour that characterised the town, from the vegetablee stalls in the market to the comfortable rooms of the Ooty Club, lingered on in a faint echo of the past. The people who had come to live in Ooty had together created something of which future generations in both Britain and India could justly be proud.

There was no master plan for nature had already taken care of that; the achievement belonged equally to all, and Chinnu was one of them. With men like him around, Ooty would remain Ooty despite its full name, 'Ootacamund', falling victim to the influence of politics.

(According to Hobson-Jobson (1886) Ootacamund itself is 'a corruption of the Badaga name of the site of Stone House' (the first European house erected in Ooty and perhaps by John Sullivan) 'properly Hottaga-mund or Ottagaimundu'. The latter meaning: Ottai (from the Canarese for dwarf bamboo), Kai (from the Tamil for fruit) and Mundu (for a Toda village). Coming from a background like that Ooty is an inspired compromise satisfying all tastes.)

The climate offers a variety of frosty nights, bright sunny days and clear blue skies. The mild scent of eucalyptus still permeates the air. The rains come in their season, falling like sheets of silver and drawing the Nilgiris within the influence of the southwest monsoon. Blending with the misty blue of eucalyptus trees and the earthy fragrance of potato fields, it is a time of dramatic change.

Landslides, inevitable along the thirty odd miles of mountain railway winding its way up from Mettupalaiyam, often reduce the speed of the Nilgiri Express from fifteen miles an hour to the pace at which work gangs, each one numbered according to location, can clear the way. Children, young and old, may be seen to dismount and race ahead to meet the train at the next station; and if, inadvertently, it should happen to out-distance them, the driver could always make an unscheduled stop.

On a raised platform at the front of the first carriage (the little engine usually pushes on the way up) the guard occupies a place of special importance. Without a signal from him there could be no movement forwards or backwards: his flags alone, one green and one red, had the power to initiate this. Four carriages down the driver waits for him and never fails to acknowledge the extended arm with an appropriate whistle – twice when taking off at speed, and once when slowing down.

The arrival at Coonoor is a moment for celebration. It is a daily event not to be missed if one has the time, and most have. Families and friends turn out in strength; relatives of the crew are there to welcome them home after another epic journey from the heat of the plains. Such goings-on attract onlookers who have no business being there at all other than curiosity, and refreshment trolleys (a board suspended between two bicycle wheels) move into position with cries of tea, coffee, and an assortment of local delicacies sufficient to demonstrate the limitless ingenuity of Indian hospitality. They do a roaring trade.

From Coonoor the gradient is less steep, the pace quickens, and all being well the Nilgiri Express pulls in to Ooty a little over half an hour later.

Chinnu was born and bred here. While others might contrast Ooty with exotic places in divers corners of the world, to him it was a world complete in itself. His outside interests were confined within the hills that surrounded the town, and he was grateful for the blessings God had bestowed on him. Chinnu knew his Ooty, most of which could be explored in a single day if one had the inclination and the energy. As a boy he would often make his way to the golf course on the off chance of being engaged as a caddy, and always in the hope of witnessing a defenceless little white ball or two despatched into a watery grave in any one of many trout streams – later to be retrieved as a small bonus for himself.

The giant Kandal Cross, watching over the downs from its own lonely hill, was a place of pilgrimage for as long as he could remember. 'When peoples go to Kandal Cross, God will give some good blessing sar,' was how Chinnu put it.

When it came to Dodabetta, the highest point in the Nilgiri Hills, Chinnu was in no doubt that it had to be climbed in order 'to see the God's place sar'. The most commanding site in Ooty had to be God's place.

But working as head cook at Anandagiri, a large country house that had once been a brewery, Chinnu had little time and, with advancing years, less drive for the adventurous pursuits of his youth. So he settled for the more sedentary activities nearer home. After a long day's work, he would slip on his shoes, the laces of which were never tied, wrap a warm muffler around his neck and set off down the drive. The main gate opened onto a road skirting the racecourse and linking Anandagiri with the main bus stand, the railway station, and the market – in that order moving clockwise. If in the mood for a leisurely walk he would follow the road round; if thirst urged more urgent action he would climb over the railings and walk across the racecourse. In either event the destination was a toddy shop which offered solace and comfort among friends. Once inside those warm and congenial surroundings, he would share a bottle or two of toddy with them before returning to his kitchen, all within the space of an hour and a half.

The only difference one noticed in Chinnu during the outward and homeward journeys was that on the way out he wore a solemn and purposeful expression, whereas on the way home he presented the more benign countenance of a man well content with life, beaming goodwill in all directions. And his work never suffered; indeed, as guests at Anandagiri would readily testify, the artistry was enhanced by the inspirational effects of the humble toddy. The chutney he prepared immediately on returning to the kitchen bore ample witness to the truth of this: a mixture of purple onions, coriander leaves, tomatoes, a little lemon perhaps, and a sprinkling of sugar. It was the speciality of the house and the quality never varied. It transformed whatever happened to be on the menu, however dull or unappetising, into something special. As we were friends, a bowlful of the stuff was always placed at my elbow, attracting jealous glances from those less fortunate.

I once asked Chinnu what he enjoyed most.

'Season time sar; then big, big people is coming and they make horse racing here sar, and it is very nice, we can see from Anandagiri sar.'

'Do you ever go to the races yourself Chinnu?' I asked.

'No sar, we poor peoples cannot go there. But we can see very nicely from here wonly.'

'What else do you look forward to?'

Without a moment's hesitation came the answer: 'Christmas time sar. Ooty that time very cold, ice yevery morning on grass. Yeverything white sar, and look very nice. Madam is give all servants one new dress and I getting long coat with one towser. Childrens get many things and we all going to midnight mass in Saint Mary Church sar. This is very nice time sar.'

'What about your daily visits to the toddy shop?' I asked. He smiled and I thought I detected the faintest sign of guilt.

'I'm not too much drinking sar,' he explained. 'In toddy shop I meet one my good friend and we can talk sar.'

'Have you known him long?'

'All the life sar. His name Rangaswami sar. He live in Mettupalaiyam, but sometime he will come Ooty and we meeting sar.'

'And what do you talk about?'

'Rangaswami tell many story sar. His family, big family sar; all toddy tapping people sar. But Rangaswami now teacher in Saint Anthony Children School sar, on Kalar Road, some two three mile from Mettupalaiyam.'

'How did he come to be a teacher?' I asked.

Chinnu laughed. 'It is long story sar. When he is toddy tapping sar, yevery evening he must want put this one toddy pot on tree, on top side, under the branch sar. His brother also doing like this. Each one must be want climbing twelve tree sar.' Here he paused, obviously putting together some sort of explanation he felt might still be necessary. 'See sar, toddy tree same like coconut tree sar. Sometime very high. Yevery morning, five o'clock maybe, this pot must be take down. That time toddy very sweet sar, but same toddy evening time too much strong sar.'

Sensing no doubt that I associated his evening visits with the strength of the toddy, he laughed. 'No sar, I am not drink too much. If too much then cannot work in right way sar.'

'Tell me about Rangaswami's story,' I urged him.

'Yes sar. One day Rangaswami is going to home. It is little bit night sar. Near Bhavani river bridge on Kalar Road sar, he see this one "Rakarchi". That one devil woman sar, she have black dress, and hair is like fire sar, and she have big tongue. Rangaswami is too much fright and fainted wonly sar.'

As he weaved his way through the story, Chinnu himself became quite agitated, and it was not easy to follow every twist and turn. However, the gist of it was that Rangaswami had been warned not to go home alone after sunset because "Rakarchies" usually appeared after dark; he was further cautioned to place some coconut, coriander and a few coins in the hollow of a tree by the bridge. As added precaution, he took it upon himself to anoint the site with red ochre and lime – which seemed to have the desired effect.

One evening, however, having celebrated excessively with his friends, Rangaswami was making his way home, accompanied by a sizeable escort in jovial mood and full voice, when, on approaching the bridge, the "Rakarchi" suddenly appeared. Fortified as they were with a generous intake of the evening toddy, Rangaswami and his friends fell upon the "Rakarchi", making flesh and bone contact.

It transpired that the dreaded apparition was none other than a fellow toddy tapper who was making a good thing out of extorting a regular toll – via the hollow in the tree – from members of the public crossing the Bhavani river after sunset. The villain was roughly handled and carried off to the local police station where he was given the appropriate treatment and thrown into a cell. Well satisfied with the evening's work the group parted company returning at four o'clock the following morning to collect the toddy pots. They had much to talk about, and the story of their encounter spread, recruiting a few embellishments en route.

A few weeks later, and oblivious to time or any threat to his person, Rangaswami was making his way home when the "Rakarchi" duly appeared, right there in front of him. But this time there was no fear; on the contrary, uttering a great cry and the most insulting words that came to mind, he adopted a threatening posture and was about to attack when the apparition vanished before his eyes. That was enough for Rangaswami! Terrified, he began to run as fast as his legs would carry him, away from the bridge, away from the road. With heart pounding and knees buckling he fell to the ground, exhausted, before the steps of St Anthony's Church. Clawing his way up the steps he knocked on the door with all his strength until it opened and there, framed in the doorway, was the white robed figure of the parish priest.

The priest helped him into the church, made him comfortable and invited him to unburden himself of his troubles. He listened patiently to what Rangaswami had to say and quietly reassured him. What he had seen was probably the spirit of a poor woman who had died and been buried by her friends without prayers or blessings to help her on her way, and she had perhaps returned to plead for such help. The priest then suggested that they return together to the site where she had appeared, armed with holy water and a candle, and bless the place. To this Rangaswami readily agreed, bravely accompanying the priest.

He was instructed to light the candle and place it in the hollow of the tree while the priest sprinkled holy water around it and on the bridge, and said some prayers in a language Rangaswami could not understand. But from that day a beautiful jasmine plant began to grow at the foot of the tree, and that was reason enough to send Rangaswami back to the church on a permanent basis. He became a Christian, just like his friend Chinnu.

'So, you see sar, Rangaswami went to father's house in Saint Anthony Church wonly, and he work there long time. Then he learn to reading and writing and father make him in charge for church and to look after the peoples. Now he is also teacher for small childrens sar.'

Some days later, while I was having breakfast in the little cottage within the grounds of Anandagiri, I heard sounds of weeping and wailing coming from the direction of the servants' quarters. I went out to find Chinnu in a state of considerable distress. Placing a hand on his shoulder I asked him what was the matter. 'My wife is dieded sar.' He spoke calmly, but that he had suffered a devastating blow was evident enough. 'I don't know how to bury her sar; it costing one hundred tonty rupees sar. I got wonly tonty rupees sar.'

I could have given this good and gentle man so very much more, with little inconvenience to myself, but, in the circumstances, offered only to make up the difference, which he accepted with quiet dignity.

It was all he wanted.

(The following year I received a letter from Rowena and Dennis Dique informing me that Chinnu had died. Having had so little in this world; having asked for so little; the only request I ever had from him was for a mincing machine made in London, four and a half inches across the top.)

Jelka and Milovan

Having placed all the evidence I had collected in favour of a Commonwealth Expedition before the first Prime Minister of Independent India, Jawaharlal Nehru, I was stumped with a simple question: 'What do they think about it in Britain?' And it was His Royal Highness the Duke of Edinburgh, who provided the answer by giving his patronage to the first expedition, with the comment that, of all human institutions, the Commonwealth came nearest to the ideal of the brotherhood of man. Yet it is not the words of the great or the actions of the humble that matter so much as a common commitment at every level, and with that thought firmly in my mind I began to make my way back via Risalpur, calling on my friend Group Captain Chowdhury.

It was a brief visit, and during lunch I expressed a wish to see the valley of Swat and Malakand.

'There's a quicker way than going by road,' he said.

It was not the best time to be diving from twenty-two thousand feet in a jet trainer piloted by a young officer anxious to impress his chief, but it was done. We swept close over the valley and saw Malakand sideways on, and then did it again to get the opposite view – but not at my insistence.

Passing through Jalalabad, between the Khyber and Kabul, my thoughts turned to the Somerset Light Infantry, whose cap badge bears the name Jalalabad as a reminder of one of the most famous battles of the first Afghan War, fought to a finish in that beautiful valley on 7 April 1842. It also earned for the regiment the title of Prince Albert's.

(It was not the only battle. When the British Indian force under General Nott marched from Kandahar to Kabul, via Gazni, in the same year, to meet a similar force under General Pollock marching from Jalalabad, there had been a lot of skirmishing along the way, and they were not singing and dancing at the end of it. The Bazaar of Kabul was blown up for a start. But these were brave men, on both sides of the battle lines, which probably accounts for the warm reception accorded to the succession of Commonwealth Expeditions that covered the same ground, with the descendants of the same people.

In Kabul, my old friend Abdullah Afghan Zade had arranged base camps for the third Commonwealth Expedition at Quarga Dam (the site occupied a few years later by Russian tanks on a quite different mission) and near the old gateway into Kabul between Sher Darwaza (the Tiger's Door) and Azamai (the Sky). When one of the larger expedition vehicles required a new engine it had to be flown out before the Afghan Government had approved legislation waiving import duty on goods in transit, leaving it open for customs to levy a charge of two hundred per cent. Abdullah simply opened his safe and invited me to help myself to as many thousands of Afghanis as I needed. 'Sometime when you are passing through Kabul you can pay me back,' he said.)

The men I met on the road – and I have mentioned only a few – were like living milestones on my travels. But there were hundreds of thousands more, of all ages, who rose to the challenge of the Commonwealth Expedition and helped to make a dream come true.

Restoring old friendships may not at first sight commend itself as a subject for adventurous treatment. But a little experience can quickly alter that view, as Kenneth Kaunda put it after twenty-eight years as President of Zambia: 'The greatest adventure of all still lies in the meeting between man and man.' And the truth of that was brought home to me in what used to be Yugoslavia, at the turbulent crossroads between east and west, where I met the Croatian lawyer, Ned Ivančević, then studying in the Law Faculty at Zagreb University, and Nikola Vrbos, a postman. Nikola was, and still is, a giant among men – perhaps even a hero. Strong, proud and independent, a one time candidate for the priesthood, he settled instead for raising a family in a house on the outskirts of the town, and became landlord to a colony of thousands of bees quartered in his garden.

The three of us became close friends and it was at Ned's suggestion some years later that I set about assembling a few stories about Nikola. But first Ned.

His family hailed from Žaluznića, an obscure little village in the bleak and rugged landscape surrounding the canyons and lakes of Plitvice, between Zagreb and the Dalmatian coast. This was to become a standing joke between us because somewhere in the archives of the Imperial Royal Ministry of War in Vienna, an adventurous ancestor of mine was reported to have made his way to the governorship of Dalmatia from Ireland – via the Austrian army – in 1804 which had the effect of introducing a more personal element into our relationship!

Ned's father had come to Zagreb as a boy, went to school there and built his own house. He spent the rest of his life working on the railway before finally returning to Žaluznića to be buried in his home soil. Ned's mother continued to live in the family home to the end of her days sustained by the love and devotion of her only son.

Although relatively poor, Ned's father was a resourceful man whose mind ranged far beyond the railways he so faithfully served, and perhaps explains why his son was steered towards a university education. Ned himself summed up their situation quite simply: 'All we had to do was to work hard. It was normal, we enjoyed it and were happy. There was no envy in the family – maybe because we were too busy to notice what other people had. And my mother was always independent and proud, as she is today.' Apart from his studies, Ned was encouraged to take part in outdoor activities – skiing and water sports in particular – which led to his becoming an international rowing coach and our meeting through a mutual friend at the British Consulate-General.

I had need of a little help unravelling the criminal law in a Communist country, and Ned was just the man. He arranged for me to meet his Dean, who lectured me patiently on the latest redraft of the criminal law, drawing particular attention to the section under Abolićija which, if successfully invoked, could dismiss at a stroke the case and all prosecution against the accused. It had been used only once before in the case of Aleksander Ranković, one time Vice-President of the old Yugoslav Communist Party.

I was to make the second call on that same formula, and with equal success (an account of which was published in *Crying Drums*) thanks largely to Ned Ivančević steering me in the right direction. But that is not the point of this story.

Ned's English was limited, and my Croatian hovered above a vocabulary of about a dozen words, so he accompanied me back to Britain and learnt enough English at Cambridge to take part in the third Commonwealth Expedition – paying for his tuition and accommodation by working in the kitchen of St John's College. He certainly learnt the quickest way of washing hundreds of plates and improved his vocabulary with a generous helping of kitchen English.

When we returned to Zagreb a year later, Ned took me to visit Zalužnica. His father's sister Jelka and her husband Milovan still lived in the little house they had built for themselves out of local stone and timber. It boasted a back extension in the form of a corrugated shelter overgrown with vine. At one corner, a large box with a hole in the top and matching lid, discreetly positioned over a deep trench and screened from view, stood ready and firm to serve the convenience and comfort of visitors, as it had done since the day the house was built. There were no flies about and no unpleasant smells. The man who constructed this masterpiece was a genius, and he was none other than the proud Milovan. He even invited me to try it, and although I was unable to avail myself of the pleasure, an inspection at least was called for, which enables me to record the matter for posterity.

To Jelka and Milovan, their house was a mansion and they would not have exchanged it for the President's palace. It had two rooms and the more functional of these was the kitchen, in which all guests were received. A large wood burning stove filled half the space, and on its broad surface there was room for logs, cooking pots – the largest was even then on active service gently warming fresh milk into cheese – and a variety of other utensils each with its own place and purpose. Above, hoisted and lowered by pulley, a rail designed by Milovan took care of the washing.

The stove was the principal piece of furniture. It served as table and worktop, and it kept the house warm. Without it Jelka and Milovan would not have survived a single winter. According to Ned, the stove had moved with the Novaković family for generations – Novaković being Milovan's family name – and had come to its present resting place just before the Second World War.

In addition to the stove, there were two chairs, each adorned with a brightly coloured cushion made by Jelka, and a small corner table. There was no electricity. When I asked Ned about this, he replied that when the local government decided to install electricity Milovan refused their help because he knew they would not have the money to pay the bills. 'So they never had radio or television, and there was also no newspaper to buy. Therefore, whenever I came to visit them the first question was: "Will there be a war?" This was because they remembered very well the last one. I offered to buy them a battery radio so they could listen to these things themselves, but they declined. For one thing, they would have to find replacement batteries; but more importantly they did not want to hear all about the bad things in a world they could not influence.'

A small adjoining room could be turned into a dining room if important guests had to be entertained, and Milovan was about to put this contingency plan into operation when Ned dissuaded him by insisting that we were neither important nor guests, and came as part of the family. The room was otherwise their bedroom, and the walls were covered with holy pictures. Behind one, of the Blessed Virgin Mary and the infant Jesus, was concealed a picture of President Tito. The explanation for this was that he had brought a state pension into their lives, and with it the few basic comforts most people take for granted. So, the least they could do in return was to pray for his salvation.

Like most peasant families Jelka and Milovan made their own plum brandy, a great favourite with Milovan, and there were several bottles in a row beside the stove. But a sortie in that direction was forbidden unless authorised by Jelka, and even then limited to a glass to start the day and one before going to bed. When guests appeared, however, all restrictions were lifted and Milovan could dispense hospitality to his heart's delight.

He was also partial to the local beer, and every time he was sent on a mission to buy flour, oil or any of the other basic necessities, he would take the opportunity of calling on the village gostionica with the sole purpose, according to Milovan, of greeting his old friend the landlord with whom he shared a long-standing interest in the latest brew to come out of Plitvice. If other friends happened to turn up, and they usually did, he might be persuaded to join them in an impromptu concert of Croatian songs and, in consequence, lose count of time, which explains why whenever Milovan set forth on one of these expeditions, Jelka would warn him about the beer: 'Milovan, Milovan, save your money for the hard days,' and she always received the same reply: 'But these are the hard days.'

On one such expedition, Milovan fell victim to a glass too many and on his way home stopped by a hayrick, perhaps to relieve himself, and then decided to roll a cigarette. Ned remembers only too well the consequences of that unscheduled assignation with nature.

'Finding the going too hazardous, Milovan sat down. Above his head the stars were bright, and in his head well-hidden thoughts that nobody but God could reach. He fell asleep with the cigarette still between his lips and in due course the hay caught fire. The flames rose in a kind of celebration of Milovan's folly, but at the same time summoned the village to his assistance. Apart from a few minor burns, therefore, and the shock of waking up in flames, he was unharmed; but Milovan was convinced that he was in hell, until Jelka was brought along to reassure him. She nursed him tenderly leaving such questions as what he was doing near the hayrick, with whom, and why, for later investigation.

The story of Milovan's narrow escape from being burnt to death spread throughout the district, and there was a great deal of sympathy for him. But the police were obliged to report the matter to the criminal court; and, far from disturbing Milovan, this pleased him, because for the first time in his life he was the centre of attention. The owner of the hayrick too was pleased that no harm had come to Milovan, for after all they were friends, and what was a hayrick or two when there was so much green grass around belonging to no one in particular. The law, however, took a different view; the owner was obliged to report the matter officially and to give evidence to the effect that Milovan had been found asleep by the hayrick. But he had already warned Milovan not to mention the matter of drinking with his friends, or that he had rolled a cigarette. Others called to give similar advice, but Milovan kept his own counsel and waited for the end of the month when the circuit judge would hold court in the village school.

On the appointed day the whole village assembled. Wearing his best suit and accompanied by the anxious Jelka, also wearing her best, Milovan took his seat on the bench placed in position for the accused. It was a brave day for both of them; never before had they attracted such public interest, not even on the day they were married.

After the preliminaries, the judge asked Milovan to stand up and explain all he knew about the burning of the hayrick. There was a long pause; people waited anxiously while Milovan rehearsed his words. Then out they came: "I did it!" he said, as he looked defiantly at the judge and around the court. There were gasps of astonishment. Even the judge was taken aback. He knew perfectly well that Milovan was guilty, but expected the community to cover up for him, and for Milovan to deny all knowledge of the fire. But the accused hadn't finished.

"Having spent a little time in the gostionica with my friends, an indulgence I allow myself from time to time like all men of goodwill, I was making my way home and felt a little tired." It was an understatement guaranteed to activate a burst of laughter. The judge responded by calling for quiet, and raised his right hand. For his part Milovan sensed that he was acquitting himself well and, looking at Jelka, smiled. She was proud of him of course, and there was a big smile in her heart, but her expression remained stern to ensure that Milovan behaved himself.

"I lit my cigarette," Milovan continued, "and was enjoying the glory of God's beautiful sky, full of stars, and thinking about all the people up there, when I must have fallen asleep. So you see comrade I, and I alone, was responsible for the fire."

There was some laughter in the courtroom and a few well wishers stepped forward to protest that Milovan was not responsible, that hayricks were burning all the time for no reason at all, and that in any case this particular hayrick obstructed the public path across the fields. All to no avail. Milovan had convicted himself and, however compelling the extenuating circumstances, the judge had to sentence him to the minimum period of labour – six months. Milovan didn't seem to mind this one bit; he left the court a hero and was for a few days employed on construction work at the state owned Jezero Hotel in Plitvice. He enjoyed the experience and commented afterwards that for the first and only time in his life God had permitted him to see the inside of a grand hotel.

The final word on Milovan and the burning of the hayrick was left to his many admirers, who drew up a petition stating that he was the most respected person in the community, and an innocent victim of circumstances. They also claimed that if anyone was responsible for the burning of the hayrick it was the owner himself. The first person to sign the petition, therefore, was the owner. It was successful and Milovan returned to his Jelka in triumph.'

Ned told me this story on our way back to Zagreb from Žaluzniča. He had spoken about Milovan and Jelka with very special affection, and it was clear that they had been an enormous influence in his life.

A long silence followed, and then Ned said, almost as an aside as he looked out over the landscape he had known all his life: 'Ya, they have no children, only each other, and when one of them dies, the other will follow within months.' In the space of a year this prediction proved to be all too accurate.

(While at Cambridge, Ned had helped to organise the Cambridge contingent of the largest Commonwealth Expedition to cross Europe on its way to the East, and in which Nikola's eldest daughter, Nena, had been selected to take part. As it passed through Zagreb, pausing long enough to make a few adjustments after the first thousand miles, an account appeared in Ned's local newspaper Vjesnik, *dated 26 July 1969.*

> *The British invented football, but the five hundred Britons on the football field at Mladost Camp left the impression that they have invented speed.*
>
> *They arrived in twenty identical vehicles fifteen minutes before midnight, and by midnight twenty huge tents, with as many lamps and gas cookers, were already up, and in the dishes there were hot soup and hot vegetables.*
>
> *They had prepared their supper before the representatives of Zagreb could offer them a welcome. They completed this without any noise, nimbly but in whispers, behaving as if they were the hosts and we the guests.*
>
> *If these were five hundred Yugoslavs [the people of all the five republics were referred to as Yugoslavs then] they would make such a noise as if they were a million. . . .*

Moreover, the reporter might have added had he been there the next day, those same five hundred men and women entertained the people of Zagreb to a programme of song, dance and drama concluding with 'Tiha Noći' – sing softly my baby sleeps – a lullaby in their own Croatian language. The response to that did sound like a million.)

Ned had come a long way from Žaluznića. He had worked hard, made many friends and found an excellent job with Zagreb television as legal adviser, whence he moved on to the Insitute of Medical Research and Occupational Medicine, and later the Institute of Anthropology.

Among his colleagues, he met and fell in love with the beautiful, dark-haired Vana Kamenarović, herself a constitutional lawyer, born in Zagreb but whose family originated from Boka Kotorska near Dubrovnik on the Dalmatian coast. They married and had two children. The first, a boy, Marko, would distinguish himself by winning a scholarship to university in Geneva. They had to wait a long time for Ivana to make her appearance, but she was worth waiting for. It soon became self-evident that she was a highly intelligent and gifted child, though there was a minor setback – her hands required remedial surgery.

In due course two anxious parents brought her to Scotland. It was a memorable visit, and I have never seen so much courage in a child. The young surgeon who operated on her (Oliver Fenton) and the nursing staff at the Aberdeen Sick Children's Hospital would readily endorse that view. Her confidence in both was as spontaneous as it was infectious. I went to see her immediately after her operation. She looked up with a smile, and raising her right hand gave me a smart salute – informing me that she was thirsty. Weeks later, in the departure lounge at Edinburgh Airport, she held out both her hands in a farewell gesture. 'Look,' she cried, eyes sparkling with excitement, 'my beautiful hands.'

(It is against this background that I think about the war in what used to be Yugoslavia. So many families have been uprooted, their lives shattered, their hopes destroyed. The Sava is awash with tears.

The men, women and children who perished in Vukovar on the Danube will have a permanent place in history for so long as brutality is despised and courage honoured. Dubrovnik has been battered for no other purpose than to deprive its people, and the world, of a priceless possession. But even those terrible tragedies were only a foretaste of what was in store.

And all this is the handiwork of men – a legacy for posterity to ponder on – and the barriers that have been erected as a result prompt me to reflect yet again on why the Commonwealth Expedition was mounted: to try and restore old friendships eroded by time and neglect by identifying the spirit of adventure with crossing the barriers that divide people.

On Remembrance Day 1991, Ned addressed a letter to The Times *in London and sent me a copy.*

> *As I listened to your Remembrance Day ceremonies on Sunday I was filled with renewed hope that Great Britain would not forget us.*
>
> *We are witness to a bloody war in Croatia which has often been described, wrongly, as an ethnic conflict between Croats and Serbs living in Croatia. I live in Zagreb, I have Serbian friends and neighbours.*
>
> *This war started under the pretext of protecting the Serbian minority in our*

country, and the so-called Yugoslav People's Army, dominated by Serbian Generals, provides all the argument they need. We have no army and few arms.

Having suspended the autonomous provinces of Kosovo and Vojvodina, and incorporated them into the Serbian State, Serbia now hopes to seize parts of Croatia, notably Slavonia and part of the Adriatic coast.

The territory in question is part of Croatia and has been since the 8th century. It was recognised by Pope John VIII as long ago as 879 A.D. The Croatian King Tomislav united all the Croatian lands in the 10th century. According to Mr Milosević, Serbia demands that all Serbs must live in one state. Where even one Serb lives the territory must belong to Serbia.

At the first free elections in Croatia in 1990, the people voted to reject Communism and to become a free, democratic and sovereign state. Croatia wishes to join the European Community. The result of this peaceful and democratic development is that towns are destroyed, villages burnt, and innocent civilians killed. Vukovar and Dubrovnik already have their place in history as a testament to the courage of ordinary people.

I have a special affection and admiration for Great Britain – as do my wife and children – and I appeal for her voice to be raised in the councils of Europe so that we may celebrate together the dawn of freedom and democracy throughout our great continent.

That is the best help you can give to Croatia. We do not ask for others to come and die for us. That, at least, we can do for ourselves.

Nedjelko Ivančević.)

I think Ned expected to see the help Aberdeen was able to offer his daughter Ivana expressed nationally in support of the Croatian cause and, like many of his countrymen, was disappointed with Britain. These feelings were deeply held and excuses did little to relieve them, but a short letter from me in *The Times* of December 1991, urging that 'better armed the Croats would be able to defend themselves and limit the fighting, if not actually stop it', pleased him and our mutual friend Nikola Vrbos enormously, and it is to the latter that I must now return.

A chance encounter

Nikola has done more for the reputation of his native Croatia than many of his countrymen basking in the comfort of more exalted occupations who regularly imbibe the wine of his labours, but know little about the processes immortalised in that single cry 'Živjeli!'

One guest or fifty, usually invited, frequently not, can be assured of the kind of welcome that inspires this story in the hope that it may one day do justice to the personality and character of a great man; great, that is, by the universal standards of hard work, generosity, humour and enthusiasm. Instant hospitality comes as naturally to Nikola as getting up in the morning or saying his prayers before going to bed. Countless battalions of bees guard his household and they have not mutinied once since they first took up residence over fifty years ago, and they repay his kindness with a continuous supply of the finest honey. Živjeli to that too!

Nikola was born in the village of Hodinci, in Vivodina, near the border between Croatia and Slovenia. His parents owned a small farm with a vineyard, and it was here that the young Nikola received his earliest instruction in the abundance of God's blessings. Life was hard, and when he left home to enrol in a Catholic seminary in Zagreb it was with the avowed intention of supplementing the family budget with a little labour of his own; but deep down he nursed a secret childhood ambition to don the habit of a monk. Fate intervened.

Born in the village of Lapac, in Lika, and making her own way to work in the same seminary was the beautiful sixteen-year-old Milka. Her presence reached out to the romantic Nikola. It was not only her smiling face and warm green eyes that captivated his heart; the many choice morsels that came his way from the kitchen may have had something to do with it too. Nikola and Milka fell in love and got married. The would be monk became a postman; the village belle became a wife and mother. Their house was restored and painted, and a spring suddenly appearing in the kitchen incorporated into the plumbing by the resourceful Nikola, when the first baby, a girl they christened Nena, was born.

It is a wooden house, carefully sited above a stream whose steep banks offer security from bulldozers and other mechanical devices that might otherwise plough into oblivion the scenes, scents and noises that come from God, free, and from which life takes on meanings and values that influence the earliest moments of conscious experience and last a lifetime. Situated at the end of a residential street in a neighbourhood of ordinary folk, but a little aloof from the others and surrounded by evergreens, the house is Nikola's pride and joy. Random footpaths mark the passage of friendship over the years; the most frequently used of these has been widened to give it status and a name of its own – Hrastovać.

Behind the house there is room enough for cherry and apple trees, a garden table and rustic benches. The bees are quartered in their own exclusive barracks to the west of the house where they are warmed by the midday sun and chorus loudly their pleasure at the sight of each sunset. They are Nikola's special friends and it is commonplace to see numbers of them promenading on his head and arms. A stranger appearing at such a moment would be at risk were he to greet Nikola with excessive familiarity, a matter to which I can bear personal testimony, and to the house-cure for any resulting injury: a liberal application of plum brandy.

A discreet warning from the gate on the other hand, and the master of the household would dispatch his buzzing comrades in a trice and advance with open arms to exchange the customary kisses, one on each cheek, made all the more eloquent by a needle-sharp growth surfacing above an otherwise boyish complexion. His favourite headdress is a navy blue beret with a little tail on top.

Looking over her knitting machine from a small hall beyond a glass fronted verandah, Milka can see little before vendors, visitors or members of her family actually arrive at the front door. But footsteps she can hear in advance, identifying those of her family with uncanny accuracy. She can often name them before they reach the gate: Nena or Miro, Nada, Zoran or Mirjana, or Stari himself. Stari means old, and Nikola, despite repeated protests, has been so addressed ever since he married Milka many happy years ago.

There are certain tell-tale features about the house over which Nikola is inclined to be reticent. For instance, beyond the hall is a dining-cum-sitting room, which doubles as sleeping quarters after lights out; lean out of the single window to the north however – overlooking Nikola's garden – and the cherry trees are at your hand. Look out of the bathroom window – the bathroom is off the hall to the right

– and the roses, if in bloom, throw up their scent to greet you. Neither of these came to their appointed places by accident.

The polka – an important factor in his courtship of Milka – is a great favourite with Nikola. And certainly those who know him would vouch for it that the dedicated postman can still rock the foundations of his wooden home after lunch, dinner, or at any other time, if asked by some unsuspecting guest whether he likes dancing. Nikola doesn't answer such questions: he just does the thing, and promptly. Ask Nikola if he likes wine and he would simply pick up a glass and say 'cheers!' or the equivalent in Croatian.

Give or take a glass of plum brandy, a litre or two of home wine, and Nikola can carry his companions away on a romantic journey into the past. And should he exaggerate, which he often does, a smiling Milka, as beautiful as when they first met years ago, will intervene to correct him. But Nikola always has the last word, brushing aside her interruptions with 'if it was not so it should have been'. And there at a glance is his philosophy on life. All the happiness is stored away intact; more is added each day. And every time their treasury of reminiscences is opened, the contents appear more beautiful, even if they were not always that way.

'Had I a thousand roses,' declares Nikola, 'I would have given them to her, so the only one I could afford speaks for the nine hundred and ninety-nine others, doesn't it?' And who would wish to challenge that? Certainly not Milka!

'He had more hair on his head,' claims Milka, which promptly sends Nikola's left hand to the still well-groomed golden locks sprouting over his ears and descending in heavy sideburns to counterbalance the little skating rink on top. More recently, a heavy blonde moustache has appeared on the upper lip to dispel further any comment about his hair being in short supply. The face is strong and pink, the eyes blue, and the frame a tribute to a hard-working man in the prime of life – rising to five feet ten inches without shoes. The little finger of the right hand was contributed to the Second World War.

Milka has put on a lot of weight, so much so that she finds it difficult to move about. Yet, perched upright on the stool before her knitting machine, she governs the family by remote control. She may not be very mobile, but sight, sound and smell serve her well. And in the end, what Milka has to say goes, and she does it beautifully. 'Bog' (God) is a word common to her vocabulary which she employs to bless a hug, a kiss, or that irresistible beaming smile that lights up her face and draws the family to her. Nikola often resists her authority, particularly when entertaining his friends, but sooner or later she sweeps him under her spell. 'Stari', in a tone guaranteed to set the alarm bells ringing, followed by 'Stari' again, with just the mildest suggestion of rebuke, and the said Stari comes bounding to her side.

In the village where Nikola was born it was too far to go for water, so they drank wine instead. About his work as a postman he has no complaints: 'For six days I serve my fellow men and the devil a little. I keep the seventh day for God and myself.'

I first met Nikola while I was driving through Zagreb on my way back to London from India. He had just completed the second delivery of mail and was hurrying homewards with an empty postbag over his shoulder when I drew up beside him and asked the way to Sljeme – as synonymous with Zagreb as the river Sava – where would-be skiers learn their business in winter and the less adventurous walk for the good of their health.

Instantly alerted to the possibilities of an entertaining encounter, Nikola looked at me with a warm and encouraging smile while muttering to himself, partly for my benefit, the word 'Britanski', followed by 'molim', a lift of the eyebrows, and a slight turning of the head to complete a question mark.

Realising that I had accosted no ordinary son of Croatia, I assumed a posture of mock importance and pointing to myself – the meaning of which was clear enough – repeated the word 'Sljeme' with an upward flourish of the right hand to make the point that I had a certain hill in mind.

This sort of exchange was entirely to his liking and he responded at once. And not being a man given to accepting defeat over a triviality such as communicating with a stranger, raised his own left hand with forefinger extended indicating 'wait', and, moving round the car, opened the nearside door and got in beside me. 'Molim', he said, eyes twinkling with merriment, and signalled me forward.

Nikola had assumed that I was a 'Britanski' because only a 'Britanski' spoke like one, whereas others, try as they might, did not. Besides, the steering wheel of my car was on the right side and that confirmed the matter. It was fortunate too that he rather liked 'Britanskis' because the plan taking shape in his mind was already ranging far beyond a simple question and answer between strangers. His daughter Nena who was studying English at the university would be at home and could act as interpreter while at the same time practising her English on the real thing. Meanwhile, gestures and hand-signals would serve their purpose and see us safely home to No 19.

'Bog! Bog!' murmured Milka softly as Nikola introduced his new-found friend, steering me past her knitting machine and into the drawing room where I was invited to take a seat. Four glasses, a bottle of plum brandy, a litre of wine – both home made – and a bottle of Radenska mineral water appeared in quick succession. Milka stumbled downstairs to the kitchen calling to her eldest daughter Nena on the way. For his part, Nikola filled two glasses with plum brandy, passed one across to me and raising his own with great deliberation uttered the word 'Živjeli'! It sounded like a victory salute, followed immediately by 'Cheerio' – the only English he had – to which I responded with a 'Cheerio' of my own.

Nikola had seen people from Britain doing this sort of thing but was never quite sure whether 'Cheerio' meant the same as 'Živjeli' – for one thing, it lacked the resonance of the Croatian word – but for the moment that was unimportant. Much relieved at being introduced into the proper way of doing things, and smiling at my host, I made a feeble attempt at 'Živjeli' and following his example drained my glass in one. The shock was as sudden as it was unexpected, and as the flames in my throat subsided I watched in amazement as Nikola, smacking his lips, calmly refilled the glasses.

Delighted that I was already tuning-in to Croatian, and to speed the process along, he came up with 'Dobro! Dobro!' (Good! Good!). And the pace would have been further accelerated had not relief arrived in the guise of plates of bread, butter, cheese, gherkins, salami, and joints of chicken fried in breadcrumbs. 'Molim' said Milka – I had by now established that this meant please – as she pushed the food towards me while Nena followed with reinforcements long before there was any call for them. 'My father says he is very happy you are here and asks you please to help yourself to everything,' she said with hands extended and an accompanying shrug of the shoulders.

A girl of striking appearance and not unlike her father: fair, tall, with blue eyes and long light-brown hair, Nena was clearly aware of her responsibilities as the eldest in a family still living close to its roots. I had asked a postman a simple question and here I was, in the bosom of his family, settling down to an enormous meal. But, as I have already indicated, this was no ordinary postman.

Sljeme is a beautiful place to spend a few days quietly and, after a long journey from India which had taken me ten days moving at a pace through Baluchistan, Iran, Iraq, Syria and Turkey, I had a mind to rest there over the weekend, and perhaps a day or two longer if I found it to my liking. With Nena acting as interpreter we made rapid progress; my presence and purpose were carefully reviewed, followed by a more general exchange of information including names – mine conveniently replaced with 'Gospodine' (Sir), which gradually gave way to the more informal 'Drug', and 'Drug', or comrade, I remained.

Nikola was dismissive of unnecessarily prolonged formalities; the sooner they were out of the way, the sooner a start could be made with the serious business of building a proper relationship. And to this end he told me exactly how to get to Sljeme, made some useful suggestions on where to stay when I got there and generally eulogised on the benefits to be enjoyed up the mountain. I learnt from him that for hill walkers the route up Sljeme was clearly marked by white circles on the trees at regular intervals, with red centres for the way up and blue for the way down. But for motorists the approach was more hazardous along a narrow winding road at a speed limited only by the horsepower of the engine and the courage of the driver. 'Drug' said Nikola earnestly, 'the record for climbing Sljeme is twenty-two and a half minutes' – he made no mention of age – 'for motorists I don't know if there is a record, perhaps not, because it would be hard to prove. But,' he added with a smile, 'you will see from the wrecks in the valley below that it is not for the want of trying.'

'Molim,' he said, pushing the food and wine towards me, as other members of the family entered, joined in the conversation for a moment and left – each in turn carrying a bottle or a plate to be added to the already overburdened table. The youngest daughter, Mirjana, put on the record player in the corner of the room; Milka abandoned her knitting machine and moved into the connecting doorway with her high stool: she disliked sitting on the divan because it was too low and once seated she found it difficult to get up.

Nikola was now making full use of his daughter's fluent English while Milka simply beamed her questions in the desired direction, repeating them several times with increasing emphasis and encouraging gestures – no doubt convinced that foreign ears must eventually succumb to such treatment. The slightest flicker of comprehension brought bursts of 'Da! Da! Dobro!' (Yes! Yes! Good!) quickly followed with yet another question.

Caught between this flanking onslaught and Nikola's frontal attack, I found myself hopelessly adrift: on the one hand trying to stay tuned to Nena's translation, and on the other watching Milka's face to glean from her expressions what I missed in her words. Nor was the problem helped by their both speaking at the same time, but, as the wine began to make its own infallible contribution, a system began to take shape. I would look at one or the other as the likely source of the next question, while Nena switched deftly from father to mother without undermining the authority of one or the enthusiasm of the other. In the corner the record player continued to play sentimental songs from Dalmatia.

Nikola now came up with 'How do you do . . . very well thank you' . . . and 'thank you very much', and, laughing at his own adventurous spirit, insisted that I learn the Croatian equivalents. I stumbled over these bravely before we moved on, inexorably, to global matters, with all the confidence that comes from excessive indulgence – but with an economy of words that did justice to us both. The family just looked on in amazement.

'Good,' said Nikola, 'now play a polka.' As it turned out, this was to be the next step in my education. In his time Nikola had won many prizes for dancing the polka, and having learnt this from Nena I relaxed, expecting to be entertained to a demonstration.

But not so. The irrepressible Nikola seized me by the arms and led me into the little hall and there, beside the knitting machine and in a space too small to swing a cat, I was whisked into the polka with firm commanding movements – one, two, three to the right, then repeated to the left – while I tried to keep in step with variations of a Scottish reel. The reverse turn was the most troublesome; but where skill was lacking, brute force was not, and the polka was well and truly executed. Too much food, a lot of wine – perhaps too much of that too – ten riotous minutes on the floor with this extraordinary postman and I had had enough. Like a matador, Nikola marched to his place in triumph; like the bull, I collapsed. But alas, escape there was none.

'Now dance with Nena and let me see how you go,' insisted Nikola. Nena could see that I had very little polka left in me and, leading the way into the arena, brought a more delicate touch to the dance. Her graceful dancing covered up the uglier movements of her partner as we went through the regulation three repetitions of the polka, interspersed with brief interludes of the waltz: the record was obviously put together in this way to give dancers a brief respite from the more rumbustious polka. The family applauded generously while Milka added her equally spontaneous 'Dobro! Dobro!' The head of the house simply surveyed the scene with the air of a man who has seen the fulfilment of an impossible dream, and, raising his glass to the dancers, unleashed a resounding 'Živjeli Drug! Živjeli!'

Whether I would, or could, find my way to Sljeme tonight, tomorrow or ever, was no longer relevant. In the face of this new and exciting relationship everything else would have to take second place. And tiring though these proceedings were, the sheer force of the bombardment – salvo upon salvo of sounds, gestures, smiles and wine unlimited – began to demolish my resistance. I found myself adapting to the situation and beginning to feel very much part of the family – a feeling I allowed myself to express with uncharacteristic exuberance: 'Dobro! Jako Dobro!' and 'Živjeli!' – all of which convinced Nikola that I had mastered the language in a single night. And although the wine was responsible for much of this, it would not have been anything like as effective without the warmth and kindness of genuinely good people.

'This was a great town,' explained Nikola. 'In fact it has been a Royal city since 1242. You must see the old and most beautiful part of it standing on its own exclusive hill; and the cathedral, next to the open market – both are in operation by five o'clock in the morning. You should visit the new theatre and the university, walk about the republic square, take coffee at Gradska Kavana and call on my favourite gostionica where they serve the best vinjak (brandy) in Croatia.'

How could I possibly do all that in two days, I asked.

'Then stay a month,' said Nikola, an invitation instantly echoed by Milka.

It was now dangerously close to the bewitching hour, not the best time to be making decisions, but I felt I ought to be making a move. 'I must be going,' I said.

'Where?' demanded Nikola. 'You must stay here and we can worry about the hill in the morning.' And that settled the matter; it also sealed the beginning of a long and lasting friendship. Just how comfortably the rest of the family slept that night I was never to know, but for me a settee was turned into a luxurious bed with sheets, pillows and duvet, and manoeuvred into position by the window. 'Laku Noć,' they called out in turn as they melted away into the night, expressing the hope that I might sleep in peace.

Glinting through the leaves of a cherry tree the sunlight fell across the bed, weaving patterns as the leaves swayed in the breeze. It brought me back to consciousness with a start. 'Good Heavens!' I thought. 'It must be ten o'clock, or even later.' For his part, having waited long enough for the first signs of life in the drawing room, Nikola walked in, clean, tidy and fully rested balancing a tray of coffee and plum brandy. My God, not again, I thought, not at this hour in the morning. There were also ham and eggs – done the Croatian way, one fried upon the other – piles of bread and white unsalted butter.

'Dobro jutro, Drug,' cried Nikola as the family trooped in echoing his greeting. 'Eat, eat,' insisted Nikola as I tried to brave through my embarrassment and present as reasonable a spectacle as a man might after a hard night – surrounded by people who had already made it safely into a new day. However, there was little room for false modesty here, so I launched into 'Cheers', knocked back the threatening plum brandy, and drawing on the lessons of the evening before added, in Croatian: 'Thank you very much' (Hvala lijepo), which went down extremely well.

To start the day with a couple of glasses of plum brandy, or any other sort, was an adventure I had hitherto avoided, but declining Nikola's hospitality dispensed with such assurance was not easy; moreover, I was no longer sure that I wanted to. The golden spirit was already stoking my inside as the sun shone through the open window; in my hand a cup of hot, very sweet, Turkish coffee was waiting its turn to be hurled into the conflagration. Such a combination had only one destination: the point of indiscretion.

Leaping to my feet and displaying a multi-coloured Indian cotton lungi wrapped about my middle, much to the amusement of my hosts, I let out the battle cry 'Živjeli!' and dashed into the bathroom. Here too the family had been active on my account. The hot water had been switched on – the type of geyser doing the job would need all of a couple of hours and I was to be the sole beneficiary of its labours; the others would have done their washing and bathing in cold water. Clean towels had been laid out, a fresh cake of soap and a new pot of talcum powder. Lying across the towelrack, my shirt had been washed and ironed. Hanging behind the door was my suit, carefully pressed and probably brushed as well. The family had obviously enjoyed doing all these things because it gave them pleasure, and knowing perhaps just how much it would be appreciated.

Sober and thoughtful I emerged from the bathroom and, catching Nikola's eye, thanked him warmly. 'Ah,' he said, dismissively, waving his hands in the air and brushing aside my thanks before they became an embarrassment to both of us, 'we must go up the hill.' Language can be a great help when you have it, and an even greater hindrance when you haven't. I wanted very much to redress the balance in some way but there were not enough words, and translation would fail to satisfy the feelings involved. As far as Nikola himself was concerned words were unimportant – except when pronouncing on matters philosophical; but I could see from the expression in his eyes that he understood my dilemma. From a case in the back of my car I fished out a silk tie and presented it to him. It was a green and gold tie, the same as the one I was wearing, and a gift he could accept without protest. His face beamed with delight and his own tie was promptly relieved of any further duties for the duration of my stay. And as we set off for the mountain, with Nena in the back seat, he commented on how well it contrasted with his fresh white shirt.

We drove along a narrow, winding road, turning and twisting its way round sharp hairpin bends; the pine-wooded countryside released its own mild perfume on the mountain air. But Nikola was more concerned with the driving habits of his countrymen.

'When the war ended,' he said, 'and for many years afterwards, there were very few cars about. Most of us travelled by tram, bus or bicycle in town, and walked up these hills. When cars became available, people rushed to acquire them, not only for convenience and comfort but also as a status symbol. And so, by the standards of these noisy, air polluting machines, the importance of one man, and in due course woman too, was measured against another – even one republic against the next – while as a whole they had the secondary effect of killing us off more quickly. A lawyer, a doctor or a judge was deemed to be more competent, and of course successful, if he possessed a car. It is also said that in our country today a man drives with one foot in jail and the other in the grave. And for most motor car owners the race is not so much against time as against the millions of miles other countries have covered while we were standing still, or just walking. But we were in better health as a result.'

Here Nikola paused for a moment, conscious perhaps of his own excellent physical condition. 'Ah yes,' he continued, 'pride is a heady medicine. Notice that car coming round the corner ahead of us' (it was a small red Fiat), 'the driver wants to go faster than the maximum speed for which the engine was built, and he can do that when coming downhill. He will come round the corner' (a right hand bend) 'on the extreme left and if you make the mistake of getting there before him – look out!' I took the hint. Right enough, the car came screaming round the corner on the left hand side and swerved sharply back to the right, while the driver, ignoring the road ahead, looked out and waved with a broad smile, 'Dobar dan!' he called out.

'Yes,' mused Nikola, his voice expressing both sympathy and understanding, 'that is how many of them go to heaven – leaning out to wave to friends – but they are happy, don't you think?'

What could I say other than to express a thought that had been in my mind since the night before. 'Not only are your people happy,' I said, 'they have a great capacity for fun and a highly developed sense of living.'

'Of course,' continued Nikola, ignoring the compliment, 'not so long ago we had nothing. Most people in our country have had their fortunes and their nationalities revolutionised by the upheavals of history. Now we are Croats, and I hope we stay that way, with enough time to appreciate freedom and peace – however little there may be in the world – and to enjoy it while we may. Do you see those people down here with their ponies?' – pointing to a group in the heavily wooded valley below –

'they are Bosnians and work very hard cutting and carrying logs from the forest. Mostly they are Muslim, extremists in their way, but very hospitable; win their love and they will give you anything; make an enemy of one and he will fight you to the death. We have many different cultures and religions in Croatia, and all are trying to live side by side, and to prosper together. It may work, it may not – not unlike India, Drug; you know that country well, don't you?' he asked.

'Fairly well,' I answered, 'and I am very fond of it, just as I have become of your country. Each generation makes its own contribution, good and bad, and moves on in the seemingly endless cycle of life, searching for the Nirvana unique to each individual according to the circumstances of his birth.'

Nikola nodded simply, and then spoke quietly, 'I should like to visit India, and Jerusalem too.'

The car had by now negotiated the final turn and was moving along a bumpy gravel road at the top of the hill. A few couples and some larger groups in coloured anoraks and walking boots, and not a few with woollen caps in the Croatian colours of red, white and blue, moved among the trees or walked ahead on the road heading towards Puntijarka, a mountaineering club-house run by Madame Keti.

'That cable car behind us,' remarked Nikola drawing attention to the pylon on the top of the hill to the east, 'Milka doesn't like it very much, but it's as safe as houses and one of the most efficient in Europe. I must take you up there some time; but if you are only staying for a day or two it will have to be next time.' He thought for a while and then went on: 'Two days, that's hardly time enough to have a proper meal. Why don't you stay longer?'

'I would love to my friend, but I have to be back by a certain date. Why don't you come to Britain?'

'Me!' he laughed, 'I've never left Croatia, and who would deliver the post in my absence? Much more important, who would look after the bees?'

'Don't forget your family papa,' prompted Nena.

'Yes, yes, and my family,' he added hastily, 'what would they do without me?'

We had now reached the end of the road. An open space fell away to the right covered with wooden tables and benches, and beyond it, timber built on a stone foundation, there stood a house with a very large window opening on to a kitchen. This was Puntijarka, and at the door stood a grey-haired lady (Madame Keti), smiling as she waved her hand towards the open door. She spoke in English: 'Good morning, please come in.' I was surprised at that – perhaps she had been forewarned – but Nikola just whipped off his cap, greeted her with marked respect and led the way inside. The girls working in the kitchen were singing, one kneading dough, another standing over the sink, and a third dispensing from a bottle for a soldier in a grey uniform leaning against the serving hatch which extended along the length of the kitchen. Without missing a note, or turning their heads, they replied in unison to Nikola's 'Dobar dan!'

We walked into the dining room, Nena bringing up the rear. It was packed with walkers eating their own picnics or enjoying the fare from Madame's kitchen. Putting his hand on my shoulder in what was clearly a protective gesture, Nikola stood still for a moment. 'Dobar dan,' he said in a loud voice after the other guests had had time to appraise the new arrivals. It sounded more like a command than a greeting. Heads nodded solemnly and a resonant blending of voices echoed 'Dobar dan' while Nikola proceeded to explain that his friend was 'Britanski'.

'Dobro! Dobro!' they fired back with quickening interest. One or two who spoke English came forward to offer a more personal welcome.

A table was cleared, a spotless white linen tablecloth unwrapped and spread over it, and without so much as a by your leave plum brandy was produced with an accompanying bottle of wine, and another of mineral water with three hearts on the label. This, according to Nikola, meant that it was good for the mind, heart and body. Glasses were filled, the liquid sparkling as brightly as the sun pouring in through the window, and up went Nikola's hand. 'Živjeli!' he cried, and then 'Cheerio'! followed by 'Živjeli'! and 'Živjeli'! again, as the uninhibited response filled the room, setting the scene for yet another celebration. In the corner an old record player was activated and made its contribution with a song I was long to remember, 'Tiha Noći', a sentimental lullaby to a nightingale. It was the song that welcomed me to Sljeme.

Madame Keti was pleased to have me stay at Puntijarka for as long as I pleased, and here, enjoying the comfort, peace and tranquillity that made me forget all about being in a Communist state, I was able to sort out my belongings and assemble the experiences of my recent travels.

Our lady of Tuhelj

(Cardinal Newman's 'Lead Kindly Light' has always been a special favourite of mine because it is a traveller's companion. And nowhere is this demonstrated more vividly than in India where lighting a lamp, or even a candle, for some special intention is commonplace.

India is a country of lights; from the most primitive to the most modern. The countless millions of little oil lamps that burst into life during the Hindu festival of Diwali, for example, are not there merely for decoration; they are there to light up the hospitable face of a great country. And it is after sunset that the real India emerges, bright as a jewel, in a wild variety of colours to soothe the accumulated stress of a busy day. There is an air of excitement in the bazaars, shopkeepers are cheerful, customers content, and a wave of human warmth flows through the streets. The dust and the squalor of the day's battlefield settle as water is sprinkled and the evening fires lit. Fears disappear, hopes blossom, temple bells ring; there is tranquillity to lean upon, and heaven descends to its constituency on earth.

My interest in the Commonwealth, and India as the largest single element of it – at least in so far as population is concerned – had taken me far and wide in the sub-continent and in the process to collect a lot of relatively useless information. I was able to establish, for instance, that there were at one stage no less than seven hundred thousand villages in India – a statistic that begins to assume some significance when one realises that the festivals exemplifying the Indian way of life are nowhere better celebrated than in those very villages. It is here that the rituals of ageless custom are observed with unquestioning faith, vindicating the commonly held view that the heart of India is to be found in her villages.

I was to learn that Indian priests – pujaris or pundits as they are traditionally called – were born and not ordained, their elevation thereafter determined by holiness and proven influence with the gods. I met doctors, teachers, lawyers and others, all of whom could stand comparison with the best in the world.

At another level I was introduced to toddy from the palm tree (Caryota urens) which, unlike its man-made equivalent, is deceptively sweet and innocuous when tapped in the early hours of the morning but, and without any interference or encouragement, lethal as plum brandy by the same evening. Nor is toddy the only drink that nature provides. A single green coconut can yield a pint of healthy non-alcoholic fluid for next to nothing, an instant meal from its kernel – and the supply is limitless. Coconut oil is widely used for cooking, and a liberal application of the stuff reputed to be good for hair and body.

Bananas are regarded as a nutritious and slow-burning food all over the world, and India is no exception. But there is a difference: India is home to a greater ethnic variety than anywhere else, and the trees require little maintenance. Their owners are not only rewarded with food, but the dried leaves can be used for thatching houses and the green ones (cut into convenient sizes) as throw-away plates. To cap it all they generate their offspring without assistance.

It was inevitable too that I should become involved in the question of spices, and not only because they lie at the very heart of the Commonwealth story, but because the word 'curry' has burnt itself into the consciousness of every country in the world. But where did the word come from? Who invented it? My research began in the home of my friend Prithi Singh – diplomat and son of the royal house of Bharatpur mentioned earlier in this narrative – and it was his mother who conducted me into her kitchen to make the acquaintance of the mysteries hidden there. The experience was evocative enough to lead me into an exploration of my own.

It was in the sixteenth century that the Dutch merchants controlling the European spice trade raised the price of pepper high enough to bring into existence the East India Company, and this may even explain Britain's reluctance to rush into Europe today. Meeting in a coffee house in London (circa 1600), a group of City merchants made a stock of seventy-five thousand pounds, armed themselves with a charter from Queen Elizabeth I, and then set sail 'to bring spices and other commodities into the realm'. This was the first step on the road to the Indian Empire. The last step came nearly three hundred and fifty years later with the independence of India and Pakistan in August 1947.

The Company brought wealth and prosperity, but it also opened the door to a world community of such excellence that when the sun set on the Empire it rose simultaneously on a new Commonwealth of nations and over a thousand million people, with a few more millions added since. This is probably the explanation for the presence in Greater London alone of more men and women from India and Pakistan than there were ever British in the Indian sub-continent at any one time during the Empire, and accounts for the incredible number and variety of Asian restaurants throughout Britain trading under the banner of an Anglo-Indian word – curry.

I first came across the word in a different form, 'kari', in Ooty. It was used by our good and gentle Tamil servants to describe a meal of rice supplemented with a little tamarind water flavoured with pepper and dried chillies, sometimes a piece of salted fish, and always two or three fresh green chillies. The word was pronounced with the suggestion of a 'd' in the 'r'; an early Oxford Dictionary *describes it as 'a relish for rice'. My own etymological labours revealed that the first memsahib to come across kari, and to risk its promotion to her Sunday table, stumbled over the word and thus, at a stroke, a thousand exotic dishes fell to the hammer of a single five letter word, and Anglo-Indian cooking was born.*

The presence of chillies was proof enough that the British never do things by half and so the affair had to be hot. Salted fish, a centuries-old tradition from the Gulf of Cambay to Cape Comorin, was quietly christened 'Bombay Duck', and the first curry lunch was served. It was destined to become a ritual of Empire on Sundays and followed the British wherever they went:

They took the humble curry and spread it everywhere
Like gold dust from the Empire, for everyone to share.
Each had his special mixture, and played it like a game,
But 'a curry', friends, is just as hot – by any other name.

Before the original (kari) made its first perilous journey from kitchen to dining room, a variety of spices were added, all beyond the means of mere servants and sampled by them only at prestigious functions when a family's fortunes might be mortgaged for a generation if honour so demanded. The result was often garnished with side dishes of chopped fruit, nuts, sambals and chutneys, or simply 'bits and pieces'. The servants, with their impeccable good manners and astonishing devotion, asked nothing more than that their masters and mistresses should enjoy Indian fare, call it what they would. And it was in Nepal that a new and interesting bit of information came my way: the thirty-two excellences attributed to Buddḫa.

I had been invited to dine with an old friend in western Nepal, we having served in the same regiment, and I had asked him whether the food would be especially good – knowing perfectly well that it would. 'Batis masala dalnu bhayo' (thirty-two spices have been used) came the stern reply. On closer examination, however, only twelve came to light, and the explanation was that perfection and thirty-two went together: if a dozen spices were required to produce the best results, then that particular dozen could be upgraded.

In twenty-four journeys down the Asian Highway I have relied a great deal on spices for comfort and health. I have learned to respect them as I would pepper and salt and, by coincidence, I have seldom been ill. Of course, Asian chefs prefer to use spices individually as they go along, but time does not allow for such leisurely practices in a Western kitchen. And while some people have a preference for the strong aromatic spices, others are more inclined towards the gentle, more persuasive variety, and a meeting between the two is hard to find. It all depends on where you are, what you are doing, the temperature, and the occasion. Sadly, the all-embracing word curry has debased much of the art and skill of Indian cookery. It is like reducing all wine simply to red, white or pink.

The Commonwealth Expeditions have taken me over some of the oldest landroutes in the world. I have eaten in the lowliest wayside eating houses (dhabas) and in the most luxurious intercontinentals. I have talked to hundreds of men and women about their simple, and often not so simple food and the preparation thereof. What started out as a traveller's interest in spices ended up in blending a mixture of my own. But it was ten years before the secret saw the light of day: a happy combination of sixteen spices (half thirty-two!) that aroused the curiosity of my friends and became known as 'the Colonel's Hot Favourites'. Alerted to the possibilities of a wider market, a North American firm wrote enquiring how many tons I could supply, and how soon. I had to confess that operations on my side of the Atlantic were restricted to a two ounce coffee grinder.

Of course, the stately homes of India would never use the word curry. To them it is a word corrupted and without meaning, while at the other end of the social scale the word kari still preserves a legitimate meaning. And perhaps the moral of the story is that the British experience in India lies somewhere between the two: we failed fully to understand the one, and undoubtedly took the other for granted – but we always admired both, and not without affection.)

Ned and Vana Ivančević had taken to the spices early and never ceased to sing the praises of the Colonel's Hot Favourites. It was not surprising, therefore, that no sooner had I emerged from my latest peregrination down the long dusty road and entered Croatia than an invitation was waiting for me to dine at their flat, Radauševa 5, in Zagreb. Not only to dine, but to prepare one of the most popular hot favourites, dry spiced venison, for the edification of any other guests who might be encouraged to sample spiced food without having to call it curry. And to that challenging assignment I descended from Puntijarka.

Vana's contribution, apple strudel, was already in the oven. Ned's part in the affair was simpler but no less important: he had made his own adventurous journey to the early morning market opposite Zagreb Cathedral and had come away with some excellent prsut (smoked ham), seedless black olives and fresh cottage cheese. Several bottles of full bodied Plavać, already uncorked, stood by together with reassuring reinforcements of mineral water. As the star turn of the evening I was expected to provide the spices and cook the venison. There were seven of us in all and as I set about the task, aproned and standing in front of the stove, it occurred to me that perhaps Ned and Vana had promised their friends more than I could deliver. Not only mine, but the reputation of two constitutional lawyers – even the whole Commonwealth – was at stake. However, the die was cast. Glasses were filled and one handed to the chef. 'Živjeli!' Ned raised his glass and the party got under way.

Questions were asked and I answered them diligently, and with the appropriate expression of authority. There was obviously a great deal of feeling for and about India, so much so that I suggested to my companions that Croatia should apply to join the Commonwealth.

'Da, Da, why not?' said Ned, and as the conversation turned to spices the venison began to sizzle and an appetising aroma fill the air. I explained how the origins of Empire and Commonwealth were founded on the flavours they were about to experience, and went on to regale them with an assortment of anecdotes until the venison was ready to take over.

Though I say so myself, it was a triumph. Crisp on the outside, soft and succulent inside, the finished product met with instant approval: 'Jako dobro' (Very good), was how Ned put it. 'I have never in my whole life tasted better venison. You are a genius,' he cried in a spontaneous outburst of enthusiasm echoed by his friends. What could I do but take a bow and pass the lettuce – apart from good bread, the only concession acceptable to dry spiced venison.

For me it was to be an especially memorable occasion, and not simply because I had been dubbed a genius for the first and only time in my life, but because Ned came up with the proposal that we should visit Tuhelj (in Zagorje), north of Zagreb, the next day in order to enjoy the hospitality of a Croatian village. 'I think you will find it similar to your experiences in India,' he said.

It would be Sunday, and Ned's friends in Tuhelj had not been consulted, but that did not seem to matter. So it was agreed that we would rendezvous outside the flat at ten o'clock, and to meet that deadline an early night was indicated. At first there was some resistance to this – choosing between an all-night celebration or Tuhelj seemed unnecessary, both were possible – but in the end good sense prevailed. I returned to base at Puntijarka driving through a clear starlit night. The single outside light, left on to welcome me, sparkled through the pine trees; I had a key and could let myself in by a side entrance. Madame Keti had asked me to turn off the light, which I dutifully did, and Puntijarka was plunged into darkness. But from my bedroom window I could see the lights of Zagreb far below, thousands of them, signalling as it were those parting words: 'Dobra večer, laku noć', wishing me a good night, and a peaceful night. In the distance, the line of the river Sava was just visible like a silver girdle encircling the city. Somewhere beyond that river was Tuhelj.

In addition to a large quantity and variety of food, Vana's mother insisted on contributing a hamper of finely sliced smoked ham, cheese, several bottles of wine and mineral water. It was more than enough for the seven well-built passengers who crowded into my station wagon, and, assuming the law would not be around to raise any objections, we set off happily reassured by Ned's final admonitions: 'So long as we are able to fit into the car, and you drive at the regulation speed on the right-hand side of the road, the militia have no business with us.'

Once clear of the cobbled streets of Zagreb and the clatter and whirring of trams, the road was clear and well surfaced. Speed limits and advertisements for rakija and wine appeared together; posters displaying barbecued pigs and sheep invited us to pull off the road and sample those delights. And there was little point in trying to compete with townspeople overtaking us as they made their own weekly pilgrimage to their villages, for they knew what they were about and, for all my experience on the long dusty road, I was no match for them; but they waved as they passed. The level of risk taking was not entirely due to an earlier appointment with sljivovica; it was more a display of native high spirits and good humour, unlikely to be fettered by the advent of the dreaded breathalyser. That, observed Ned with a laugh, would merely encourage a new and more dangerous sport.

'You see that little church, like a pimple on the hill,' he said pointing, 'at the bottom of that hill is Tuhelj, we turn off here.' A narrow winding road, first gravel, then dirt, led us all the way to a wooden farmhouse. There was space to park the car under a walnut tree.

Gabrijel, the youngest of eight brothers and sisters of the Posavec family, had a little English and helped his eldest brother, Pepek, to play host. His four sisters were nuns, one brother a priest, Gabrijel and the brother next to him Dominican lay brothers. Pepek, married to Stefića, managed the small family farm.

While living with the Dominican community in Zagreb, Gabrijel worked on repairing church organs – a skill that accounted for the fine parquet façade of an otherwise plain farmhouse. Pepek's children, two girls and a boy – Ivića, Mirića and Jožek – instantly obedient, stood behind their parents on a raised verandah before the entrance door.

Having embraced his guests, Pepek led the way into the house. Their possessions were modest: the new calf in the shed opposite, the little white kitten no more than two days old in the arms of Mirića, an old rubber ball and a small accordion were the immediate symbols of a family united in everything it did. Survival depended on everyone playing a full part in working the farm under the guiding hand of the much loved and respected Pepek.

Ignoring Ned's protests that there was a large hamper in the car, food and wine of the house had to be offered and could not be refused. And while we ate and drank, Gabrijel strapped on the accordion and played. The children sang.

The polka apart, repeated frequently, the songs were sentimental and hauntingly beautiful. I happened to mention that the only Croatian song I knew was 'Tiha Noći' and that immediately evoked a great chord from the accordion followed by the two brothers and the children singing in perfect harmony. Then came a local favourite 'Hvala' (Thank you) a compliment to visitors set in the same soulful tempo. The melody was simple enough for the rest of us to pick up and join in, and with that the preliminaries were concluded. Ned rose to his feet and suggested it was time we made our way to the top of the hill. 'We must look at the church,' he said, 'it is over a hundred years old and we shall be able to see the purple, grey and blue hills that separate Croatia from Slovenia.'

In single file we made our way up a narrow path, the imported hamper on Gabrijel's back and Ned's small son Marko on mine. 'I'm used to this,' said Gabrijel, brushing aside offers of help. But no one volunteered to relieve me of Marko so I made him walk part of the way. It was a fair climb.

'Who owns all this land?' Ned asked, pointing to the small vineyards, potato, corn and wheat fields dotted about the area. 'Are services held in the church?'

Gabrijel explained that each family owned a small piece of land, demarcation fences were unnecessary. 'At harvest time we help each other. If anyone wants some potatoes, or a cabbage or anything else they simply help themselves from where it is most convenient; there is no need to ask. My brother markets very little. Most crops are used for the family; but when we need a little money some of the farm produce is sent to the local market, or even to Zagreb. As to church services, these are held on special occasions or whenever a priest happens to be visiting.'

The church was closed. It was painted white and occupied no more than about a hundred square metres of that little hill; but looking up, one could see its weaponry raised high like an arrow aimed at heaven, with the bell primed and ready to rouse the people in the valley below. Our party moved across the flat top of the hill to a point whence the surrounding countryside was exposed in every direction. Blankets were spread on the ground, a sheet unfolded and laid in the middle, and the hamper unpacked. Witness to these activities, the bell came alive, thundering out its approval. 'Do you hear?' said Ned. 'The bell is welcoming us.'

Ned, Gabrijel and I left the others and walked over to the church. The door was now open. A short, square man of about sixty years, with paint on his trousers – from working on his or a neighbour's house perhaps – and a cap on his head, came out. Surprised, and obviously pleased to see us, he removed the cap with a polite 'Good day' in Croatian, smiling in turn at the three of us, and proceeded to explain, in response to a question from Ned, that for forty-two years he had rung the bell four times a day during summer and three times during winter. 'It is the voice of the church,' he said shyly but not without pride. 'Should there be a death, a marriage, birth or some other event in the village, people come and ask me to ring the bell, and I try to vary the sounds so that most people can identify what is happening. What you have just heard is a routine call to the parish that there will be a service this evening.'

Inside, the church looked like a cathedral in miniature. There were no kneelers or seats, only a cold concrete floor, but there were two side altars and at the high altar a statue of the Blessed Virgin Mary beautifully dressed. 'The statue has come home to its own church,' said the old man whose name we had by now discovered was Konrad Stanković. 'It is famous and greatly revered by the local people; but during the war it was removed from here and taken to a church in Austria, and there it remained until the priest had a dream in which he was told to return the statue to Tuhelj. Not even a Communist government could prevent that happening,' he added with satisfaction. 'Now there are no problems, and many people from Austria come here to visit the statue which we call Our Lady of Tuhelj. So I thought you were from Austria,' he smiled as we moved out into the sun.

Approaching from the opposite end of the hill with a bottle in one hand and picking his way cautiously along the path leading to the church was a man of uncertain age. This was Pepic Pukljak. 'Who are your friends Konrad?' he called out to the bellringer.

'Come and meet the Britanski,' answered Konrad.

'Good day,' said Pukljak, removing his hat, 'I have just finished work and am on my way home. I always leave when I hear the bell.' He was a gentle man, fragile in appearance and confirming by his over-cautious movements that he had taken a fair quantity of wine. Despite that, he was not the habitual drunk, and his manners were impeccable. 'Will you please accompany me to my hut, just beyond the vineyard here, and take some wine?' he asked. 'It is only a hundred metres away.'

'Good!' said Ned, turning to me, 'it will be a new experience for you to try our natural wine, which is much better than the wine you can buy in the shops.' Pukljak led the way and we followed.

Built of stout bamboo poles with a makeshift wooden door and thatched with vine leaves, the hut was minute, tucked away into a cutting in the bank above his vineyard, and hidden from view. Inside, a small rickety table, a bench and several nondescript bottles, all empty, and two enormous wooden barrels filled the available space.

In one corner, a small natural spring had found its way to the top of the hill and into Pukljak's hut; it kept him supplied with pure fresh water. For security reasons perhaps, its presence was concealed by the top of a winebarrel, and it occurred to me that Pukljak had probably built the hut around what must have been for him a miraculous bit of good fortune. I asked him whether he had considered bottling the water for sale with the brand name of Tuhelj; it could prove very popular in view of its proximity to the church! He laughed aloud and said that anyone lucky enough to find a spring immediately wanted to bottle the stuff and endow it with extravagant benefits. As far as he knew only one had been successful, somewhere in Bosnia, where the owner had claimed sexual virility for his water and had at once attracted a flood of German tourists – until the militia discovered what he was up to and sent him away on a short holiday as a guest of the state.

So Pukljak's spring remained hidden and served its master exclusively – with who knows what properties – before and after the taking of wine. Accordingly, we were invited to clear our palates with the purest of waters before turning our attention to the wine.

Apart from the courtesy of exchanging good wishes every time a bottle was raised to waiting lips, this was no place for formality. The wine itself was white and cloudy, untouched by the clearing processes which, according to Ned, improved the appearance but never the quality.

'Cheers! Živjeli!' and the ritual of good comradeship began.

'Ah!' sighed Ned, 'You can drink as much of this as you like without having a head like a stone the next morning. Isn't that so comrade?' he asked, turning to Pukljak.

'Da, da, there are no enemies in these barrels,' declared the said Pukljak, caressing the flank of the barrel nearest him like an old friend.

Ned then invited him to come and share our picnic.

'Thank you comrade, I should like to very much if you will allow me to contribute the wine,' and without waiting for the offer to be accepted, he solemnly set about filling several bottles. It was as much an expression of confidence in the quality of his wine as a gesture of native hospitality.

As we came over the brow of the hill the sight of a sumptuous spread of food, the breathtaking view of the valley of Tuhelj, the jolly faces of what now seemed like half the village, and Pepek's son Ivića singing as he accompanied himself on the accordion wiped out any lingering restraint. The singing swelled into a chorus with everyone joining in.

'You are very lucky to be working so close to the soil,' I said to Pukljak, 'it must be immensely satisfying.'

'Yes, that is true,' he replied. 'The work is hard and, like the rest of my friends, I am poor – but quite content.' His smile confirmed that. 'I have no worries because not a single hair of my head will fall unless God wills it, and I accept His providence in all things. I come up the hill every morning and work in the vineyard. On a clear day I can see the spires of the great cathedral in Zagreb where my brother is a priest. At about midday I finish and sit in my hut drinking wine. When I have had enough – about the time Konrad rings the Angelus – I fill a bottle and take it home.'

Ned was obviously moved by this and I could see that he was struggling with his thoughts. 'I wonder how many bells, throughout the world, ring out their messages to countless numbers of people every day; and surely if Heaven wished to communicate, it would not choose some ghostly revelation, or a miracle that might alarm us, but an ordinary, everyday means easily understood such as a bell. As Konrad says, it is the voice of the church, even of Heaven perhaps!' Like a good lawyer, Ned paused to reflect on the impact of his words. No one spoke.

'Indeed,' he continued, 'it could have been a message to remind us that we are enjoying a wonderful day under a clear blue sky, with a beautiful view, excellent food, and wine from the very hill on which we are sitting. What is more, we can enjoy all this again whenever we choose.' Ned had certainly started something. Everybody became involved in making extravagant promises. There was even talk about buying a part of the hill on which to build a house that would welcome us back every year. More wine and we would certainly not have stopped at only part of the hill!

I suggested that whether we met every year was not as important as just meeting whenever we could, and, in order to give notice of that, might it not be a good idea to commission Konrad to ring a special message as we departed. And perhaps we should ask him – I too was getting carried away – to light as many candles as the little stand in the church could accommodate in honour of Our Lady of Tuhelj.

Making our way slowly down the hill, the thought of those candles led me back to 'Lead Kindly Light', and, as the bell rang out across the valley, the words came unbidden: 'The night is dark and I am far from home, Lead Thou me on.'

There is much more to remember of that enchanting day on the hill overlooking Tuhelj that must remain a memory, except perhaps for Pepek Posavać saying to me, as I accepted a farewell glass of wine in his hospitable house, 'Don't be unduly anxious over just one more glass, because between you and the wine there is only the grape, Živjeli!'

CHAPTER FIVE
NIKOLA

Double Martini

(Among the many adventures stored away in my memory is a tram ride in Calcutta. The weather was excessively humid, and the tram overcrowded with barely enough standing room as we rattled along what is generally recognised as being the busiest street in the world – Chowringhee.

It was a hair raising experience, and one had to marvel at the extraordinary courage of people – whether on foot, pedalling furiously on a rickety bicycle, or more comfortably transported in an amazing assortment of vehicles – attempting to cross the tramlines for the safe haven of the maidan beyond, well knowing that the only consideration they could expect from the driver was a quick flick on the tram bell as he bore down on them. What is more, the protagonists on and off the tram seemed to enjoy the experience, laughing merrily every time there was a near call. Like so much else in India, it was a game, and I must admit to enjoying it very much.)

The last time I climbed aboard a tram was in Zagreb, in the Republic Square (now called the Ban Jelačić Square) with Ned, and the principal difference between the Calcutta and Zagreb trams was that whereas in Calcutta passengers travelled on the running board, and on the roof if they could secure a perch there, filling the time with loud conversation and much laughter, in Zagreb there appeared to be a greater sense of discipline and very little conversation.

When I put this to Ned, he pondered over the matter and then came up with: 'Ya, if some of our people had got up on the roof it would be because they had drunk too much sljivović; they would be happy of course, and may even claim a democratic right for their actions, but the militia would take a different view. Inside the tram, people don't talk too loudly because it is considered impolite – or perhaps because the ears of the authorities are everywhere – though the natural inclination in their hearts is not only to talk but to sing. So we are not all that different from those people in Calcutta.'

That was a reassuring thought, but for the moment the only sound that exercised a democratic right to be heard came from the whirring of steel on steel as the tram rumbled on towards the terminus at the foot of Sljeme. And for us there was the pleasing prospect of Nikola's company; that adventurous spirit guaranteed to inject a little happiness into every step of his daily rounds – whether to celebrate the good news or ease the pain of the bad.

The time we had spent together was still fresh in his mind and he went over the experience in some detail emphasising that the absence of a common language had not been an impediment. Indeed, he insisted, there had been a complete meeting of minds. And when Milka reminded him that we hardly knew each other his answer was emphatic: 'Nonsense šef [chief]! There are some people you know at once, as though they have always been part of your family.' Well, if that's how Nikola felt, it was all right with me.

Now Nikola was a sworn opponent of the gostionica (pub) culture, claiming that it served more headaches than good drinks – reason enough for making his own wine and sljivovic to enjoy at home with his friends – but he made an exception in the case of Debeli Martin (Fat Martin) on grounds of 'licentia poetica' because I had christened it 'Double Martini', and the name stuck. Moreover, he was much taken by the similarities with the Union Inn in Denbury and even expressed the hope of visiting that pub one day.

Although Double Martini was the place for examining matters of international importance, we had come to pass on the news that the Cambridge contingent of Comex 3 had decided to invite Nikola's daughter Nena to join them. He seemed pleased but his mind was elsewhere, on the 'saga of the motorbicycle' and he wanted to talk about it – after a welcoming glass of sljivovic!

Nikola had for some time been toying with the idea of acquiring such a vehicle which would add something to his image and efficiency, and reduce the excessive wear on his shoes and energy. But while his savings might accommodate that small outlay, it would mean pedalling hard to help the little motor uphill on the way back from the main post office because there would not be room enough on the tram for himself and transport. However, he would have to wait and see.

A second hand moped was acquired and the work of reconstruction began at once. Like everything else that went on at No 19, the whole family joined in.

The frame was a bit rusty but otherwise sound enough. Only the skeleton of a saddle remained, but Milka could soon put that right with a small rubber cushion in Croatian colours. Tyres and tubes were perished and would need replacing; some spokes were broken and there were no brake linings. The chain looked serviceable. For a few dinars the deficiencies could be made good, and with the application of a little oil and paint the machine would be as good as new, or if that was putting it too high at least operational.

No sooner said than done. Milka began work on the cushion and saddle cover, Zoran was dispatched to the shops to get the spare parts and paint while Nikola and the girls began cleaning and oiling the frame and wheels. A pump and head and tail lights would also be required, but these extras could await the outcome of the trial.

At 5 o'clock on a fine Monday morning Nikola was mobile. With the glow of achievement flooding his senses and the good wishes of his family ringing in his ears he rode off into a new dawn turning neatly into the main road leading to the central sorting office.

He moved at a modest speed, the engine ticking over gently to a pleasing rhythm and both his feet firmly planted on the pedals ready for any emergency. And not at any time did he forget to sound the horn or make the proper hand signals. Nor did he fail to wave politely to passing acquaintances or to acknowledge their greetings.

Before a set of red traffic lights he stopped and waved towards the militiaman on duty. But the latter reacted in the most unfriendly manner: 'I hope you've got a licence to ride that old crock,' he shouted at Nikola.

Furious at this insult, not only to himself but to the love and devotion of his family, Nikola shouted back: 'Where's your partner, the one who can read and write!'

It was a disagreeable start to the morning and a great rage began to take hold of him. The more he thought about it the worse it became: 'I was riding along these roads on a homemade wooden scooter long before some unfortunate mother gave birth to that cretin,' he muttered to himself.

Free-wheeling down the hill lifted his spirits. He crossed the tramlines, touched his cap to the cathedral, and then cruised comfortably on towards the post office. Apart from the earlier exchange the operation was a total success, living up to all the loving attention that went into its launching. Nikola parked the moped with meticulous care and went in to collect the mail without giving the slightest thought to the possible hazards of riding uphill with a large bag balanced on the handlebars.

Twice he narrowly missed being hit by a car shooting across his front, and he very nearly fell off when the militiaman near the gasoline station suddenly turned to stop the traffic advancing with Nikola at its head. Cruising downhill had been an exhilarating experience, operating in the reverse direction quite another matter. However, confident that the prayers of his family were guiding him he applied full throttle, pedalled hard and made the summit without mishap. But his pulse had risen alarmingly, and the pounding in his ears warned him that he had pushed himself to the limit. His cap had slipped to the back of his head and he was sweating profusely. As he turned the corner leading into his own district, with the blissful prospect of moving effortlessly for several hundred metres down a gradual decline, he thought it might be sensible to freshen-up: to dry his face, tidy his clothes and relieve himself. Then he could demonstrate his mobility where it mattered most.

It was during the latter operation, i.e. relieving himself, that the selfsame militiaman, 'the pig-faced provocateur' of an hour before, now on his way off duty, stopped to ask Nikola, in an authoritative and threatening manner, what he was doing.

Now it was perfectly obvious that Nikola had not parked and found a discreet corner behind a hedge simply to play hide and seek with passing militiamen. What's more, he was already too far embarked on the matter to put it on hold, and was obliged to turn his head as far as his neck would stretch before confronting the militiaman with a question of his own: 'What the hell do you think I'm doing?' – something of the morning's anger apparent in the tone of his voice. But the militiaman feigned indifference to this.

'Do you realise that you are causing a public nuisance?' he demanded.

Adjusting his trousers and buttoning-up leisurely, Nikola fixed his adversary with a look that might have warned a more intelligent man not to fumble for his notebook: 'I am relieving myself out of view of everybody except those who cannot mind their own business,' he replied with heavy sarcasm, and then proceeded to deliver a few observations in the knowledge that he had his man cornered.

'I have been delivering mail in this district efficiently, punctually and to the entire satisfaction of all my clients for twenty-five years. People who live around here are wise enough to know that there are times when a man simply must relieve himself and, in the circumstances, are civilised enough to look the other way.

If a horse were making its way down the middle of this road, and without warning proceeded to flood the entire surface, splattering your boots with dung in the process, would you address it in the same disagreeable manner you have adopted towards me, a public servant? Would you threaten it with your notebook – disregarding for a moment the question of whether you are able to write?

And finally, the chief of police lives at the end of the street, I have some letters for him and will make a point of bringing to his notice that I have been impeded in the discharge of my legitimate duties – hence the delay in delivering his mail – by the wilful interference of a junior member of his force.'

That final shot found its mark reducing the militiaman's countenance to the colour of ashes. 'Nikola,' he began to grovel, 'surely you know that I was only joking and wouldn't dream of booking you! After all,' he pleaded, 'we serve the same district and we are, you might say, old friends.'

They were not friends, old or new, not by any stretch of the imagination, nor were they ever likely to be; but there was little to be gained from kicking a man when he was down. 'Very well then,' said Nikola, 'I will now continue my rounds,' and turning his back on the militiaman remounted and moved forward slowly savouring the flavour of a complete victory.

When he arrived at Double Martini, Vlasta, the blonde behind the bar, realised that something was amiss: 'Is something the matter?' she asked.

Nikola drank a glass of plum brandy, chased it down with the appropriate quantity of mineral water, and then began to recount the events of the morning. Some of the customers went outside to examine the moped and returned to join the others gathered round to listen.

'I have often thought about the law,' he said, pleased to find himself the centre of attention. 'It is neither a science nor an art, and evolves in step with the sins on which it is founded. It is a code of conduct for us all fashioned by wise men – who are themselves sinners – but too often interpreted by fools with little or no understanding of the letter, let alone the spirit, of the law they are paid to enforce.

If I am taken short and found peeing discreetly against a tree or wall, accepting that neither is a proper place for that purpose, I may be accused of violating the letter of the law but certainly not the spirit of it. A civilized man or woman, any of you for example (the compliment went down well) would appreciate the difference, but not a fool. Do you get my point?' They nodded: yes, they had got it.

'It takes a man, or woman, of ordinary common sense to make the distinction. Now listen to me,' he went on, 'suppose I am riding a bicycle and find myself moving across a pair of tramlines but fail to notice a tram approaching; a quick witted and helpful militiaman would shout clearly: "Look out for the tram!" I would react instinctively, engage full throttle and pedal hard, and the militiaman would probably raise his hand against the oncoming tram, as he might in any emergency, and then signal it on with a courteous "Dobar dan" – perhaps wagging his finger at me in a friendly fashion: "You were lucky that time Nikola!" He would probably know my name for having served, like me, in the same district for many years. In these circumstances I would have committed an offence against the letter of the law but hardly against the spirit of it, and would still be alive to talk to you today. But, had the militiaman screamed unintelligible abuse at me while fumbling for his notebook, I would most probably have been killed, deprived of your company and left him with no one to book. The responsibility would be his which of course he would deny vehemently.'

'Have a drink Nikola,' said a friend and admirer for whom the idea of Nikola being run down by a tram was not very pleasant.

'The law my friends,' he lowered his voice as if confiding a secret, 'is the instrument of freedom not oppression. It is not to be upheld simply by twirling a small white baton or pointing it in a threatening manner at a citizen of Croatia. A militiaman is not the law, he is a servant of the people and the hand of their law. And, as you know, God made hands to work and to help.'

An old man sitting in the corner murmured 'Dobro!' and after a brief pause raised his glass: 'Živjeli Nikola!'

The bishop's dream

Never having absented himself on account of sickness, or for any other reason, Nikola continued to carry out his duties with a sense of responsibility that won for him the admiration of his customers and the reputation of a rising star in the post office. Over the past two years many new experiences had come into his life adding to the fund of stories he carried from door to door as he went his daily rounds, leaving at each a cheery greeting and an anecdote or two to relieve the impending boredom of the day.

Today he had something else to talk about. A large number of students from twenty British universities were bound for India with the object of demonstrating that the greatest challenge of the twentieth century lay in crossing the barriers between people – a journey that would take them across the borders of eight countries through the lands of a thousand million people – and Nena, his eldest daughter, was to accompany them.

I had of course given him prior warning of this and he had reacted enthusiastically; but being by nature cautious, and inured to the possibility of good fortune ever entering his door by way of a miracle or the benevolence of the state, Nikola hadn't taken the matter seriously. And now it was actually happening, just as Nena was about to finish her degree course in Indology.

The news caused considerable excitement among Nikola's immediate neighbours and quickly spread throughout the district. It was the most talked about event since the end of the Second World War. Everyone wanted to help and, with a stream of advice pouring in from all quarters, the indefatigable Milka was busy making plans in which she was anxious to incorporate every bit of advice, and every suggestion. So much so that Nikola was forced to intervene, even at the expense of dampening her enthusiasm and upsetting her friends. Nena was not going to the moon, he pointed out, only to India; it would be hot there, and lighter clothes might be more suitable. There was no need, for instance, to step up production on the knitting machine, because she was unlikely to find much use for three heavy cardigans – even if they were in the Croatian colours of red, white and blue.

However, having made his point he left her to it and hurried away to Double Martini, where he was always assured of an attentive audience. But before sharing the news with his companions, he waited for that precise moment when the warming glow of sljivovića would signal that they were ready to assimilate the revelation that Nena would be travelling overland to India. 'Comrades,' he said, 'I am proud to tell you that she will be the sole representative of Croatia, and will be meeting face to face the people whose history, culture and customs she has been studying for the past four years; whose language she has learnt and will now be able to put to the test.'

He accepted their congratulations with a mixture of parental pride and pleasure that touched their hearts, and promised that immediately Nena returned she would accompany him to Double Martini to give them a full account of her experiences. Meanwhile, having studied the background material sent to his daughter – illuminated with a little research of his own – he thought a few words from himself might not be out of place.

'The world,' began Nikola, drawing an imaginary globe in the air, 'is a small or big place, depending on how you look at it. People say that the jet age has made the world smaller because in a matter of two days you can fly around it. In little more than two hours you can fly from Zagreb to London, in nine hours to India, in six to the United States and in four to Moscow. and the great airports where these planes land and take off are windows on their countries and people – gateways to friendship and understanding you might say. Yes indeed,' he mused, 'one can fly from place to place very quickly; but there is an awful lot of land, mountains, valleys, deserts and coastline between one airport and another where most of the human family lives.

For this reason, I am overjoyed that Nena will be travelling overland to India as part of the Cambridge contingent of the largest single convoy to cross the Asian Highway since Alexander's great march from Macedonia more than two thousand years ago. Like him, she begins her journey from our heartland, unlike him she will be armed with a song and not a sword.'

Nikola could see that his companions approved of this by the way they looked at him, raising their glasses in his direction. He was a popular figure at Double Martini, his friends enjoyed listening to him and, predictably, they responded by insisting that Nena and all her companions should be their guests when they returned to Zagreb. 'That is no more than I would have expected of you my friends,' said Nikola, touched by such a spontaneous and generous invitation, 'but there are five hundred of them, so I had better just bring the particular group to which my daughter is assigned, about twenty-five I think, and all of you must come to her school where they intend to perform excerpts from Shakespeare on the day after their return.'

Nikola had a final drink and wished them all a very good day before hurrying home earlier than usual to supervise preparations for Nena's departure. As he walked home he recalled how often he had heard it said, particularly during catechism classes in his village school, that light came from the East, and as he turned that thought over in his mind it took shape as a suitable subject for Double Martini sometime after Nena's return.

Nena had been warned that each member would be allowed fifteen kilograms of luggage to include all personal requirements for a hundred days. But the first attempt at assembling these essentials covered the large settee in the drawing room and by Nikola's reckoning weighed over fifty kilos; and Milka had only just started.

'Nena is not setting up house in India,' he pointed out tactfully. 'She will not need sheets and pillows and blankets.' Milka's look of hurt and disappointment pierced his heart but what could he do? She meant well, but if allowed to carry on like this Nena would require a truck to herself. 'You see,' he said gently, 'what is required is a careful assessment of the important items, and once that's done the balance can be made up with as many extras as weight will allow. This is something only you can do satisfactorily, but first Nena must explain exactly what has been written in her joining instructions.

Then,' Nikola continued reassuringly, 'when the men and women from Cambridge come to collect her, they will be very impressed to see that she alone is not carrying any excess weight. She will be starting-out on this new and exciting adventure by setting a good example to the others. And bear this in mind šef, they will be looking to you for hospitality and encouragement during what will be their first major stop away from home. And even more, the success of the whole enterprise could well depend on how they are treated here.'

This was another small victory for Nikola. Milka liked it when he spoke quietly and she was visibly stirred by the challenge in his words. 'Bog! Bog!' she said, hugging Nena unexpectedly. The family knew that this was her way of expressing the deepest emotions. It was the same when greeting friends, saying goodbye or demonstrating a mother's love. It was her personal password to heaven, and it never seemed to fail.

By the evening, Nena was ready for the road – two days ahead of time. Cambridge was due to arrive the following evening and camp in the local stadium, Mladost, for two days before setting off for the Middle East and Asia. All members of the contingent would be brought to the house and entertained to dinner. If the weather was good, tables could be arranged outside, under the plum trees. The menu, standard for the family on all festive occasions, would be noodle soup, turkey and mlinci, and apple strudel. Nikola planned to visit his village the evening before and collect a twenty-litre demijohn of wine, and the neighbours had already offered to bake bread, cakes and other extras.

In the event everything worked according to plan. Cambridge duly arrived in a cream and gold coach with the word Cambridge on the sides and flying a little green flag. It looked very smart. On one side of the flag was the wheel of King Asoka embroidered in gold, and on the other the letter P for Prince Philip. It was later explained to Nikola that every one of the twenty vehicles was identified by the same flag which represented a symbolic link between the oldest and the largest democracies in the world – Britain and India.

Accompanied by the family and close friends, Nena met Cambridge and was duly introduced to the other members. She was given an outline of her duties and allocated a place on the coach specially designed to accommodate five crews of five, each crew operating two hours on duty and eight hours off. This meant that everyone had a specific task as driver, mechanic, navigator, radio operator or cook/steward/stewardess – Nena was to be one of the latter – a division of duties designed to ensure that responsibility for the well-being and safe passage of Cambridge was shared by all its members.

The addition of a pretty face with a welcoming smile did not go unnoticed by the men and women on board, each for their own reasons, but when Nena announced that her parents would like to invite everyone to dinner the following evening all other thoughts were banished. Accordingly, Cambridge began preparing not only for its first encounter with foreign hospitality, but to celebrate the successful completion of the first thousand miles. Precisely at six o'clock the next evening Nena arrived to collect her companions. The coach had been washed down and looked like a large block of polished marble tinted pink by the setting sun.

Dressed up for the evening, they embarked in silence, affecting a mildly superior attitude as they paraded before the envious gaze of the other four hundred and seventh-five pairs of eyes. This was Cambridge, a cut above the rest! At the end of a short journey they were received, not by a President, as in India a month later, but by a simple postman and his wife, and they were to learn there a lesson in hospitality to be remembered for the rest of their lives.

Nena tried to remember their names: Peter, Richard, Hilary, Janet, Mike, Dave and so many more. Huh! What did it matter? They would all get to know each other soon enough she thought as she waited for them to disembark outside the house.

The neighbours had lined the little street: not out of curiosity but simply to wave a welcome to a group of young people which now included one of their own. They would all be represented by their own dear Nena from Hrastovać, which merited, in addition to baking bread, cakes, and doing anything else they could to help, a demonstration of solidarity.

The Vrbos children stood dutifully behind their parents. Papa, dressed in his best suit, looked immaculate, outshining his guests in every detail. Mama was equally impressive in a navy blue dress with red and white polka dots. Everyone wore a smile.

Having rehearsed his words carefully Nikola took charge: 'I am glad to see you,' he said, which released a flood of greetings. Nena did her best to tell each one exactly what the other meant. Nikola then fired a barrage of 'how do you dos' and other pleasantries, part in English and part in Croatian – Nena weaving and ducking between them with a running translation – before planting a kiss on both cheeks of the girls. Milka simply repeated the words 'Bog! Bog!' and smiled into the eyes of her guests.

Having ensured that a glass of plum brandy was in each hand, Nikola raised his own: 'Cheers! Živjeli!' he repeated often enough for everybody to tune in and join him in a great chorus of 'Živjeli!' And that, in Nikola's book, meant that they had grasped the very foundation of the Croat language.

As they gathered round the table, candles were lit. Large glasses were placed before each one, filled with wine from Nikola's village, and the great demijohn moved into position within easy reach for all to help themselves at will. Nikola sat at the top of the table with Nena at the opposite end while Milka and the younger children shuttled back and forth to the kitchen. There were little baskets of homemade bread, plates of salami, cheese and salad spread around to cushion the impact of the plum brandy and to stimulate appetites.

The meal followed quickly, plates were filled and refilled; there was no need to ask for more and little use refusing when served. Compliments were showered upon Milka, and Nikola beamed over the scene, as a good man might whose hospitality is rewarded with spontaneous appreciation. Conversation moved swiftly from food, to drink, to Croatia and then to India.

The East was a mysterious place to most of them. None had been there before and they were careful not to claim to have done so. Nikola's knowledge came from what little he had read since Nena's involvement, while natural modesty, despite the fact that she was studying Indology at the university, prevented her from dominating the conversation. In any event, she had enough to do translating what her father and the others had to say. Communication flowed easily; they talked about the myth and the mystery that are so much part of the East: Maharishis came into it, the days of the British Raj, weddings, and even funeral rites – a subject arising out of someone commenting on the Chinese custom of scattering rice to lay a false trail for evil spirits.

'Do you believe in ghosts?' one of the girls asked Nikola. It was a casual question, prompted perhaps by the want of something better to say, but Nikola responded thoughtfully.

'I am not sure whether I do or not,' he replied, pausing long enough to hold their attention, 'but I was once told a story which may interest you.' The master story-teller knew his business, his timing was perfect, and there was a twinkle in his eye.

'O do tell us,' urged the girl, and Nikola noted that all eyes were turned on him.

The conversation had wandered thousands of kilometres away from Zagreb and had suddenly returned to the scene where candlelight reflected eager young faces: 'like stars lighting up the world,' he later recounted.

Nikola drank deep from his glass, licked his lips, brushed his moustache thoughtfully to right and left, and then began.

'A number of men were sitting in a room after dinner one night, drinking and smoking – not unlike ourselves. They represented many professions; lawyers, policemen, doctors, teachers and a bishop. There may also have been a postman,' he smiled. 'They were talking about ghosts, when one of them noticed that the bishop had fallen asleep. He was rudely awakened and asked, as a spiritual leader, to speak about the existence or otherwise of ghosts.

"That's funny," said the bishop. "I have just been having the strangest dream. I saw a man walking along a road peeling an orange; a large golden orange. Oblivious to his surroundings, he threw a particularly large piece of the orange peel over his shoulder; it was caught in the air-stream and hovered for a moment before falling like a meteorite on an ant hill. The lookout at the frontier immediately telephoned the military guard to report this extraordinary phenomenon. It defied description; the world had suddenly gone dark.

For his part the commander of the guard decided that such an occurrence called for immediate action and, buckling on his sword, ordered the trumpeter to sound the general alarm. He then telephoned the commander-in-chief. That great man, a five star general, called for his horse, and with the aid of stirrup lights, galloped to the scene of the action. His immediate military appreciation was that a giant flying saucer had landed. It was clearly a national emergency to be communicated to the Prime Minister without delay, which he did, adding a personal observation that the end of the world was at hand. Frightened out of his wits, the Prime Minister summoned his cabinet but as they had nothing constructive to say he telephoned the Queen.

Her Majesty, ever mindful of her duty, called for her state coach and bravely drove out to be confronted by ministers at a loss for words and unable to offer any plausible explanation for what had happened. Exasperated, the Queen turned to the bishop who, by coincidence, had been asleep, but awoke with a start at the sound of her voice. Noting the anxious expression on her face, he gave his opinion – choosing his words with care.

Your Majesty," he said, pleased to be addressing the Queen in person, "this is nothing more alarming than Buckingham Palace."' And there the narrative ended.

Above the ensuing laughter and derision, a young voice cried out: 'He's having us on! How does that explain your attitude to ghosts?'

'Well,' said Nikola, 'the bishop was not entirely right as you yourself have gathered. Something had undoubtedly come from the man's world into the ant's world – thus far he was right; but what he described as Buckingham Palace was, after all, only an orange peel.

There are undoubtedly many similar instances of communication between the spirit world and the man's world; it is only our interpretation that is at fault – often wildly so – and that was the purpose of the bishop's story.'

Though there was much good natured barracking and laughter, they had got the point and with it a rare insight into Nikola's sense of humour; but he had not finished: 'I have told you this story because you are moving from the developed world into the developing world. It won't be easy for you. You will see many things in the East that you have never seen before and, similarly, you will hear many things; try not to jump to conclusions too quickly. They may not always be what they seem, or mean what you think, and remember that light came from the East.

'Now you must learn the polka,' he said, getting to his feet and seizing the girl nearest him, 'so that when you come back safely to my house we may have a bigger and better party.'

A civic reception

It was something more than an expedition: Great Britain had invaded Croatia, there was no doubt about it, and, even more alarming, had taken the postman's daughter hostage. This was the sort of jolly tale that Nikola bandied about among his colleagues at the post office, and even more eloquently in the warm and congenial atmosphere of Double Martini.

But etched in his mind was the spectacle of a great convoy of ivory vehicles, each with its own little distinguishing green flag, moving out of Zagreb like an army of occupation on completion of an historic mission. He noted the famous British names emblazoned on the sides of the vehicles as they moved slowly in alphabetical order before the bemused gaze of the locals lining the road out of the Mladost stadium: Birmingham, Bristol, Cambridge, Cardiff, Durham, Edinburgh, Exeter, Glasgow, Keele, Kent, London, Leicester, Lancaster, Liverpool, Manchester, Newcastle, Oxford, Sussex, St Andrews and Yorkshire.

By virtue of their personal involvement, Nikola and his family were in the unusual position of VIPs with a perfect view whence they caught sight of Nena as she waved to them from Cambridge. Milka had cried a little and Nikola had found it very difficult not to join her. They were glad, of course, that she had been given the opportunity of taking part in something so exciting, but sad too because they would miss her. She had never left home before.

Nikola had read somewhere that time passes quickly and that the memory is short. How different it was for him. His psyche was in turmoil, the house seemed empty, and time stood still. His memory was full of a carefree evening and happy voices, overshadowed by visions of what might be happening on the road.

When the first postcard arrived from Istanbul, all the excitement of preparing for the journey came flooding back, and Nikola not only felt part of the expedition, but spoke as though he had physically arrived in Istanbul. Other postcards followed, from Ankara, Samsun, Tehran, Meshad, Kandahar and Kabul, each one pasted carefully in its proper place on a large map now adorning the drawing room wall.

Nena reported that everything was going well, apart from a few cases of diarrhoea and one of appendicitis. The latter was a medical student from St Andrews University who had been operated on by a Pakistani surgeon, somewhere in the Murree Hills behind Islamabad, but had been able to complete the final lap into India stretched out on the back seat of her coach.

In Kabul they had staged an entertainment. It was so widely publicised that members of the then royal family announced their intention of attending, but were advised against it on the grounds that it was only a trial run of what was to be inflicted on audiences in Pakistan and India, and might not be entirely suitable. In the event it was such a success that the organisers regretted their advice, and admitted as much next day on the front page of the *Kabul Times* under the banner headline: 'A Commonwealth Village on Wheels.'

One of Nena's postcards talked about making camp at least a dozen times since leaving home: the spectacle so attracted visitors, she said, that they had adopted the policy, whenever possible, of entertaining the public in the middle of the camp site, using the coaches to mark out the stage and supply the lighting. She went on to amplify that piece of information by saying that the light-green tents, 'spreading their wings like giant moonmoths around our improvised auditorium' had prompted the headline in the *Kabul Times*.

As these situation reports arrived Nikola relayed them to his friends at Double Martini with a few embellishments of his own. If she reported something as being successful, he passed it on as outstandingly so, always giving the news more credit than she claimed.

He painted for them a picture of a long white caravan finding its way across the great desert between Damascus and Baghdad, much in the fashion of a camel train, exposed to the heat one moment, enveloped in sandstorms the next, or moving steadily through the cool of the night under stars hanging like jewels from a blackened sky, touching the horizon at every point. He asked them to imagine that desert filled with the great silence of the night and broken only by the inter-communicating radio reporting progress from the front, and the all clear from behind. It was like a military operation; there was no other sound. 'Anyway,' he broke the spell, 'such a journey has never been attempted before.'

According to one report, an entertainment staged in India had attracted an audience of about ten thousand people every night on six consecutive nights. Nikola found that hard to believe, but there it was, clearly stated in Nena's letter. 'Ten thousand people a night for six nights', Nikola reminded his friends, 'is sixty thousand people, and that is in only one place. How many people do you suppose they have met in all?' He let them ponder that question for a moment before continuing: 'I am so glad Nena is forging this link between Croatia and the Commonwealth. And how appropriate it is since we have such good relations with both Britain and India at either end of this great trek into a world we can only dream about.

We all have dreams comrades but, according to my daughter Nena, she and her companions are witnessing an impossible dream come true. Perhaps, comrades,' he continued, a solemn note creeping into his voice, 'the Commonwealth is the real superpower after all because its strength is people; just ordinary, everyday people like you and me, hundreds of millions of them.'

The passion and eloquence of their favourite postman held them in thrall. Words were the only means available to him; words to express the pride he felt in his daughter and the great enterprise on which she was embarked. His friends understood this and remained silent. Single handed, Nikola was doing in Double Martini what Nena's expedition had been trying to do along the length of the Asian Highway, and time did pass quickly – almost unnoticed but for the change in the weather heralding the coming of Christmas.

Nikola had received a telegram from somewhere in Turkey to the effect that Nena and her companions would be arriving in Zagreb at five o'clock the next morning. It actually read: 'Arriving tomorrow morning. Expect to be outside the cathedral at five o'clock. We are the same number. All is well. Lots of love. Nena.' A shrewd calculation and reference to the expedition map in the drawing room placed the convoy, at best, on the frontier between Salonika and Skopje, or between Edirne and Sofiya, depending on the route they were taking. Nena must have meant the day after tomorrow, 'unless', as Nikola joked with his youngest daughter Mirjana while studying the telegram, 'they are flying on their moonmoth'. And he was right.

The first thing to consider was food and wine. That was priority one. Nikola would also make a start with the cooking to ensure that everything would be all right, knowing perfectly well that there was no need for any such initiative. The truth was that he was too excited to sit still.

Milka and Mirjana would proceed to the cathedral, having first visited the market to collect supplies of cream, cheese, vegetables and ham, and bring the whole party back to the house, where they would have breakfast and a little rest before making their way to Double Martini. Zoran would carry a message to that hospitable establishment warning Vlasta and her clientele to expect twenty-five guests at one o'clock, or a little later depending on circumstances.

Mother and daughter arrived at the forecourt of the cathedral at the appointed hour, and there was the coach, not as clean as it had been when they last saw it, but safe and well. The little green flag was in its place. The occupants were asleep, but Nena had been looking out for them and rushed out to hug her mother and sister, and to shed a few happy tears. Noticing little movement inside, Milka insisted on going into the cathedral to light a few candles in thanksgiving before returning to the coach.

'Good morning, how do you do,' she called out in Croatian as she stepped aboard, beaming her warmest smile at the weary faces within. They smiled back and the girls among them came forward to hug Milka with as much warmth and affection as her own daughter. The men followed shortly, and then it was more kisses and hugs all round. 'Bog! Bog! Come, we go home,' said Milka as she occupied a seat near the entrance. Nena sat beside her and they talked about everything at once, sharing each morsel with the rest of the coach. As far as Nena and her mother were concerned they were all part of one family and coming back to Zagreb was coming home.

On the home front meanwhile, Nikola had been busy preparing a reception fit for heroes. His elder son, Miro, and second daughter, Nada, had come in to help. Zoran, the youngest, and in permanent residence, was put in charge of the ablutions. But the facilities in the house were insufficient for such a large number so he was out negotiating with neighbours for a bath here and a bed there, and in the process came away with offers of hospitality not just for twenty-five but for all five hundred. Or so it seemed to Zoran. Many of them had sons and daughters of their own, about the same age, so the simple matter of providing a bath grew into everything from accommodation to clean clothes. And each house insisted on contributing something, or a bit of everything, and certainly enough to turn the occasion into a national celebration. 'We have food enough; and wine, and music,' protested Nikola, 'but not enough young people to do justice to all three, so you must bring your sons and daughters as well,' he insisted.

The most remarkable feature of these proceedings, however, was how a postman, whose English had progressed no further than a single confident sentence: 'How do you do,' with variations of 'Very well,' and 'Thank you very much,' supported staunchly by a wife with a vocabulary of little more than 'cornflakes', because she liked cornflakes, could cope with a house full of people all speaking a foreign language. But it soon became evident that a few of the neighbours were students of English too and could be deployed to speed up communication. Milka managed with food, smiles, and her eternal invocation 'Bog! Bog!' while Nikola concentrated on the wine, a hearty laugh, and the polka!

There was more than a little philosophy in all of this. People are people, and young people more obviously so: their needs simple, their responses to kindness spontaneous and their enthusiasm infectious. No one understood this better than the postman.

Hosts and guests moved about in relays; here to have a bath, there to help themselves to ham and eggs, cottage cheese with sour cream, home made bread, strudel and coffee. A few stayed put, seeking instant relief from the weariness of the night in a glass of plum brandy. In due course the majority came to rest in the drawing room, filling the available space on the floor. Others stood in the connecting hall. The moment was at hand for Nikola to raise his glass:

'Živjeli!' he began, and they all responded to that. 'We are all very happy to see you back safe and well. Since you were last here, three months ago, you have travelled about forty thousand kilometres and you have met hundreds of thousands of people. They will all remember you because you had the courage to go; despite the weather, health hazards, unusual food, and very little personal comfort. You went to all those countries to make friends. What a wonderful thing you have done.

We followed your journey on this map here, as you will see from Nena's postcards pinned up all over it. We were often anxious for you, and Milka went to church every day to pray for you. So, as the bells of the cathedral were ringing today you came home to us. I congratulate you, and I thank you for looking after my daughter.

It was my hope that you and your comrades would receive a civic reception on your return to Croatia. Unfortunately, that has not happened, but I assure you that the heart of Croatia beats strong in the breast of this postman, his family and friends. Please remember this. And one day, when you occupy important positions in your own country, please remember Croatia too.'

And that did it; suddenly everyone was doing the polka – in the drawing room, the hall, the verandah and outside under the plum trees where Nikola's bees watched without protest. They too were in action singing tunefully as they went about their labours.

(At the time no one could have foreseen the events that lay in store for the old Yugoslavia. We are all much wiser now. My wife and I visit Croatia from time to time as a gesture of solidarity with our friends, and Nena has been to Edinburgh – perhaps with a similar purpose in mind. But she came armed with a seven foot candle – which at first sight looked like an outsize billiard cue – as a blessing from the Holy Land taller than the recipient. I have not yet dared to light it.

A review of the Vrbos family fortunes occupied much of our discussion: Nikola has retired from the Post Office; the children are married and gone their separate ways but return with seasonal regularity to raid Nikola's garden and to replenish their supplies of wine and honey. There are many grandchildren, and Milka watches over them from heaven. Nena has completed her postgraduate studies in Jerusalem and is now a teacher, married with children of her own.

The remorseless brutality that engulfed the old Yugoslavia has left Croatia wounded but proud to be free. Nikola still lives in the house on Hrastovać. Despite everything that has happened to his country he remains indomitable, with few complaints, leaving the final word to an infallible judge, while he continues to make his own wine and sljivovića.

He still enjoys a regular rental from his bees, currently celebrating over fifty years of freedom under his inspiring leadership, and he never fails to raise a glass to the memory of the Commonwealth Expedition. Živjeli!)

CHAPTER SIX

CHARWALLAH

(Tea-vendor – chiefly British and informal)

When the mind has nothing better to do it is inclined to wander aimlessly, occasionally coming across a little gem or two long neglected and crying out for attention. And then the action begins. Perhaps it was my obsession with the circumstances of my friends in the old Yugoslavia that triggered the process! In any event, that is how I came to be thinking about the charwallahs of the Empire, great men all, attached to British regiments stationed in the sub-continent before the war, and the enormous contribution they made to the morale of those regiments.

These thoughts began to take shape as I marched across the Dean Bridge in Edinburgh with a firm grip on my old trilby hat (the wind from the North Sea blows hard here) lest it become dislodged from my head and end up in the Water of Leith below. Pace quickening, I had reached George Street and was moving purposefully in the direction of the Edinburgh Book Shop when a familiar voice stopped me in my tracks, and I saw Tom Lewin advancing towards me with a broad grin.

'Remember me?' he asked.

'How could I forget?' I retorted, quickly turning over the pages of my memory to check that I had his name right.

Without actually testing Tom's recollection of events, the particular subject being a delicate one, I had little doubt that he would remember leading a disparate group of Commonwealth volunteers from Britain, Canada, India and Zambia through the centre of Ooty, working hard on his bagpipes for nearly two hours at an altitude of seven thousand feet. It was a spectacle guaranteed to capture the wondering, amused, and even astonished gaze of the locals – all of whom clapped not knowing what else they were expected to do. And Tom's performance may well have evoked many old friendships along the Commercial Road; but at journey's end he expressed himself in a distinctly unfriendly manner: 'The person who dreamed up this idea,' he declared, 'needs to be put away.' And, as I had played a part in the dreaming, it was as well to distance myself from close contact until he had regained his own composure and a piper's good humour.

Besides, there was another factor that made my role all the more suspect, for while the others had marched, spruced up in jeans, salvar kameez, saris and suits – Tom himself was kilted, with a glengarry atop his head – I alone rode in a rickshaw, looking like a relic of empire, excused marching on grounds of having my left leg in plaster. It had happened in this manner.

We were assembled with our Indian hosts in the state guest house in Chandigarh, the capital of Punjab at the opposite end of India, for a briefing by Kamaljit Singh Garewal, a young lawyer from the Punjab High Court. The programme included Simla and Amritsar, which had something to do with the former having been the unofficial capital of the Empire, and the latter the point of no return for its demise. And he expressed the hope that we would survive both without mishap before being transported to Tamil Nadu, and thence the Nilgiris, in the *Mountbatten* – a train so named in honour of the event. We asked the obligatory questions and then followed our leader into an adjoining room to sample the first instalment of Punjabi hospitality, not very different from the rest of India but pepped up with a strong man's ration of alcohol.

This was an agreeable start to the adventures ahead and we naturally set out to express our appreciation in the approved manner. Representing the African continent, the Zambians opened the proceedings with some exceptionally fine singing; the Canadians followed with equal enthusiasm and insisted on teaching the rest of us to sing 'O Canada' – which we dutifully did.

When it came to the turn of the sons and daughters of the old mother country, I found myself being propelled into the centre of the arena to perform the Highland Fling on a hard concrete floor. With national honour at stake caution was not an option. Tom piped with enthusiasm. Now if a display had to be given, it was as well to give it wholeheartedly, and, bowing to that principle, I shot up into the air with turns and high kicks that must have been impressive, because there was much vocal encouragement, until something like an explosion took place behind my left leg. I thought at first that someone had deliberately kicked me, but it soon became apparent that this was more in the nature of a self-inflicted wound – my left leg was no longer operational on account of an Achilles tendon having just been sacrificed in the service of the Commonwealth. But the party went on while I was transported to Kamaljit Singh Garewal's house. His wife, Gurjeevan, is a doctor – the scientific kind more interested in research than repair. Nevertheless, she was in no doubt that a surgeon's hand was called for.

Back at the guest house, Tom continued to play and others stepped in to fill my place, while in the Garewal household a conference was called. The programme in Punjab and Himachal was scheduled to last ten days, and I was expected to appear, along with my friends, before an invited audience in the Gaiety Theatre in Simla. At the Agricultural University in Ludhiana, it had been put about that having been made an honorary Sikh, for no greater reason than writing a lighthearted poem about the Sikh truck drivers on the Grand Trunk Road, I would be joining my bearded brothers on stage in the Bhangra – a dance calling for even greater agility and stamina than the fling – and they could not be disappointed!

In Amritsar, an entertainment for the general public had been planned and published, and an impressive list of dignitaries invited. That show too had to go on. A telephone call to Parmjit Singh Grewal, a leading orthopaedic surgeon in Amritsar, confirmed that surgery was unavoidable and that the leg should be suspended without any weight being placed upon it.

To me personally he communicated the following message: 'Please bring your leg safely to my hospital and I will underake the operation,' adding that there was nothing to worry about. My friends expressed their approval of these arrangements and presented me with a solid walking stick.

The Gaiety Theatre owes its origins to the days of the viceroys and the goings on in Simla during the summer months – which included an amateur dramatic society. That tradition continues, more or less, and no violent activity was expected from me. But an early appearance on stage did draw audible murmurs of sympathy and I was let off the hook after a loudly acclaimed 'Captains', as it was now called, delivered in the manner of 'The Charge of the Light Brigade'.

At the Agricultural University in Ludhiana, however, it was a different story. Carried away by an overdose of enthusiasm, the Dean announced that not only would I be joining in the Bhangra, but I would be doing so on one leg, which qualified for loud and prolonged cheers. Of course, many of my friends in the Commonwealth have done their share of crossing the barriers that divide people – an example I was about to emulate – but none could claim to have done so on one leg!

The leader of the Bhangra dancers was an enormous Sikh who wore his beard with a challenging double twist under the chin. It somehow suited the gold and red turban that adorned his head, towering proudly above all the others. And to this great man I had but a moment in which to whisper a desperate plea: 'Bhai Sahib,' I said, 'you will have to steer me through this ordeal or my leg is finished for ever.'

The Bhai Sahib (respected brother) did the trick. 'Don't vurry!' he reassured me as the cry went up, 'Sat Sri Akal' and we were off. My feet barely touched the ground. His right arm held my left in a vice-like grip that carried me through the air, legs dangling with every turn, as the drummers hammered out the deafening, accelerating rhythm of the dance of the warriors celebrating their harvest festival. I came through that ordeal with no greater damage to my person than an armful of bruises, although the operation in Amritsar next day took much longer than it might otherwise have done: the severed tendon having worked its way up the back of the leg and very nearly out of reach of the surgeon's fingers.

'We are very glad to have been of service to you,' said Parmjit after the operation. Food was brought from his house and a member of the family watched over my welfare day and night. They had never met me before, but Kamaljit Singh's father was a cousin, and that was enough to treat me as one of their own without thought of cost or convenience to themselves. They too, and who can tell how many more, had not lost touch with old friendships.

The entertainment scheduled for Amritsar did take place, switched at the last moment from hotel to hospital, under a colourful shamiana (decorative cloth canopy) on the hospital lawn, so that I could attend in a wheel chair. This was yet another example of how India responds instinctively to people who have won a place in her affections. The entertainment was made all the more enjoyable by the nursing staff presenting an item of their own, which encouraged the management to come forward with the suggestion that 'without doubt there must be another show in hotel tomorrow only'. And to that venue I was transported in my surgeon's car, and wheeled into the auditorium by his own hand.

These events had taken place a long time ago, as I have already indicated, and, if Tom needed reminding, he could always refresh his memory with a long sentimental look at the pipe banner presented to him on behalf of the state and people of Himachal by the Governor at a reception in his residence in Simla.

As we walked down Hanover Street to continue our discussion over a cup of coffee at Henderson's, I could sense that Tom's outlook had matured. But his appearance was much the same: clean cut, lean and fit with a steady smile befitting the personality of a dedicated young officer in the Lothian Police. He was also a member of the pipe band, he told me, and when I asked him whether he had ambitions to become the Pipe Major he was modest enough to admit that that was unlikely; he was more concerned about trying to keep his place in the band.

It crossed my mind then that Tom might even bring to the Edinburgh police a different view of the Commonwealth than was provided by the Commonwealth Games, when more than half the member states chose to decline the hospitality of this ancient and royal city. The welcome so beautifully sung by thousands of children, the kilted Sir Yehudi Menuhin playing with the Scottish fiddlers, and the comradeship so readily offered in every public meeting place had been spurned in favour of staging a protest against the British Government's attitude to sanctions against South Africa. However, that is yesterday's story.

Tom mentioned that an ancestor of his had been an officer in the East India Company and had written a book about his experiences during the Mutiny which he promised to lend me one day. And with that, having exchanged addresses and telephone numbers, we parted company – Tom to pick up his car from a much-prized parking space on George Street, and I to pick up a couple of fresh loaves from the Italian bakers in Stockbridge on the way home.

As I walked along the cobbled street replaying much of our conversation, I could not help wondering why so many Commonwealth leaders sought to acquire political merit, even personal satisfaction, from knocking the old mother country. Britain had done them no harm, indeed the contrary could be true, and may even have contributed something towards their progress. Besides, was it not an entirely voluntary process that led them out of the British Empire into the Commonwealth? My thoughts moved on to the Indian Mutiny and I wondered, as most people do I suppose, what it is that drives human beings to the point of slaughtering each other, and often total strangers, for no better reason than that they happen to have been caught in the sights of a self-repeating rifle.

But one can easily be drowned in such thinking, and what has it got to do with the Charwallah anyway? I'm not sure, but when searching for those old friendships on which the Commonwealth was built, there maybe some merit in listening to what he has to say.

And perhaps it was for this reason that the Mutiny remained fixed in my mind; so much so that when I got home I picked up Vincent Smith's *History of India*. Page 663 sets out the events leading up to 15 May 1857.

The East India Company's Army was two hundred and thirty-eight thousand strong, of which only thirty-eight thousand were British. Half of them were killed. The causes of the Mutiny are clearly set out, and the writer concludes with these words: 'The pity of it is that the issue should have been put to the test of battle, to be decided at the cost of so much blood, and the flowing of so many tears.'

For nearly a century after the Mutiny, British troops continued to be stationed in India: enlisted soldiers to serve seven years with the colours and five on the reserve, their officers bound only by a code of honour. And seven meant seven, there was no going back on the deal; no walkouts, no working to rule or anything of that kind. Every hour, every day, every month was mortgaged to the Crown and accounted for to ensure that the contract was properly honoured.

It is difficult to imagine those soldiers today, thousands of miles from home, cooped up in barrack rooms accommodating a platoon of about thirty men each. But it is important not only to imagine them but to remember them, because out of the bone of their discipline grew the tradition of professionalism, comradeship and courage that were to become the hallmarks of the Commonwealth and Empire armies.

Every soldier had an iron bedstead, a light-blue Indian durrie and a wooden kit box. Chairs and tables were not allowed. But there was a coir mattress which came in three sections for easy stacking known as biscuits. On top of these, every morning, two sheets, two blankets and a mosquito net, folded neatly to match precisely the size of the regulation pillow, were carefully arranged in the order: blanket, sheet, mosquito net, sheet, blanket and pillow.

Kit boxes and beds were dressed in line from one end of the barrack room to the other. A towel was draped over each kit box. Highly polished boots and spotless white canvas shoes were tastefully arranged on the forward edge of the bed. 'Boots on the inside, shoes on the outside!' was how the platoon corporal called out the morning routine. Nothing was ever out of place and everything had to be ready for inspection by 7 a.m. Such was the start of each day.

Immaculately blancoed, brasses sparkling, and stretched across supporting bamboos with the bayonet suspended in the middle, personal equipment hung on two hooks to one side of the bed. The greatcoat too had its appointed place behind the equipment, with arms reversed and tucked neatly inside the back straps. At night, mosquito nets were tied to wires running parallel down both sides of the barrack room. Inside the mosquito net lay privacy and a place to dream. In the centre of the barrack room a riflerack held one rifle per soldier, chained through trigger guards and locked at the free end. An ammunition box, secured to the concrete floor, contained a maximum of five rounds per rifle.

This was home for years on end. The average salary was about fifteen shillings a week and the accommodation free. Supper was not included.

Although there was no charge for unironed laundry, the khaki drill for parade required not only ironing but starching – if it was to pass first the platoon sergeant's and then the platoon commander's inspection, and once or twice a week the more discerning eyes of the company sergeant major and the company commander – and for this purpose, a facility known as 'flying dhobie' was available at a penny a piece. Soap, toothpaste, cleaning materials and other essentials also came out of the weekly budget leaving very little to nourish a weary and well exercised body.

Entertainment, such as a visit to the local cinema, restaurant or dance hall, consumed a week's wages. Female company was a rare luxury and came only to those lucky enough to make a good impression in the railway colony. For some, the end of the rainbow lay in the seedier quarters of the bazaar, with all the attendant risks. The majority soldiered on with remarkable equanimity.

But a stripe made all the difference. Picked out of a list of hundreds, the unpaid lance corporal emerged tottering on the first rung of a long ladder that could carry him up to the stars, or as easily drop him into oblivion. That single stripe attracted universal contempt, the wearer thereof becoming known to all and sundry as a 'lancejack', and for him the period of trial and humiliation lasted for about a year. He was never out of someone's sights. If he failed to impress his many superiors, or to discipline the private soldiers who despised him – without the inducement of any extra pay – the stripe would take wing like a mosquito disturbed at work and be gone for ever.

The list of his duties was endless: supervising the sweeping of barrack rooms and verandahs; lining up beds, beddings, boots and shoes; ensuring that the rifles were clean and that the contents of the ammunition box had been checked and found correct, or otherwise; marching fatigue parties to their appointed place of labour. There was also the regimental side of standing in for the corporal of the guard: posting and changing sentries every two hours throughout a twenty-four-hour period without indulging in a little nap between times. Checking in all late-comers against the company orderly sergeants' rosters while the guard commander himself enjoyed a full quota of sleep; or parading squads of soldiers not otherwise gainfully employed in drill, physical training, musketry, map reading or afternoon education classes, which most of the men needed but resisted by every means possible – these were just a few of the extras that came his way.

All these duties, carried out meticulously, could hasten that sunny day when an announcement in regimental orders that he had been appointed paid lance corporal would change everything. Congratulations flowed from every quarter; instant recognition followed. A stripe on both arms instead of just one signalled a dramatic change in status, respect came from above and below, earnings went up by a shilling and nine pence a day and access to the platoon sergeant was available without an appointment.

Promotion to corporal was unlikely to happen for many years; but when it did come, he would no longer be working class but part of the management, riding up front with the men who manned the guns, and second only to the platoon sergeant. The doors to the outside world would slowly swing open to admit him. Henceforth, contact with his former comrades would be conducted through the medium of orders. He would no longer visit the canteen, except on duty, and would be a permanent member of the Corporals' Mess. His sights would be raised, cautiously at first but none the less raised, to the giddy heights of sergeant, to be reached with any luck in another five years of exemplary service. For the ordinary private soldier, it was a long and perilous journey, and only a few made it. An officer might be trained in two years; it took every bit of five to produce a good corporal.

The daily routine began with reveille at six, followed by a mug of tea – dipped out of a camp kettle fetched from the cookhouse by the room orderly for the day and placed in the centre of the barrack room – and a biscuit. This early boost to the day's activities went by the name of 'gun-fire', dating back to the older tradition of frightening soldiers out of their dreams by firing a gun. The working day ended twelve hours later with the sounding of retreat. The time between was filled with parades in the morning: physical training, some drill perhaps, weaponry and an inspection or two – with time allowed for education and general fatigues in the afternoon. Sport was confined to the evening.

Roll call commenced at first post, sounded by the duty bugler at 9.30 p.m., and was usually completed by last post at 10 p.m. Lights out followed at 10.15. After a year's service, a soldier who had attained the required standards of military and educational proficiency could qualify for a permanent pass which permitted him to stay out of barracks till midnight – always assuming he had somewhere to go. But he was required to check in through the guardroom on his return, sober and properly dressed. The roll call ensured that the names of all those absent from their beds would be on the guard commander's table, and there was no way of sidestepping the rules.

Now the purpose of this story is not so much to record the lifestyle of the British soldier during the days of the Empire – important enough though that is – as to pay a small tribute to the men who made his life tolerable, while at the same time focusing on the quality of friendship the Commonwealth Expedition was designed to restore.

The charwallahs who followed the British Army wherever it went have a special place in history. Each company had its corps of charwallahs, appointed by the regimental contractor, but they agreed among themselves on the barrack rooms they would adopt, usually two. Once that relationship had been established, the bond became so strong that it was more than the contractor's life was worth to reshuffle the arrangement.

Shortly after sunset, as the mosquito nets were hooked up to keep the mosquitoes at bay and over-zealous NCOs from bringing charges against their room mates for failing to comply with anti-malaria orders, two sounds brought comfort and hope. The bugler sounding retreat: Ta-ta-ta, ta-ta-ta, ta-ta-ta, ta-ta-ta, descending in regular stages as from sunrise to sunset, signalled the end of the working day. And, as the last notes faded, another call took over: Charwallah-ooo,' the 'ooo' lingering long enough to reassure the loneliest spirit that relief was at hand and would remain on call for the rest of the evening.

And right enough, there in the distance, carrying a brass urn in one hand, a hurricane lamp in the other and a tin box slung over his shoulder, was one of the men behind such a call: Lakki Zaman, the charwallah of No 8 Platoon, B Company, known to one and all as 'Lucky', heading for his place on the verandah as he had done for nearly three years – whatever the weather.

His coming had a deeper and more lasting effect on morale than almost any other single factor. And although it was not within the means of every soldier to avail himself of Lucky's services, he felt a certain responsibility towards them all. They were his customers, but his friends too, and he was always ready to underwrite any temporary cash flow problems so that no one in the platoon should retire for the night without at least the semblance of a supper.

His tin box contained supplies enough to meet the first rush on eggs, fish, liver or steak, encased in a large bun that would today be called a hamburger but then rejoiced in the name 'Banjo'. It was always of high quality and enough to satisfy a modest appetite, and Lucky was ever solicitous for the well-being of the younger soldiers, advising them to husband their resources carefully to last out the week – even to bank a part with him to achieve that purpose.

In addition, madeira and rock cake, current buns and chocolate-coated biscuits were available as a second course. On pay day most soldiers would splash out and have both, otherwise it was one or the other. A large mug of tea, sugar and milk added to suit the average taste, cost the equivalent of tuppence, a banjo thruppence, and any cake or biscuit a penny. The bill for a five star supper, therefore, was the grand sum of sixpence, or a tanner. On that basis, supper for the whole platoon would cost one pound and eighty pence in today's money, and the whole battalion about forty-three pounds. Not bad.

The tea was kept hot over a charcoal fire in the bottom of the urn. Additional supplies could be produced quickly from the main canteen, transported by a fleet-footed apprentice with ambitions of becoming a charwallah himself in the fullness of time.

Lucky was a Punjabi Mussalman of Pathan origins and wore the traditional baggy pyjamas with shirt hanging outside. His headgear consisted of a small cap, sometimes called a kullah, with a turban tied around it leaving a two foot tail behind. On special occasions, when the old turban had been freshly washed and starched, or a new one brought into service for the first time, one end would be pleated and encouraged to stand upright like the back end of a fantail pigeon. He sported a colourfully embroidered waistcoat with large inside pockets in which he kept his money and records. He wore a moustache but no beard. For his feet he preferred Peshawari chaplis (or chapals) manufactured in Peshawar with soles cut out of old motor car tyres and much favoured by units of the Indian Army serving on the North West Frontier.

For most of the soldiers serving in No 8 Platoon, strangers in a strange land with few sympathisers to turn to when morale was low, Lucky was friend and counsellor, and, as I have mentioned earlier, banker too. He seldom sat alone; there were always a few customers to keep him company: some to negotiate an evening meal pending pay day, Friday, which would be recorded in the little book tucked away in the waistcoat; others to talk about home, India, the North West Frontier – Lucky's home state – or regimental events forecast in daily orders.

It was generally understood that credit before Wednesday was bad for business, and equally bad for personal budgeting; and not to pay up on Friday was considered dishonourable. In special circumstances, however, deferred payments could be arranged, no interest was charged, and everyone was happy with the rules. Few, if any, defaulted. Come the sound of first post and Lucky would call for final orders; by last post he was on his way.

Whatever the origins of this remarkable association, there could be little doubt that few friendships were founded on a more clear cut standard of behaviour, understanding and respect than that between the charwallahs of the Empire and the British soldier – humble men both, but of rare quality. To the members of No 8 Platoon, Lucky was the best. He would follow his platoon on manoeuvres, appearing as from nowhere when most needed. At the end of a long day's march, Lucky would be seen jumping off the back of the contractor's lorry fully loaded and ready for action, and always with a wave and a cheery smile.

Nor was his interest in the platoon limited to selling tea, cakes and banjos. He would appear unobtrusively to join the spectators on the touchline when B Company was playing an important football match. At regimental boxing tournaments he had a ringside place – though he didn't much care for the sport – and he always produced a small present for members of his platoon going home, never failing to wave them goodbye as they marched out of barracks for the last time, kit bags slung over their shoulders.

Now Chalky Saunders was one of Lucky's best customers. Between them there was a special relationship dating back to a never-to-be-forgotten New Year's Eve when Lucky was attacked by a gang of drunks on his way back home. They must have come from C Company just across the road running through the barracks, but close enough for the noise to be heard in No 8 Platoon, B Company.

Lucky was alone, he had some money in his pocket and what remained of the evening's fare in his box. They seized the box, and one of them grabbed his right arm as he swung the hurricane lamp at them, while another held him around the chest and tried to remove the money from his inside pocket. In the struggle, his turban was knocked off his head; but his cry of 'Array Bhaiyo!' (Oh Brothers). 'Don't do like this, you are devil people,' was loud enough to have Chalky Saunders out from under his mosquito net and racing towards the scene. Fortunately for Chalky, and most unfortunately for Lucky's assailants, he was the regimental welterweight boxing champion with a long-established reputation for handling difficult situations inside and outside the ring. He was therefore in his element and demonstrated those skills by knocking two drunks to the ground, grabbing the other two by their shirt fronts and addressing them in time-honoured fashion: 'You bastards!'

No great harm was done; Lucky recovered his turban and retied it muttering, half to himself: 'You do like this, all charwallahs go away.' But as the consequences of the night's work began to dawn upon them, in large measure induced by the hugely effective ministrations of Chalky Saunders, the four repentant sinners were profuse in their apologies and insisted on accompanying Lucky back to the main canteen.

13. Master model of The Commonwealth Green Pennant Awards. (*Hamilton and Inches*)

14. Love Mtesa, High Commissioner for Zambia in London, receives the master model of The Commonwealth Green Pennant Awards from the Managing Director of Hamilton and Inches, in Edinburgh on behalf of the Government of Zambia. (*Joyce Murdoch*)

15. The first Green Pennant Awards by His Royal Highness the Duke of Edinburgh, at the Commonwealth Institute in London hosted by Times Newspapers.

Kamaljit Singh Garewal, India. (*Frank Herrmann*)

Facing page:

Piper Tom Lewin leads the way flying the Himachal banner. (*Frank Herrmann*)

Lionel Gregory announces the awards watched by Sir David Hunt, HRH and Sir Denis Hamilton. (*Frank Herrmann*)

Sir Denis Hamilton receives an award on behalf of Times Newspapers. (*Frank Herrmann*)

Ron Ward, The Chase High School, Malvern. (*Frank Herrmann*)

Lynda Tamm, Canada, on behalf of Buntie Bidie. (*COI*)

16. Tabla player Kamal Kant Sharma and Sarod player Promod Shanker performing The Commonwealth Raga (*Madan Mahatta*).

An incident of this kind was worth at least fourteen days' defaulters, and a regimental entry in the personal conduct sheet which remained in place for a year. It had the added disadvantage of erecting a barrier between the individual and all privileges, including any prospect of promotion. And somehow the news had got around. Company sergeant majors have a nose for such things and questions were asked. Nor was there any problem over extradiction between C and B Companies; the same justice could be handed out in both places. All that was necessary was an identification parade and the charwallah's presence to pick out the guilty men. Lucky heard about this and quickly made his way to his own company sergeant major's office. He knocked on the door discreetly and was ordered to come in. Having made the customary salaam he began his appeal to the sergeant major in the knowledge that only some obvious benefit to B Company could persuade that rod of discipline to take a lenient view of the matter.

'This our B Company sergeant major sahib, we don't do like this. In the new year time soldiers thinking about home and maybe drink too much pint this beer. Maybe they not know I am B Company charwallah Lakki Zaman. Now they are very sorry for that sir.'

'But saying sorry is not enough, they must be punished.' The sergeant major was not a man for this kind of soft talk.

'No, no, sir. When everybody know that sergeant major sahib for B Company is not making charge to C Company it is good for B Company sir. Soldiers will maybe better and I am too much glad for that sir. Mauf karna [do forgive], I cannot make identify sir.'

The sergeant major was not entirely unimpressed by the charwallah's reference to the reputation of B Company; and although the charwallah had not dared to say so, there were hidden benefits in having C Company in B Company's debt: the last thing that the sergeant major of C Company wanted was a District Court Martial on his hands for an assault on a regimental charwallah. In the event nothing further happened apart from a visit from the four men of C Company who appeared on the verandah of No 8 Platoon, B Company after sunset to make peace with Lakki Zaman, alias Lucky, the charwallah.

Chalky Saunders was an able soldier and a fine sportsman, but he failed to make the grade to lance corporal because he drank too much; and in any case he had no ambitions in that direction. Most Fridays would find him teetering on the brink of transportation to the cells for an excessively vociferous rendering of 'The Rose of Tralee', challenging the authority of the orderly sergeant at closing time, taking over the reins of a tonga (pony trap) and galloping through company lines after lights out, or returning late from the local cinema and disputing the time with the guard commander.

But these were no more than an outline of the variety of exploits that got him into trouble under Section 40 of the Army Act: 'Conduct to the prejudice of good order and military discipline.' And yet he was popular, not only with the NCOs and men, but with the officers too, because despite the unpredictability of his behaviour he was a big man and a brave soldier. When he did collect a stretch of seven days' defaulters it worried him little, and was much less arduous for him than anyone else because the regimental police supervising his extra duties took care not to provoke him: so he got away with the minimum effort extended over the maximum time. On the football field and in the boxing ring, Chalky Saunders was the pride of the company and the hero of every recruit.

He and Lucky would spend long hours trying to sort out his accounts and his career. And despite depositing most of his pay with Lucky, it was seldom enough to get him out of the red: he would unfailingly need the price of a few pints of beer on Fridays. It was always provided, and without rebuke. Whatever the state of his finances, a liver banjo and a mug of tea were on the menu every night, whether ordered or not, and Chalky would settle down to his supper seated on the verandah. There could be little doubt that the quality of friendship between these two men, then as now, spread up and down and sideways, would certainly make the world a better place. But for that to happen the leaders of the day would have to bend low enough to listen to the likes of Lakki Zaman and Chalky Saunders, and only the truly great can do that.

'This is no good you drinking too much,' Lucky would remonstrate with his friend, and back would come the answer: 'Just because you're a Mussalman and don't drink the stuff doesn't mean that the beer's no good now does it?'

'Yes, I am Mussalman charwallah, but you what? Not corporal, not lance corporal, only private – not enough pay to drink.'

Down would come Chalky's arm on the charwallah's shoulder: 'No offence Lucky, but you're quite right. I've got to get those bleeding stripes and more money, otherwise you'll never get paid, you crafty old scoundrel.' The dialogue was routine and well rehearsed.

'You don't drink then maybe sergeant major give you good recommendation to company commander sahib, then you be lance corporal, maybe one day platoon sergeant.' He dangled that prospect before his friend with an incredulous smile.

Clearly the charwallah saw in Chalky Saunders qualities that the sergeant major and the company commander were soon to discover because, not long after a discussion along those lines, a stripe did appear, and then a second in record time, and the drinking stopped. No one was more sincere or generous in his praise than his friend, the charwallah.

When the battalion left for a routine tour of the North West Frontier, covering Bannu, Gardai, Damdil and Razmak, Chalky Saunders was the platoon corporal of No 8 Platoon, B Company, and Lakki Zaman was never happier than accompanying that platoon. Between the camps at Damdil and Gardai, life was very much the same; tents replaced barrack rooms and no one went out. But following his platoon around was not so easy; at least half were deployed for days at a time on a bare hill overlooking the camp from the far side of the perimeter wire. It was protected by a 'sungar' (a rude stone breastwork for defence) with an eighty pound tent for use against inclement weather.

These posts were known as pickets. They were fuelled and fed on a routine basis by cooks and water carriers, and always accompanied by armed escorts, which presented Lucky with the opportunity of visiting his platoon even when there was no call for his usual services. There were other commissions he could undertake such as posting letters, or ordering special requirements from the base canteen in Bannu. And for him it was a risky business because his style of dress would pick him out as a collaborator qualifying him for a bullet from the unseen tribesmen lurking behind boulders at every strategic point. Sniping was so common that everyone just ignored it. The snipers were disinclined to expose themselves for fear of being picked out instantly, and so fired at random in the hope of a lucky shot. Occasionally, a mule or a horse, tethered in the animal lines outside the inner perimeter, might be hit but not very often. Boredom sometimes found a soldier leaning over a picket wall and the field ambulance would have a casualty on its hands, often fatal.

There was seldom a pitched battle, except possibly on road opening days when the hills from Bannu to Razmak would be manned by temporary pickets to allow large convoys of personnel and stores to move through without hindrance (a tactic that might well have suited Bosnia given enough well trained troops). These convoys displayed a green flag in front and a red one behind. As the red flag passed it was time to withdraw which often provoked a quick response from tribesmen reclaiming the hill before the picket was completely clear. On such occasions both sides would have to stand and fight, and not infrequently it might be necessary to re-establish the picket. At the end of the day each side would count the cost and it was not unusual for a few tribesmen to appear at the entrance to the camp looking for medical treatment, which they always found, before returning to the hills to fight another day. Such was the chivalry of the North West Frontier. A successful day, from the tribesmen's point of view, might be followed up by an attack on a permanent picket at night. Tribesmen closing in on the stone wall made it difficult for the men inside to see exactly what was going on and random shooting only added to the confusion.

It was just this sort of situation that befell the No 8 Platoon picket under command of Corporal Chalky Saunders. The sun had gone down, the bugler in the camp below had sounded retreat and the sentries inside the sungar had been posted, when the sniping started. There were a few shots from one side and then the other. By day a faint puff of smoke would sometimes betray the direction of fire, but at night it was impossible to see anything, there were no searchlights, and tribesmen moved in silence. Chalky Saunders walked around his picket trying to establish the source of the firing, and he telephoned down to company headquarters with what he thought was the likely direction. But there was little that could be done apart from the mountain battery dropping a shell or two on pre-arranged targets, which did little damage, while the noise itself provided cover for the tribesmen creeping closer in towards the picket. They would know too, from their own intelligence sources, that a new battalion had recently moved in – a good time for a little action.

As the firing increased, coming from several directions, it became clear that when the sound came from the north, a few tribesmen moved in a little closer from the south, and vice versa. Chalky Saunders ordered a general stand-to and arranged his men around the inside of the wall with orders not to fire unless they could actually see something move. The younger soldiers were nervous, the night was pitch-dark and the shooting continued. The platoon commander came on the line to ask if all was well. 'We're on stand-to sir, and ready for anything. I think we are more or less surrounded,' was how the platoon corporal reported the situation.

'Well, don't fire unless you're sure of a target. I'll see what can be done from here.'

'OK sir!' And Chalky Saunders returned to the task in hand.

For the moment reinforcements were out of the question. It was too dark – the men would make a hell of a noise stumbling over the boulders and there were enough tribesmen waiting to inflict heavy casualties on any such adventure. A Very pistol would have been useful but was beyond the standard provision of a routine picket. The skirmishing continued until the early hours, only the wall stood between the tribesmen and the men in the picket. A few testing shots from both sides heightened the drama and Chalky Saunders had his work cut out trying to maintain control.

Suddenly a few shadowy figures appeared on the sungar wall. 'Look out!' one of the sentries cried as he received a bullet in the head. At the same time one of the tribesmen got his number and fell back outside the wall. Wild firing took over. Chalky Saunders shouted for the firing to stop, just as another wave of turbaned figures came over the wall.

'Shoot to kill and give them the bayonet,' yelled Chalky Saunders as he set about doing much of it himself. Two, three, four tribesmen fell before he himself took a shot in the shoulder and another in the leg. But he was now operating at fever pitch when these things made little impression. To the right a young recruit scored his first hit and got a 'well done lad' from his commander.

'Come on you bastards!' The corporal's battle cry rose above the sound of the fighting as he threw a grenade, and then another, before leaping onto the wall and calling on his men to follow him. The effect on No 8 Platoon was electric, they were on the wall and over in pursuit, firing as they went and hurling grenades down the hill at the tribesmen trying desperately to extricate themselves from a bloody mess. It was at that precise moment that a single tribesman, badly wounded, turned and fired a last defiant shot as he slithered down behind some rocks. In his hour of triumph, Chalky Saunders fell dead. As dawn was breaking, the news was relayed to the camp and spread like wildfire, as such things did on the frontier. The picket was relieved and funeral arrangements made. Of those who survived, seven were wounded.

Chalky Saunders and the three young soldiers who died with him were carried down the little hill they had so gallantly defended. Later they were moved to the base camp in a special convoy – with an escort from No 8 Platoon – to be buried in the garrison cemetery. The new picket stood to and saluted their departing comrades. Lakki Zaman accompanied them. Ironically, his own home town, 'Lakki,' was just thirty miles from Bannu.

In accordance with the custom among British soldiers serving abroad, the whole of B Company gathered in the canteen on Friday for the auctioning of cap badges. It was a tradition that came naturally to those generous-hearted men: to collect as much money as they could for mothers, wives or families back home. All the bids, successful or not, would be surrendered.

Chalky's badge was the first to be put up. Some placed all they had on the table, which was not much, ranging from two to twenty rupees. Others just bid a week's salary. As the bidding grew, two members of the platoon pooled their resources and upped the bidding to thirty rupees. It was then, from the back of the tent, that a lone voice called out: 'I give one hundred rupees.' Astonished heads turned to see Lakki Zaman holding up ten ten-rupee notes – in those days a lot of money. The bidding stopped; he came forward slowly to collect the badge, looked at it for a moment, and then turned to face the whole company with an expression of intense grief. The depths of affection within the heart of this good man for the young soldiers who had come to serve, and if necessary die, in his country was revealed for all to see.

Slowly he raised the badge to his forehead, then held it across his breast and spoke softly: 'Salaam-a-lekum,' words of greeting intended for his friend Chalky Saunders. 'I give for you this badge, No 8 Platoon, B Company. Khuda Hafiz [God be with you].'

CHAPTER SEVEN

THE CAPTAINS OF THE ROAD

I had lost contact with Kamaljit Singh Garewal until I tracked him down in Ferozepore, dispensing justice among his fellow countrymen, who enjoyed nothing better than a good bit of litigation to keep everyone happy. My needs were simpler. I had already consulted him on the correct spelling for 'charwallah' and been advised that it could be either chaiwallah or chaewallah, whereas my version was essentially British and informal. As to the matter of 'The Captains of the Road', on which I now sought his opinion, he thought it might be a good idea if I were to furnish him with a copy of the manuscript, which of course I did: 'Meanwhile, you may proceed with impunity,' he said.

These captains are to be found on the Grand Trunk Road that crisscrosses the Indian sub-continent; their spirit of adventure is legendary, and they rank high among the most hospitable people one is likely to meet on the ancient land route between Britain and India.

A warm welcome always awaited me in Punjab: the land of the five rivers and the home of the Sikhs – the Khalsa Brotherhood. And that figure five is no ordinary numeral either; it is dignified by the number of religious symbols worn by a Sikh on receiving amrit, or being baptised into the brotherhood. These signs are: Kes, hair; Kangha, comb; Kirpan, dagger or sword; Kara, steel bangle; and Kachh, shorts. Their religion is a synthesis of Hinduism and Islam. The word Sikh means disciple; Singh means lion.

It is the presence of these men, straddling the frontier between India and Pakistan, that seemed to offer the best insurance against those two friendly Commonwealth countries falling out with each other. But they did just that, for all sorts of reasons: they went to war, and friendship was consigned to the rubbish heap.

My diary has this to say:

> Once across the Khyber I had always felt at home in Pakistan, a founder member of the new Commonwealth with a great knowledge and understanding of Britain. How could one ever forget her comradeship in battle?
>
> Sentimental tosh perhaps, but not when one acknowledges indebtedness to countless thousands of men who fought and died in support of an Empire's cause, which was essentially Britain's, during one of the most challenging periods in her history.
>
> Out of this was Pakistan born, an equal partner in the new Commonwealth of nations. Now, bruised and faced with an impossible situation, her last act of defiance had been to back out of that same Commonwealth. Humiliation was complete.
>
> Whatever the politicians thought expedient, whatever the rights and wrongs of the case, there could be no blemish on the record of her fighting men. Defeat does not suggest cowardice nor courage victory. What a pity it is that the Commonwealth, with its centuries old tradition of friendship, was unable to come between warring friends before it was too late.

Oddly enough – and I mention it not for the first time – the purpose of the first and subsequent Commonwealth Expeditions was to revive that very tradition of friendship. And Pakistan did return to the Commonwealth, but by then Zambia and other East African countries were already gearing themselves up to launch the Fifteenth (Pan African) Commonwealth Expedition in celebration of the twenty-fifth anniversary of the first, with the prospect of a multi-racial contingent from South Africa joining its ranks. The Zambezi, I was told in Livingstone, was a river of destiny (an epithet that might well be applied to the Indus as well), and the African continent a bridge between Empire and Commonwealth, with Britain and India standing at either end. If that is the case, then South Africa's return to the Commonwealth serves only to strengthen the claim.

But it is in the green and fertile valley of the Indus that the seeds of this tale must be sown; for it was here, between India and Pakistan, that I first met the Garewal family. The two sons, Kamaljit and Manavjit, were studying at Mayo College in Ajmer, well known for its public school traditions. Their father, Sarjit (son of the first Indian Deputy High Commissioner of Simla, Balwant Singh Garewal, earmarked to take over as Prime Minister of Patiala in 1938 before his sudden death), having switched a lifelong interest in journalism and the law to fruit farming and home-made wine, now lives in Balwant Palace in Solan, on the road to Simla.

His wife, Davinder, draws her strength from fasting and prayer, and directs all her energies towards keeping the family happy. The Commonwealth too has benefited from her unshakable faith, which she demonstrated by herself joining one of the Commonwealth Expeditions with the express purpose of looking after the sick. When her sons were old enough they too were dispatched to maintain the family tradition; not to look after the sick perhaps, but to represent the people of Punjab. And it was their proud claim to have been responsible for organising the *Mountbatten* which carried Comex 10 from Amritsar to the Nilgiri Hills. To return to Davinder, so long as she was present, arguments, angry disagreements, and even wild celebrations – with so many friends these were not infrequent – never failed to reach a peaceful conclusion. The *rakhis* that decorate my study are a reminder that I am an honorary brother.

My long association with this family instilled in me a fellow feeling for all Sikhs and led me (quite irrationally) to expect of all Sikhs the same degree of understanding and affection for Britain to be found in the Garewal household. This may explain my sense of disappointment whenever I read or saw anything that diminished that view; as for instance when I attended a Sikh wedding in London, and found the makeshift gurdwara decorated with slogans about Khalistan, demonstrating that the Sikhs of Britain were bent on embarrassing India from the sanctuary of the old mother country of the Commonwealth.

These thoughts were sharpened by a letter I received from Kamaljit: 'Quite unexpectedly, I have been transferred to Ferozepur as Additional Sessions Judge. The move was in a sense a journey through two hundred years of Sikh history: from the garden of our faith, in Amritsar, to the battlefield of the fiercest fighting in the first Sikh War in 1845/46.'

I turned to Vincent Smith's *History of India* and there, right enough, found the Sikh army crossing the river Sutlej on 11 December 1845. I read on: 'It was a soldier's war, brief and bloody. The Sikh thrust on Ferozepur was driven back; a dash towards Ludhiana was thrown back at Aliwal, and the Sikh army was finally broken up at Sobraon on 10 February 1846. The principal military lesson of the war was the fighting quality of the Sikh soldier which came as a revelation to many on the British side.'

There was a Second Sikh War which started on 10 February 1848 and raged across the river Ravi for five months, ending with the outright annexation of Punjab by the British in 1849. I was present in 1947 to see Punjab divided along religious lines; west Punjab passing to Pakistan, and east Punjab remaining in India to be further divided into the new states of Punjab and Haryana. The Garewals were in the middle of that carving up operation.

Kamaljit's letter continues:

> I have enjoyed my stay in Amritsar and in the surrounding towns on ground hallowed by the footprints of our saints and gurus. It was here, so runs the popular view, following the massacre at Jallianwallah Bagh on 13 April 1919, that the demise of the Empire began.
>
> There have been other massacres before and since, not least during the communal riots of 1947, guilt for which we must all share. But the Golden Temple, standing on a site given to the fourth guru, Ram Das, by Akbar, has testified to the ultimate goodness of man, and explains why the recent assault on this holiest of all our holy shrines is an event that can never be erased from the hearts and minds of ordinary people.
>
> It was in the Golden Temple that my mother attended prayers during your operation for a damaged Achilles tendon, while my father kept watch by your bedside for the first signs of you regaining consciousness so that he could celebrate your recovery at the hands of a Sikh surgeon!
>
> He was probably feeling a little guilty too for having persuaded you to attend that function at the University of Ludhiana where you found yourself on stage with the Bhangra dancers – not the best preparation for an operation the following day! My father of course was very proud of you, and the university has not forgotten the gesture.
>
> The problem of Punjab has become a stalemate without any encouraging signs for lasting peace, though there is a noticeable decline in boastfulness. History is unlikely to be kind to those men (and women too) who had the opportunity of influencing events and did nothing; they just waited and watched the Punjabi spirit disintegrate.
>
> On another plane, ninety-five per cent of the common people – the Sikhs you have admired so much and who, among other things, inspired 'The Captains of the Road' – have displayed remarkable good sense by keeping cool and not getting carried away by events. So there is some hope.
>
> I once suggested in a letter published in the *Indian Statesman* that the government should invite expatriate Sikhs and their friends to visit India and see for themselves our struggles, challenges and achievements. The abundance of cultural and spiritual stock is open for all to see, and to make a judgement on whether India breathes hope or despair for eight hundred million humble folk who are, by and large, cheerful in their daily labours.
>
> Such exposure would provide the best counter-claim to those cries of Khalistan generated far from home. We don't enjoy the same benefits as those of our people who have chosen to settle in the West. Most, if not all our motor cars would fail your MOT tests! We have to rely too much on do it yourself

methods and the results are to be seen on the G.T. Road! For all that, we manage quite well, and if all else fails there is always the bicycle.

Buses rattle rather more than they do in London or Edinburgh, but the people inside are cheerful and the drivers, as you know, are no longer mere drivers but 'Captains', while the bullock-carts, 'preserving in their way a thousand years of history' you once said, move along the Grand Trunk Road shaded by Neem and Sheesham trees as living proof that in essentials our way of life has not changed.

But most of all we have the inestimable and irreplaceable satisfaction of being close to the soil in which our history is buried, and out of which our hopes rise. We can laugh at ourselves too. For instance, a short while ago there was a case of a Sikh farmer who boarded a train without a ticket:

It was a small enough matter had he not been accompanied by a pony, on which he sat claiming that it was the pony and not himself that had boarded the train. The story appeared in the morning papers and one of the more affluent readers paid the fine.

You will certainly remember the reaction of a couple of thousand of my countrymen and women at the Tagore Theatre in Chandigarh when you introduced Kenaki [a popular choice of title taken from 'ki kehna' meaning what can I say], a musical based on the experience of the first Commonwealth Express to run in India, with the words 'Bhaiyo aur Behanon' and how the place erupted.

The newspapers next day claimed that you had conquered Punjab with just two words! And the Indian National Theatre promptly made you an honorary life member.

That is the natural reaction of our people to gestures of affection and courtesy. Don't lose sight of us. To your friends you are important, and you have many in India – not least in Punjab. Moreover, Sikhs have a special regard for Britain demonstrated during the Mutiny, two world wars, and by winning the piping championships in Edinburgh not so very long ago. Does that alone not entitle us to a special place in your hearts?

After such a letter, one begins to think about the Commonwealth and how it would be if the many ethnic communities in Britain could stand back from the prevailing obsession with differences, and concentrate instead on the part they can play in improving relations between the countries of their origins and the country of their adoption. The Commonwealth too might begin to see in Britain, the home country of the head of the Commonwealth, a microcosm of what the Commonwealth itself should be like. An impossible dream perhaps, but one that is nurtured in Balwant Palace, on the road to Simla.

There are many anecdotes that might serve to illustrate this story. For instance, walking in the grounds of Hopetoun House, a short distance from Edinburgh, I was struck by the notion of a single family home which, when completed in 1703, did not house its original owner Charles, the first Earl of Hopetoun, but his son John, the second Earl. Now Hopetoun no longer serves just one family but a nation; not unlike Britain building an Empire and then handing it over to the Commonwealth.

These are just fanciful thoughts of course, but to give them some relevance take a closer look at Hopetoun from the first design by Sir William Bruce in 1699 to the present magnificent edifice, Scotland's greatest Adam mansion, radiating the vision and creativity of one family over a period little short of three hundred years. Measured against that, what might a nation not achieve given a similar sense of purpose over an equal period? Does that not point directly to the Commonwealth which, of all human institutions, according to the Duke of Edinburgh, comes nearest to the ideal of the brotherhood of man?

In 1900, the seventh Earl of Hopetoun was created first Marquess of Linlithgow and became the first Governor-General of Australia. His son, the second Marquess, held the office of Viceroy and Governor-General of India from 1936 to 1943 – the longest serving viceroy – succeeded by Lord Wavell and then by Lord Mountbatten, who was to become the first head of state of independent India. Can there ever have been a greater gesture of friendship?

As Viceroy, the second Marquess of Linlithgow would have spent a great deal of his time in Lutyens' great building, the Viceregal, now Presidential, Palace in New Delhi, and the Viceregal Lodge (now the Indian Institute of Advanced Studies) in Simla, some seven thousand feet above sea level. These great houses, built long after Hopetoun, have their own stories to tell in the drama of Empire and Commonwealth.

In 1974, the third Marquess established a charitable trust 'to own and preserve the house with its historic contents and surrounding landscape for the benefit of the public for all time'. I took particular note of what he had to say: 'My family are no longer the owners, but we have a home in part of the house as tenants. I like to think that Hopetoun will prove an important factor in educating the young and teaching them to appreciate our great historic heritage.' Similarly, when Great Britain stepped out of the Empire (but still lived in the house), disrobing itself of superpower status, it left a Commonwealth in trust to an ever-growing number of nations in the hope that they would be equal to the challenges of our time. The Commonwealth responded by acknowledging the British crown as the symbolic head of the Commonwealth.

In the library at Hopetoun, I looked at some of the albums of photographs – one of a state visit to Hyderabad by the Viceroy and Vicerene – and noted a list of viceroys who had served India. There were twenty-eight in all, but as five were only officiating, the real number was twenty-three in a little over a hundred and thirty years. As I walked out of the library, a Sikh family was about to enter, as much at home as anyone else. They were smiling happily, perhaps at the prospect of visiting the home of someone who had once ruled their country! The man of the family wore a royal blue turban over a dark blue under-turban, with shirt to match, and a blazer. His beard, freshly dressed, was rolled back neatly under his chin and tied in the traditional manner. His wife was dressed in a dazzling green and gold salvaar kameez with a light green chiffon scarf draped about her head and shoulders. They looked very distinguished indeed, and complemented the scene perfectly. I would not have been surprised to learn that some of their own ancestors were safely tucked away in the scrap books inside.

You do not have to travel far in Scotland to encounter a very different environment, of hills and lochs, grazing sheep and peat fires, where the national sentiment of the Highlands and Islands comes across in crisp resonant tones contrasting with the more dulcet voice of Edinburgh. And there are few more pleasing journeys than being transported aboard the Lord of the Isles from Lochboisdale to Oban on a clear morning, when the air is still, the sky blue and the water an unblemished sheet of reflecting glass.

Here again, leaning on the rails of the upper passenger deck with his gaze fixed on distant horizons, his native Punjab perhaps, was a lone Sikh with black turban and red under-turban adorning a Harris tweed jacket and trousers, which indicated that he had more than a passing interest in the region. My inclination was to go over and greet him with 'Sat Sri Akal!' but I held back, thinking that it might sound offensive coming from a stranger of a different race, and that he might not appreciate being singled out as an object of curiosity. There must have been half a dozen other nationalities on board, so why pick on a Sikh?

Now if the legendary host of the Lochboisdale Hotel, where most travellers pause to take a little something before boarding the ferry, had spotted a Sikh entering his hospitable house, he would have made him welcome at once, and brought him into the same cosy atmosphere enjoyed by the fishermen for whom it is a kind of conference centre for their adventures with fish and fishing. What would he have made of the fisherman who talked of going up and down and across the loch several times and not catching a 'sausage', only to find the sausage miraculously reappearing as a fish in the retelling, and to be landed triumphantly? The Sikh sense of humour would surely have risen to that. He might even have enjoyed himself so much as to miss the ferry; and can one not imagine him instructing his new friends on the use of that historic Sikh cry, 'Jo Bole So Nihal', and departing to the sound of a comradely 'Sat Sri Akal' ringing in his ears – flavoured with a strong Scottish accent?

Alas it was not to be, nor was the host of the Lochboisdale, Major Finlay Simon Mackenzie, around to bid him welcome. For, having looked after all comers from 1928 to 1960, the Major bade a final farewell to his friends on the seventh day of December 1963, followed by his wife Millicent on the twenty-first day of January 1964. A plaque, erected by his friends under the flagstaff outside the hotel, provides that bit of information. It was the sort of gesture my unknown Sikh friend would have approved.

Kamaljit Singh's letter from Ferozepur reminded me of yet another Sikh I had met, not gazing over the peaceful waters of a Scottish loch but in action, under altogether different circumstances. Nand Singh, Sepoy and Acting Naik (Private and Acting Corporal) of the 1/11th Sikh Regiment, formerly of the 14th King George's Own Ferozepur Sikhs, was with his battalion when it was ordered to clear the Japanese blocking the Maungdaw-Buthidaung Road during the Arakan Campaign – a minute corner of the Second World War in Burma.

Those orders settled on Nand Singh, and the citation states that he led his section of a handful of men under heavy rifle and machine-gun fire, and was wounded. Despite this, he took the first trench at the point of a bayonet. He then crawled forward, alone, accepting additional wounds to his face and shoulder, to capture the second stronghold. With all the members of his section now killed or wounded, and with a complete disregard for his own safety, he stormed the final position, killing all its occupants. The road was cleared and the 1/11th Sikhs rode into Buthidaung on the tanks of the 25th Dragoons. Nand Singh was awarded the Victoria Cross. There are many such instances of bravery; to this one I can personally testify.

But it was not only in war that the Sikhs have displayed courage. Their land is a breeding ground for warriors: green and fertile in favourable weather, swept under flood waters during the monsoons, or dry and parched under a scorching sun – temperatures ranging from below zero to a hundred and fifteen in the shade –

Punjab is the land of the Sikhs. The rivers that feed the land draw their waters from the snow capped mountains that stand guard at the entrance to the Indian subcontinent. The greatest of these is the Indus, synonymous with India.

As to their antecedents, piecing together the stories I was told by the Garewal family with a random glance at the literature available, it was not difficult to establish that the Sikhs go back to the Aryan people who invaded northwest India around 1500 BC. With their fair skins and thin noses, the Aryans were much concerned to preserve the purity of their race, a process that was to throw up the Brahman or priestly caste, Kshatriya or warrior caste, Vaisya or merchant caste, and Sudra or labouring caste. The Brahmans cleverly established themselves at the top of the social pyramid but were challenged time and again by the Kshatriya, who were opposed to the caste system. In time, the Kshatriya all but disappeared – perhaps as a result of resisting the endless invasions of India – but reappeared as Khatris, Rajputs and Jats. The ten gurus who founded the Sikh religion came from the Khatri class.

To the first guru, Nanak, goes the distinction of founder of the faith. He lived from 1469 to 1539 and travelled widely, preaching and learning in Assam, Ceylon (now Sri Lanka), Nepal, Tibet, Mecca and Baghdad, journeys far from easy in those days. Then followed Angad, Amar Das, Ram Das, Arjan, Hargobind, Har Rai, Har Krishan, Teg Bahadur, and the tenth and last, Guru Gobind Singh, the only son of Teg Bahadur, born at Patna on 22 December 1666.

Gobind's father was martyred in 1675 – an event which had a profound effect on him – and he was taken to Anandpur (also the home of Naik Nand Singh perhaps), in the foothills of the Himalayas. Here, at the age of nine, he was proclaimed guru and instructed in Persian, Sanskrit, Hindi, Gurmukhi and Arabic, and introduced to riding, archery and musketry – which seems to indicate that something more than preaching was expected of him. Guru Gobind established his court at Anandpur and had his own private army. He was the model of a saint-soldier who wrote martial poetry (which suggests that he would not entirely have disapproved of the Captains!) in order to fire his followers with the spirit of resistance against injustice and tyranny.

But the Muslim rulers of that time were not over-pleased with these developments, and the imperial troops were sent to close in on Anandpur. Gobind, meanwhile, had decided that the time had come to organise his followers into the 'Khalsa', or the 'pure and sincere'. Appearing before them at Anandpur in 1669, armed with a kirpan, he called for a volunteer to give his head for his faith. There were no ready volunteers for this kind of invitation until a man called Daya Ram, a Khatri from Lahore, stepped forward. He was led into a tent and there followed the swish and thud of decapitation by the sword. Blood flowed from under the tent and the guru reappeared, his kirpan dripping blood, to call for a second volunteer. Forward came a Jat from Saharanpur, by the name of Dharam Das.

The same procedure followed with three more volunteers: a barber, Sahib Chand, from Nagal Shahidan, near Hoshiarpur; a water-carrier, Himmat Chand, from Patiala; and a calico-painter, Mohkam Chand, from Ambala. The tent was then thrown open to reveal five headless goats, while the five volunteers, dressed in splendid robes, were still alive. They were baptised, each taking the surname Singh, and proclaimed 'the beloved ones'. This then was the beginning of the Khalsa Brotherhood, and there is a lot more to be found on the shelves of most libraries, but here, I hope, is enough to associate the origins of Sikhism with courage, faith and humour.

I must now return, for the last time, to Kamalijt Singh's letter, in which he mentioned the entertainment in Ludhiana which had me dancing the Bhangra on one leg. What he failed to mention was that the dancing, the singing and the clowning were all part of the Commonwealth Expedition's aim of crossing the barriers that divide people – perhaps because he himself saw no barriers! However, that aim had been carefully built into the programme presented at the Punjab Agricultural University in an open stadium specially prepared for the occasion. And although the details had been cleared with the authorities, and the entertainment itself thoroughly rehearsed, it was lacking in that single indispensable element, a clown. Finding a man to fit the bill, and one good enough to win over an audience of two thousand Sikhs, was a major problem unless a certain Kevin Lacy was well enough – he had been nursing an upset stomach for several days – and could be persuaded to take the risk and adventure.

Kevin was an old friend; short, solidly built, with a generous moustache drooping at the ends. His blue eyes sparkle with merriment behind spectacles that make a habit of slipping down to the ends of his nose. Exuberance characterises everything he does; his generosity of spirit and bubbling good humour have won him friends all over the Commonwealth.

At home, in the village of Brent Pelham in Hertfordshire, he presides over a cottage farm with his wife Shirley. They have three children, Sarah, David and Emma. The whole family enjoy looking after the sheep. The goat guarantees an adequate supply of milk, butter, cheese and yogurt in house, while a fine stock of Sussex and Rhode Island Reds supply family and friends with free-range eggs; vegetables are grown on site. Self-sufficiency is Kevin's watchword. He enjoys cooking too, turns in a useful tune on the guitar, and sings for himself, his friends and all within earshot of the farm. He is also much given to versifying, at which he is especially good, displaying a talent for acting as strong as his instinct for the land. Come the cricket season and his cheery voice is transported to the village green; the Christmas pantomime commands his full attention. Such a man would have no difficulty appearing on stage dressed as a Sikh, so I put that proposition to Kevin.

'What, me?' He roared with laughter knowing full well that I would not have thought of asking anyone else, and, moreover, that he would agree. Rehearsing him was important, but impossible. Every line was buried in paroxysms of laughter, every gesture adding to the hilarity; so much so that we had to abandon the attempt and 'leave it to the Gurus' that all would turn out well on the night. And I had little doubt that it would for I had seen Kevin in action often enough. His style and commitment were irresistible; even when lost for a line, he would keep the action alive while his mind chased around looking for it. When all else failed, he would simply stand still and grin. And it always worked. At the time he sported a small beard, which a Sikh student was only too willing to tie in the appropriate fashion. In addition, he very kindly kitted Kevin out with a colourful turban, kurta, and white cotton pyjamas. He certainly looked the part, and was ready enough to act the part. His only concern was for the opening scene, when he would make his appearance chasing a pretty girl across the stage. How would the audience react to this? We need not have worried. A great cheer went up, followed by even louder applause as Kevin leapt in the air and flicked his heels together before continuing the chase. During the singing and the dancing, and the various sketches devised with this particular audience in mind, Kevin appeared at intervals: lurking first in one corner and then another, joining the singers when appropriate, or taking his place among the dancers without upsetting their carefully planned choreography.

When the moment finally came for 'The Captains of the Road', he introduced the poem with a mastery that brought the audience to its feet: 'Now I must tell you about the truck drivers on the Grand Trunk Road.' (The audience knew very well that those drivers would be Sikhs, and not only the truck drivers.) 'They wear turbans of bright colours [pause to accommodate the audience], and they wear beards [more laughter]. Sometimes they drive, like everybody else, on the left of the road [pause]; sometimes, unlike everybody else, on the right of the road [pause, and there is a ripple of laughter]; but more often down the centre of the road [the hand emphasises the direction and the audience erupts].' Kevin now leads the audience down the G.T. Road with carefully controlled gestures, and is interrupted time and again with wild cheering and the slapping of thighs:

Upon the national highways, along the Grand Trunk Road,
In an endless trail advancing come the Captains of the Road.
I see their headlights flashing, their horns are blaring still;
Their thunder dies in passing – the echoes never will.

From Bombay to Calcutta, Lucknow to Katmandu
I've convoyed with these gallant men, these noble hearts and true.
We've chased the stars together and watched the setting sun;
We've had our testing moments but we've also had our fun.

Beware the coloured turbans, the beards with sex appeal;
Flags and pretty lights proclaim a sardar at the wheel:
'Flee the road or perish!' more appropriately they might say
Than the commonly favoured slogans: 'Horn please! Thank you! OK!'

In the lowlands, on the hillside, over mountain pass and fell,
These gaily painted chariots thunder on to Tunikel.
The dust bewails their passing, each village bears the scars;
If they terrorise the bullock carts they petrify the cars!

About the highway tandurs, at morning, noon or night,
Their merry gossip babbles on and hearts are ever light.
Tales of high adventure, of men, and fancy free:
Of love and laughter, song and dance, and living dangerously.

Arrested by a puncture or overbalanced load
Defiant stands the gallant steed in the centre of the road.
Protectively, a ring of stones lays claim to highway keep;
Behold, beneath the chassis a bearded captain sleeps.

Ahead repeated tragedy might catch the roving eye
The price of taking endless risks – to triumph, or to die.
The Sheesham claims its victim yet quite incredibly,
Unscathed, the smiling charioteer, sits brewing fresh his tea.

Now codes of honour have their place and one might rightly guess
That Captains of the Road don't fail a fellow in distress.
No chain? No rope? No gasoline? When others helpless feel
Off comes a purple turban to be fitted to the wheel.

The grinning face, the sparkling eye, ambassadors of cheer,
Each one a living likeness of the Laughing Cavalier.
The core of every mischief, the butt of every joke,
A little tale with due respect, I finally invoke.

Many years before his time a jaunty sardar went
To face the Courts of Heaven – by misadventure sent.
'You have come, my friend, before your time,' the judge in session said.
The sardar smiled, he stroked his beard, and sadly bowed his head.

'I have driven sir, a million miles, through every kind of hell
And once, just once, unwitting, to temptation's call I fell.
She spoke so softly, gently, and coyly looked at me;
Then all the way to Heaven drove that pretty Sardarni!'

At the conclusion, a formidable looking Sikh stepped on stage raising his arms. Kevin immediately took cover, but was seized about the waist and hoisted high while the big man announced: 'This is my brother, the little sardar.' And that clinched it.

The success of 'The Captains of the Road', and its subsequent popularity, was such as to call for a brief postscript on what might have happened after the 'Captain' and the 'Sardarni' (lady) got to heaven. And I am happy to leave the reader to ponder that question in the company of Kevin Lacy.

The Captain was young and handsome, the judge wise and old,
The Sardarni was acquitted – or so we are told!
No need for counsel either, no need for argument:
When Sardar faces Sardar, only the brave comment.

'Kya baat hai, Sardarji! this simply will not do!
However coy Sardarni she may not sit with you.
You took a risk, my dear sir, of that there is no doubt;
Ensuing garbaration is what this trial's about.'

'Hazur-e-ala ka, hukum main manta hun:
But running on the G.T. Road calls for some risk too!
Yeh sacha pyar hai, quite absolutely true,
So kindly sochna Bhai Sahib and see what you can do.'

'Mukadama mushkil hai, shaid sach bhi ho,
But what to do about it I simply do not know.
If there is a jurum, some saza there must be
But, within my jurisdiction, handled differently.

Mitigating circumstances have their place in law,
And moreso here than elsewhere, of that you may be sure:
Some consideration to courage must be given
And the million miles you drove – all the way to Heaven.

Ah! Ho! You are a Captain, a Captain of the Road;
Is karan your story so fully has been told.
Let jury now consider: Jo bole . . . so nihal,
And announce the verdict boldly: Sat Sri Akal.'

Glossary:

Kya baat hai = *What is the matter? (i.e. What is going on?)*
Garbaration = *Confusion.*
Huzur-e-ala ka = *Your Honour.*
Hukum main manta hun = *I will obey orders.*
Yeh sacha pyar hai = *This is true love.*
Sochna = Think.
Mukadama mushkil hai = *A difficult case.*
Shaid sach bhi ho = *It is probably also true.*
Jurum = *Offence.*
Saza = *Punishment.*
Ah! Ho! = *Yes! So!*
Is karan = *For this reason.*
Jo bole so nihal = *He who speaks (thus) will be victorious.*
Sat Sri Akal = *Truth is timeless.*

CHAPTER EIGHT

LET'S SING A SONG

A bird in the hand is worth two in the bush,
the idea is a thousand years old.
So a heart that is warm, the riddle might add,
is worth more than one that is cold.
Extending the moral and widening the theme,
a smile is worth many wise frowns.
As judges, politicians, parsons and kings,
achieve less in their labours than clowns.
Let's sing a song, what shall we sing,
the birds and the bees and the flowers in spring.
Let's sing a song, what shall we sing,
the moon and the stars and everything.
Let's all sing it together,
the weak hand in hand with the strong.
Let's all sing it together,
the choice of a sword or a song.

This was the sort of thing that had brought us together, and, although the practice of translating experiences into songs is by no means novel, it was for us a great adventure. What we had in mind was an album entitled *The Choice of a Sword or a Song*, taken straight out of the song above which would encapsulate the spirit of Comex and carry it to the remotest corners of the Commonwealth. In the event, we toned that down to *The Story of Comex in Song*. Even so, it was an ambitious undertaking, and we were mere amateurs entering a world where even the brave fear to tread.

Behind us lay the experiences of a dozen Comexes once described as a replay of the exploits of the East India Company, but this time trading in goodwill. Armed with Elizabeth I's charter, the EIC had succeeded in bringing into being the largest empire the world has yet seen – the forerunner of today's so-called superpowers – and the even more remarkable Commonwealth that followed in the name of friendship on a world scale. Comex, by contrast, began with a group of two hundred and ten men and women from the universities of London, Edinburgh, Cardiff, Oxford and Cambridge setting out to test the reality of that friendship in an increasingly hostile world. And, while singing and dancing may not be everybody's idea of adventure, they at least represent a language that is universally understood, even without a charter.

But a message there was, which served just as well. 'It is a splendid achievement that Comex is at last ready to go,' said Prince Philip. 'The media may prefer more newsworthy issues, but for those who go looking for the Commonwealth it is still the most remarkable exercise in human relations on a world scale mankind has yet witnessed.' We had been looking hard and long for twenty years, and it was time to compress the experience into the language we had chosen; and, regardless of whether or not it is a cliché to say that songs are the best way of communicating between people, that was precisely the Comex experience, at every turn of the road and on every sheet of the map.

Coming face to face with the ups and downs, the joys and sorrows of ordinary people exploring together the wilderness of human relations, our own songs began to emerge; some of them were even whistled over what was then Her Majesty's Post and Telecommunications system into the ear of Christopher Nichols studying at Oxford who came up with suitable arrangements. And the whistling didn't stop there: it found its way into the consciousness of friends at home and abroad, and we could already hear the sound of what had hitherto been only a dream.

(At home: Brenda Stevens of BAFTA in London, Judith Parkinson – a designer in Twickenham, Roy Truby of the Dartington College of Art in Devon, Kevin Lacy – a farmer in Hertfordshire, Charles Holme – a doctor in Somerset, Ron Ward – a music teacher at the Chase High School in Malvern, Norman Leigh of the British Council, Jane Boston – a drama teacher in Brighton, Celia Congdon – a children's teacher in London, Angus MacDonald of the School of Piping in Edinburgh Castle, John Cranston and St Margaret's Girls' School Choir in Edinburgh, the band of the Coldstream Guards in London, Fred Fayling-Kelly and the Leith Community Band in Edinburgh.

And abroad: Mary Abendroth – building log cabins in Minneapolis, Stephen Burnett – a jazz pianist in Toronto, Kamal Kant Sharma – tabla player and teacher in Delhi, Promod Shanker – sarod player and MUSIC TODAY in Delhi, the Delhi University Girls' Choir, John Mwesa and the Heritage Singers in Lusaka, the Croatian Singers in Zagreb and the band of the 2nd King Edward VII's Own Goorkha Rifles in Hong Kong.

I list these people, and there were many more, merely to illustrate the variety and range of help available, and the kind of fuel that fired our enthusiasm. They, and thousands more like them from many Commonwealth countries, provided the bricks and mortar for the great edifice of song we hoped to build.)

But to dream a great dream, as Africans do, is one thing; to bring it to life quite another. We had neither the resources nor the kind of talent likely to attract popular attention. All we had was an idea and a lot of volunteers willing to push it along; and it was the tabla player, Kamal Kant Sharma, who brought it to life with a philosophical comment in Hindi: 'Singing is adventure without frontiers. It is not only for pop stars or the Bombay film industry. Like birds, people too have voices with a wide variety of sound and texture, and they like very much to sing. That is why God gave them voices.'

So full marks to Kenneth Kaunda, the first head of state to offer practical encouragement by promising 'to sing in the streets of Lusaka' in support of Comex. And if the Zambian President was going to be singing in the streets of Lusaka in support of Comex, then that was where Comex had to be – with the Zambian National Broadcasting Corporation (ZNBC) on hand to record the event. The whole process began to generate a jolly atmosphere, the kind of co-operation that found its way even into the studios of the BBC's Radio Scotland, in Glasgow, with a comradely gesture from Chilton Ingles – many blessings on his head – and at each stage the songs were revamped to accommodate the talents, styles and idiosyncrasies of the performers. Together they tell a story.

Bent low over an old rustic table in the back garden, with sheets of music spread out before him, John Mwesa was busy humming to himself while arranging a number of songs for the Heritage Singers of Zambia to record with the aid of a few British voices, an Indian sarod player, a tabla accompanist and a selection of African drums. Inside, sitting on a sofa in what looked like the lotus position, with a benign expression on his face, was the tabla player, Kamal Kant Sharma, a Brahman who took his morning prayers seriously. Seated, and still wearing his cotton khurta and pyjamas, was the sarod player, Promod Shanker, otherwise known as the Khan Sahib, waiting impatiently for the Punditji to complete prayers and ablutions and to get on with the business of making the morning tea – a duty that had somehow fallen to Kamal Kant, which he accepted cheerfully and without protest. These three men were friends, and my guests, and a most enjoyable coming together of Africa, Britain and India – a sort of combined operation. The Indians had come to London with the help of the Commonwealth Foundation; the Zambian was already in Britain completing a musical scholarship. We were in the planning stages of an operation that would take us to the African continent.

But first 'the album'. The easiest part was the choice of a title and by coincidence the song with a natural claim to first place became identified with Prince Philip. Endorsing the confidence he had expressed fifteen years earlier, His Royal Highness had been persuaded to present the identification mark of Comex to a number of people at the Commonwealth Institute in London. And this is what he had to say: 'I have watched the development of Comex since it started as a gleam in Colonel Gregory's eye. The Ten Tors expeditions which he pioneered I think made him realise just how much young people could learn by travelling and exploring together.'

And he went on: 'Sixteen years ago Comex was a completely new idea. It was revolutionary in the best sense of the word. But, as everybody who has tried to get a new idea accepted knows, you need very considerable powers of persuasion. Colonel Gregory has, of course, always been the moving spirit, but even he could not have succeeded without some help, and over the years he has been fortunate, or perhaps I should say persuasive enough, to find many people whose faith in the Commonwealth was as strong as his own.

And some of these people (ten in all) are being recognised today by the award of a green pennant, the little flag which has been the symbol of each of the ten Commonwealth Expeditions, and I am very pleased to have been asked to present them today.

In a world which is being torn apart by men of narrow ideological and nationalist horizons, men who seem to believe that they can reform the world by violence and terrorism, and by the destruction of communications; in this sad and depressing situation the Commonwealth ideal of the brotherhood of man, of peace and co-operation, stands out like the beam from a lighthouse on a stormy night, and I hope that the spirit of Comex, represented by these little green flags, will help to keep that light shining brightly, giving hope and encouragement to all who share the Commonwealth ideal' – then over a thousand million people and growing fast.

Thus, by bending low enough to touch the activities of humble folk, Prince Philip had triggered an idea whose time had come; the hope he expressed took root and grew into a massive assignment.

Now, Prince Philip had been piped into the Commonwealth Institute with a little tune specially written for the occasion, and although not over keen on being ushered in like a haggis, he entered into the spirit of the thing with royal equanimity. The tune hardly warranted a name, but the moment he used the words 'little green flags' an idea flashed into the mind of Promod Shanker, who reached for his sarod: 'This is perfect for raga,' he said, and the raga 'Little Green Flags' ('Nannhey Harey Dhwaj') – 'across barriers of class, colour and creed, of wealth and of caste' – was born.

It really was quite remarkable that this little tune, which had been produced simply to warn the audience of the Duke's approach, and limit the pace to the mobility of my broken leg, should find its way across the Commonwealth as the herald of the story of Comex in song. With a little help from the BBC, Radio Scotland, Pipe Major Angus MacDonald began the process on the bagpipes from Edinburgh Castle; it was then carried across India on the sarod and tabla by courtesy of All India Radio, and rebroadcast by the Heritage Singers of Zambia with the help of the Zambian Broadcasting Corporation, thus forging a link between three continents.

In addition to 'Little Green Flags', Promod was to accompany most of the other songs – a challenge for the sarod, but Promod was no ordinary player. Meanwhile, Kamal Kant Sharma was working on a tribute to those thousands of tabla wallahs who make an indispensable contribution to life in the Commonwealth, and that had to be a ballad entitled 'Tabla Wallah' – embracing all those occasions when the absence of a tabla would be unthinkable. The following lines give some idea of how it worked:

Play when the people are crying,
Play when they dance and they sing,
Play when the seasons are changing,
Play when the temple bells ring.
Tabla Wallah, play your drum . . .

Apart from his other commitments, John Mwesa volunteered to solo in two songs, 'How Many' and 'My Friend': 'How Many' because it dealt with every day events, and 'My Friend' because it singled out the humble bullockcart driver as the symbol of friendship – with its origins in the Nilgiri Hills. Both songs appealed to John and were perfectly suited to his rich baritone voice. We enjoyed listening to him rehearsing because he sang, like his fellow countrymen and women, without inhibition, placing great emphasis on the words. Just listen to this:

How many babies will be born today?
How many lives will fade away?
How many hearts will laugh or cry?
How many hopes will fade and die?
How many words in anger or kindness?
How many decisions with vision or blindness?
How many rebukes, how many smiles?
How many journeys, how many miles?
How many dreams are meant to come true?
How many old make way for the new?
How many ideas will take root and grow?
How many winds of change will blow?
How many deeds will have been in vain?
How many bridges will be built again?

How many sins, how many prayers?
How many worries how many cares?
How many of these O Lord will there be,
In the day we offer today to Thee?

'It is like a prayer, don't you think?' he asked, and we agreed with him, before he went on to entertain us with 'My Friend'. And it is not difficult for anyone who has visited India to visualise convoys of bullockcarts grinding their way along the Grand Trunk Road with John's voice serenading their passing:

My Friend, we have met a thousand times,
And your image comes vividly to my mind.
With unaltering pace, patience personified
You journey on content and I am left behind.
The creaking of your cart, the bumps, the grinding wheels,
The rhythmic footfalls of your bulls portend
The tenor of an endless way,
Beneath your gentle hand my lonely friend.
My Friend, hark to the modern chase,
And its message demanding you give way
In homage before the mood of passing time,
And end the thousand years that went before today.
The blinding scourge of dust from traffic roaring by,
Provokes your anger, wins a kindly smile,
Comforting your bulls, now briskly coaxing,
You journey on forgiving, for yet another mile.
My Friend, when heart and limbs are tired,
And your hopes lie still within your breast,
Lay aside your reins, and put your trust in God,
And ask of Him the blessing of some rest?
The hurricane lamp swings, and gently beckons still,
Symbol of comfort, of hope, and of light,
Scatter your doubts and fears forever,
Forever shining brightly through the night.
My Friend, it is time to say farewell,
We shall meet again but parting I confess,
Of all the things you see and others miss,
I treasure most your memory, timelessness.

The very thought of an African singing about the bullockcart drivers of India appealed enormously to our Indian friends, and they promptly came up with the idea that the sound of a boy playing a bamboo flute – while tending his herd of buffaloes in a field beside the Grand Trunk Road – would provide the perfect accompaniment. We never did find that boy!

Enthusiasm is an infectious disease, particularly among Africans, and once the news got around that we had started work on the project, the Heritage Singers promptly laid claim to two songs and set about recording them. I was never quite clear about the reason for their choice, but suspect that the drums of Africa (Crying Drums or Baba Noma) calling out to the rest of the world had something to do with it.

Baba Noma, Alla Muta, Baba ici ano luka,
Ke mazumba, itchawalele, ke mazumba zumba o-i-eh.

Crying Drums, everywhere,
Their moaning sets a rhythm on the air,
If the good life ever really is to matter,
Time to pause a while and start to care.

Crying Drums, everywhere,
Echo sadnesses that everyone must share,
But the drums of hope will sound again tomorrow,
When we start to build new bridges and to dare.

Chimame chumbulumba, Chimame chumbulumba,
Chimame chumbulumba o-i-eh,
Chimame chumbulumba, Chimame chumbulumba,
Chimame chumbulumba o-i-eh.

It called for a big African sound and got it. But the second choice ('Faith, Hope and Charity') was quite different, and yet seemed to follow 'Crying Drums' as surely as day follows night. The lead singer, Lydia Lufungulo, with a powerful soprano voice, did more than simply sing the words: she fired them like bullets, everyone hitting its mark:

Day dawns with fresh resolution,
Sifting hope from the ash of yesterday,
Offering again the occasion
To laugh, to sing, to dance, to pray.
Hope fades with evening shadows,
Victim to life's decay
As pleading, wailing, tears unavailing,
The body journeys on to meet its clay.

Give us faith; give us hope; give us charity.

Faith lives guardian of tomorrow,
And life itself will never end,
Till outliving life and all that thrives upon it,
Man comes to see in God his friend.
Swept forward on perilous wings of fortune,
To gamble on the battlefield of chance.
What hope is there of faith surviving,
When death looks out from every glance,

Give us faith; give us hope; give us charity.

Charity glows through the blinding darkness,
Anchored in life's stormy seas,
A golden straw for clutching fingers,
A healing touch to painful reveries.
A last reprieve from chains of anguish,
A way through jungles of despair,

A kindly voice to whisper softly:
The elixir of life still fills the air.

Give us faith; give us hope; give us charity.

There were many other songs, some of which we sent to the United States, Croatia (traditional friends of Comex), the West Indies and Singapore, to be recorded and returned for inclusion in the album: in particular 'Life is Empty Without Love', because Mary Abendroth of Minneapolis, who had joined Comex 3 while studying in Britain, was especially fond of it, and sang it beautifully, and 'Tiha Noći' ('sing softly, my baby sleeps'), which we had adapted from an old Croatian folk song. There was also 'Do It In Style', specially written to express the flamboyant style of most West Indians, and 'No Problem La Bole Juga' ('no problem we can do it'), a play on words which we thought might suit Malaysia and Singapore.

A song we found particularly difficult was 'Together Unafraid'. This was the theme chosen for Comex 10 to describe a journey on what used to be known as the Silk Route, now the Asian Highway. It called for a large choir and a military band. What we really had in mind I suppose was some kind of Commonwealth march; but what kind of march would it be without an army? The Chase High School in Malvern came up with the answer by recruiting nine hundred volunteers to have a go. Even the local authority was sufficiently impressed to provide funds for the acoustics in the gymnasium to be brought up to studio quality for the recording. And those nine hundred young voices certainly played their part by making a noise loud enough to be heard in London. More than that, they inspired the Coldstream Guards to play 'Together Unafraid' at the changing of the guard outside the home of the head of the Commonwealth. For their part, the guards were expecting the children to join them in the forecourt of Buckingham Palace but, alas, at that additional cash barrier, the County Council failed.

But the example set by the children and the Coldstream Guards lived on, drawing to our ranks St Margaret's School and the Leith Community Band in Edinburgh, and the band of the 2nd King Edward VII's Own Goorkha Rifles in Hong Kong. It would, of course, have been marvellous to assemble a Commonwealth army to march down the Asian Highway filling those desert lands with the sound of its passing, and lifting the spirits of its thousand million inhabitants; but where reality falters, perhaps the imagination can take over.

Where the sands of the desert touch the sky,
and the mountains rise to heaven from the sea.
Where the wild green earth with its rivers and its streams,
speak for freedom and for liberty.
Where a dozen different nations raise a hand,
and smiling faces kill hostility.
Where kindnesses like moonbeams, silver bright,
overflow the bowls of hospitality.
Where the rhythmic beat of drums evokes the tune,
and every village dance a story tells.
Where the hills echo sounds of laughter and song,
and sunsets fall on temple bells.
Where the saddest sadness lives and hope is gone,
and dreams may never see the light of day.

Where poverty's forgotten and wealth survives,
and the future seems so far away.
Together Unafraid,
overland, in the air, or on the sea.
Together let us march, hand in hand my friend,
and ring the bells of victory,
Together Unafraid,
for a hundred nights, a hundred days.
Together let us go where the green pennant flies,
and friendship's banner raise,
Together Unafraid.

Real or imagined the great march was now heading for the African continent. And although John, Promod, Kamal and I had been on Comex 10 together, Africa was something new, where singing is the traditional means of mass communication. John would, of course, have the responsibility of leading, and he was convinced that if the story of Comex could be told in song it would capture the minds and hearts of Zambians, and the rest of the continent. For this reason, he insisted, we needed a strong input from Britain and India – in addition to the African voices available.

The Heritage Singers were already in place in Lusaka and many of them had taken part in Comex 10. Promod and Kamal Kant knew their business. John was now looking for additional soprano voices and a guitarist. A quick glance at the Comex list and we opted for Brenda Stevens, holder of 'the Comex star with bar' and instinctively loyal to her many friends, who was working for the British Academy of Film and Television Arts. She had a strong, confident voice and a vivacious personality.

It took a single telephone call to get her on board, and there were two songs ready and waiting for her. One of these was 'Tabla Wallah' – mentioned earlier – at which she worked very hard with Kamal and Promod. An English voice singing about the tabla wallahs of India was not an everyday occurrence and carried a powerful message of its own.

The other song for Brenda was 'Another Day', associated for some reason with Canada – perhaps it was because Canada is the largest and yet one of the younger countries in the Commonwealth, and still full of hope. To do justice to this, we invited the 2nd Goorkhas to accompany her and, as they happened to be stationed at Queen Elizabeth Barracks in Church Crookham at the time, they were only too happy to oblige. Besides, the Gurkhas enjoyed having Brenda sing with them.

Another day, another dream come true,
for everyone, for me and you.
The sun will shine, the clouds will drift away,
your dream, my love, is the dawn of each new day.
So on and on, as the seasons go their way,
be sure my love, they're coming back one day.
All else may fail, but this at least is true,
the dawn of each new day is a dream come true.
Stand high my love, and all your hopes renew,
reach for the stars and they'll belong to you.
And the world will smile, as sweet winds kiss your brow,
and you'll know my love that the time to dream is now.

So far so good. But we had still to find another voice and a guitarist. What about Jane Boston? She was a product of Dartington School in South Devon, had been on Comex 7 and was an accomplished guitarist – as well as a very fashionable singer with boundless energy and enthusiasm. Her name too was on the list, but where was she? She was somewhere in Europe touring with a theatre company, but a telephone call to her parents changed all that; hopping a lift in a van coming our way she reported for duty.

With her theatrical background Jane was lumbered with 'Village Lights' ('Gaon Ki Jyoti'), to be sung in Hindi – another first for Comex – and 'Silver Train'. According to our Indian friends, there were between six and seven hundred thousand villages in India, and they were confident that 'Village Lights', led by Jane and backed by African voices, would be one more step on the road to greater Commonwealth awareness.

The lights of my village are my planets and stars,
As the flowers of heaven are Venus and Mars.
Dispelling at night my fears and my blindness,
They replace them with warmth, comfort and kindness.

The lights of my village are always at hand
For the tailor, the grainshop, the tonga stand;
The fruitshop, the teashop, the trays in the street,
The Panchayat hall where our elders all meet.

The lights of my village feed the soul of our nation,
And thus it will be till the death of creation.
So I hope and I pray, I plead and I shout,
The lights of my village must never go out.

The last line always produced a resounding 'Waha, Wa!' – the nearest Hindi equivalent of 'Bravo!' – from Kamal Kant.

Jane Boston was equally enthusiastic to have a go at 'Silver Train' (in English!), which had to do with the twelve silver vehicles that carried Comex 8 all the way to the Blue Mountains (Nilgiris) to celebrate the Queen's silver jubilee, accompanying herself on the guitar and with Kamal Kant on the tabla. But, while the performers and instruments were exactly right, it was very hard work for the guitar. The tabla on the other hand was in its element, the player's hands moving like the wings of a butterfly, modulating pitch and tempo to the sound of carriages lurching on an uneven track. Even British Rail would have been impressed by Kamal's high-speed train. It was a bravura performance. They even invited me to blow a whistle at suitable intervals!

The miles have gone behind us,
Far away but still remind us,
That some journeys have a beginning, but no end.
Till that final destination,
Every man in every nation,
Learns to call a wayside brother blessed friend.

Silver Train on lonely highway, Silver Train, Silver Train,
Silver Train on sun parched desert, Silver Train . . .
Silver Train on snow capped mountains, Silver Train . . .
Silver Train through flooding waters, Silver Train.

Let it storm and let it thunder,
There's a reason, and no wonder,
For the devil's army marches in the night.
The rain will wash the blackness
And the lightning light the darkness,
Till the sun comes out to put the night to flight.

Most, if not all the songs had their origins in some particular experience, and none more so than 'There Must Be A Reason' – the associations of which were of special interest. It was inspired by the Franciscan priest (Joshua Sterk) for whom Kamal Kant had the highest regard, dating from the Queen's Jubilee Comex 8 when Kamal was detained in Quetta and prevented from continuing the journey through Pakistan to India on the grounds that he could have been a spy. The intervention of Fr Joshua, and his personal guarantee that Kamal was a man of great integrity, secured his release. This, I believe, was the reason Kamal insisted on having the words translated into Hindi by a professor of English at Delhi University and sung by a group of Indian girls studying at the university. But his influence fell short of having the song recorded by All India Radio and we were obliged to fall back on the Heritage Singers, who recorded it in English. However, the thought remains active and will one day honour a joint effort by a Franciscan priest and an orthodox Hindu.

There must be a reason, but who can tell you why,
For men to be born, and for men to die;
A place and a purpose that makes it all clear,
Where the end of the journey is the end of doubt and fear.
For if there's no reason, it surely will seem,
This life is a nightmare, or at best a bad dream,
And a better tomorrow, ever one day away,
But without that tomorrow there's no hope anyway.
So there must be a reason, and all we need know,
A day is a lifetime, nothing less, nothing more,
So fill all the hours with joy and with love,
And leave the rest of the matter to the Heavens above.

Despite our unflagging optimism, bringing all this together was becoming increasingly difficult, so we trimmed our ambitions and got on with the immediate task of sorting out all the material we had managed to collect and transporting it to Zambia. It would then be up to John and the Heritage Singers to take it on from there.

But it was essential to find someone, not actually involved in the singing, who could anchor us to earth and co-ordinate the work at both ends, in London and Lusaka; in fact a sympathetic producer familiar with Comex and the songs. There was no need to look further than Judith Parkinson – Comex star and two bars! – whose considerable knowledge of the theatre and music was an enormous help. Moreover, she had already played an important part in producing much of our material. Initially, she was reluctant to be drawn in, on the grounds that she would not be up to the job. But much pleading, expressions of affection, and the promise of a broad-brimmed floppy hat finally did the trick, boosting her confidence to the point of her embarking on her first visit to Africa.

The goodwill and enthusiasm generated by this little group so impressed Kenneth Kaunda that he invited them to lunch at State House and later offered to record one of his own favourite songs with them. This remarkable African had already impressed a much grander audience with his singing and dancing at the Lusaka conference that signalled the birth of Zimbabwe, and his offer was snapped up in the hope that other Commonwealth leaders might follow, if not by singing, then at least by supporting the project in other ways. He chose to sing 'Tiyende Pamodzi' ('Forward Together'). In telling me about his own early life, John Mwesa had something to say about that choice.

'During the final stages of colonial rule, Kenneth Kaunda's life had not been easy, or particularly safe. He was constantly on the move, keeping out of the line of fire, while relying on his friends for safety and succour. One of these, a fisherman, or perhaps not a real fisherman but someone who fished like the rest of us living in the area, had written a song dedicated to Kaunda whom he admired very much. It was called "Tiyende Kaunda" (forward with Kaunda), and became very popular, not least with Kaunda himself, who most of us then referred to as KK. After he became President, I think it was his own decision to replace the word Kaunda with Pamodzi, which means together, and that is the version we sing today. It was not unknown for the cabinet of the day in Zambia to break into "Tiyendi Pamodzi" at a given signal from the President.'

As far as I could gather, the words of the song talked about moving forward together with one heart, and crossing the Limpopo with arms outstretched in friendship to Zambia's brothers in the south. But this is only a crude summary. And whatever may be said of Kenneth Kaunda himself, it is worth remembering that he came to power with a song and not a sword, answering the call of his people – a fact of history that cannot be changed – while in recording the song, he inserted the words Comex Tiyendi (forward with Comex) quite spontaneously in order to express his own personal commitment. And now I must return to John.

'Our family lived by Lake Laungwa on the border between Malawi and Zambia. We were a large family and quite poor. My father was a minister and church music played an important part in our lives. In fact we all sang, which explains how the Heritage Singers came into existence. My own interest in music went some way beyond the others, which is the reason why I finished up in the Ministry of Higher Education as the Director of Music. Some of the schools I now visit were exclusively for white children when I was a boy. But it didn't matter; that was the way things were. I certainly feel no bitterness, nor have I any desire to get involved in activities that divide people or lead to violence. I abhor violence of any kind, and would prefer to serve my fellow men, through music perhaps, if I had the chance and to be remembered in that way.'

We were having tea together with his wife Jennifer and their youngest daughter Grace in their little cottage on the outskirts of town. Other members of the family appeared and disappeared. It was a surprisingly modest dwelling for a man in his position when compared to the very much larger houses occupied by Asian businessmen. I commented on this and asked John whether the Asian community had taken over from the British. 'Something like that,' he smiled, 'most indigenous Zambians are poor and our currency does not attract foreign exchange (pause) hence the black market.' At no stage did I sense frustration, anger or envy. This was a true African, a Bemba, a man of quiet pride and goodness doing his very best in a difficult world. My admiration for him grew.

'We used to do a lot of fishing you know. We had to in order to eat. I remember acquiring a kind of boat made from the trunk of a tree; it was primitive and cost us the equivalent of about two shillings. I was out fishing in this one day, with my younger brother, but we could not find any fish. So I rowed close into the bank where other people had put out their nets and from one of these I took two fish. Just then a snake slithered into the boat, it was about four feet long and began dancing about my feet. I became afraid, remembering what my father had told us about these snakes, that they danced in this way in order to frighten their victims into jumping overboard and drowning. I might have done so too, but I had my young brother with me and he was crying. So I began beating that snake and drove it out of the boat. Maybe I even killed it; but I was never again tempted to steal fish.'

A dazzling white smile accompanied this confession, and he laughed out loud when I suggested that the snake – he couldn't give me a name for it – was probably acting on behalf of a crocodile. 'Yes,' he said, pausing for a moment as if to consider that possibility seriously before continuing, 'and we always ate fish with our hands, because that way all the flesh can be removed from the bones, without breaking them, and there is no waste.' This was not an idle boast; a few days later, at a fish tasting in the Ridgeway Hotel – a worthy relic of the colonial period – John gave me a personal demonstration.

Our sarod player, Promod Shanker, had come to be called Khan Sahib because he was introduced to the sarod – an instrument not unlike the sitar but a little smaller and without frets – by the father of Amjad Ali Khan reputed to be the greatest sarod player of all time. According to the notes on the reverse side of an LP given to me by Amjad Ali Khan, his great great grandfather (Ustad Gulum Bandegi Khan Bangash) had come to India from Kabul in the early eighteenth century, bringing with him the Rabab which his son (Ustad Gulum Ali Khan) modified, 'giving India the precious gift of the sarod'.

Promod's story goes something like this: 'I was not very strong as a child and spent some time with an uncle who was a doctor. One day Khan Sahib came to consult him about his health, and seeing me there asked what was the matter. My uncle explained that I was very weak and run down, and seemed to be showing no signs of improvement. The Khan Sahib suggested that it might be a good idea to interest me in something and promised to have a sarod made for me. Some weeks later the sarod duly arrived and I was given my first lesson. My health improved immediately; I enjoyed playing and made excellent progress. Years later, when I went to college, I came under the influence of my class fellows, the guitar and pop music were very popular, and I forgot all about the sarod.

One day, I happened to pass the Khan Sahib in the street. I had not seen him for some years and he seemed to be very old, and didn't look well. But he smiled in his kindly way and asked me how I was getting on with the sarod. Feeling very ashamed I had to admit that I hadn't played for a year or more. "That's bad," he said. "The sarod will keep you well and make you happy." He died shortly afterwards. In our custom such events are considered prophetic, in this instance that the Khan Sahib was destined to meet me before he died. I have not given up the sarod since, and it is the best way I know of communicating with people. It is for this reason too that I enjoy playing the raga "Little Green Flags" for the Commonwealth. It was meant to be so.'

Promod is a big, strong man, not easily disturbed by emotional problems, and the sarod is probably the greatest single influence in his life. 'Although I am an accountant, the sarod is my first love, and I wish I could make a living exclusively from playing, but that is not possible. Playing the sarod I have been able to make more people happy than I ever could as an accountant. What to do?' He was not to know then that a place was waiting for him in the studios of Indian television, or that he would move on to a top position in *Music Today*.

John Mwesa and Promod Shanker are highly talented and dedicated musicians; both are blessed with a warm sense of humour. But it is Kamal Kant, or the Punditji, who bubbles with fun. Unmarked by avarice or envy, he lives his life practising happily on the tabla for up to five hours a day. The middle fingers of both hands are bent outwards – these are the striking fingers – with a crop of corns at every other point of contact, and he is proud of them because, presumably, they are the marks of a great tabla player. He plays with the touch of feathers and the speed of a quivering wing, and claims to be able to reach as many as thirty-two beats to the bar. He certainly understands all about rhythm.

One morning, having taken it upon myself to make the tea, I asked Kamal whether it was to his liking. 'Woh yes,' he replied, lips pursed and eyes opening wide – accompanied by the head rocking sideways – as he reached out to caress the teapot, using an expression reserved exclusively for those occasions when something is beyond praise: 'ki kehna' (which could be spelt ki kena), meaning 'what can I say?', a sort of superlative of superlatives. It had the effect of sending our imaginations on a wide ranging quest for other examples that might qualify for similar treatment. In the process, we came up with an anagram, 'Kenaki'. It had a pleasing sound and fitted comfortably into three notes of a possible chorus line. And so, a new song was born.

Where do they come from and where do they go,
The fruit and the flowers, the rains and the snow?
Who presses the button, who 'plies the brakes?
Who gives the orders, who makes the dates?
For the summers to warm, and the winters to cool,
The grass to grow green, and the leaves to turn gold.
For fishes to swim, and birds to fly,
Children to play and lovers sigh:
Kenaki, Kenaki, Kenaki.

From the deserts of hate to the mountains of love,
From the gutters of living to the Heavens above,
Relentlessly onwards, these footsteps don't change,
Deaf to all pleading they pass out of range:
But the summers still warm, and the winters still cool,
The grass grows green, and the leaves turn gold,
Fishes still swim, and birds still fly,
Children still play and lovers sigh:
Kenaki, Kenaki, Kenaki.

The pendulum swinging to the passage of time,
The wheels of life turning, mile upon mile,
Like streams flowing out to the wide open sea
Men pass on to eternity:
But the summers still warm. . . .

Satisfied with that piece of work, Kamal informed me that the song was very much in the tradition of *Qawalis*, or Urdu couplets, sung by the street singers of India and Pakistan, which encouraged us to explore other possibilities. And why not? Having dealt with everyday events in 'How Many' and the seasons in 'Kenaki', our thoughts raced on towards nothing less than God's creation and that is about as far as thoughts dare go. But we were being driven by enthusiasm, the ordinary, uninhibited enthusiasm that knows no bounds, and came up with 'The Living'.

That thought was straightforward enough, and while we would not claim to have done justice to the subject perhaps heaven might be persuaded to grant that we had at least tried our best; and with offence to none:

Swans glide on the water so majestically,
Birds of every feather flying high and free,
Butterflies flaunt their beauty on the summer breeze,
Squirrels scamper wildly 'mong the autumn leaves.

We then slipped in a chorus to match that line of thought:

O the living, living, living that surrounds me,
On the land, in the sea and on the air.
O the living, living, living that astounds me,
In every little corner everywhere.

'Woh yes,' said Kamal, 'it is very fine,' and with that assurance the pace quickened:

Cornfields bowing lowly for the harvesting,
Flowers give up their colours and their scents to spring,
Orchards heavy laden, and the fruit hang ripe,
Hopfields and the vineyards add a spice to life.

Elephants and the tigers and the kangaroo,
Lions, giraffes and monkeys in a common zoo,
Reptiles lie in waiting in the marshy lands,
Camels move in silence on the desert sands.

Dwelling in the rivers and the deep blue sea,
Crabs and fish and oysters live in harmony,
Whales are raising fountains, sharks await their prey,
Still the world keeps turning through another day.

Insects chorus loudly when the day is done,
Crickets chant a pibroch to the setting sun,
Frogs croak evening vespers as they go to bed,
Life still goes on living though the world seems dead.

Having thus stretched our imaginations as far as they were prepared to go, Kamal turned his attention to his drums, invariably the source of some new inspiration. 'I will tell you one story,' he said, as he set about tuning the drums, tapping the rims with a small chrome-plated hammer, and he spoke in a mixture of English and Hindi, choosing from both languages with a fine economy of words. The word 'yes', used frequently to check progress, is given the resonance of a prolonged 'a' and comes out sounding like 'yeas'. He has mastered the word 'actually' to perfection and uses it as often as possible.

The start and ending of a story are never clear, gaps are left for the listener to fill, and at strategic points history is bent a little to satisfy the requirements of his own imagination. But his expressions, inflections and infectious laughter are very nearly vocabulary enough. The story begins.

'Yeas; these people make too much fighting. Both people, Muslim and Hindu. Ac-tu-ally, I think so in that time, so many hundred years before, people have nothing to do, so they fight, or do something else! Aha, ha, ha, ha!' This apparently naughty afterthought prompts the laughter and brings a sparkle to his eyes. Another tap or two on the drums. 'Paniput is there only, on Delhi-Ambala road, nearly about thirty miles from Kurukshetra and that one big story of Mahabharata – yeas.' His eyes open wide and the head moves from side to side as he contemplates this epic of Indian civilisation. 'Ac-tu-ally, in this Paniput only, one big fight, more than two hundred thousand people killed. What kind of war? Yeas; hundreds of elephants, thousand-thousand bullock-carts, camels also; many, many horses. They are killing, that's all. You see? Yeas.'

I had become used to listening to this dear old friend and never attempted to hurry him along. The story and his purpose in telling it would become clear in due course. Another tap, tap, a sound test to see how the tuning was coming along and on with the story. 'Yeas, three big fight in Paniput. This last time Maratha people nearly win empire from Moguls. Then why not?' Now I got the message. Kamal Kant had been with me when circumstances had obliged me to climb the statue of Shivaji, in Kolhapur, the capital of Maharastra, to garland the great Maratha chief on his birthday. The Marathas were so pleased with me for accomplishing this feat without breaking my neck that they hailed me as one of their own by tying a kesar patka (saffron turban) on my head, much to the amusement of Kamal Kant. Though he thought it hilarious at the time, he was secretly pleased, and it was this connection he was on about.

'Ac-tu-ally, you see, Viswas Rao, he was big general and leader for Marathas. He was Peshwar's son, you know, like prime minister, and he bring too many peoples with him. Muslim commander is very cunning man. He is Ahmad Shah. He is also king's son, yeas. It was too big fight. Marathas is also winning. Viswas Rao is sitting on very big elephant with too much decoration. Some peoples say Viswas Rao shot down. When soldiers see this they all run away.' He looked at me and smiled, a signal that some mischievousness was at hand.

'Ac-tu-ally, I don't think so. Viswas Rao like too much this mango fruit, and in Paniput there is only one tree with mango. When he see this he become too much happy and jump down from elephant. Soldiers think he is killed and run away. One empire for one mango! So this is story of mango tree in Paniput.' Slapping his thighs he roared with laughter and had me in stitches too. What he was trying to do here was to convince me, if I needed convincing, that the Marathas had shown me special consideration, that they were a great and brave people and were prevented from becoming the dominant power in India by an accident. I established later, by referring to Vincent Smith, that he had been describing the third battle of Paniput that took place on 13 January 1761, and that Viswas Rao had indeed been wounded and unhorsed. The mango tree was Kamal Kant's own invention to point a finger at the futility of war.

He lived with his parents in a back street in Old Delhi called Nai Sarak (New Street) – one of the most densely populated districts of the capital. They had just one room with facilities for cooking in the corner. The room immediately above also belonged to the family but had been rented out to a friend. Water and toilet facilities were provided on a communal basis outside. But when he was given charge of the percussion section of the department of music at Delhi University, his prospects improved dramatically. So much so that the family were able to reclaim the whole house for their own use. Not much for five people, but a great deal better than before. The comment he made to me at the time was characteristic: 'I can tell my mother drink how much milk you like, now I can pay. I am very happy.' The day dawned too when he was able to acquire a motor scooter and celebrate the event by taking me on a tour of the city riding pillion. That was an adventure fraught with risk, but one that had to be taken in the face of his irrepressible excitement.

Kamal Kant's father worked for the *Hindustan Times* as a compositor, and was very skilled at the job. He seldom made a mistake in assembling those heavy lead letters, despite being unable to read or write. Those luxuries had to wait for his retirement when there would be more time. Once unleashed, however, the adventurous spirit could not be stopped. He bought himself a bicycle and informed Kamal Kant that he was off to visit the holy places in Banares – never having left Delhi in his life – a journey of around three hundred miles, without any means of repairing the machine in the event of breakdown, and with a small cloth bag for all his personal needs. Fortunately, Kamal Kant's marriage to the orphan Premlatta and the birth of a daughter were events of sufficient importance to outweigh his own inclinations. But the bicycle remains chained to the door, and one day, perhaps, before the sun rises over the Jumna, he will be off.

Kamal Kant, Promod Shanker and John Mwesa were to demonstrate that the British, Indians and Zambians could still find friendship across the barriers of colour, class, creed, caste and politics that sometimes blur our vision, and they can take some credit for the invitation that went out from State House, Lusaka, to heads of Commonwealth Governments asking them to join in 'setting in motion a tide of goodwill from the Zambezi to reach people all over the world'.

I like to think that they also influenced the remarkable initiative of Devon County Council (nudged by a council officer, David Burchfield, who had in his time helped in training young people to take part in Ten Tors) in offering to provide a base for the British end of operations in the county of Drake and Raleigh. Not only was this a brave acknowledgement of the spirit of Comex and Ten Tors, but proof that local government is not without its reservoir of enthusiasm. Accordingly, the Chairman of the County Council, who had met my African and Indian friends at County Hall when I took them on a visit to the West Country, wrote to the Zambian High Commissioner in London. Here is part of his letter:

> We would be more than grateful if you would convey the appreciation and good wishes of Devon County Council to His Excellency, Dr Kenneth Kaunda, President of the Republic of Zambia, for inviting us to send a contingent to represent the United Kingdom on Comex 13 in Zambia.
>
> We are proud to be the home of the Green Pennant Council [the body set up to mastermind the British contingent] extending our interest in national affairs beyond regional boundaries and into the life of the Commonwealth.
>
> Invited to send an 'unlimited' number we had hoped to muster something in the nature of an 'Expeditionary Force' from Ten Tors and Comex veterans as well as other regional authorities.
>
> The immediate response was over 200 with a few more every day. Inspired by these numbers, and bearing in mind the limited number and cost of direct flights, we requested the government to consider the provision of a Royal Air Force VC10 transport plane. A copy of the Prime Minister's reply is enclosed.

Margaret Thatcher was then Prime Minister. She wrote:

Colonel Gregory has been to see Malcolm Rifkind at the Foreign and Commonwealth Office and briefed him on the background to Comex 13 Zambia. Malcolm, himself a member of Comex 1 to India in 1965, confirmed to me the great affection in which he holds Comex, and the enormous value of what you are doing.

I was delighted to hear that Devon County Council has provided a permanent home for the Green Pennant Council and I congratulate you on commissioning such a striking model [by Garrards] for the Green Pennant Awards [this was later redesigned in copper by Hamilton and Inches of Edinburgh – the same regiment! – incorporating the African continent] which I was pleased to see. It is particularly appropriate that President Kaunda should be making these awards for the first time on the African continent at the conclusion of Comex 13 Zambia.

The Zambian initiative is timely, and exciting. It is a development I warmly welcome, and I congratulate all those who have worked hard to make it possible. I am sure the whole Commonwealth would endorse President Kaunda's call for a demonstration of friendship on African soil and it was for this reason that we looked long and hard into the possibility of an RAF aircraft to lift the British contingent to Lusaka.

I am afraid however that an RAF VC10 could only have been provided at inordinate cost, and would have involved a division of scarce resources from other essential needs which, in the event, we could not justify.

Will you please give my very best wishes to all the participants and congratulate them particularly for forging this adventurous link with the African continent in the best Commonwealth tradition.

There was no mistaking Margaret Thatcher's genuine desire to help – I was experienced enough to measure such things – and, although an aircraft was not forthcoming, we were invited to Downing Street (the inside of which I never expected to see in my lifetime) and a cup of coffee with the Prime Minister, who did as much as she reasonably could to boost the spirit of the enterprise. That too was a first in twenty-five years.

(A large map of Zambia in copper, surrounded by all the flags of the Commonwealth enamelled in the appropriate colours, is to be seen in County Hall today as a permanent reminder of this bit of co-operation, presented to Devon in the name of the President and people of Zambia.)

In all, eleven governments responded: Botswana, Britain, Canada, Cyprus, India, Kenya, Malaysia, Nigeria, Tanzania, Zimbabwe, and of course Zambia. Two hundred and fifty men and women, including those I have been writing about, took part. Their exploits will be remembered for something more than any words of mine can describe. The Zambians understand this, the thousands of people who welcomed us understand this, but none more so than Kenneth Kaunda himself, who said: 'I am proud to welcome Comex to Zambia. Your performance has given us some idea of what you have been able to do together in thirty-one days by road and rail, from Lusaka through the Central Provinces to the Copperbelt, and then down to Victoria Falls.

You have seen us in all aspects of our lives; as a people, as a nation, as a continent, as a Commonwealth. And you have demonstrated, successfully, that the brotherhood of man is not an impossible dream.

I want to assure you that the message has been loud and clear, and not least because the language of Africa is the language of song. This is as true of Zambia as anywhere throughout the continent. So I welcome the songs of Comex to Africa. They represent the experiences of thousands of men and women from many Commonwealth countries . . .

They have reached a thousand times that number and will now become part of our folklore to live as long as the Green Pennant Awards continue to remind us that the greatest adventure of all still lies in the meeting between man and man.'

Kenneth Kaunda himself began his political career bicycling from village to village with a guitar on his back singing to the people he was destined to lead for twenty-seven years. So it was surely appropriate that he should leave in the same manner with the sound of 'The River Of Destiny', constructed from an input of suggestions from John Mwesa, Kamal Kant Sharma, Promod Shanker and myself, and sung by the Heritage Singers of Zambia, to accompany him:

A stranger on the river, I asked some passers-by
What they called the river and they looked up in surprise:
'Have you not a notion friend, and do your eyes not see
Reflections in the water of the river of destiny?'

The sun rose to the surface, a ball of crimson flame,
The world renewed its struggles in a never ending game;
While etched upon the landscape, as far as eye could see,
Pilgrims bowed in homage by the river of destiny.

Praying for peace tomorrow, forgiveness for today,
Deliverance from the fears that never go away:
Until the final battle, and cries of victory
Resound across the waters of the river of destiny.

When summer turns to autumn, and winter turns to spring,
Wild winds blow defiance and storm bells start to ring:
For fishermen to return from the perils of the sea
And contemplate their labours on the river of destiny.

The day had long departed, the night owl sang its song,
Deep in the darkened waters the stars now brightly shone,
And then I heard a whisper that made all clear to me:
Living is forever on the river of destiny . . .

Yes, everyone has a river of destiny:
Searching for nirvana somewhere in a timeless sea,
Murmuring ageless mantras as they course along their way,
To ward off evil spirits – so the jolly pundits say.
Yes, everyone has a river of destiny:
From the sacred Ganges to the singing Zambezi
Forever moving onward, yet forever standing still,
A paradox to comprehend – perhaps one day we will.

Maybe it was the combined support of eleven Commonwealth governments – for the first time on such a scale – that inspired the decision; or maybe the prophetic words of Kenneth Kaunda calling on his fellow Commonwealth leaders 'to help set in motion a tide of goodwill from the Zambezi to reach people all over the world'; or maybe it was simply a timely gesture of encouragement from the unseen hand that saw the master model of the Green Pennant Awards take wing from Edinburgh for its permanent home in Zambia whence to set in motion that tide of goodwill, if not to reach people all over the world then at least the Commonwealth Heads of Government Meeting – as this extract from Malcolm Rifkind's letter dated 31 December 1994 demonstrates.

> I wrote to Douglas Hurd about your ideas for the 1995 CHOGM [Commonwealth Heads of Government Meeting]. He commented that, should the Commonwealth Foundation take on responsibility for the Green Pennant Awards, as you have proposed, CHOGM might consider the scheme when examining the Foundation's report.
>
> Douglas and I both like your idea of arranging a Green Pennant Awards Ceremony during CHOGM, and thereby bringing young people involved in Comex into contact with Heads of Government. We stand ready to commend these ideas to other Commonwealth Governments and in particular to the Secretary General and the New Zealand Government who will make the arrangements for CHOGM next year [1995].

On 10 January 1995 a long and encouraging letter arrived from the office of the Secretary-General in response to a letter from me which included the following:

> At their meeting in Islamabad in November 1994, Commonwealth Senior Officials considered and supported the proposal concerning the Commonwealth Expedition [COMEX] and the Green Pennant Awards which had been made by the representative of Zambia. The Secretary-General is, of course, delighted that this contribution from Zambia was so warmly endorsed . . .
>
> The Commonwealth Foundation is not a part of the Commonwealth Secretariat; it is a separate international organisation in its own right.
>
> We applaud your efforts to arrange for the stands for the awards to be manufactured in Zambia and 'the little green flags' in India. It is an excellent idea that the awards should be presented following each CHOGM.

On 27 March – following a piece in the *Sunday Telegraph* – I wrote to Malcolm:

> I was so pleased to see Douglas Hurd quoted in The Sunday Telegraph – after the Queen's visit to South Africa: 'The barriers have come down and the Queen is back,' and his further comment that he was now determined to review Britain's approach to the Commonwealth in the upward direction – good, that's the way flags go!
>
> Could a friendly nudge to the Commonwealth Foundation be incorporated in that review? In my opinion, a more positive attitude towards the Commonwealth would be hugely popular among the majority of people at home, attract an immediate response from our friends abroad – rich and poor alike – and do the government a lot of good . . .

On 18 April 1995 Douglas Hurd wrote to Malcolm:

> Thank you for sending me a copy of a letter dated 27 March from Colonel Lionel Gregory.
>
> The next Commonwealth Heads of Government Meeting in Auckland from 9 to 13 November offers an opportunity for all Commonwealth Governments to re-assess how the association can make a more imaginative and creative contribution

to issues of broad international concern, especially now that quarrels over South Africa are behind us. We intend to play our full part in this and are in close touch with the Government of New Zealand and other Commonwealth countries and the Commonwealth Secretary-General. Colonel Gregory may be interested to read the speeches that the Prime Minister and I made at the Chatham House Conference last month on 'Britain and the World' both of which highlight the role the Commonwealth can play. I also enclose a speech I gave before the last CHOGM in 1993 which takes up a similar theme.

Colonel Gregory asks that we give more support to the Commonwealth Foundation. We are already the largest contributor and earlier this year made a special contribution for their NGO Conference in Wellington in June. We see the Foundation as a vital part of Commonwealth activity and will continue to support it.

We will also keep nudging the Foundation and the Secretary-General, as we have already done, to find a way of incorporating Colonel Gregory's Green Pennant Awards proposal into the CHOGM proceedings.

On 22 September Love Mtesa, the Zambian High Commissioner in London, wrote to the Commonwealth Secretariat:

I would be grateful if you would include an item 'The Commonwealth Expedition and The Green Pennant Awards' on the CHOGM agenda to be discussed by Heads of State and Government in Auckland, New Zealand from 10 to 13 November 1995.

You will recall that Zambia introduced the item during the meeting of Senior Commonwealth Officials in Islamabad, Pakistan in November 1994. The meeting unanimously accepted the proposal. The idea is to have it endorsed by the Heads of State and Government so that it may be implemented.

Spurred on by this letter, a copy of which Love Mtesa had kindly sent to me, I wrote to my old friend Kamaljit Singh Garewal, urging him to drop everything and set about finding an embroiderer with the necessary skill and enthusiasm to have two little green pennants made in time for the CHOGM in New Zealand. On 20 October 1995 I received the following reply:

You asked me to have two little green pennants embroidered for the Zambian version of the stands for the Green Pennant Awards designed by Hamilton and Inches of Edinburgh. The urgency of the matter was not lost on me, not only because the stands – original and copy – are to be on display at the Commonwealth Heads of Government Meeting in New Zealand, but because the honour of embroidering these 'little green flags' in the future comes to India, while the stands themselves will be manufactured in Zambia. This, of course, presupposes that our Commonwealth leaders decide to adopt the Green Pennant Awards and I personally cannot see how they can do otherwise.

India loves stories like this and whatever happens in Auckland the green pennant has already found a place in the heart of my country. In Bulwant Palace in Solan, my father's house, a Green Pennant Award has a place of special honour.

But that is only one of many, nineteen in all I think, awarded to places and people from Ooty to Simla, and modelled on the original commissioned by Devon County Council. Others have similarly gone to Australia, Britain, Canada,

Pakistan, Singapore and Zambia. The Edinburgh model forges an interesting link between Devon and Scotland, and extends it to Zambia which in turn brings together the African continent and the largest and oldest democracies in the world. What a story.

When I related it to my young lawyer friend Guravtar Mann and asked his advice on producing the pennants in record time he informed me that there was only one man who could undertake the work in a manner that he and I, the Punjab and indeed India could be proud of, and that man was one Habib Mohammad, embroiderer to the late Nawab of Malerkotla. Saying which, and with a resounding 'Jo bole so nehal', to which we both responded with 'Sat sri akal', Guravtar was off to Malerkotla.

I think you had better have the full story, and you may find a map useful:

Malerkotla, an Afghan citadel in predominantly Sikh country, is an excellent example of ethnic tolerance. After the establishment of the Khalsa brotherhood by the 10th Guru, Guru Govind Singh (1666-1708), in the town of Anandpur in the foothills of the Himalayas, word got around that the Guru had created a new order. Feeling threatened therefore, the hill rajas, in collaboration with the Governor of Sirhind, Wazir Khan, and the Emperor Aurangzeb, adopted a policy of harassing the Guru and his followers by means of a succession of military skirmishes.

In due course, Guru Govind, who had considered leaving Anandpur in order to continue the struggle elsewhere, received a message from Aurangzeb expressing regret for the behaviour of his troops and promising safe passage should the Guru decide to quit Anandpur.

The Guru's mother, Mata Gupri, and his two younger sons, Zorawar Singh (8) and Fateh Singh (6) were entrusted to the care of a retainer with instructions to conduct them to safety, while the Guru himself, with his two elder sons Ajit Singh (18) and Jujhar Singh (14) and about 500 followers, made his way separately to the plains.

Mata Gupri and the boys were taken to Ropar were they were met by a man called Gangu who had been a cook with the family. He conducted them to a village near Sirhind and betrayed them to the aforesaid Governor Wazir Khan so that he could dispossess them of the money and jewellery the Guru's mother had about her person.

The Governor offered those young boys the choice of Islam or death. But remaining true to their faith, they chose the latter and were ordered to be 'bricked' alive at a place near Sirhind where the Gurdwara Fatehgarh stands today and a feast is held in the last week of December to mark their martyrdom.

The only nobleman to protest at such barbaric behaviour was Sher Mohammad Khan, the Nawab of Malerkotla, and the Sikhs of Malerkotla remembered that act of grace. Consequently, when Bandu Singh Bahadur led them in sacking and destroying Sirhind, Malerkotla was spared.

While the execution of the Guru's young sons (the Sahibzadas or princes) was taking place, the Guru, together with his own men, had taken shelter in an improvised mud fortress at Chamkaur where a bloody battle was fought. He lost all but five men, and his elder sons too fell – fighting valiantly – before their father's eyes. Guru Govind then offered a simple prayer: 'O God, I have surrendered to Thee what belonged to Thee.'

During the worst riots of 1947 when Hindus, Muslims and Sikhs migrated en masse to their respective homelands midst so much carnage, not a single Muslim of Malerkotla was touched, and they were persuaded to remain along with their Nawab, Iftikhar Ali Khan, who later became a member of the Legislative Assembly and died in 1982.

Malerkotla has traditionally been a centre of music and dance (qawali and mujra) and is also renowned for its folk singers. And I am so glad that 'the little green flags' were embroidered in such a place nearly 290 years after the events I have outlined. Worked in untarnished gold on a grass green silk background they have been much admired in my office. But today they are on their way to you with many blessings.

When Habib Mohammad was told that his work would go first to Edinburgh, then to London, New Zealand, and finally to Zambia, he remarked modestly: 'If you had given me a little more time I would have made a better job of it.' He started the work the moment Guratvar arrived and finished by midnight. Is this not a story worthy of Comex?

Kamal had expressed the hope that the little green flag would arrive on 23 October, the Hindu festival of Diwali (the festival of lights), but it was early by two days; so, and very properly, the Zambians were to be the beneficiaries of both the little green flag and the blessings of Diwali. On 31 October Love Mtesa wrote as follows:

I acknowledge with thanks the little green flag sent under cover of your letter of 21 October 1995. I am also pleased to inform you that I have received the two samples of the master model of the Green Pennant Awards from Lusaka which the Minister of Sport, Youth and Child Development, the Hon Patrick Kafumukache had made in Kitwe, Zambia.

They are beautiful, but I will only take one to Auckland together with the one I received from Edinburgh.

I trust that all will go well.

On 29 November Love Mtesa, who had returned to London via the Republic of Ireland and was about to take off for the Vatican, telephoned to give me one of the most encouraging messages I had ever received. This is what he had to say: 'Hullo! Hullo! How are you? I am so happy to tell you that the Green Pennant Awards received unanimous support in Auckland. Everything went very well indeed and, remarkably, the next awards are likely to take place in Edinburgh at the conclusion of the 1997 Commonwealth Heads of Government Meeting. So I have sent the models back to Zambia to have more made! I am sure this news will make you very happy.'

Whether administered and organised by the Commonwealth Foundation and hosted by the country hosting the biennial CHOGM, or administered, organised and hosted by those countries in turn, the Green Pennant Awards Ceremony could be modelled on the trial run at the Commonwealth Institute in London on 18 December 1980 (later repeated in Delhi and Lusaka) which received a generous accolade from Brian MacArthur, representing Times Newspapers, who hosted the event: 'I felt I had to write to congratulate you on the brilliant organisation – and your brilliant performance – at the presentation of the Green Pennants today. I could not wish to have been associated with something more heartwarming and uplifting. So many congratulations.'

Mission accomplished, I leave the reader with a summary of the Commonwealth Expeditions, Comex, which brought together the oldest and largest democracies in the world, and the African continent, on the wings of an eagle.

CHAPTER NINE

ON THE WINGS OF AN EAGLE

On the wings of an eagle is as good a way as any of viewing the ground covered by the Commonwealth Expedition, Comex, over thirty years. Many have come, many have gone; but the spirit of Comex lives on in the Commonwealth Green Pennant Awards endorsed at the November 1995 Commonwealth Heads of Government Meeting in New Zealand.

The journey from Denbury – where the idea was conceived at the same time as Ten Tors – to Auckland had a single purpose: to restore old friendships eroded by time and neglect which in time settled into 'identifying the spirit of adventure with crossing the barriers that divide people', the purpose of the awards. And it was the success of Ten Tors, bringing together as it did thousands of young people from all walks of life to test themselves against the rigours of Dartmoor, that inspired the more ambitious venture.

'It is fitting,' said the Chairman of Devon County Council, 'for Devon to be associated with the Awards, both as the birthplace of Drake and as the place where the twin projects of Ten Tors and Comex were started. It is particularly gratifying that Devon's name will henceforth be linked with adventurous activities across the barriers that divide people.'

And yet the very idea that the barriers that divide people might be a legitimate target for adventurous treatment ran into trouble. An Indian minister kicked off with 'A hippy trail led by a colonel', which was loud and clear enough, and hippy was the in-word at the time. A British Council officer went even further: 'A latter day Muhammad trying to restore the British Raj' was his view of the matter.

But there were others who saw it differently. In terms of international friendship and Commonwealth understanding, His Royal Highness the Duke of Edinburgh dubbed it 'the most worthwhile programme ever devised', while the first Prime Minister of India, Jawaharlal Nehru, gave practical expression to that view by inviting young people 'to organise a new consciousness in the Commonwealth through cultural and intellectual activities as well as in common adventure' – starting in India.

Organising a new consciousness in anything is not the easiest of assignments, and certainly not without a proper strategy! And that was how an adventurous journey, in tandem with equally adventurous entertainment, came to be the means of meeting thousands of people. Now, singing and dancing and clowning may not grip the imagination as a high-risk adventure, but to those who have never thought to do that sort of thing in public before it most certainly is, and on that premise the operation got under way.

The comradeship that came off the battlefields of the Second World War was still fresh enough for the armed services to take the lead in coming forward, followed shortly by the universities, industry, local government, the medical and teaching professions, the Fire Brigade and British Rail. The Royal Commonwealth Society, the English Speaking Union, the Royal Overseas League and the Commonwealth

Institute all stood by in case reinforcements should be required. The services and industry helped with training, the universities and local government with venues for meetings, and the Foreign and Commonwealth Office with good advice.

The military men in charge of training were well experienced in handing over all manner of recruits, and made available specialist instructors for everything – apart from the singing and dancing, which fell outside their remit. But so impressed were they with the results of their handiwork that Comex was christened 'the Duke of Edinburgh's Own Volunteers' and treated with the appropriate honours. It was a jolly notion that had to be scotched before the Ministry of Defence got on to it. Nevertheless, it did lead to the first expedition securing His Royal Highness's patronage and every convoy thereafter being identified by a green pennant with his personal cypher on one side and King Asoka's wheel on the other. By any standards this was a prestigious symbol, serving as a link between the oldest and largest democracies in the world, but with sights raised that high, 'the P and the Wheel' had to be embroidered in gold. The Eagle came later.

Of course, symbolism is all very well; it is there to encourage, even inspire. But the key to success lay in crewing and commitment: crewing to ensure that Comex got to its destination; and commitment to ensure that what was done in the process would not lead to an international incident. A crew consisted of driver, mechanic, navigator, radio operator and cook – who also served meals on board. And, in accordance with good military practice, every vehicle had five crews working in shifts of two hours on and eight hours off. The remainder were assigned to the less attractive duties of loading and setting up camp. If lucky, they could count on a little help from the others.

Commitment, as the Canadians so aptly put it, was something else. In the early days, the idealism of the sixties rose to the surface ready to put the world right; but as the heat, the dust, an Indian monsoon and the shortage of home comforts took their toll, it was much less in evidence. And it was in this context that real leadership was called for, coming more often than not from the women, who not only inspired the men, but in a few brave instances took them on for the rest of their lives.

Organisations wishing to be represented were responsible for selecting their own candidates by agreed criteria. And they were also required to give those selected the opportunity of presenting an account of their experiences on return, no matter how well or badly they had acquitted themselves. The principle here was that each person would know just when, where and how he or she fell short; and whatever blame or praise might be levelled at the expedition as a whole, there was no escape from that. In a way, the success of Comex grew out of those failures, because in them were sown the seeds of a renewed sense of purpose: a determination to do better next time, and the next time after that.

The first signs of success came like the sun rising in a clear blue sky: the drivers returning to base no longer as trainees but proudly displaying their HGV badges. It put them in a class by themselves. Their personalities too seemed to change: they were somehow remote and aloof, with a noticeable disinclination to participate in the more basic chores. Yet without them, there could be no movement, and that fact alone contributed to their authority, no matter who was appointed contingent leader. When something went wrong, it was the mechanic, or perhaps tbe navigator, the state of the roads, the whole plan of operations, or heaven itself that might be to blame; never the driver! If the vehicles attracted attention, which in their striking ivory and gold livery they invariably did, much of it focused on the driver, who might oblige his wayside audience with a heroic smile and a toot on the horn as he waved them goodbye. But time soon brought him, and all the others, down to earth.

At the end of a long day it was the cooks who lifted the spirits by producing some excellent meals out of an assortment of onboard supplies supplemented by local purchase. But soya, however ingeniously disguised, was not a favourite, despite its proven nutritional value. And any arguments about its being cheap and better than the diet most people in the host countries enjoyed fell on deaf ears. Generous quantities of powdered milk, tea and coffee, donated by well-wishers, facilitated a round-the-clock service on the move as well as hospitality for guests climbing aboard or visiting the camps.

It was sometimes claimed by the jealous and less chivalrous that the women in charge of the commissariat laid a snare for travel-worn, hungry men, and that it was around the kitchens that most romances blossomed. Such gossip was usually aimed at the mechanics, who worked long hours under appalling conditions, unfailingly cheered on by their companions anxious not to get their own hands dirty. And the inter-contingent rivalry was such that the slightest breakdown was an event to be broadcast gleefully to the rest of the expedition. But by working those unsocial hours, and often late into the night, the mechanics were much admired and did receive sympathetic attention. There were other unexpected benefits, too, which separated the men from the boys.

When the driving, the navigating, the cooking and the maintenance were over, it was time for the stars to shine on stage. Here too there was a lot of competition, and unless one was able to play an instrument competently, or to sing, dance or act to an acceptable standard, there was no way of muscling in on those activities. For the majority, however, there was a niche among the stage hands, while the numbers recruited into the choir swelled noticeably as confidence grew, drowning the bum notes in the noise!

Very often the convoy would drive straight to the place of entertainment and all preparations had to be completed on the move. This included rehearsing, frequently over the telecom, the ironing of clothes, washing of hair, dressing, make-up and the myriad details that make the difference between cheers or jeers when the curtain goes up for the first time. Twenty-five people milling around a coach on the move, each one with his or her own image uppermost in mind, is not the most comfortable environment in which to cultivate dreams of stardom, but it is at least a challenging start. And under these circumstances the only privacy possible was a discreet turning of the blind eye whenever a sensitive target presented itself.

Billed in advance as *The Story of Comex in Song*, audiences were led to expect more than was on offer, with the result that local talent had to be brought in – usually camouflaged as a gesture to hosts – to help out. But these were the early days.

Having a good clown was essential, for nowhere is the Comex adage 'A smile is worth many wise frowns, as judges, politicians, parsons and kings achieve less in their labours than clowns' better understood than on the Asian Highway. Once the clown had learned his business – absorbing something of the regional ambience in the process – and the singers, dancers and actors had rehearsed their parts to as near perfection as talent would allow, the prospects of survival, even success, were greatly enhanced.

The practice of singing songs about the host country, sometimes in its own language, and introducing a topical sketch or two, became progressively more common. Subjects such as the villages of India, encompassed in a ballad called 'Gaon Ki Jyoti' or 'Village Lights'; the activities of Sikh drivers of Punjab in 'Captains of the Road'; or the bullockcart drivers in 'My Friend', were all highly acclaimed. Simple, rhyming verse was always popular – depending largely on the skill of the local translator – with the clown and the actors giving the words a visual dimension. In this way audiences were sometimes able to follow the narrative without the translation.

Radio operators argued that as communicators they were the proper people to look after public relations. But contingent leaders were only too keenly aware that PR and perks were closely allied, not least in the matter of hospitality, so they naturally saw it as their duty to hang on to those responsibilities. However, radio men, and women, are by nature persistent and not easily satisfied. They even complained that the single channel system was hugely frustrating because as one spoke the other nineteen were silenced. This led to acrimonious exchanges far beyond the perceived function of keeping the convoy together by reporting hazards ahead and the all clear from behind. Like media men everywhere, the boldest got in first and stayed there.

When it was proposed that the lead vehicle should do the reporting of hazards and the tail the all clear – the remainder observing radio silence – this was immediately challenged on the grounds that hazards could occur after the lead vehicle had passed and before the tail caught up. There was nothing for it but to allow time and experience to dictate a sensible procedure. And, as a salve to well-nourished ambitions, radio operators were assigned to the exclusive role of diarists.

The nights brought peace, drawing a mantle over the deserts, the mountains and the streams that are there to deter, to encourage or to inspire, according to one's own inclinations. Hostilities suspended, camaraderie is restored. The stars reaching down from a desert sky like jewels have invaded the dreams of travelling people since time immemorial. And, as the night waits for a new dawn, all is quiet on the long dusty road. In the distance the Khyber beckons. If the speedometers get it right, the expedition should cover over twenty-five thousand miles in three months – a lot of miles and a lot of time for making friends and enemies. What was that aim again?

Sooner or later it was inevitable that the combined expertise of the radio operators and the navigators would lead the convoy, or part of it, up the garden path, where there was neither garden nor path but a lot of no man's land. Misreading Kandahar for Katmandu, or Chandigarh for Lahore, are navigational errors of immense proportions demanding immediate action: either to press on regardless or to call a conference and put the leader on the spot.

For the leader there are only two options: to disappear into the desert, or to shower praise on his followers for having crossed the barriers of colour and class, creed and wealth, and, but for a case of diarrhoea or two, the barrier of health. And given that asssurance, they could move forward with renewed confidence in a leader who, drawing on the principles set out in the handbook of leadership, bursts into song, but with eyes firmly glued to the camel tracks.

The sight of India raises the temperature. Crowds gather out of curiosity, always cheerful, always questioning: 'Hullo! How are you? Where you come from? What is your good name?' It is standard and continuous. After the bleak and empty landscape of a desert, a crowded Indian city is a contrast that defies the most versatile imagination.

Buses, lorries and cars heave and rattle through the crowd like waves impatient to be done and die on a rocky shore. Bullockcarts, tongas, trishaws and cyclists lace themselves about the heavier vehicles, scrambling for space, ignoring the shrill exhortations of a policeman's whistle. Amber, red and green lights flash dutifully to little avail. Mobile stalls move through the milling mass of humanity, cheerfully oblivious to any danger. All eyes turn towards the convoy, everyone waves; miraculously, no one is hurt.

There are a hundred places to visit and thousands of people to meet from Simla in Himachal to the Blue Mountains of Tamil Nadu, and Sri Lanka. And beyond that there are Malaysia and Singapore. The convoy moves on, the relentless routine continues: crew changes every two hours, greetings and how-do-you-dos in every village and town, and loo stops with unpredictable frequency. The latter bring home the lesson that whereas toilets to accommodate five hunded people are readily available in a desert, they represent a formidable challenge in a town. Nor are these the best reasons for reclaiming old friendships. And while the armed services may preach the battlefield ratio of five holes in the ground to a hundred men, a mixed bag of civilians have much higher expectations.

Campsites too are different. In a desert they can be awe-inspiring, but in the more populated areas the choice varies from schools, to stadiums, to universities; from the banks of the river Ravi in Punjab, to the Cauvery in Mysore.

The guests in the Intercontinental Hotel in Lahore may have been startled by the appearance of twenty ivory and gold vehicles forming a circle and making camp on the main lawn. But they also enjoyed the entertainment. And the camps themselves attracted many visitors – the majority young men armed with invitations aimed at the young women, for whom it became a simple matter of weighing the risks against the adventure, and accepting all invitations on behalf of a few men as well.

It was not always possible to foresee a problem. The Burmese Government having closed its borders with India, the shutters were down and the officials hiding behind them reluctant to reveal their presence. Nor was there any way of bypassing Burma without the help of the Royal Navy. It was therefore time to test the latter's boast never to have failed its countrymen in distress with an SOS calling for immediate action! This unexpected switch in the mode of transport did not please the drivers; not one little bit. Sailors taking charge would diminish their own authority to the point of mixing with the common herd; unless, of course, they could somehow contrive to occupy separate tables – as between officers and ratings.

At first light all eyes were turned on the horizon to watch as the LSL *Sir Lancelot* burst through the early morning mist at the mouth of the Hoogly with orders to lift Comex to Penang. What seemed like a miracle was no more than co-operation, as unique as it was British, providing the excuse and the occasion for men and women to indulge a long-denied thirst for a pint of beer. Unfortunately, Landing Ships Logistics are notoriously buoyant and the *Sir Lancelot* was no exception. When the Captain mentioned the matter tactfully to those intrepid travellers who had crossed deserts and moutains in what was the largest overland expedition in history, they were but mildly amused. However, before India sank below the *Lancelot*'s stern, and despite the commanding presence of a large Green Pennant flying aloft, retribution struck. It was as swift as it was effective and the party disappeared below decks to deal with the casualties in private.

Reports that Lee Kuan Yew was a good and generous host but did not much care for long hair on the male head had the girls up early snipping at honourable heads bowed to the inevitable. Safely ashore, the drivers are back in the driving seat; the radio operators perform a few test calls to impress the onlookers; and the navigators walk about studying maps of the well signposted route to Singapore.

Rumours about 'ronging' in Malaysia spread quickly. 'What is this?' they demanded to know and were told: 'It is an older and more elegant form of rock-'n'-roll.' Aha! Here was something to work on and, influenced perhaps by the encounter with the Bay of Bengal, 'ronging and rolling' was launched on a short lived career down the Malaysian peninsula to Singapore and a welcome with orchids and green coconuts, followed by a lavish breakfast. The People's Association did it in style, steering Comex through a labyrinth of rules and regulations that preserve a certain excellence in the island. The medical college, schools, the orchid conservatory, industrial complex, private homes and visits to the surrounding islands were all on the agenda.

(By coincidence Alan Dexter was commanding the Queen's Gurkha Signals now stationed in Singapore. He and his wife Celine rose to the occasion bolstering our presence with the pipes and drums and all ranks not otherwise employed! Their hospitality too was of a quality worthy of old friends: open house round the clock. And when the regiment was marshalled for a scheduled inspection by the Commander-in-Chief, Comex was on parade with the rest.)

Kilted Chinese girls dancing the Highland Fling was a pleasure as it was a surprise; but most significant of all was the giant banner of welcome outside the university: 'Yu Yee Wan Swee', it said, meaning 'friendship for ever'.

All too soon it was time to say goodbye. The LSL *Sir Galahad* (later lost in the Falklands War) had taken over from the *Sir Lancelot* and lay at anchor waiting to take Comex on board after a final word from Prime Minister Lee Kuan Yew: 'The Commonwealth Expedition is an adventure, with all the excitement with which the Commonwealth began. Long may it continue,' he declared, waving to his guests as they embarked, misty eyed and wiser for the memories they carried with them.

Responding to the ebb and flow of political events along the long dusty road, a quick change of direction is indicated. When war comes, peace departs, and the quickest way of doing that is by air, which brought Comex to Bombay to embark on the first *Commonwealth Express* at Victoria Station, and the longest single rail journey in history.

Crewing was out, communication of another sort in. Every station became a meeting place for hundreds, if not thousands, of people. Impromptu entertainment brought alive the humblest platform; more than once the express was delayed. But did it matter? Not in the least! Concessions were made, time-tables altered, and the express thundered along tracks where other trains ought to have been. Such is the way in India.

A quick change, wash and brush-up is much easier on a train. There is more room for one thing, also more experience to call on, and more time for rehearsing. There is to be a reception in Bangalore and an audience of thousands to entertain. But the performers are by now seasoned troupers and take it all in their stride. The old repertoire is revamped and reinforced with bagpipes, sarod and tabla.

To take in a country of eight hundred million people and rising, embracing a variety of castes, creeds and languages, is an immense assignment. But Comex has its methods, its priorities and, of course, its strategy! That strategy included enchanting Kanniyakumari, sometimes called the virgin queen of the sea; Trivandrum University, whose students were on strike but called it off to welcome their peers from abroad; the Military Staff College in Wellington, catering for potential staff officers from all over the Commonwealth; and Ooty, at the heart of the Blue Mountains. At the other end of the country, Simla and the old Viceregal Lodge (now Rashtrapati Nivas), arguably the crossroads of the Commonwealth story, and Mother Teresa's homes for the poor and the dying.

The clatter of the train subdues the mumbles and the grumbles: Jaya hai! Jaya hai! Jaya hai! Stations flash by, their names indistinguishable. Villages appear and disappear in a timeless landscape. A blast of steam rises sharply, followed by a triumphant whistle signalling that the *Commonwealth Express* is running on time. As the sun sets over the Rajastan Plain there is another long blast followed by three short ones, and the engine slows down. Platform cries fill the air: 'Hot tea! Hot coffee! Cigarettes! Cadbury Fry!' And a thousand voices cheer: 'Jaya hai! Welcome to Old Delhi Station.'

News of the next port of call sends shock waves through the Canadians on board. It is their country next following in the footsteps of Sanford Fleming's expedition through Canada in 1872 (brilliantly recorded in *Ocean to Ocean* by the Revd George M. Grant of Halifax, N.S., Secretary to the Expedition, and published by James Campbell and Son, Toronto, in 1973) but they need not have worried. The largest country in the Commonwealth remains intact, the maple leaf still adorns the Governor-General's house and Comex sang 'O Canada' without a single bum note.

Meanwhile, in the home country of the head of the Commonwealth, British Rail is moved to acknowledge Indian Railways' part in these momentous events by naming Locomotive 47555 *The Commonwealth Spirit*, and sending it on a trial run to Derby, before taking up Kenneth Kaunda's invitation to help set in motion that 'tide of goodwill from the Zambezi to reach people all over the world'.

In Lusaka, the Heritage Singers were already waiting to express their President's welcome and yet another train (the *Spirit of the Commonwealth in Zambia*) stood by to complete the final leg of the journey to Kitwe and Victoria Falls – where the song of the river of destiny was born. 'Comex Tiyende! O Yea!' the Zambians cheered in their thousands. They sang, and they danced, and stayed to the end, watching in silence as their guests finally departed, moving away into the night on the road to Mazabuka.

Dressed in scarlet and black, his warriors in their traditional leopard skin uniforms and armed with spears, Mazabuka's great chief, Mwanachingwala, was waiting to offer his own brand of hospitality by slaughtering a cow. Handing over his fly-whisk and fixing the leader with an uncompromising eye, he invited him to face the initiation ceremony of a chief: a full-blooded charge! However great the desire, it was not a matter to be sidestepped by claiming some previous engagement.

With a stamping of feet and a blood-curdling roar, the warriors of Mazabuka charged. Lest their leader should lose his nerve, turn tail and run, his comrades stood behind him, loyally blocking all avenues of retreat. But Mwanachingwala's advice had been to stand firm and wave the whisk, and that is what he did, not once but twice – just in case the message had not got through the first time. The waving may have lacked conviction, but it was effective: the charge stopped dead in its tracks and a look of disappointment spread across the faces of those warriors. For his part, Mazabuka's chief was well pleased and named his 'brother' Chief Makumba!

At the end of this memorable celebration of the Commonwealth, the first of its kind on African soil, Kenneth Kaunda insisted on everyone – African, British, Canadian, Cypriot, Indian, Malaysian and the official representatives from other Commonwealth countries – joining him at State House in a toast to friendship. Comex had seen and experienced many things, but never a head of state playing a guitar and singing a duet of welcome with his daughter.

Consciences were stirred. Too often the heat, the flies, the sandstorms and the monsoon rains had scored their victories over human frailty, relegating goodwill and understanding to second place. But such victories were short lived. When the aches and the pains had been too much to bear the healing touch of comradeship was always at hand. Even the diplomatic corps, not noted for its enthusiasm towards visitors, played a crucial part – provided its resources were not raided too often – and an hospitable door would be opened by a sentimental soul far from home flooding the mind with the strains of 'Auld Lang Syne'.

And so, the curtain comes down on the long dusty road; the imagination takes wing to distant places; bells ring out in salute to all who made the great trek possible. Farewell dear Babylon and the Garden of Eden! Farewell ancient Nineveh! Farewell to the deserts, the mountains, the people.

When the time came to celebrate the twenty-fifth anniversary of Comex, and the thousands of men and women who had made it possible, what would those other hundreds of thousands who watched their passing think? What would their epitaph be? The Duke of Edinburgh put it this way.

'Comex has proved that the Commonwealth is still the most remarkable exercise in human relations, on a world scale, mankind has ever witnessed.' And speaking as an African, Kenneth Kaunda had this to say: 'Comex has demonstrated that the brotherhood of man is not an impossible dream.' That dream is now enshrined in the Commonwealth Green Pennant Awards: no longer manufactured in silver but in Zambian copper, and mounted on a wooden base displaying the Zambian eagle, thus identifying the oldest and largest democracies in the world with the African continent.

That then is the achievement. But for those who might be amused to hear the same story, expressed as it evolved, by narrators, musicians, singers, dancers and actors, from many Commonwealth countries, here it is, spoken by Norman Leigh of Exeter University and the British Council in sixty-six cantos, with an impressive array of gestures from the Union Inn in Denbury to the Tagore Theatre in Punjab, the YWCA in Ooty, the Military Staff College in Wellington, the Gaiety Theatre in Simla, the Royal Albert Hall in London, and other places too varied and numerous to mention.

We'd a date at the end of a long dusty road,
To sing, and to dance, and to laugh.
And the men who took to this ancient land route
Were not men, but men and a half.

It would not of course do to describe women thus,
Though they played their own subtle parts:
By stirring the blood, and upsetting the peace,
And paving the road with male hearts!

The reconnaissance over, recruiting began,
Far horizons beckoned us still.
And plans were drawn up; but plans to succeed
Call for patience, good faith and goodwill.

We assembled at Denbury, gateway to the moors,
The West Country welcomed the news.
The Home Office raised its incredulous eyebrows,
'Old hands' activated the loos!

From all over the Commonwealth, volunteers came
Answering the call of the hour.
With a glint in the eye and a spring in the step
They marched on the Union Inn bar.

The ups and the downs were all part of the game,
The weak hand in hand with the strong.
But the factor most common, and shared by them all,
Was the choice of a sword, or a song.

The drivers just drive with aplomb and with style,
Aloof and remote men of steel;
Never to blame for anything going wrong
As they heave on the smooth steering wheel.

A wave of the hand, a toot on the horn,
And away to their revels in dust.
Then a hearty 'hooray', or a sombre 'I say'
When a window or bootlid is bust.

Ah! But there are times on the long dusty road
When the heart is uplifted with joy:
The cooks have made supper with Smash and dried mince,
A naan, and an onion old boy.

The will and the skill, and the struggle uphill
Get there, yes indeed, in the end.
But trapped in her glance and kitchen parlance
The man is cut down to boyfriend.

The mechanics submerged in mud, sweat and oil,
Discover faults where once there were none!
And they don't seem to mind, not being of that kind,
That their comrades are out having fun.

Yet the filth and the grime have been known, in their time,
To have benefits some may not see:
In the feminine heart, contradictions apart,
The mechanic's a capital He.

The culture-performers are highway reformers,
Refined, and genteel, and discreet:
The heart of the matter (no matter, no matter)
Where the East and the West chance to meet.

Now hark to the voice, the contingent's own choice,
Going out on the still desert air:
'Britain for India! Canada for Zambia!
Malaysia, Singapore, are you there?'

'But of course I am here you silly old fool!'
The rejoinder comes back loud and clear.
Radio operators are non-co-operators
When it comes to the sensitive ear.

And so we march on down the long dusty road,
Past deserts, o'er mountains, through streams;
And when the sun sets on the Khyber at last
We march through the valley of dreams.

But that does depend, as it must in the end,
On whether we know where we are.
Has my navigator friend gone right round the bend?
Katmandu? Chandigarh? Kandahar?

The debate carries on and questions are asked,
Gestures and words rise and fall.
Till light suddenly dawns, the navigator yawns:
'It's Lahore, I believe, after all.'

But the time has now come for joking to cease;
And the leader aroused takes the chair:
'Now look here you chaps,' he pleads and he chaffs,
'Let's not give way to despair!'

'We've crossed all the barriers of age and of class,
Of colour, of creed, and of wealth.
And, but for a case of diarrhoea or two,
We've crossed the barrier of health.'

'So forward! Non-stop! Let us move! Let us go!
It's the travelling that's getting us there.'
And he rouses their spirits to burst forth in song:
'Crying Drums' on the soft scented air.

We're in Delhi at last: hear the bustle and noise
Of scooters and lorries and buses.
Cycles and people and all things galore
Turn out to see what the fuss is.

'Comex argaaye! Hullo! How are you!
Where you come from? What is your good name?'
We've heard it before, the familiar old style,
And by God we'll hear it again.

To Simla, the Nilgiris, Nanital and Ceylon;
To everywhere – come, let us go.
To Bangladesh, Burma, the moon and the stars,
Each man has his own seed to sow.

On, on, ever on, down the long dusty road,
Like a village on wheels rolling by;
The loo stops, the crew stops, the 'how-do-you-do' stops,
I'll remember them all till I die.

Hospitality boundless, in camp site and out,
Overwhelming or simply absurd;
But the sort most common to Comex, alas,
Is the sort that is aimed at a 'bird'.

Gathering momentum the convoy moves on,
Destinations are not always clear;
But the leader's decisions still carry the day
With a promise of Commonwealth beer.

Now campsites are something to write home about,
Whether mission school, desert or shack;
Hotels, Motels, or Intercontinentals,
And those where we're not coming back.

There's an ambush ahead, now that's something new,
The Burmese do not want to know:
'To the sampans chaps, and the Bay of Bengal,
For Malaysia and Singapore.'

The drivers don't like it, don't like it one bit;
Indeed! And they make themselves heard:
'To step down from the heights of leaders-in-chief
And mix with the plebeian herd!'

An SOS goes to the RNFA:
'We're stranded in Eastern Bengal.
Burma intransigent. Stop. Action at once.
Will someone please answer this call?'

As the sun and Hoogly rise with the tide
The *Sir Lancelot* steams into view;
Flying the Green Pennant as much as to say:
'Bole juga! What about you?'

The Bay was too rough for this peaceful crusade,
But 'drink-up' we did just the same;
Until the good ship, pitched and tossed by the sea,
Unsettled the rest of the game.

Discharged at Penang Comex took to the road,
Some thought it a bit of a laugh;
But memories and guilt still flooded the mind:
'Where now are those men and a half?'

Crossing the causeway to old Singapore
And welcomed without ifs and buts:
Lee Kuan Yew's message is delivered on trays
Of orchids and green coconuts.

The People's Association steered us ashore
And taught us a good thing or two;
Till the *Galahad* docked and took us on board
Horns sounding a sailor's adieu.

'You're an adventure,' the Prime Minister said,
'With which the Commonwealth began,'
Waving us goodbye as we put out to sea,
Sadder to a woman and man.

Alas, it's goodbye to the long dusty road,
The war drums are beating 'Distress'.
So we take to the air for Bombay V.T.
To board the first Comex Express.

A trial run this, never happened before:
'All aboard!' The green flags are out;
A blast of hot steam and the whistle blows twice:
'We've made it, O yes, without doubt!'

To the longest rail journey since records began,
And memories that live with the day;
The clattering sound of the track's distant echoes:
Jaya, jaya-jaya, jaya hai!

At last, there ahead, Kanniya-kumari,
Sometimes called the queen of the sea;
Udagamandalam, or Ooty for short,
Trivandrum University.

Wellington Staff College, Rashtrapati Nivas,
And Simla way up in the snow.
Mother Teresa's homes for the poor and dying;
For people with nowhere to go.

The grumbles and rumbles will come later on,
About water, food, and the heat.
And goodwill abandoned will bow its way out
With friendship – in hasty retreat.

Until the sun sets on the Rajastan Plain
And everyone comes down to earth.
The message is simple, there's no turning back,
And the cure for ill-humour is mirth.

The leader survives by the skin of his teeth,
A feat of endurance and skill;
And tells us to take a firm grip of ourselves
'Because, comrades, no one else will.'

With order restored the express thunders on
To wild cheers, and calls of encore.
The great audience waits, rehearsals begin:
'Welcome please to our Bangalore.'

Village after village, the stations flash by,
Each day brings a new revelation:
To cries of 'Chae Garam!' and 'Cadbury Fry!'
We pull in to Old Delhi Station.

As news spreads abroad of our next port of call
Canada is greatly alarmed.
But ocean to ocean, 'no problem' at all,
The maple leaf blossoms unharmed.

While *Across the Atlantic* 47555
Warms up at St Pancras Station.
And the *Commonwealth Spirit* is ready to roll
On to the next destination.

The African continent: hip, hip, hooray!
We're all set to do the right thing.
But as good intentions are not good enough
We'd better stop talking and sing.

The Heritage Singers in sparkling form,
Tiyende Pamodzi comes strong
And Kenneth Kaunda picks up his guitar
To speak in the language of song.

'You're welcome,' he says, 'to whatever we have',
And goes on more boldly to say:
'A tide of goodwill will be set in motion
From the river Zambezi today.'

That's fair enough, metaphorically speaking,
As the story of Comex recalls:
The River of Destiny, fabled in song,
Was born at Victoria Falls.

Too many committees near scuppered all that,
One for 'discipline' – how absurd:
When the Chairman himself, staggering from grace,
Was given the African bird.

Mwanachingwala, the great African chief,
Honoured us by killing a cow;
Then handing his fly-whisk to our leader he said:
'My warriors will charge you down now.'

With their spears raised high and a stamping of feet,
They charged with a roar as they came.
But forewarned by the chief, he just brandished the whisk
Since when he has not been the same.

At State House in Lusaka the farewells began,
Remembered to this very day:
It brought out the Zambians in their thousands to cheer:
'Comex Tiyende! O Yea!'

Shouts of 'Crossing the barriers! Bravo! And well done!'
Are not always quite what they seem.
And the brotherhood of man, believe it or not,
Is not an impossible dream.

What matter if sometimes things went a bit wrong
And tempers gone mad hopped about?
When we'd bunged up the loos with queues upon queues
And few taps had not given out.

In this way had we left a mark of our passing,
Hoping that memories would die.
And so, having stooped to the gutter of living,
Thanked God for the stars in the sky.

There were some with ideas and others with none;
Motives were frequently mixed:
Goodwill, understanding, had only to wait
Till our creature comforts were fixed.

And the doctors were slick, armed with every new trick
On how to avoid consultation:
They diagnosed ills with available pills
Invoking divine dispensation.

The heat and the flies and the storms raging wild;
Eyeballs an ominous yellow.
When the aches and the pains were too much to bear
God was there – 'Capable Fellow'.

And when, in the end, some disaster befell:
No passport! No visa! No wine!
The diplomatic corps would open its door
To the wailing of 'Auld Lang Syne'.

The curtain comes down on the long dusty road,
The great, the good, and the regal.
And the little green flag flies proudly aloft,
High on the wings of an eagle.

Farewell Babylon and the Garden of Eden;
Farewell ancient Nineveh too;
Farewell to deserts, to mountains, to people:
And farewell, dear friends, to you.

INDEX

Butt maidan
Marlimund Lake
Marlimund R F
7584
7500
7250
Aramby R F
Club Hill
8040
Tudor Hall
7416
Golf course
Kandalmund
Club
St Stephen
7440
PTO
Bank
PS
Hospital
Market
Kandal
Sewage farm
7230
Mettucherri
RS
Race course
RH
St Thomas
Fernhill
Fernhill RS
7500
Cairn Hill
7619
Cairn Hill R F
Fernhill Shola
Manjanakorai
Batri Shola
Lovedale Lake
7000
Institute
Lawrence Asylum
0
1/2
1 mile
Scale 2" = 1 Mile